Family Communication

Custom Edition for
Portland State University

Taken from:

Family Communication, Theory and Research
by Lorin Basden Arnold

Understanding Family Communication, Second Edition
by Janet Yerby, Nancy Buerkel-Rothfuss, and Arthur P. Bochner

Learning Solutions

New York   Boston   San Francisco
London   Toronto   Sydney   Tokyo   Singapore   Madrid
Mexico City   Munich   Paris   Cape Town   Hong Kong   Montreal

Pearson Learning Solutions, 501 Boylston Street, Suite 900, Boston, MA 02116
A Pearson Education Company
www.pearsoned.com

Printed in the United States of America

10   16

000200010270728260

MT/JG

ISBN 10: 0-558-78312-0
ISBN 13: 978-0-558-78312-9

Contents

Section III

Chapters taken from: *Family Communication, Theory and Research*
by Lorin Basden Arnold

Section I

The following chapters are taken from:

Understanding Family Communication, Second Edition
by Janet Yerby, Nancy Buerkel-Rothfuss, Arthur Bochner

CHAPTER 3

THE FAMILY AS A
MEANING-MAKING
SYSTEM

NANCY VADER-McCORMICK

THE MARTIN FAMILY

The Martins live in a suburban neighborhood near Chicago, where Paul Martin works as a city planner. Jane Martin teaches reading readiness part-time at a nearby elementary school and spends much of her free time as a volunteer for a local hospice. The Martins have two children: eleven-year-old Julie and fourteen-year-old Anne. Both girls attend junior high school.

A neighbor and close friend of Julie's recently moved away, which was a tremendous disappointment for her. To compensate, Julie began to hang around and probe into the affairs of her older sister. Anne had been developing an increasing need for privacy as part of her emergence into adolescence and resisted Julie's new interest in her.

In an attempt to free herself of her sister's constant company, Anne tended to be curt with Julie and to say things that hurt her feelings. Julie usually retaliated in some way and their interactions frequently ended in conflict. Both parents tried to be understanding, but sometimes they would get angry and frustrated with the girls.

The girls' mother, Jane, began to make an effort to spend time with Julie in activities that were intended to keep her away from Anne. Jane taught Julie how to knit, for instance, and took her to the indoor pool at a local community center one or two times each week. Jane was not always comfortable, however, with the demands that this made upon her time and energy. She had been thinking about going to graduate school. She now worried that such a change in family routine would be too disruptive at this time.

Jane wished that Paul would take more of an interest in the girls. She would get irritated whenever he suggested that the girls were simply "going through a stage" and would probably return to being friends in a few months. Jane accused Paul of being a workaholic and tried to pressure him into spending more time with the family. From his point of view, Paul felt unappreciated for the hard work and long hours that he put in at his job, something that his own father had never done for his family. Conversations that began as discussions about the girls often turned into arguments about the larger issue of how much time each parent should spend with the family.

To ease some of the demands made upon her, Jane began to rely more on Julie and Anne to help her with the tasks around the house. Initially, Jane asked the girls to help with the dusting, vacuuming, yardwork, and some of the cooking. The girls complained at first, but Jane developed the habit of treating them to dinner at a restaurant, a movie, or some other reward when they did an exceptional job. These rewards seemed to motivate them. Eventually, Julie assumed more of the housekeeping chores as a matter of routine. Anne took charge of much of the meal planning and even suggested that she, Julie, and their father do the cooking together on weekends.

The girls began to work together more cooperatively, to feel good about their increased responsibilities, and to enjoy their father more. Paul realized that he enjoyed cooking with his daughters on weekends and noticed that the household seemed more tranquil with the girls getting along better. He shared his perceptions with his wife, thus opening the lines of communication between them. Jane began to realize that she and Paul quarreled less than they had a few months earlier and she began to think again about going back to school. With less energy focused on internal family problems, at least temporarily, family members began to attend more to other relationships outside of the family: work, school, friends, and others.

UNDERSTANDING THE MARTINS

Families function within a certain range of day-to-day predictability. As illustrated by the Martin example, family members continually negotiate their relationships with each other as the family strives to reach its goals. Families also evolve and constantly change as members interact with each other, with their extended family, and with the environment.

What are the causes of the Martin family's problems? Is Julie to blame for the conflict that occurs between Anne and her? Should Paul feel guilty because he believes that his work prevents him from helping more around the house and spending more time with his family? Can we say that Jane is selfish because so much of her behavior seems to be guided by a desire to attend graduate school? How you answer those questions depends, at least in part, on the theoretical perspective you use for understanding family communication.

In the previous two chapters, we indicated that our preferred view of the family includes a systems theory orientation. This chapter will discuss systems theory and will apply the tenets of systems approaches to family communication. The first section of the chapter will examine the notion of causality and its relationship to a systems perspective. The second section will describe the elements and processes that underlie all family systems. The third and final section will examine current perspectives in the systems view of the family.

CAUSALITY AND FAMILY SYSTEMS

Every theoretical perspective brings with it some assumptions about the world and the events that occur within it. A major assumption underlying systems theory is that all components of a system are interrelated and interdependent. They work together to perform various system functions. Consequently, when we consider family communication, a systems perspective requires that we focus primarily on the relationships between family members and the ways in which family members work together to attain family goals. We think of communication messages as interwoven patterns of interaction that stretch through a family's history together rather than as singular events. Each message is simultaneously a response to someone else's message (real or anticipated) and a stimulus for future responses.

These interactions become patterns that tend to be repeated in family relationships. Thus, communication between family members can be studied as an interactive phenomenon in which all family members participate. When we examine the family from a systems point of view, no one person or one thing in the family can realistically be identified as the "cause" of a problem. Instead, we try to understand situations, problems, and "ways of being" in families. We examine the influences impinging upon the family, behaviors that are evoked between and among members, the sequencing of events over time, and how family members fit together.

As is evident from the opening example, individuals frequently talk about their families only in terms of what specific family members did and how they felt. Julie turned to her sister when her friend moved away. Jane was resentful because she believed she would have to postpone graduate school. Paul found that he enjoyed cooking with his daughters. People describe their own families this way: "My younger brother doesn't like competition." "Mother gives Dad 'the silent treatment' when her feelings are hurt." "My sister has been much easier to get along with lately."

To understand events in the Martin family, however, it is important to think about their behavior from the perspective of the family as a whole rather than just from the perspective of the individual. Consider what happens when behavior is viewed as emerging from what Hoffman (1981) calls "the social field" in which it occurs. Rather than acting independently, family members invite responses from each other through their actions, conversations, and place in the social unit. Jane became more content about Paul's involvement in the family when she saw how much he enjoyed cooking with his daughters on weekends. When Julie started to become dependent upon her sister, Anne pushed her away, hurting Julie's feelings and producing a retaliatory response. Although these episodes must necessarily be phrased to sound as if there was a cause (Paul became more involved with the family) and an effect (Jane became more content), these statements merely describe arbitrary starting and ending points for the episode. We could just as easily observe that Paul's desire to help his wife drew him into a closer relationship with his daughters or that Anne and Julie encouraged their father to work with them out of their needs to both help their mother and feel closer to him. The connections between and among family members and the need to maintain the family system produced the communication episodes just described.

People, however, typically perceive their own behavior only as a response to other members in the family. Imagine Anne Martin saying, "You've got to do something about Julie; she is driving me crazy!" From Anne's point of view, it is Julie's persistent attempts to pry into Anne's affairs that are the source of the problem between the two girls. From Julie's point of view, however, Anne's secrecy and lack of interest are the major problems.

While the responses of each sister reflect authentic feelings and experiences, the girls also tend to justify each of their behaviors by blaming the other. Behavior of all family members is evoked by other family members in significant ways. When behavior in the family is seen primarily as interactive, then it is possible to conceive of episodes as occurring within a sequence of events. How members and subgroups in the family are connected and how the family makes adaptations in their relationships over time also become more apparent. Notice, for example, how Anne and Julie were drawn closer together when they became involved in managing the cooking. When they included their father in the task, some of the distance between Paul and his family was also reduced. Because Paul was more involved in the family, Jane may have felt a little more comfortable putting more distance between herself and her family so that she could go back to school. You can begin to see that the influences affecting the family are complex—influences impinge upon the family from outside the nuclear family, from responses to each other's behavior within the family, and from the individual predispositions of family members.

As we discussed in an earlier chapter, concepts related to *causality in the family* are viewed differently in thinking about how family members, through their communication, are related to each other over time. From a communication perspective, there is little value in blaming Julie, or the neighbor who moved away, for the problems that developed in the Martin family. Why not begin with the fact that Julie had only one close friend in her neighborhood instead of two? Nor do we decide that Anne is the cause for the stress in the family because she needed privacy and pushed her sister away. Why not, instead, blame Paul's investment in his work or Jane's resentment over the increased demands on her time for the tension in the family? Blaming individuals does not help much to understand the family and the processes that influence family behavior.

A focus on the social unit allows you to think of family interaction as ongoing, choice-governed, and somewhat circular. Communication episodes isolate bits of the family's interaction but all episodes are tied together by an ongoing family history. Each episode builds on some prior event rather than beginning anew. In addition, it should be clear that choices about behavior are made in concert with responses received from other family members. Anne chose to be short with Julie partly because her curt responses achieved the desired reaction from Julie: distancing in their relationship. Had Julie's response been different, Anne may have selected another strategy. These episodes reflect overall family functioning and communication rather than individual messages and responses. Family members can predict outcomes in a given situation based on outcomes from prior episodes, which provides a sense of circularity. Thus, family communication can be seen as somewhat patterned and predictable.

Focusing primarily on the social unit rather than on the individual will lead you to think less in terms of causes or of blaming individuals for problems that develop and will change the interpretations of what you observe. Different kinds of concerns are, instead, addressed: what influences do family members exert over each other through their actions and their conversations? How do family members display their connectedness to one another? How does this family manage conflict? What patterns of interaction are repeated and what function do those patterns serve for the family system? What needs do family members satisfy for each other; how are these needs identified; how do they change? How does the family's communication influence and reflect the degree of integration and individuation of family members? What influences outside the family exert pressure on family members and how does the family system cope with those influences? Questions such as these help to identify the interrelatedness of family members. As we will discuss in the next section, the systems view involves a focus on a set of systems elements and the processes that make the systems work.

FAMILY SYSTEMS THEORY: ELEMENTS AND PROCESSES

An early theory of systems called general systems theory (GST) was developed largely by Bertalanffy (1968) and expanded by other social and physical scientists (Buckley, 1967; Laszlo, 1972; Mesarovic, 1970; Pepper, 1972). According to Bertalanffy, the development of systems theory met a need of biologists to describe biological systems and organic phenomena. In particular, the need arose to describe systems that, unlike mechanical or physical systems, are changed by input from the surrounding environment and, in turn, exert an influence on that environment. These biological systems—phenomena like tide pools, insect colonies, various animal habitats, and families—exhibit a number of traits not easily studied using cause-and-effect models. Capra (1982) has called general systems theory a "turning point" in how we think about living organisms and about life in general on our planet.

GST was extended by Miller (1978) in his benchmark work on general living systems theory. Miller argued for the construction of a general theory that would allow researchers to examine hierarchical relationships between the smallest possible unit of analysis (the individual cell system) and the largest (the supranational system).

Because human families are living phenomena that both influence and are influenced by changes from within and without the family unit, they can be studied effectively using a systems approach. In their article in *Contemporary Theories About the Family,* Broderick and Smith (1979) argued that the "systems perspective seems to have no peer among the theoretical perspectives available to family scholars" (p. 126) for examining family communication.

The shift in focus from interest in individual entities to studying relationships as they exist in systems was not lost on therapists and researchers working with troubled families. Although trained from a psychoanalytic perspective, which calls for diagnosis of mental illness within a single identified patient, early therapists began to consider the influence of other family members on their patient's behavior. (For a detailed description of this evolutionary process, see Guerin, 1976.)

This application of a family-centered approach to family therapy emerged simultaneously in several areas of the country. In California, Gregory Bateson and colleagues Jay Haley, John Weakland, and Don Jackson—known as the "Palo Alto Group," began an investigation into the role of communication in the family system. In Washington, D.C., Murray Bowen undertook his pioneering project to study the families of schizophrenics in an effort to explain the fact that improving patients frequently regressed after returning to their family systems. In Atlanta, Carl Whitaker and colleagues went into a private practice in which they acted as co-therapists to work with troubled families. In their therapy, family members were added one at a time to the therapeutic unit, until whole families and, eventually, members of the suprasystem were included in the sessions. In Chicago, Charles and Jeannette Kramer formed the Chicago Family Institute, now affiliated with the Northwestern University School of Medicine. In Pennsylvania, both the Philadelphia Family Institute and the Philadelphia Child Guidance Clinic provided centers for the study of families, eventually focusing on intergenerational family networks as a place for intervention. Ivan Boszormenyi-Nagy, Geraldine Spark, Salvador Minuchin, James Framo, Ross Speck, and Carolyn Attneave have all been part of the pioneering work in family therapy that was undertaken in Philadelphia. In New York, Nathan Ackerman began to examine the influence of social forces, family roles, and other environmental influences on families, although he retained a psychoanalytic focus in his therapy.

In the sections that follow we describe characteristics of family systems theory that were developed in the formative decades between the 1950s and 1980s. The terminology and concepts we describe reflect what could be identified as traditional family systems theory and provide the theoretical background for much of the current discussion of family systems. Family systems, like all living systems, incorporate two types of characteristics: (1) a set of system elements, and (2) a set of processes that help the system function.

System Elements

System elements are the physical features of the family system. Six types of system elements comprise family systems: (1) interdependent components, (2) inputs and outputs, (3) boundaries and hierarchies, (4) rules for operation, (5) system goals, and (6) feedback mechanisms.

Interdependent Components

The **components** of a human system are simply the parts that work together to create the system as a whole. In the case of the family, the components can be people and the functions or roles that they perform for the family system.

One way to organize your thinking about family systems is to consider the components of a family system to be family members: spouses, parents, children, stepchildren, in-laws, grandparents, and other relatives or nonrelated individuals who function as family members. People can also enter and leave the system at various times as family members are born, marry, divorce, and die.

The size of the family can influence how a family functions. As Broderick and Smith have observed (1979), "Large family systems are structurally so different from small family systems that they should be considered separately in making any generalizations about how family systems operate" (p. 113). Clearly, the four-person Martin family will differ in significant ways from the twelve-person Lueder family. Similarly, there will be many differences among single-parent families, blended families, ethnic families, two-generation families, and gay families that will not be reflected in just their sizes.

Roles are sets of functions that individual members are expected to perform in the system, such as caregiver, breadwinner, or scapegoat, based on the rules established for specific relationships. We discuss family roles in Chapter 10.

By *interdependent* we mean that the actions of each component affect in some noticeable way other components in the system. The behavior of one family member has an influence on other members. When Jane returns home from a frustrating day at school, her frustration will invite responses (or nonresponses) from Anne, Julie, and Paul. The ways in which they respond (or fail to respond) to her

FIGURE 3.1   System elements.

1. **Interdependent components:** people and/or sets of role functions.
   Examples of people components: parents, grandparents, newborns.
   Examples of roles: wage earner, nurturer, problem child, initiator, scapegoat.
2. **Inputs and outputs:** information that flows into the system and the products or energy of that information returned to the suprasystem.
   Examples of inputs: newspapers, radio broadcasts, phone calls.
   Examples of outputs: work, volunteering, money to charity, attendance at church services, support for friends and family.
3. **Boundaries and hierarchies:** a series of ever-wider arbitrary dividing lines separating subsystems, systems, and suprasystems.
   Examples: marital dyad subsystem, sibling subsystem, nuclear system, extended family suprasystem, community suprasystem, world suprasystem.
4. **Rules for operation:** guidelines that prescribe what is expected, allowed, and prohibited in a given set of circumstances.
   Examples: parents make the rules, when a parent has been drinking the rest of the family compensates, children may solve conflicts using physical force with each other but never with parents or people outside the system.
5. **System goals:** desired outcomes of family functioning at a particular time.
   Examples: prosperity for family members, happiness, social recognition, promotion of self-worth among family members, maintenance of an unhappy marriage, support for a parent's alcohol dependency.
6. **Feedback mechanisms:** devices that indicate the degree to which family systems are headed toward (or away from) satisfaction of their goals.
   Examples: conflict between spouses may indicate movement away from self-worth goals, chores left undone may indicate movement away from family harmony, cheerful participation in family events may indicate movement toward a goal of happiness.

---

feelings of frustration will, in turn, affect her responses to them. Similarly, when one family member is ill, absent from the family, or otherwise unable to perform the behaviors usually expected from and associated with that person, the entire family system is altered. Because roles help to structure family interaction and stabilize the family system, family members will compensate for each other when roles are not performed.

To fully grasp the concept of interdependence, imagine large, stretchable rubber bands linking family members to each other. For example, imagine strong bands connecting Jane and Paul Martin. As a married couple, they feel strongly tied to one another. As one partner moves, the movement tugs on the other partner, resulting in some movement on his or her part. For example, Paul's long hours at work pull on Jane's rubber band, resulting in tension and frustration in their relationship. Now imagine rubber bands stretching from each parent to each of their children and bands connecting Julie and Anne to each other. As one family member experiences a change—for example, the loss of a close friend who moves away—the bands that connect that family member to all others may stretch. This increased tension in the system will affect each of the other three system components. If the influence is temporary, the tension in the rubber bands might be released, requiring no systemic change; if the change is major, the tension in the rubber bands will eventually be sufficient to move others in the system in some way. Again, returning to our opening example, Julie's loss of a close friend resulted in tension, or a tightly stretched rubber band, between Anne and her. Anne's attempts literally to pull away from her sister resulted in considerable tugging on the rubber band connecting Anne to Julie and, in turn, on those rubber bands connecting both girls to their parents. To ease some of the tension, Jane and Paul engaged in numerous activities that had the effect of moving them closer to both girls, thus reducing the perceived tension.

In our definition of family, we call the interdependence among family members mutual influence. As a natural consequence of exerting mutual influence over each other, being interdependent means that even the absence of a family member will have a profound effect on the family system. The relationship, for example, between a teenaged son and his parents can change dramatically when the older of two sons leaves for college. The boys' parents might find that they have more time to spend with their younger son. They might also begin to use the departure of one of their sons as an opportunity to begin letting go of their children as they make the transition to adulthood. The brothers, in turn, may find that they are closer, even though they see each other only on holidays, because the competitive edge of the relationship is softened with distance.

Thus, family systems can be thought of as sets of people and roles that are inextricably bound by invisible ties. When one element of the system is affected, all others are influenced in some way.

System Inputs and Outputs

Inputs and outputs are the "matter" that moves in and out of the system. **Inputs** are received and used by the system to perform its designated function or achieve its goals. **Outputs** are the outcomes or by-products of the system's activity that are returned to the environment. Inputs and outputs of family systems can be treated as forms of information or communication or can be thought of as requiring communication (Kantor & Lehr, 1975).

For the typical family system, inputs include information from the media, visits from friends, money from employers, mail, and goods and services. When Anne receives a pleasant phone call from a friend, or Jane brings home a new idea that she struggled with in graduate school, or the family watches a natural disaster on their television screen, the result is an input of feeling, information, or meaning into the family system. Incoming information is dealt with and compared with family images and meanings; some is incorporated and some is discarded. When there is disagreement among family members about the value of the information or how to interpret it, conflict may occur. Similarly, issues concerning money enter the system and decisions are made, usually through negotiation, about how it eventually will be converted to interest or hard goods. In the Martin family, inputs may take the form of values held by grandparents that are communicated to Julie and Anne, television news programs that convince Paul and Jane that Chicago is a safe city in which to raise their children, books that entice them to travel to foreign countries, and unwanted intrusions from the too-friendly next-door neighbors.

Family outputs include work and service in the community, money spent on goods and services, participation in politics (voting), support for friends and relatives, and socialization of children. In families with antisocial members, outputs might include damage to the neighborhood, intense noise, or violence. Outputs from the Martin family system might include Paul's efforts at work, Julie's and

Anne's contributions to their classes and helpfulness to their friends, Jane's volunteer work at the hospice and her financial support for her aging parents, and time that all four of them devote to cleaning up the neighborhood park each spring.

As we discuss in Chapter 6, which explores the family's ecosystem, the amount and kind of influence that a family system receives from its environment can significantly affect its functioning. The quality of outputs a family system provides to its environment affects its place in that environment. Examining the ways in which inputs and outputs are processed by the system allows you to identify the rules of operation that influence the family system as a whole and to understand better its place in the larger environment.

Boundaries and Hierarchies

A system **boundary** is an arbitrary dividing line that defines the inside and outside of a given system. The boundary differentiates inputs and outputs and identifies the components that will be considered part of the system. The system **hierarchy** defines the relationships among two or more system boundaries.

The boundary may be an arbitrary dividing line that is drawn at the discretion of the person who wishes to describe that system or it may be a shared perception that family members hold regarding elements that belong inside and outside of the family system. In general, it is most useful to think of boundaries as separating system elements that have frequent interaction with one another. In our opening example, we arbitrarily drew a boundary around the four members of the Martin nuclear family system as our unit of analysis because, using our earlier definition of family communication, these are the four individuals of central interest to a family analysis. If our definition of family were broadened to the extended family, we might have included grandparents, aunts, uncles, and cousins within the boundary.

A systems approach to the study of the family often makes distinctions between subsystems and suprasystems in the family. A **subsystem** includes components of a larger system. The nuclear family is composed of several subsystems. Parents and/or spouses, two sisters, four children and their mother, and a father and son are examples of subsystems in the nuclear family. A **suprasystem** is defined as a larger system that is composed of other identifiable systems. The extended family network, the neighborhood where the nuclear family lives, and the larger community within which the nuclear family functions are included in the family's suprasystem.

Systems have commonly been thought of as containing a **hierarchy of subsystems** and as being embedded in a **hierarchy of suprasystems.** As Miller (1978) discusses in his book on general living systems and Haley (1976) describes in *Problem-Solving Therapy*, this notion of hierarchy can help you to understand the structure of the family system in relationship to the structure of its internal organization and outside environment. Just as a family contains a variety of subsystems (individuals, parent–child relationships, the marital dyad, and child–child relationships), each family is one system in the larger suprasystem hierarchy that contains families of origin (grandparents, aunts, uncles), the community system, and the social system. The relationships of interest (child–child, family–neighbors, or family–society) differentiate the "system" of interest from the supra- and subsystems. We discuss the concept of a hierarchy of subsystems and suprasystems further in Chapter 6.

Please note that families create boundaries by the designs of their houses, locks on their doors, fences that surround their yards, and through the dozens of ways that they stake out and defend family "territory." In some family systems, grandparents, aunts, stepchildren, and even nonrelatives are considered part of the system. These individuals nap in the porch swing, borrow the cars, and feel free to drop by whenever they feel like it. They may even live in the same house with the nuclear family. In other family systems, only parents and children qualify as "family"; other family members function as part of the larger suprasystem. These "outsiders" call ahead and schedule time to be with nuclear family members.

The *permeability* of the boundary that surrounds a family indicates the degree to which that system is open or closed to its environment. In "open family systems," many inputs are sought and there is significant interaction with the outside environment. In such families, members expose themselves to many viewpoints and make attachments outside of the system. In "closed family systems," the boundaries are more rigid and are used to screen inputs and outputs more rigorously. Family members keep to themselves and information may be carefully filtered, with only information consistent with family values being allowed to enter the system. Family behavior may be monitored with equal care, with outputs being restricted to a fairly narrow range of acceptable behavior. A relative degree of openness is important for understanding family functioning (Broderick & Pulliam-Krager, 1978; Constantine, 1986; Kantor & Lehr, 1975).

Boundaries also help to identify how individuals and subgroups are differentiated within the family system. They help to distinguish, for instance, what is unique about the relationship of Julie to her sister Anne; they indicate what is shared only by Paul and Jane; and they prescribe ways in which Anne may be considered to be her own person. Anne and Julie may share secrets as a way to differentiate their relationship from other relationships in the family and thereby define their boundary. Anne may keep a diary that her parents are not permitted to read as a way of establishing a boundary between herself and other family members.

Boundaries may be clear in some families and not clear in others. **Rigid boundaries,** or boundaries that are clearly defined and difficult to penetrate, produce different communication interactions than **diffuse boundaries,** or boundaries that fluctuate freely and are easily permeated. For instance, the mother and father in a family may differentiate themselves from the rest of the family by setting aside one evening per week to spend alone together or by making their bedroom off limits to other family members. In their case, the boundary is clear. Another couple may not have defined their boundary as a couple as clearly. As a consequence, they may allow their conversations and conflicts to be interrupted by their children or they may openly disagree about how to handle the children.

Recognizing characteristics of system, subsystem, and suprasystem boundaries can provide considerable information about family functioning. Boundaries differentiate the family from the environment, maintain the uniqueness of subsystems (i.e., dyadic, triadic, relationships, etc. in the family), and preserve the individuality of family members.

Rules for Operation

Rules specify which operations or behaviors are allowed, recommended, expected, and forbidden within the system. The rules for operation provide the framework or structure within which the system components are connected and must operate (Ford, 1983).

The specific rules governing a family are unique to that family and change as that family evolves (Constantine, 1986). Family system rules pertain to such things as roles for family members, subjects that can and cannot be discussed, ways of expressing anger or affection, and authority among family members. In the Martin family, both adults work but Jane divides her time between paid employment and volunteering, suggesting some rule about who is to be the "breadwinner" for the family. We also learn that it is acceptable to talk about one's frustrations in that family, that efforts are made by all family members to maintain some sort of family harmony, and that affection can be expressed by participating in activities with other family members (cooking, going to a movie, etc.). Each of these observations provides insight into the rules that structure the Martin family system. We discuss various types of family rules, their origins, and their influence on family system functioning in more depth in Chapter 7.

Family System Goals

The system **goal** is quite literally what a system attempts to accomplish or achieve at any given point in time. As such, identification of family goals tends to direct family interaction toward attainment of those goals. The goal of a small antique business may be fairly fixed and generally well understood: to sell enough merchandise at prices that will allow the owners to cover their costs and make a modest profit for themselves. Family system goals may not be as clearly articulated: a goal might be to raise the children in a loving environment or it might be to confirm the belief that men cannot be trusted.

A characteristic of family system goals is that they are not absolute. Family goals may change before they are met, a new goal may emerge as an old one is achieved, or two conflicting goals may compete for the family's attention. For example, in the Martin family there appears to be a structure of rules that promotes family harmony, leading to the conclusion that the Martin system has a goal of maintaining harmonious relationships among its members. Achievement of that goal involves family members doing things together, such as cooking, attending sporting events, and going to movies. It also involves intervention by one or more family members when difficulties erupt in one of the subsystems. As you see in the example, however, as relationships improve, family members begin to focus attention on goals that require family members to draw somewhat apart (Jane begins to anticipate graduate school). The goal of family harmony directs family activity inward; the goal of satisfying individual family members' needs draws family members apart. Sometimes family goals are revealed in conversational themes or in the stories they share and the metaphors they use to describe their life together. We discuss family stories, myths, metaphors, and themes in Chapters 8 and 9.

Goals in family systems continually change as the family evolves, and a family system may work toward multiple goals at the same time. A newly married couple with career aspirations for both spouses may be excited about moving to a large urban area where each of them will realize the goal of being employed in a new, challenging job. Once settled and involved in the demands of their careers, they may find themselves needing to spend time working on problems in their relationship. As we will discuss in Chapter 6, the addition of children to the family system necessitates further modification of family system goals, as does every other major life event to follow.

Feedback Mechanisms

Feedback is any response to an operation or behavior that provides information about that operation or behavior. In communication terms, feedback is simply the response to a comment a speaker has made: the answer to a question, a nonverbal confirmation of listening, or any other communicative act that allows for a communication episode to move ahead. In systems terms, feedback provides information to the system about its progress toward or away from system goals.

In family systems the ability to monitor progress toward goals and make changes in structure or behavior with the intention of improving this progress is important. While families are systems, similar to other living systems that are constantly changing, some family members may attempt to stabilize or regulate behavior within the family in ways that keep the family oriented toward specific goals. Other family members may press for faster change, suggest alternative family goals, or resist previous patterns of relating. Communication in the family often provides the family with information that goals have shifted, that taken-for-granted patterns are changing, or that roles are evolving. In traditional systems theory terminology, the regulating mechanisms in a family help indicate member satisfaction, adherence to family rules and norms, and general progress toward family goals. In some families, conversations among family members perform this function on a regular basis. In other families, quarrels and emotional outbursts provide the needed information. As you might expect, not all deviations from family goals are correctable, even when detected by feedback mechanisms.

In the Martin family, conflict between Anne and Julie served as a regulating mechanism to alert family members to a potential problem. Changes in responsibilities and ways of relating to each other helped to put the system back on course.

System Processes

System processes are the characteristics of human systems that describe how the system functions through time. System processes describe the day-to-day conduct and evolution of the family as it maintains itself in some working order and adapts to the course of events and to the environment. In this sense, families, because they are social systems, are constructed, maintain themselves, and adapt to their environment through their communication.

Four types of systems processes are especially relevant to our discussion of family communication: (1) nonsummativity, (2) stability, (3) change, and (4) equifinality. Each is discussed in the sections that follow.

Nonsummativity

The principle of **nonsummativity** refers to the fact that "a system cannot be taken for the sum of its parts" (Watzlawick, Beavin, & Jackson, 1967, p. 125). To understand the family as a system we need to do more than describe the characteristics and behaviors of individual family members. Each member's behavior is influenced by the behavior of other family members. We cannot, therefore, understand how the family operates by merely "summing up characteristics of individual

FIGURE 3.2   System processes.

1. **Nonsummativity:** developing the patterns and relationships in which the whole is greater than the sum of the parts.

    Example: Those who know Eric Morris and his parents perceive them as relaxed individuals who are easy to get along with. Whenever the three of them are alone together for a holiday, however, they all begin immediately to irritate one another.

2. **Stability:** establishing a balanced state that will ensure maintenance of the system.

    Example: The Millars have two young sons who frequently get into physical fights with one another. Their parents typically ignore these combats until one of them gets hurt and begins to cry; then one of the parents will separate the two boys in order to restore peace.

3. **Change:** adapting to the growth and maturation of family members and to novel circumstances for which no roles currently exist.

    Example: When the Robinson twins started kindergarten their mother went back to work full-time as a maternity nurse and their father reduced his hours at work in order to participate more fully in household tasks.

4. **Equifinality:** reaching similar goals from different pathways or achieving different goals from similar origins.

    Example: The Cohen family achieves a feeling of connectedness among family members through frequent hugs and kisses, while the Quinn family achieves the same feelings through frequent arguments, political debates, and heated discussions.

members" (Walsh, 1982, p. 9). It is important to attend to how family members function as a whole, the patterns that they develop in their conversation and interaction, and how they are connected to one another.

For example, the positive changes that occur in the Martin family are not simply the consequence of the separate behaviors of individual family members but of changes in how the Martins relate to one another. Anne and Julie begin to share more of their mother's role and begin to behave more cooperatively toward one another. Paul and the girls develop tasks that they can share. Paul and Jane share positive feelings about the girls and become more comfortable with their parenting relationship. If we wish to understand the Martins, it is important to understand their relationships. It is not enough merely to indicate that Julie gains maturity or Paul opens up more or Jane becomes less stressed.

Nonsummativity is the outcome of interdependence. System components working together can often achieve what individual components working alone cannot. Integrating their parenting styles is something that Paul and Jane can only do together. Regulating the closeness and distance of their relationship involves both Julie and Anne. The patterns of parenting that the couple develop and the rules regulating closeness and distance that Julie and Anne create describe aspects of their family system that "transcend the qualities of individuals" (Watzlawick, Beavin, & Jackson, 1967, p. 135). Because family systems identify boundaries, establish hierarchies, develop rules, and set collective system goals, they are able to accomplish as a system what cannot be accomplished alone. By recognizing the importance of this system principle, we begin to attend more to characteristics that help us understand the family as a group or a set of relationships.

Stability

The tendency for families to seek stability means that they seek enough regularity, order, permanence, and predictability in relationships outside and inside the family to ensure the maintenance of the system (Watzlawick, Beavin, & Jackson, 1967). Families are continually confronted with information and events from outside their system. At the same time, individual family members are growing and maturing. The patterns that create a sense of predictability in the family enable the family to maintain some degree of "relative constancy" in an environment that is constantly changing (Jackson, 1970, p. 1).

Information from outside the family or deviations in behavior from within the family that might threaten its stability are resisted by feedback mechanisms (Walsh, 1982). As we indicated earlier in the chapter, **feedback mechanisms,** sometimes called *homeostatic mechanisms,* are the system-regulating processes that reinforce family rules and patterns. As Walsh (1981, p. 10) explains, "Too great a deviation from the family norm may be counteracted in the negative feedback process in order to regulate tension and to restore the family equilibrium or homeostasis." Parents who "ground" their teenaged daughter for two weeks after she comes home intoxicated one evening are using a feedback mechanism to discourage such behavior in the future. When one component of the family system deviates from expectations or desires, other family members may intervene to ensure the maintenance of the family system. Rather than allow Julie and Anne's subsystem to break apart through their conflict, both Jane and Paul moved in to try to rectify the problem; they assumed roles that allowed the system to establish stability once again. The family's tendency to seek stability or equilibrium is called **morphostasis** (Speer, 1970; Ariel, Carel, & Tyano, 1984). A system that cannot maintain some degree of stability may eventually disintegrate, but stability is different for every family.

For most families, maintaining stability is an ongoing process that is continually challenged. A family that is going through obvious changes may experience the challenge to its stability as more obvious than a family in which changes are more subtle. The tendency to restore order and equilibrium in the family can be seen following any of the many life crises to which families are prone: the birth of the first child, death of grandparents, divorce, unemployment, and so on. Returning to our opening example of the Martin family, it would be apparent that instability began to be a problem for the Martins shortly after Julie's friend moved away. Jane felt overworked, Paul felt harassed, Anne was feeling pestered by her younger sister and unable to attain the degree of privacy and independence she desired. Left unchecked, these feelings could have escalated into a serious explosion among members of this family. Fortunately, the system reorganized to avert a breakdown. Jane, for instance, shifted some responsibilities to Julie and Anne, thus giving Julie something important to do and satisfying Anne's desire to be recognized for her increasing maturity. In system terms, one component (Jane) shifted some of her functions (housework and shopping) to two other system components (Anne and Julie). This shift in responsibility helped the family system to achieve some degree of stability once again. As new roles were incorporated into the rules for operation, a new sense of order was created and the system took on more organized patterns of interaction.

Change

While some level of stability is necessary for the self-maintenance of the family, it is apparent that some flexibility is also necessary as the family evolves over time. Change refers to the tendency of family systems to reorganize themselves and adapt new patterns in response to new "developmental imperatives" within the family (Walsh, 1982, p. 10). A system tends to evolve over time, usually as it encounters novel events for which it has not yet developed standardized ways of responding (Dell, 1982; Speer, 1970; Carter & McGoldrick, 1980). In other words, family members change how they relate to each other as the system encounters surprising inputs from the environment and as it moves through the family life cycle. The family's tendency to change as it evolves through time is called **morphogenesis** (Speer, 1970).

Family systems can generate feedback and can respond to that feedback in ways that may alter goals, functions, and/or rules of operation as well as maintain them. Components of human systems may modify their behavior, appearance, and relationships. They exhibit interdependence and interconnectedness, and their relationships can be modified if necessary. A couple with a new baby may make some dramatic changes in the roles they assume toward one another, the goals they have as a couple, and the patterns that characterize their life together. Such changes are made possible through the couple's ability to communicate and to act on the basis of their conversations and interactions with each other.

It should be clear that a struggle between the need for stability and the inevitability of change across the life cycle involves the family in a dialectical process that highlights the importance of communication. In Chapter 1 we introduced the idea that stability and change may present contradictory demands on the family. Change may be resisted in the family as it attempts to maintain a stable system. Stability evolves from consistency, familiar patterns, and predictable behaviors. However, systems do not stand still in time. Change naturally occurs as the family goes through various life cycle stages. The addition of children, the aging of parents, and myriad other family life cycle crises push the family system into new forms, new patterns, and new pathways. This change, which we discuss in more detail later in this book, makes the struggle for stability more difficult.

Families continually negotiate a balance between stability and change. There is a constant tension between the forces that resist too much novelty in the family and those that cause the family to adapt as it grows, matures, and responds to the environment. Paradoxically, families that cling rigidly to familiar patterns of relating at the expense of adapting to change can be dysfunctional and may precipitate a family crisis that threatens the integrity of the family (Steier, Stanton, & Todd, 1982). Conversely, families that fail to develop adequate levels of constancy and predictability in their patterns of relating may not be able to maintain the stability necessary to keep the family intact.

Clearly, the degree to which families cope with changing circumstances influences family form and functioning. We discuss some of these variations when we describe family patterns in Chapters 10 and 11.

Equifinality

A fourth and final consideration for understanding family system processes pertains to the ways in which families reach goals. **Equifinality**, a term coined by Bertalanffy (1968, p. 40), refers to the fact that the "same final state may be reached from different initial conditions and in different ways." As Walsh (1982, p. 10) illustrates, "Thus one family may be disabled while another family rallies in response to the same crisis; or two well-functioning families may have evolved from quite different circumstances." Similarly, two different systems may attain the same goal by beginning at different starting points and selecting different strategies.

Return for a moment to our opening example. A goal for the Martin family system appears to be to maintain family harmony. When tension was felt following the departure of Julie's friend, harmony was restored through a series of episodes designed to strengthen relationships and bring family members closer together: cooking together, sharing responsibilities, and having honest conversations about feelings. You can probably think of other strategies that might have been used to achieve the same effect: making new friends, getting professional help, taking a family trip, installing a backyard swimming pool, and so on. Family harmony might have been restored in many ways, depending on the characteristics of the Martin family system described in this chapter.

In the Scarzoni family, for example, family harmony is tied to independence. Rather than finding new ways for the family to join together when the tension becomes troublesome, the Scarzonis look for ways to allow family members the freedom to function outside of the family. Family harmony might be achieved by allowing Dad a special fishing trip with his buddies or by saving the money for each of the three children to go to separate summer camps.

Knowing that the same goal can be achieved in a variety of ways allows for creativity in family functioning. The degree to which family members employ the principle of equifinality is tied to the flexibility with which they meet challenges. Similarly, recognizing the potential for two families to achieve the same goal via differing pathways could provide you with more tolerance for different family styles. Rather than labeling the Martins as a "better" family because they solve their problems without shouting and tears, you may want to consider that such outbursts could provide the same outcome for another family—and they might enjoy the outlet that yelling and crying provides!

THREE APPROACHES TO FAMILY SYSTEMS THEORY

In the previous section, we presented the basic terminology of family systems theory in our description of systems elements and processes. It is important to point out, however, that the window through which one may view communication in the family system may differ depending on the particular approach to systems theory one takes. Bochner and Eisenberg (1987) outline three models, originally identified by Carlos Sluzki, which differ in their approach to family systems theory: (1) interactional, (2) structural, and (3) constructivist or constructionist (p. 544; Sluzki, 1983). Each of these approaches to studying family systems adds to our understanding of family communication.

The **interactional view** emphasizes the importance of message transactions in the family system. In particular, this approach analyzes how *patterns of interaction* in the family help to define the nature of relationships in the family system. It is the relationship-defining aspect of messages rather than the content of messages themselves that is important. For example, Colleen almost always initiates suggestions for how to discipline the children in the family, while her husband, Jay, almost always supports her decisions without commenting very much. In this case, the interaction pattern in which the wife's "dominant" moves are typically

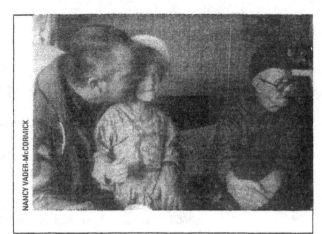

NANCY VADER-McCORMICK

The constructionist view of
the family focuses on
meaning making in the family.

accepted by her "submissive" husband is viewed as more important than the specific content of their talk. The persistent occurrence of reciprocal patterns of interaction among family members within a particular context of episodes that tend to
be repetitive is the focus of interest for this approach to family systems. The
exploration of family rules as they relate to repetitive patterns of interaction in
Chapter 7 is especially relevant to this view of family systems.

The **structural view** focuses on the social organization and role structure
of the family system. This view emphasizes how various dyads are organized in
the family, examines patterns of triangulation and role conflict, and attends to
issues related to how families manage boundaries and negotiate psychological
distance and closeness in the family. The structural view also identifies the
functions that particular members of the family perform for the family. For
example, a family therapist with a structural view of the family would be interested in the extent to which the parents in the family are able to work together so
that they can present a "united front" to their children. The therapist would be
concerned, for instance, if he or she noticed a coalition between a mother and
daughter, who are very close and involved in each other's lives, against a father
who tends to be "blamed" for the problems in the family. The therapist might
also try to identify the roles that various family members play in an alcoholic
family. Fitzpatrick's (1988) work on types of marital role structures is an example of research compatible with this view of systems theory. We address some
of the concepts related to the structural view of systems theory in our discussion
of the family ecosystem in Chapter 7 and in our discussion of family roles in
Chapter 10.

The **constructionist view** of the family tends to focus on meaning-making
processes in the family. How does the family construct its particular social reality?
What is the family's view of the world and its relationship to it? How do family
members' belief structures, their paradigms for living, and their interpretations of
events help us to understand their behavior? How is the family's social reality
revealed in the narratives or stories that family members construct of their experience together or in the content of their conversations? For example, how do Alice
and Ted tell the intensely emotional story of their personal crisis of going through
an abortion together (Ellis & Bochner, 1992) or how do a couple's conversational

APPLICATION 3.1

THE BROWN FAMILY

Using systems theory terminology, analyze the communication in the Brown family system:

Sara and William Brown lived in an older neighborhood in downtown Detroit, Michigan. William worked on the assembly line in a steering gear plant that recently began rehiring employees after a series of layoffs. Sara stayed at home, caring for their four children: two-year-old Teddy, four-year-old Robby, and the twins, Lauri and Melissa, both ten.

Sara's parents recently moved back to Detroit after living for eleven years in Arizona. Although she and her mother had always been close, Sara found it difficult to adjust to the daily phone calls and surprise visits that she received from her parents. She disliked that her parents, now retired, seem intent on spoiling their four grandchildren.

To make things worse, William was clearly disturbed by what he perceived to be his in-laws' interference with his family life. He resented the gifts that the maternal grandparents showered upon his four children. He also feared that Sara was too closely tied to her mother and, because Sara's mother had vigorously opposed their marriage, that this would cause marital problems at some point.

Sara felt caught between her parents and her husband. Although she felt loyal to her mother and father, she recognized that she and William had to maintain a life separate from that of her parents. She found herself defending her parents' behavior to William and his attitudes to her parents. She and William frequently engaged in loud arguments that added to Sara's stress. Although she did not agree with her parents' actions, she felt disloyal whenever she perceived herself to be siding with William against them.

Whenever Sara and William began a verbal battle, the younger children became disruptive and somewhat hyperactive. They would frequently run through the house yelling and screaming at each other. Sometimes the older son would throw toys or hit his younger brother. This behavior usually postponed the couple's argument, but it frequently resulted in a redirection of the anger and frustration felt by the parents toward their children which, in turn, made both William and Sara feel guilty.

William's dissatisfaction with the situation continued to grow for some time. He began working overtime to try to keep a little distance between himself and his problems at home and to make extra money for a camping vacation at a nearby lake. Between the long hours he kept and the tension at home, William frequently found himself worn out. The more tired he felt, the more he found himself resenting the fact that Sara could not straighten things out with her parents and make life a little easier for him. At work, instead of concentrating on his job, he found himself wondering what was going on at home and worrying about the long-term effects of living so close to Sara's parents. His blood pressure rose to 180/95 and he frequently complained of headaches.

themes reveal their orientation toward separateness and togetherness in their relationship (Sillars, et al., 1992). The constructionist view is based on social construction theory, which we describe in Chapter 1. Our discussion in later chapters of marital reality construction and of meaning-making in the family as a process of telling stories, as well as our description of family stories, myths, metaphors, and themes in Chapters 8 and 9 are also related to the constructionist view of the family.

According to general systems theory, families can be productively thought of as family systems because they incorporate all of the systems elements and processes we have thus far described. As we have indicated, systems theory terminology provides us with a vocabulary for thinking about communication in the family. For example, you can begin to think about how your own family defines and regulates its boundaries; or try to identify the extent to which particular family systems goals are shared or integrated in the family; or notice how inputs in the family, such as information from the media, are filtered, screened, or processed by the family. Depending upon your approach to family systems theory, you can analyze how the interaction patterns in the family define the nature of relationships in the family, examine the functions that various family members perform for the family, or examine how meaning is generated in the family. In the following section we discuss current perspectives, primarily from the constructionist view, that have made important contributions to the evolution of family systems thinking.

CURRENT PERSPECTIVES IN THE SYSTEMS VIEW OF THE FAMILY

Systems theory began as an innovative way to think about human experience. Instead of perceiving problems in terms of linear causality, that is, as a consequence of the effects of one person's behavior on another, we can pay more attention to the mutual influence that family members have on one another. Systems theory can make us more aware of our interdependence, help us avoid assigning "blame" in the family, show us how to recognize patterns of interaction which often get repeated in the family, teach us about such issues as how families maintain boundaries and monitor and process incoming and outgoing information in the family, and help us to observe how the family regulates the behavior of its members.

However, while the systems view is useful in providing a set of concepts about family process, we do not want to suggest that this view is a way to "decode" daily interactions and communication in the family. Hoffman (1990) has called this the Rosetta Stone fallacy. This fallacy assumes that if we analyze the family's inputs and outputs, rules, feedback mechanisms, roles, repeated patterns, and other dimensions of the system, we will be able to decipher the "real meaning" of communication in the family. Current discussions in the literature of systems theory view this formula approach to the application of systems theory as somewhat simplistic.

Some researchers have expressed the concern that, taken as a whole, the language of family systems theory may give one a sense of the family as a kind of mechanistic organism (Hoffman, 1990). For example, an image of a mobile hanging from the ceiling has been used as a metaphor to describe the family as a system; if one were to bump one part of the mobile, all the parts would jiggle. This image represents the interdependence of family members; there is the danger, however, that it also presents an image of the family as a kind of machine made up of parts that have some kind of permanent relationship to one another.

It is useful to caution the reader against assuming that the categories, types, and generalizations we describe here somehow capture "what a family is *really* doing." The language of family systems theory, in actuality, offers the reader ways to represent family process and metaphors for thinking about family process (Rosenblatt, 1994). That is, family systems theory provides us with a set of ideas and a language for having a conversation about interactions in the family.

Just as with any conversation, discussions of family systems theory concepts are constantly evolving; ideas evolve, just as families do. What we have presented in the previous sections of this chapter are concepts and ideas generally associated with general systems theory. In the following section we discuss some of the more recent ideas and reevaluations of systems theory. These include ideas that have been developed by gender-sensitive family theorists, researchers influenced by social construction theory, family therapists, and those who have a dialectical view of family communication. The critique of systems theory can be thought of as a *shift in emphasis* in several areas of particular importance. There are six characteristics we have associated with some of the newer prevailing views of systems theory: (1) emphasis on an individual–system dialectic, (2) the significance of change over stability, (3) the importance of narrative in the construction of meaning, (4) the focus on language in the construction of social reality, (5) the attention to intergenerational influences and interconnectedness, and (6) the need for awareness of how culture and gender bias relates to our interpretations of family life.

The Dialectic Between the Individual and the System

New systems thinking tends to emphasize the *dynamic interplay between the individual and the family*, which can be related to an individual–system dialectic. Several family systems theorists have made the point that the tendency of traditional systems theory to compare an individual perspective with a systems perspective can create a false dichotomy between the individual and the whole family system (Weeks, 1986; Nichols, 1987).

In focusing on characteristics of the whole family unit, we can see family systems theory as an alternative to social theory that focuses exclusively on the problems and inner experiences of individuals. However, instead of thinking of systems theory as an alternative to an individual perspective toward problems in the family, it may be more appropriate to take a dialectical view of the relationship between the individual and the family system. In contrast to the either/or approach (represented by an individual *versus* a systems perspective) is the dialectical view that suggests that one needs to move back and forth between the individual and relationships in the family to have a full appreciation of how meanings develop in the family. As Weeks (1986) has argued, there is a need to "fully integrate" both individual and whole family perspectives in order to understand problems in human relationships (p. 6). Nichols (1987) has used the phrase "the self in the system" to focus attention on the importance of the individual in the family.

Families are made up of individuals whose habits of relating and identities can appear to be enduring and permanent but who also have the potential for spontaneous change and growth. In Chapter 1, we indicated that the family is an "abstraction" (even definitions of the family are somewhat arbitrary). Understanding what occurs in families is a matter of understanding what transpires between and among individuals. For example, one of the author's students indicated how frustrated she was over a rule prescribing that she and her mother were not to talk about the daughter's struggle with alcoholism. The resolution to this problem was not a consequence of confronting and changing the pattern but a consequence of the daughter's own grieving, forgiving, and coming to terms with her mother's inability to discuss the issue. The pattern, which one might call rule-governed, remains the same, but the story that the daughter tells about the pattern is different than it was several years earlier because of how she has explored her own experience. Family systems theory provides us with a language for talking about mutual influence and patterned behavior, but knowledge of individual experience is equally important.

The Dialectic Between Stability and Change

Current systems thinking has also tended to emphasize the idea that *change is just as significant, or more significant, in understanding family process as is the family's tendency to strive for stability*. Stability and change are viewed as inextricably bound together rather than as different dimensions of family life, a view compatible with our discussion of stability and change as a dialectical process. Earlier in the development of family systems theory, stability—the striving for equilibrium or homeostasis—was typically presented as the primary goal of family life (Jackson, 1970). This view sees families as developing typical patterns of interaction which help to maintain predictability and help its members to resist change. Families are seen as using feedback mechanisms, such as sanctions for rule violations, primarily to control members so that stability can be maintained at the expense of change.

Reevaluations of family systems theory, however, have tended to view change as a primary characteristic of family functioning; stability is seen as a secondary function (Anderson & Goolishian, 1988; Hoffman, 1990; Gilligan & Price, 1993). The previous tendency to place stability in the foreground and change in the background has been reassessed in part as an idea compatible with Western cultural values. Some have argued that, in Buddhist terms, "change is the constant and stability is an illusion" (Chang & Phillips, 1993, p. 104). While it is useful to be able to identify patterns in the family's interaction, it is also important for us to remember that families are in a constant state of motion and flux. Our ability to identify stable roles and patterns may solidify our view of the family at a point in time and help us talk about what we see happening in the family, but, in actuality, time and motion, like a river, keep the family in a continuous state of change.

The Importance of Narrative

Recent approaches to understanding family systems have emphasized the importance of *narrative in understanding family process* (Anderson & Goolishian, 1988; Bochner, 1994; Bruner, 1986; Doherty, 1986; Friedman, 1993; Gilligan &

Price, 1993; Hoffman, 1990; McNamee & Gergen, 1992; Parry, 1991; White, 1993; White & Epston, 1990). One way to understand current ideas about the relationship between stability and change is to think of stability as grounded in the stories that family members tell about their lives together. The predictable family patterns that we identify can be considered important pieces of a family's history, which give the family a sense of communal identity. In this sense, a family's stability is the set of shared memories that help to make behavior in the family predictable.

A **shared memory** represents how family members recall their previous interactions; memories are related to the stories that they create about their experiences together.

The following example helps to illustrate the relationship between experience, memory, and family stories. Jack is a senior in college and is about to graduate; he is concerned about finding a job after graduation. Jack's father is worried about Jack's future also, so he frequently offers Jack advice. Jack's car is ready for the junkyard and Jack is planning to ask his father to loan him money for a new car. Jack's last discussion with his father about money helps him to predict what the upcoming discussion might be like. In the past, when Jack has asked his father for money or a loan, his father usually "comes through," but not without asking Jack a lot of questions about how he manages his money and how Jack is going to use the money he is asking his dad to loan him. This usually makes Jack defensive and angry, which he tries to hide. The rule seems to be, "Whenever Jack asks for a loan, Dad gives Jack a lecture." As a consequence of this rule, which describes a pattern that has occurred in the past, Jack is anxious and nervous about asking his father for a car loan, even though he knows he will. The rule seems to reflect a stable pattern in their communication.

Jack remembers previous episodes and constructs a scenario, a story, that represents how the interaction in the present is likely to go. He assumes that his father will quiz him about whether he actually needs the car, criticize the type of car Jack would like to buy, and indicate to Jack that buying a new car at this time is a big responsibility, especially now, when Jack has not yet found a job. When he talks to his father, Jack is tense and hesitant. In response to Jack's request, his father is quiet for a long time and then tells Jack that he would like to buy his son a new car for graduation. Furthermore, he thinks that Jack should make his own decision about what car to buy, within a reasonable price range. Father and son agree on a price range, a figure that turns out to be very close to what Jack wanted, and end their transaction agreeably. Jack is elated—and very surprised. The story of Jack's interaction with his father has taken a new twist, and Jack knows that, in the process, their relationship has changed.

In their conversations with one another, family members shape the present moment from the memories of past interactions. These memories become family stories. **Family stories** are the narratives that family members construct about their life together, just as Jack's memory of a discussion with his father is a story that he remembers, or a conversation between two family members that reflects a family theme. But there is a tension between memory and the flow of life as time moves forward. Jack has a memory of the pattern, but the story keeps evolving. One can grasp the simplicity of this concept by noting that every day they are together, family members are getting older, their biology is changing, and the concerns related to their particular stage of life are changing. All of these changes make interaction in the present a little different from conversation in the past. As a consequence, the stories that family members create from the memories of their experience are constantly evolving.

An infinite variety of factors can affect the evolution of family stories. Even your own exposure to the ideas in this book will influence the story that you tell about your family. As you think about the ideas discussed here, you may begin to look for rules in your family or think about other aspects of how your family functions as a system. By paying attention to your family's communication, you may put a different construct on what you observe in your family and on your own family experience. When you finish reading this book, you may view your family a little differently; that is, you may tell a story about your family that is a little different from the one you might have told six months ago. Consequently, as your understanding of your family changes, the rules and patterns in your family will have the potential to change, too.

White (1993) has summed up this narrative approach to understanding family process:

> The idea that it is the meaning which persons attribute to their experience that is constitutive of those persons' lives has encouraged social scientists to explore the nature of the frames that facilitate the interpretation of experience. Many of these social scientists have proposed that it is narrative or story that provides the primary frame for this interpretation, for the activity of meaning-making: that it is through the narratives or the stories that persons have about their own lives and the lives of others that they make sense of their experience. Not only do these stories determine the meaning that persons give to experience, it is argued, but these stories also largely determine which aspects of experience persons select out for expression. In addition, inasmuch as action is prefigured on meaning-making, these stories determine real effects in terms of the shaping of persons' lives.
>
> This perspective should not be confused with that which proposes that stories function as a reflection of life or as a mirror for life. Instead, the narrative metaphor proposes that persons live their lives by stories—that these stories are shaping of life, and that they have real, not imagined, effects—and that these stories provide the structure of life (p. 36).

Social Reality as Linguistically Constructed

Recent approaches to systems theory have tended to emphasize the importance of *families as meaning-making systems whose reality is linguistically constructed through conversation* (Anderson & Goolishian, 1988; Hoffman, 1990). While this concept may seem overly technical, it describes the relatively simple idea that the interpretations or meanings that family members assign to actions and events are directly related to the language or discourse they use. For example, imagine a scenario in which a sixteen-year-old daughter who has just gotten her driver's license asks her mother if she can drive alone to visit a girlfriend who lives eighty miles away. The mother deems the daughter's request "utterly ridiculous." This mother's response attaches a different meaning to the request and to the relationship between mother and daughter than a response that would present a series of questions to the daughter: "Do you think you are an experienced enough driver to travel that far alone? Isn't it dangerous for a teenaged girl to be going that far by herself? Shouldn't you find someone else to go with you and try to stay overnight at Sharon's house?" Each mother in this illustration is resistant to the daughter's suggestion. In the first case, the mother holds an implicit judgment that the daughter's request is not legitimate or reasonable. Imagine that the daughter walks away, feeling foolish. Imagine also an alternative scenario in which the daughter gets angry at her mother and accuses her mother of being "overprotective"; mother then argues that her daughter is being immature and self-centered and the argument escalates until the daughter stomps off to her room and slams the door. Different experiences have emerged from these two different scenarios of conversations between mother and daughter.

Current family systems analysis sometimes refers to this process of attaching meaning to events (including requests like the one in our example) as a description of how families **frame** such encounters through their conversations with one another. Similar encounters between mother and daughter may be framed as "fights," "unreasonable suggestions," "rebelliousness," or "overprotectiveness," depending upon the conversation between mother and daughter. Family systems therapists and researchers often try to understand how family members talk about their experience. How do family members frame their experience or tell stories of their encounters with one another in ways that may be painful or adversarial and how can they be helped to generate different meanings through their conversations?

In her work analyzing conversations between family therapists and the families they are trying to help, McNamee (1989) has described the way that a family therapist can help a family reframe the interpretations that they make of their experience by questioning and expressing curiosity about the taken-for-granted meanings that have been generated in the family. One example McNamee gives shows how a son's "bad behavior" is reframed by a therapist as "lively." The therapist expresses curiosity about the adversarial nature of the son's relationship to his father and frames it as an "interesting" way for father and son to connect. In conversations with the family, the therapist explores different possibilities for how the *family* might describe what is happening in their relationship. The therapist helps the family to reframe their experience through conversations that use language in a different way. How the mother and daughter in our example interpret or frame their experience depends upon how they label, describe, and talk about the daughter's request. Thus, the patterns, rules, and other aspects of the system can be seen as linguistically constructed through their discourse. The emphasis on meaning and reality as linguistically constructed suggests that systems characteristics, such as rules and patterns, stem from how family members communicate with one another. The conversation produces the pattern as much as the pattern produces the conversation.

The Significance of Intergenerational Influences

Current perspectives on family systems theory have also tended to focus *more attention on intergenerational influences* on the family (Boszormenyi-Nagy & Spark, 1984; Kramer, 1985; Framo, 1992). As Boszormenyi-Nagy and Spark have argued, "If one accepts the premise that it is essential to study the interconnectedness between an individual and his family system, then the boundaries of the family must be extended to include the interlocking between a nuclear family and families of origin (including the in-laws)" (p. 216). Families are not viewed as closed systems but as intimate communities with histories that extend beyond one generation. It may be helpful to analyze how a family functions within the framework of concepts that we have described in this chapter, but it may be equally helpful to include an examination of the influence of previous generations on the family.

The family's history includes the experiences that the parents, or the spousal dyad, have had in their family of origin. The conversations among family members in the present may be influenced by relationships and experiences in previous generations. Framo (1992) has made the point that "individuals incorporate aspects of their parents' marital relationship as well as characteristics of their individual parents" (p. 125). Attention to intergenerational influences on the family includes recognizing that rules and styles of communicating as well as gender orientations often get passed down from one generation to the next (Fink, 1993).

In addition, the struggles of one generation of parents often have an impact on the problems that children, as adults, have in relating to their own mates and children. As Framo (1992) suggests, "The invisible bonds of loyalty to the family of origin exercise their irresistible influence throughout one's lifetime" (p. 123). In order to understand and appreciate fully what has happened in the current generation, it is often useful to understand intergenerational patterns and influences. In a later chapter, we discuss the "baggage" that couples inevitably bring with them as they create their own families. Framo (1992) describes the influence of his family of origin on his own first marriage and offers testimony that most of us can relate to:

> I think that in some ways, in my marriage to Mary, I felt similar to my father in his marriage to my mother. On a deeper level, I suspect that our hostility to each of our opposite sex parents got displaced onto each other. . . . It took me years to rework the image of being a man that I got from my father, and this change may have something to do with why, in my second marriage, I am more free to give and get love (p. 227).

In the passage above, Framo poignantly describes the influence that his family of origin had on his first marriage. Kramer (1985) provides an example of the way that the different patterns that each spouse learned in his or her family of origin can influence communication in the nuclear family:

Dan: My mother came over the other day. She was repeating things three or four times—I mean, she *repeated* them. I can look at it more objectively now.

Helen: I could see how it was affecting me. I can accept her doing it more than I can accept Dan's needing it. When I tell him something and then he comes back and says, "Now, what did you say?" or "Tell me that again," I just think: "You baby! I told you! Damn it!" But, interestingly enough, and this is really fascinating, the school wants to test our oldest son, Jeff, for learning disabilities. They think he has an auditory difficulty—that he cannot process what he hears the first time.

Dan: Is it connected to my family? My family did not write notes and Helen's did. And there was the need to repeat and reinforce things from my side, versus Helen's side. It happens with my brother or sisters or mother.

Marian will call me up and tell the story, then Ann will call, and then if I talk to my mother, she'll tell the same story—it's repeated and I can't say, even at this time, "I heard it."

Helen: She'll ask if you heard it and you'll say, "Yes," and she'll tell it anyway . . .

Dan: . . . and it goes on and on to the point where I need less and less of that, but those patterns are still there.

Helen: Your mother was always there as the source of information. That wasn't true in my family—we were always coming and going so if you wanted to tell someone something, you wrote it down. And his dad did it, too, and his uncle did it.

Dan: Also, since the family did not read a lot, vocabulary was limited. We used words as simply as possible and as repetitively as possible to get the message across.

Helen: Did they repeat because they knew they needed to repeat, because they all needed it? Because they had trouble processing auditory things? Or did they lose the ability to process things because they didn't use it? Which came first?

Jan: Then it becomes a pattern in which children are taught that it is so difficult to process things auditorily, even if it isn't difficult for you, that it really *is* difficult, like it is now for Jeff.

Dan: You are taught that the first time around you don't have to catch it.

Jan: It will come around again—as a matter of fact, if you catch it the first time, you're going to be bored!

Dan: That's it! Isn't that Judy!

Helen: Yes, our daughters—none of them are like that, but our son *is* like that.

Jan: It looks like it's coming down the male line.

Helen: Oh, yes. They couldn't be more different in terms of what their abilities are. Judy gets real annoyed when you tell her something twice. She says, "I heard you!"

Jan: (to Helen) But that's like you.

Dan: Oh, ho! The parallel's there!

Helen: I know she's a mirror. It's funny and scary at the same time (pp. 14–15).

In discussing this dialogue, Kramer comments, "As Dan and Helen were able to step back and see the patterns in their families, there bubbled up an escalating enjoyment in discovering the parallels and the process" (p. 15). When we include a description of patterns in previous generations in our search to understand behavior in the present we often "discover the parallels." In subsequent chapters, we explore further some of these issues in our discussion of marital reality construction and the family's ecosystem.

Given the importance of intergenerational issues in the family, you might wish to find out more about the relationship of your parents to your grandparents. Shawn, one of our students, tells the story of her father, Quinn. Quinn used to get irritated every time his mother, Shawn's grandmother, would look disapproving and leave the room when his father told a joke or shared a story about his youth on the farm. Quinn appreciated his father's jokes and stories, as most people who knew him did. His mother's disapproval of his father bothered Quinn so much that if his wife was not totally enthralled when Quinn, on rare occasions, told a joke or story of his own, he would get irritated with her. His perceptions changed, however, when he heard a cousin of his mother's share a story of her own.

Apparently, Quinn's mother at one time was quite pretty, loved to dance and sing, and before she was married she acted in community theatre groups. Quinn's father's family, however, never approved of Quinn's mother's theatrical interests; after they were married, all of her in-laws, who lived nearby, put pressure on Quinn's mother to end her amateur acting career. And Quinn's father refused to go dancing with her because dancing was against his religion. However, he captured the attention and admiration of friends and family through his teasing, humor, and skill in telling jokes and stories. Quinn's father got the kind of attention and admiration that Quinn's mother had experienced in her theatrical adventures. Quinn began to understand that his mother's "disapproval" had much more to do with her own disappointment and sense of being denied attention than it did with her "sour disposition." When Quinn heard his mother's story, he developed compassion for what must have been difficult years early in her marriage. As a consequence of the compassion he developed for his mother, his wife's response to his own occasional bid for attention seemed much less important to him. Shawn also felt more connected to her grandmother, who had been somewhat stern with her, and she understood something about the tension between her parents that she sometimes observed at social gatherings. Sometimes one's own behavior can change as a consequence of curiosity about the previous generation.

Concern for Gender and Culture Bias

Family systems theorists have, in recent years, emphasized the *need to examine family systems terminology for potential gender and cultural bias*. Feminist family theorists and researchers argue the importance of examining the extent to which a systems theory view of the family may reflect male cultural values or minimize the power differences between women and men and between adults and children (Ault-Riche, 1986; Goodrich, Rampage, Ellman, & Halstead, 1988; Gouldner, 1985; Hare-Mustin, 1978; Leslie & Glossick, 1992; Luepnitz, 1988; Libow, Raskin, & Caust, 1982; MacKinnon & Miller, 1987; Morgaine, 1992; Taggert, 1985; Walters, Carter, Papp, & Silverstein, 1988).

Walters, Carter, Papp, & Silverstein (1990) suggest that a common understanding of what is meant by "feminism" is important in discussing this issue. They offer the following definition:

> Feminism, we agreed, is a humanistic framework or world view concerned with the roles, rules, and functions that organize male–female interactions. Feminism seeks to include the experience of women in all formulations of human experience, and to eliminate the dominance of male assumptions. Feminism does not blame individual men for the patriarchal social system that exists, but seeks to understand and change the socialization process that keeps men and women thinking and acting within a sexist, male-dominated framework (p. 17).

Using this definition as a starting point, Walters and her colleagues (and others as well) have explored the ways that systems theory may have been used to "disadvantage women" (p. 17). One example of this problem relates to the issue of family violence. We must take care that in discussing the tendency for family members mutually to influence one another, we do not make the mistake of "blaming the victim" or believing that the victim of abuse is just as "responsible" for the problem as is the perpetrator of violent acts. This caution does not mean that one cannot feel compassion for abusers, who were often abuse victims themselves, or that violent couples do not sometimes participate in mutually destructive communication patterns. However, it does mean that individuals who behave violently should be held accountable for their actions and that cultural values and mores, which may reinforce violent patterns in the family, should be examined.

Furthermore, feminist family theorists and therapists caution us to question taken-for-granted assumptions that may emphasize certain systems processes at the expense of others. Gilligan (1982), for example, has argued that there are differences in values between men and women that suggest they inhabit two different cultural worlds. If gender differences in values exist, it is important to attach equal worth to each set of values. Women often tend to value connectedness, relatedness, expressiveness, nurturing, caretaking, and interdependence more than men. In taking a systems perspective of the family, it may be equally important for us to be consciously aware of the need for interdependence and connectedness as it is to understand how well a family establishes clear boundaries among family members. We may also need to take care that our acceptance of a father who is somewhat aloof and distant is not *greater* than our acceptance of a mother who may be perceived as overinvolved in her family members' lives. Researchers may also need to emphasize the qualities of male expressiveness and emotion in their exploration of the effects of a crisis on intimate relationships (Ellis & Bochner, 1992).

In addition to acknowledging the potential for gender bias in our study of family process, it is also useful to be aware of how our view of the family might

---

TABLE 3.1   Current perspectives in the systems view of the family.

1. *The Individual–System Dialectic*
   Emphasizes the need to view individual and relationship dynamics as interrelated, rather than take an either/or view of individual and whole family perspectives.
2. *The Stability–Change Dialectic*
   Emphasizes a view of the family in which families are thought of as in a constant state of motion and flux rather than striving primarily for equilibrium.
3. *The Importance of Narrative*
   Emphasizes the idea that the lives of families are shaped by the constantly evolving stories that family members construct of their life together.
4. *Social Reality as Linguistically Constructed*
   Emphasizes the idea that the meanings that are generated in the family emerge from the discourse and conversations that they share.
5. *Intergenerational Influences*
   Emphasizes the influence and interconnectedness between the patterns of one generation and another as the family's story unfolds.
6. *Gender and Culture*
   Emphasizes the need for an awareness of how one's taken-for-granted assumptions about the family or what one chooses to notice or value can be a reflection of gender and/or culture bias.

reflect cultural bias (McGoldrick, Pearce, & Giordano, 1982; Sue & Sue, 1990). This issue becomes increasingly important as cultural diversity increases in the United States and as the planet becomes more of a "global village."

Shon and Ja (1982) provide an example of the importance of understanding the influence of culture on communication in the family in their discussion of Asian families. In Western culture, we tend to value individuality, argumentative skills, and admire someone's ability to express their ideas and feelings. Most Asian cultures, however, do not attach the same values toward openness and free expression of one's thoughts and feelings. Instead, communication that contributes to the harmony and peace of the family are valued. The idea that there is a dialectical tension between differentiation and integration in the family (as we describe in Chapter 1) is a concept that one should view differently in Western culture than in Asian cultures. In Asian cultures, family members are not expected to differentiate themselves from the family but to behave in a way that will promote the family's integration. Direct confrontations are avoided, face-saving behaviors are important, and talking around a point is often more highly regarded than directness because people in Asian cultures believe that directness might lead to disagreement and confrontation. Shon and Ja (1982) tell the following story to illustrate the importance of indirectness in Asian culture:

> For example, consider this story of two Malaysian families. A daughter from a higher-class family fell in love with the son of a lower-class family. The son approached his parents and told them that he wanted to marry the girl from the higher-class family. His mother said she would approach the girl's family to see if it were acceptable to them. She made an appointment with the girl's mother and went to the home on the proper day. She was greeted by the mother and was shown into the sitting room. Refreshments were brought in consisting of tea and bananas. The two mothers talked about the weather and other things, but they never mentioned their children. After a period of time the boy's mother thanked her hostess politely and left. Upon returning home she told her son that the marriage was unacceptable and, therefore, not possible. The boy's mother knew this because in Malaysia tea and bananas are not generally served together. The girl's mother had given the message that her daughter and the other mother's son did not belong together. By doing it in this way she avoided direct discussion, which may have led to hurt feelings and a loss of face, not only for the boy's mother, whose son was rejected, but also for the girl's mother, who would have caused the other mother embarrassment and shame (pp. 216–217).

Family interaction may be influenced by the cultural background of the family, by differences between various subcultures that often exist side by side, and by differences in values between the generations. Differences in family forms and the impact of economic disadvantage are just as important as an awareness of cultural differences in understanding the family (Chilman, Nunnally, & Cox, 1988). Gay and lesbian families must cope with a culture that can be homophobic and that may stereotype family members. A new stepparent may have difficulty relating to her stepchildren because she feels that she has to live up to the cultural expectations of a natural parent. How does one apply systems concepts to the rules and communication patterns of a homeless family? Without

APPLICATION 3.2

CURRENT PERSPECTIVES IN THE SYSTEMS VIEW OF THE FAMILY

Describe a significant event, circumstance, issue, or conflict in your family. Indicate how the episode or situation illustrates one of the six characteristics that summarize current perspectives of family systems theory. For example:

Tory is a 24-year-old divorced Caucasian woman with a toddler. She is going to school while she is living on welfare; her plans are to complete a nursing degree. Her parents who live nearby help her out by babysitting their granddaughter, occasionally buying groceries, and helping with car repairs. Tory has met an African-American student in one of her math classes and has begun dating him. Edward is considerate and funny and gets along well with Tory's baby. Within a matter of just a few months the relationship has become serious. However, Tory's parents do not approve of interracial relationships and argue continuously with Tory about her relationship with Edward. They like Edward well enough, but they do not believe that interracial marriages can be successful and they do not want to see Tory fail in a second marriage. Some of Edward's friends—especially his female friends—do not hang out with him anymore because of his relationship with Tory, but Edward's closest friends and family are generally supportive. Despite her feelings of guilt and obligation toward her parents, Tory is considering breaking off relations with her family if they cannot accept her growing love for Edward.

1. How does the situation illustrate the dynamic relationship between the individual and the whole family?
2. How does the situation illustrate the family as a system that is continually changing?
3. How does the situation illustrate how families are shaped by the stories that they construct?
4. How does the situation illustrate the way that meanings emerge from the conversations that family members share?
5. How does the situation illustrate the influence and interconnectedness of the generations as the family's story unfolds?
6. How does the situation illustrate the influence of cultural and/or gender bias in the family's interaction?

an acknowledgment of the influence of culture and economic disadvantage into a systems approach to understanding the family, the identification of the family's rules, role functions, and communication patterns may seem abstract and inconsequential.

One additional point needs to made: Sometimes the need to avoid gender bias and respect cultural differences may be contradictory, especially if one is attempting to appreciate a family whose parents grew up in a culture with a more rigid patriarchal structure than our own. We would like to suggest, however, that sometimes contradictions such as this cannot be resolved. Ultimately, each family must be understood in terms of its own complexity and uniqueness. What we can do, however, is become more sensitive to our own biases and assumptions and to appreciate that those theories that are most useful in understanding any phenomenon are probably those that are still evolving.

In conclusion, this discussion of current perspectives of family systems theory should indicate that conceptual approaches to understanding family process are constantly unfolding. As Hoffman (1990) suggests, recent views of family systems make it clear that "the development of concepts is a fluid process" (p. 3). The sense that ideas about family systems are fluid and constantly unfolding helps to keep them vital and alive by inviting you to think about your own family experience and consider what fits for you. In this way, we hope that you come to see these ideas as opportunities for further dialogue and conversation rather than as rigid prescriptions about family process.

SUMMARY

The purpose of this chapter is to describe the systems perspective for understanding the family, because this perspective underlies the chapters that follow. The systems perspective, based on general systems theory, stresses the interdependence of family members and the importance of communication in the family system.

Six types of system elements compose family systems: (1) interdependent components, (2) inputs and outputs, (3) boundaries and hierarchies, (4) rules for operation, (5) system goals, and (6) feedback mechanisms. Communication is linked to all six in specific ways. Communication skills differentiate system components (family members) and allow them to develop relationships with each other, manage their designated family roles, and interact with the various suprasystems. Communication messages and other types of information form the inputs and outputs that flow through the family system. Nonverbal markers such as fences and door locks help to designate physical boundaries around family systems, just as messages differentiate one subsystem from another within the nuclear system. Family rules emerge from family interaction and govern future interaction. Similarly, communication makes it possible for families to establish goals and seek information about their progress toward or away from these goals.

Four types of systems processes are especially relevant to our discussion of family communication: (1) nonsummativity, (2) stability, (3) change, and (4) equifinality. Again, the messages that permeate a system provide the vehicle through which individual system components are able to combine their abilities into a collective whole that allows the system to accomplish more than the components could accomplish independently. Furthermore, family systems tend to strive for stability even though they are constantly changing.

In this chapter, we also discuss the influence of current perspectives related to the systems view of the family. Recent discussions of family systems reflect the influence of social construction theory and the dialectical view of family process, as well as influences from feminist family theorists and therapists and those concerned with the variety and diversity of family life. Six issues were identified in our discussion of current perspectives in the systems view of the family: (1) the individual–systems dialectic, (2) the stability–change dialectic, (3) the importance of narrative in understanding the family, (4) social reality in the family as linguistically constructed, (5) the significance of intergenerational relationships in the family, and (6) the importance of an awareness of gender and culture bias in one's thinking about the family.

Overall, the notion of a system provides the theoretical groundwork for the material to follow. Treating family interaction as an ongoing set of episodes with no beginning and no ending point avoids many of the pitfalls common to an analysis of family functioning such as blaming one family member for problems in the system. From a systems perspective, it is generally possible to identify functions that problematic behavior serves for the larger structure. A systems perspective allows you to appreciate the incredible complexity of family communication. Messages perform many functions on many levels; focusing on just one message or one episode in a family's collective history is futile. Finally, a systems perspective unifies a number of seemingly diverse topics such as rules, roles, themes and narratives, family types, and the family life cycle, which allows us to achieve a degree of relatedness and continuity in our approach to family communication.

KEY TERMS

boundary	interactional view
components	morphogenesis
constructionist view	morphostasis
diffuse boundaries	nonsummativity
equifinality	outputs
family stories	rigid boundaries
feedback	role
feedback mechanisms	rules
frame	shared memory
goal	structural view
hierarchy	subsystems
hierarchy of subsystems	suprasystem
hierarchy of suprasystems	system elements
inputs	system processes

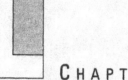

CHAPTER 4

COURTSHIP
AND
COMMITMENT

JANET YERBY

ANITA AND CARL

Anita Morales was dating someone else when she started going out with Carl Tyrrell. She and Carl were introduced by a mutual friend; Anita was a freshman in college and Carl was a sophomore. At the time they had started to date each other, neither of them was involved in a relationship that they really cared about. From their first date, their relationship was very intense. They were very physically attracted to each other; they also liked to do the same things together and they liked the security of being together. Anita was outgoing, funny, and intelligent. She had never before experienced the kind of feelings for anyone that she felt for Carl. She felt excited and alive when she was around Carl. Carl was attractive and serious. He made excuses to see her whenever he could and spent every free moment with her.

Their relationship progressed very quickly—it was exciting but a little scary, too. Carl planned to transfer to another university to study engineering the following year and Anita was wondering how they would take the separation. That summer they each had jobs near their families and within traveling distance of each other. They saw each other when they could on weekdays and on every weekend. Toward the end of the summer, Carl and Anita began to quarrel with one another over inconsequential issues; their conflicts seemed to emerge suddenly and without warning.

When she went back to college in the fall, Anita decided to join the staff of the college newspaper. She threw herself into the responsibilities that she was given. Carl came to see her on weekends, but it seemed to him that all Anita talked about was her work and the new friends she had made on the newspaper. He accused her of not being interested in anything he was doing. Anita felt betrayed by his accusations since it was Carl who had transferred to another school and encouraged her to get involved in other activities in order to meet new people. She accused him of being possessive and jealous. Carl began to call long distance more frequently during weekdays. If Anita was not home when he called, the next time that he called Carl would ask where she had been. These conversations always had an edge to them.

Anita began to date a friend on the newspaper staff without saying anything to Carl. One weekend when Carl came to visit, Anita announced that she was dating someone else. Carl exploded and they spent most of the evening arguing. Anita told Carl that she thought they should quit seeing each other for a while. Carl left at the end of the weekend feeling angry and despondent. He called her every night the following week. Their conversations were stormy. Carl would plead for Anita to try to work things out and Anita would try to hold her ground. She said that she really cared for Carl, but that she needed some distance between them right now. Carl accepted Anita's wishes and started writing occasional letters instead of calling. After a few months, the intensity of Carl's letters began to diminish and he began to share more factual information about what was going on in his life. Carl also began to date other women occasionally. Anita wrote to Carl from time to time, sharing what was going on in her life and inquiring about his.

One weekend when Anita was home to celebrate her mother's birthday, Carl stopped by to see her. The school to which he had transferred was not far from the town where Anita's family lived. They spent an evening together. At first, they were a little more formal with each other than they had been in the past and they did not get physically involved with each other. They had a wonderful evening, however, and parted without saying much about what would happen next. Anita went back to school expecting Carl to call her that week. When he didn't call, she finally called him. She said that she thought they ought to start seeing each other again to see if they still had strong feelings for each other. Carl said that he would come up that weekend. They spent the entire weekend together. Three weeks later Carl proposed marriage and Anita accepted.

UNDERSTANDING ANITA AND CARL

Do Anita and Carl have a solid foundation on which to build a successful marriage? How confident can they be about their decision to marry? Out of all the millions of people in the world, how did they happen to find each other, fall in love, and decide to get married? What factors will determine whether their decision will prove to be right? Did they choose each other rationally or were some irrational factors involved in their selection of each other as mates? These questions draw attention to the functions of communication in the process of courtship and commitment to marriage.

Why do some marriages succeed and others fail? This vexing question has frustrated students of the family for a long time. Scholars have searched and probed, queried and pried, examined and reexamined, trying to unlock the mysteries of a happy marriage. Yet little ground has been gained in the battle to triumph over the interpersonal perils of marriage. The divorce rate remains extremely high and each year thousands of adults and children experience the pain and suffering that go along with breaking up a family.

Ironically, there is no shortage of advice about what constitutes a good marriage, how to form one, and what to do to make it last. The problem is that the experts have many different versions of the ideal marriage. The range of conflicting advice found in trade books and primers on marriage is bewildering. It is also

depressing. There is so much contradictory evidence, so many different sociological and psychological factors correlated moderately, but not substantially, with
successful marriage, that it is easy to be left not knowing who to believe or what
advice to follow. The information is so confusing that you may be left wondering
whether there is anything more to say than, "It takes a lot of luck to have a happy
marriage!" This remark may sound like something a cynic would say. But before
dismissing the possibility that the "good luck" proposition contains a grain of
truth, let us consider what is involved in the decision to get married.

This chapter examines patterns of premarital interaction associated with the
decision to marry. The first section reviews theories of mate selection and interpersonal attraction. A distinction is drawn between why people are attracted to
each other and what people say and do to facilitate attraction. The development of
a relationship is problematic because its course largely depends upon what each
person says and does. The second section builds on the idea that the development
of a relationship is a problem that hinges on what people say and do to each other
as they move toward commitment. The problem of resolving issues of ambiguity
as the couple negotiates how to characterize their relationship in its early stages
and the importance of momentum in carrying the relationship forward will be discussed. Five forms of escalation are presented, which advance the view that
courtship involves persuasion. We also explore the ways in which a relationship
becomes objectified, idealized and, occasionally, functions as a resolution of an
identity crisis for both partners. The third section discusses decisive episodes
called turning points, which can make or break a relationship. These decisive
moments center attention on whether the relationship is sufficiently loving, the
partners are sufficiently virtuous, and the bond between partners is sufficiently
resilient to make the relationship "marriageable." The fourth section describes
four uniquely different patterns of courtship that revolve around different relational themes. These quite different patterns may lead to the same result: the decision to marry. Overall, this chapter attempts to dispel some of the myths that exist
about what brings people together. As we look at what people say and do to each
other during courtship, it will become clear that if logic and rationality were
insisted upon, all communication would have to cease (Freedle, 1975), and far
fewer people would be willing to commit to marriage.

SELECTING A MARRIAGE PARTNER

Courtship as Decision Making

On what basis does one person decide that another person is "marriageable"? *The
decision to marry is a prediction about how one person's life with another person
will evolve in the future based largely on how it has evolved in the past.* In this
sense, we can conceive of **courtship as decision making**. Each person assumes
that he or she can rely on the past to predict the future. It is taken for granted that
the attitudes, feelings, and experiences that bring two people together are the same
ones that will keep them together. If you ask a couple why they want to get married, they are likely to give you one or more of the following reasons: (1) we have
a lot in common; (2) we get along really well; (3) we are very attracted to each
other. But how do they know that they still will have a lot in common five or ten
years from now? How do they know that they will be able to talk as freely and as

effectively then as they do now? What makes them think that they will stay attracted to each other as they grow older together?

The cynical view is that most people contemplating marriage for the first time have no real idea of what is in store for them. Dating couples sometimes face issues related to religion, racism, abortion, class, and gender. Too frequently, however, the toughest decisions a couple will face include what to do when close friends fail to support the relationship or whether or not to engage in sex before marriage (not including the decision to marry itself). Are these experiences a sufficient foundation for anticipating how they will cope with the many unforeseen events that can alter the course of a marriage? How well will they function if she loses her job; he becomes critically ill; they have a child born with a severe handicap; or they are forced to move to an unfamiliar place where they have no friends. Considering these possibilities, it is difficult to anticipate the course a marriage will take. In Bergman's famous film, *Scenes from a Marriage*, Marianne and Johan look upon the marital selection process as something akin to "luck of the draw."

Perhaps the secret to predicting whether a marriage will turn out to be happy is that there is no secret. Marriage is a calculated risk. Even though the decision to marry may place your emotional health in jeopardy, marriage is nonetheless a ubiquitous experience. More than ninety percent of all people will get married. Not only will most people get married, but those who marry unsuccessfully probably will marry again. This odd pattern of "repeating the error" makes it apparent that the selection of a marriage partner is not an altogether rational process.

Mate Selection

You might like to think of courtship and commitment as moderately rational; however, the events that move two people toward marriage sometimes seem to have a life of their own. Consider the following testimony from a study conducted by Rubin (1976):

> We met at this place and I kind of liked her. She was cool and kind of fun to be with. Before I knew it we were going steady. I had this class ring from high school and she kept wanting me to give it to her. So finally one night I took it off and did. And the next thing I knew, she took it down and had it made smaller. She made a big thing out of it, and so did her family. Don't get me wrong; I liked her good enough. But I just didn't think about getting married—not then anyhow. But then, after we were going together for almost a year, it just seemed like the thing to do. So we did. (p. 164).

In Chapter 5, we will describe how a relationship develops after two individuals decide to marry. Our discussion of the marital relationship will explore the expectations that each individual brings to a marriage. But as important as expectations may be to the future of a marriage, this factor alone cannot explain how two people become committed to marriage. If marriage is viewed as the development of a relationship, then the entire history of the relationship needs to be examined. Taking a relationship perspective on marriage draws attention to the importance of considering what happens *before* two individuals commit themselves to each other.

For many years the selection of a mate was viewed as a psychological act in which certain measurable traits could account for why one person chooses to marry another. Two theories were advanced, one which hypothesized that mate selection could be explained by **homogamy** (similarity), the other which emphasized **heterogamy** (complementarity of differences) (Altman and Taylor, 1973; Knapp, 1978). Do birds of a feather flock together or do opposites attract?

Both of these theories have been shown to have some merit, but neither theory provides a forceful explanation of why one person selects another. The research on mate selection suggests that the most crucial factor is **differential contact**—typically, the "field of eligibles" is a confined social network. This may explain why demographic factors such as race, religion, education, and social class usually are more predictive of mate selection than social-psychological variables such as attitudes or personality profiles. For most individuals, the field of eligibles is narrowed considerably by socialization experiences that limit the range of other persons with whom one will interact. Since individuals with more similar demographic profiles are more likely to hold similar attitudes and values, demographic similarities tend to cancel out social-psychological factors.

While studies of complementarity have produced some evidence that certain types of individuals will match up with certain other types, the strongest support involves atypical cases in which one of the individuals has a "psychological deficiency," such as a weak ego, which is counterbalanced by a mate with a very strong ego. While this "neurotic" pattern has been found to occur frequently among couples who marry at a young age, it is not characteristic of the broader range of "normal" marriages (Bolton, 1961).

Mate selection has also been viewed as a **filtering process** in which individuals apply different tests of compatibility to each other as they progress toward increased commitment (Kerckhoff & Davis, 1962). The test of whether or not the other is regarded as sufficiently compatible tends to change as time passes and experiences are accumulated. Filtering theories provide a richer conception of complementarity, but they do not adequately explain how individuals will respond to particular combinations of personal attributes.

Even if empirical support for these theories were more convincing, we would not know precisely how similarities or differences affect individuals during premarital interaction because inferences about the selection of a mate must rely on measures taken after the mate has been selected. This standard procedure begs the question of whether or not these traits were important during the process of selection. Did Anita choose Carl because his political, religious, and moral values were similar to hers, or did their attitudes merge after they were attracted to each other?

There is another line of research that has examined the question of whether or not similarities between attitudes leads to interpersonal interaction (Byrne, 1969, 1971). These studies have tested the hypothesis that "the more similar another person's opinions, interests, or personality characteristics [are] to those of a perceiver, the more will the perceiver come to be attracted to the person" (Fishbein & Ajzen, 1975, p. 255). The studies that have been conducted to test this hypothesis have followed a standardized procedure. First, each subject in the study is asked to complete a questionnaire dealing with attitudes and opinions on a variety of issues. A few weeks later, subjects are given a copy of the same form and told that it has been completed by some other person. This person is sometimes referred to as a "bogus stranger," since no such person really exists. But subjects are not told that they have received fictitious forms.

The questionnaires are systematically distributed in such a way that some subjects receive forms with responses that are nearly identical with those they

Theories of mate selection often overlook the importance of communication and the progression of a relationship toward the commitment to marry.

gave earlier, while others receive questionnaires containing responses that are highly dissimilar to their own. After the subjects are given an ample opportunity to look over the "stranger's" responses, they are asked to report the degree to which they would tend to like this person and how willing they would be to work with this person in an experiment. The results of these studies repeatedly and conclusively show that the more similar the bogus stranger's attitude profile is to the perceiver's, the more "attractive" the bogus stranger is likely to be to the perceiver. Under these restrictive circumstances, then, attitude similarity leads to attraction.

Unfortunately, studies of interpersonal attraction underestimate the *significance of conversation* (Bochner, 1984). The fact that people talk to each other should not be taken for granted; it must become a part of the attraction equation. The problem is that research on interpersonal attraction is not interpersonal at all. As Levinger stated, "research on interpersonal attraction has tended to confine itself [to] . . . the target of attraction as an object of contemplation rather than a human being who stands in vibrant reciprocity" (1974, p. 100).

The sequence of interactional experiences that typifies the development of a relationship reveals that most of the time individuals become attracted before they know each other's attitudes and opinions, and rarely, if ever, does one person gain access to another person's attitudes through a written mode of communication. Most of what we learn and what we surmise about another person's behavior comes from talking to the person or observing his or her behavior. When research procedures have been modified to include conversation, the association between attitudinal similarity and attraction has been shown to be considerably more complicated. For example, Sunnafrank (1984) found that attitudinal similarity predicted interpersonal attraction only under circumstances in which conversations were highly atypical of what people say to each other when they are getting acquainted. Following more typical encounters, individuals tend to become more attracted to dissimilar people once they have the opportunity to interact with them (Sunnafrank, 1984). As Stephen (1985) has suggested, there is increasing evidence to support the view that it "may be as much the communication exchange between partners that determines the progress of their relationship as the background factors themselves" (p. 956).

To sum up, neither the research on mate selection nor the research on interpersonal attraction can tell us very much about *how* Anita and Carl's relationship

evolved to the point where they were prepared to commit themselves to marriage. This is because mate selection and interpersonal attraction have not been considered as processes that evolve over time. Bolton (1961) was one of the first writers to point this out:

> Perhaps mate selection must be studied not only in terms of variables brought into the interaction situation but also as a process in which a relationship is built up, a process in which the *transactions between individuals* in certain societal contexts are determinants of turning points and commitments out of which marriage emerges. Seen from this viewpoint, the development of a mate selection relation is a problematic process. By problematic is meant the outcome of the contacts of the two individuals is not mechanically predetermined either by the relation of their personality characteristics or the institutional patterns providing the context for the development of the marriage— though these are both certainly to be taken into account—but that the outcome is an end-product of a sequence of interactions characterized by advances and retreats along the paths of available alternatives, by definitions of the situation which crystallize tentative commitments and bar withdrawals from certain positions, by the sometimes tolerance of and sometimes resolution of ambiguity, and by the tension between open-endedness and closure that characterizes all relationships that have not been reduced to ritual. In short, the development of love relations is problematic because the product bears the stamp of what goes on between the couple as well as of what they are as individuals (pp. 235–236).

Viewing the development of a relationship as problematic brings into focus the importance of examining what goes on between the two individuals; that is, what they say and do to each other. Once a relationship begins, its members are faced with the problem of making it work. The metaphor of "work," in fact, has become part of the ordinary language of relationships. When Jane says to her boyfriend Bill, "We need to spend some time working on our relationship," she is expressing a need to talk with him about what's happening between them. She may also be implying that the relationship has become a problem. If they let the relationship run its natural course, Jane thinks the problem will become worse. She assumes that by talking about their relationship, they can "work things out" (fix the problem).

In one episode of the former television series "Moonlighting," Maddie says to her lover (and colleague), David, that she doesn't know where the relationship between them is going. She has strong feelings toward David, but she cannot be content with a relationship that is confined to the bedroom. The relationship has to move forward. David is ecstatic about the relationship. He is crazy about Maddie. But he also has a nagging fear that it could end at any moment. David wants to bring some of his things over to Maddie's house, where they've been sleeping together. His response to her concern about where the relationship is going is to say jokingly that he could move some of his things in with her. Then, the relationship could move from the bedroom to the bathroom and on to the living room and the kitchen. That's how relationships move for him. David's response is more than good-natured sarcasm about Maddie's anguish. He is concerned about the ambiguity of their relationship. He knows that Maddie's willingness to have him bring some of his things over would signal a more definite commitment on her part.

Each of them is trying to influence the other to extend the boundaries of the relationship, though each defines the problem differently.

MOVING TOWARD COMMITMENT

The communication or relational perspective treats the development of a relationship as a problem in its own right. The problem is that once some initial attraction occurs, individuals must say and do something to facilitate the development of their relationship. This section focuses on how communication can escalate a relationship toward increasing commitment.

Every relationship has a unique history. Some people fall in love at first sight and others move slowly and cautiously toward a commitment to each other. In many relationships affection is asymmetrical. One individual is more attracted to the other, feels more strongly about the other, or is more uncertain about the other's feelings. When one person likes the other more than he or she is liked by the other, this person faces a difficult interactional situation with a lot at stake. Most of us like to think that falling in love is a natural and spontaneous process. But not many of us actually experience our relationships this way. The probability of being discovered by "the one person you were meant to be with" seems rather remote. More often, when you become attracted to a person you think of ways to get that person to notice you. When you like a person, you will probably say and do things to make the person like you.

The point should be obvious: *courtship involves persuasion*. There is a considerable amount of interpersonal influence that takes place as the relationship between two individuals intensifies. The influence is more covert in romantic relationships than in other interpersonal experiences, and frequently, the commitments to which the process is directed are established more implicitly. But the indirect nature of persuasion in close relationships should not be allowed to conceal what is going on. Six factors influence the movement toward commitment: (1) ambiguity, (2) momentum, (3) forms of escalation, (4) objectification of the relationship, (5) defining the other as marriageable, and (6) the relationship as a resolution to an identity crisis.

Ambiguity

Once a relationship moves beyond a state of casual acquaintance, some ambiguity about the definition of the relationship is bound to exist. There are no institutional constraints making the continuation of a relationship compulsory (such as there are in marriage); generally, the individuals proceed voluntarily. The institutional constraints of marriage carry certain premises about the closeness of the spouses and their commitments to each other. This is not the case in a premarital relationship. The meaning and value of the relationship are considerably more ambiguous. This tends to make premarital relationships even more precarious and fragile than marriages. The individuals have to figure out what the relationship means to each of them and then gauge their own perceptions of the relationship against their partner's. Anita may be crazy about Carl, but if she thinks he is not yet wild about her, she may measure her reactions carefully so as not to give the impression that she is rushing him.

CHAPTER 4   COURTSHIP AND COMMITMENT   93

evolved to the point where they were prepared to commit themselves to marriage. This is because mate selection and interpersonal attraction have not been considered as processes that evolve over time. Bolton (1961) was one of the first writers to point this out:

> Perhaps mate selection must be studied not only in terms of variables brought into the interaction situation but also as a process in which a relationship is built up, a process in which the *transactions between individuals* in certain societal contexts are determinants of turning points and commitments out of which marriage emerges. Seen from this viewpoint, the development of a mate selection relation is a problematic process. By problematic is meant the outcome of the contacts of the two individuals is not mechanically predetermined either by the relation of their personality characteristics or the institutional patterns providing the context for the development of the marriage— though these are both certainly to be taken into account—but that the outcome is an end-product of a sequence of interactions characterized by advances and retreats along the paths of available alternatives, by definitions of the situation which crystallize tentative commitments and bar withdrawals from certain positions, by the sometimes tolerance of and sometimes resolution of ambiguity, and by the tension between open-endedness and closure that characterizes all relationships that have not been reduced to ritual. In short, the development of love relations is problematic because the product bears the stamp of what goes on between the couple as well as of what they are as individuals (pp. 235–236).

Viewing the development of a relationship as problematic brings into focus the importance of examining what goes on between the two individuals; that is, what they say and do to each other. Once a relationship begins, its members are faced with the problem of making it work. The metaphor of "work," in fact, has become part of the ordinary language of relationships. When Jane says to her boyfriend Bill, "We need to spend some time working on our relationship," she is expressing a need to talk with him about what's happening between them. She may also be implying that the relationship has become a problem. If they let the relationship run its natural course, Jane thinks the problem will become worse. She assumes that by talking about their relationship, they can "work things out" (fix the problem).

In one episode of the former television series "Moonlighting," Maddie says to her lover (and colleague), David, that she doesn't know where the relationship between them is going. She has strong feelings toward David, but she cannot be content with a relationship that is confined to the bedroom. The relationship has to move forward. David is ecstatic about the relationship. He is crazy about Maddie. But he also has a nagging fear that it could end at any moment. David wants to bring some of his things over to Maddie's house, where they've been sleeping together. His response to her concern about where the relationship is going is to say jokingly that he could move some of his things in with her. Then, the relationship could move from the bedroom to the bathroom and on to the living room and the kitchen. That's how relationships move for him. David's response is more than good-natured sarcasm about Maddie's anguish. He is concerned about the ambiguity of their relationship. He knows that Maddie's willingness to have him bring some of his things over would signal a more definite commitment on her part.

APPLICATION 4.1 ———————————————

ESTABLISHING A RELATIONSHIP

Think of a movie or television program that you have seen in which two people develop a relationship with each other that seems to be leading to some sort of exclusive commitment. Some examples are *When Harry Met Sally, Frankie and Johnny*, and *Sleepless in Seattle*.

Trace the development of the relationship in terms of the six factors that move the relationship toward commitment.

Escalation

Our understanding of how commitments evolve has been greatly advanced by Charles Bolton's (1961) study of premarital interaction patterns that move individuals toward the commitment to marriage. **Escalators** are defined by Bolton as sequences of action that have a built-in momentum. Once the first step is taken, the individuals may feel as if they are being swept away as the relationship glides inexorably toward commitment to marriage. The hidden dangers of this process may have been what the famous sociologist Georg Simmel (1950, p. 328) had in mind when he warned individuals not to allow the enchantments of intimacy to lure them into "sending the last reserves of the soul after those of the body."

Five forms of escalators have been described by Bolton (1961): (1) involvement, (2) commitment, (3) addiction, (4) fantasy, and (5) idealization. We identify and provide examples of these five forms of escalators in Table 4.1. Each provides information about the nature of the relationship.

The first form is referred to as **involvement**. The relationship is escalated by interpersonal sequences that have the effect of coordinating one individual's activities and plans with the other's. The more each individual takes the other into account in working out a daily routine, the more involved they become with each other. In the beginning of the relationship, this may mean only that Anita and Carl try to arrange their schedules so that they can walk each other to class or have lunch together. As time passes, they may begin to talk about their career aspirations in relation to each other. Consequently, they may begin to conceive of a future that involves the other person. Some of each individual's personal goals may be revised in light of these conversations, but the important discovery is that the other's goals are complementary to one's own.

The second form of escalation is called **commitment**. Commitment refers to private and public expressions of the special meaning of the relationship and the feelings that define it. These two domains of experience, private and public, are woven closely together. At first, it may be sufficient for Carl to confine his expression of strong feelings for Anita to her alone. But after a time, she probably will want others to know. The promises or pledges that one person makes to another privately carry with them an implicit agreement to define the relationship in

TABLE 4.1   Phases in the escalation of a relationship.

1. *Involvement:* Interpersonal sequences in which two people coordinate their activities, agendas, plans, and schedules in order to spend more time together.
   Tracy and Patrick usually have lunch together on Tuesdays and Thursdays, meet each other after work, and leave their weekends free in order to spend time with each other.

2. *Commitment:* A couple makes private and public declarations of the importance of the relationship for them.
   Gary and Jay make it clear to their parents that they view their relationship as permanent and declare their feelings of love for each other.

3. *Addiction:* Two people become psychologically and physiologically dependent upon each other such that withdrawal can evoke anxiety or feelings of longing to be with the other person.
   When Carl was gone for three days on a job interview, he called Anita every evening on the telephone and would usually talk to her for over an hour. He could hardly wait to see her when he got home.

4. *Fantasy:* Individuals in the relationship daydream or develop mental images of their sexual, romantic, and/or day-to-day life together.
   Shawna thinks about the kind of stepfather that Cory might be for her small son: she pictures Cory taking the boy to baseball games, helping him with his homework when he starts school, and giving him advice about girls when her son is older.

5. *Idealization:* The tendency of individuals to focus on the positive qualities and overlook or minimize the negative qualities of their partners.
   Jake is aware of how much fun he has with his fiancée and how good she makes him feel; he overlooks the fact that she often drinks too much and tends to avoid conflict.

broader terms. She may want him to have dinner with her family. He may invite her to spend a vacation with his parents as an indication that their relationship is exclusive.

Moreover, a time will come when one person says "I love you" to the other. The commitment to love ordinarily precedes the commitment to marry, and in many cases, this message can be perceived as a sign that one is contemplating marriage. It is important, however, to understand how incredibly ambiguous the statement "I love you" can be. Henry (1973) expressed this point vividly in the following passage:

> If a man says "I love you" to a woman, she may wonder whether he means it, whether he loves only her, how much he loves her, whether he will love her next week or next year, or whether his love only means that he wants her to love him. She may even wonder whether his love includes respect and care, or whether his love is merely physical (p. 191).

A third form of escalation consists of what Bolton calls **addiction**. Love is like a potent drug insofar as it can produce a constitutional dependency that the individual eventually becomes terrified to lose. This dependency can have both psychological and physiological manifestations as the term "love-sick" suggests. The individual is afraid of experiencing the withdrawal symptoms that have accompanied the ending of an intimate relationship in the past. The relationship is perpetuated in order to avoid the pain and suffering of withdrawal. Carl remembers how bad he felt and how he suffered when Susan, his first lover, broke up with him. He may do almost anything to avoid feeling like that again.

A fourth form of escalation occurs through **fantasy**. The relationship becomes a symbol for a privately held fantasy to which the individual attaches substantial importance. The relationship is an embodiment of the fantasy. Love and marriage are supposed to go together "like a horse and carriage." Thus, the fulfillment of a romantic or erotic fantasy may lead naturally to the desire or need to broaden the definition of the relationship by institutionalizing it through marriage. Individuals can also daydream about what life would be like with the other person, creating visions of domestic bliss or a life without loneliness.

A fifth form of escalation arises from a process of selective perception referred to as **idealization**. As a relationship evolves, each person tends to inflate the image of the other. Negative qualities of a person are likely to fall outside the other's field of direct perception, while positive qualities are blown out of proportion. A person's self-esteem may become dependent on the degree to which the mate he or she selects is considered to be a person of moral, intellectual, physical, and/or social value. The other side to this is: "if such a terrific person loves me, then I must not be bad after all." Once the relationship becomes so much a part of one's own self-esteem, the continuation of the relationship takes on added importance.

APPLICATION 4.2

ESCALATING THE RELATIONSHIP

Consider the movie or television couple you selected in the last application. Describe the ways in which their relationship escalated, as well as the communication at each step in the escalation process.

Objectification of the Relationship

Escalation pushes a relationship forward by producing certain images about the quality and type of relationship in which the individuals are involved. The first of these is referred to as **objectification** of the relationship. As the relationship escalates it begins to be perceived as something that is as objectively "real" as the individuals who constitute it. The relationship begins to assume an identity of its own, apart from and in addition to the separate identities of the individuals in the relationship. The individuals arrive at the point where they refer to themselves as "we" and this subjective definition of their bond is reinforced by achieving an objective public existence as "a couple." The forms of address used as modes of reference help to legitimize the relationship for the individuals as well as for outsiders. Gary and Jay are a gay couple who provide an example of this process. Gary recalls:

> I think that our relationship took on a real permanence for us when we
> decided to buy a house together. As soon as we told my parents and took

them to see the house, they seemed more accepting of us as a couple. They talked about how "we" could have them over for dinner now and asked questions about our mortgage and how we were going to finance the house. Making a commitment to "home ownership" made them see our relationship as stable and almost conventional.

Objectification of the relationship removes the fundamental problem of premarital interaction. The ambiguity of the relationship is greatly reduced. Commitments no longer need to be expressed; they can be assumed. The question becomes not *whether* they will marry, but *when*. This level of objectification is achieved in three ways. First, the two individuals differentiate themselves from the field of eligibles composing the general dating complex. They take themselves "off the market." Second, this process of differentiation as a couple must be respected and fortified by the public reactions of others to the relationship. Their network of family and friends now considers them as a couple and treats them as a unit. Violations of exclusivity can threaten the viability of existing friendships. By this time, the other has become "the significant other par excellence" (Berger & Kellner, 1974). This may explain the "Romeo and Juliet effect" in which parental attempts to divide or break up a relationship often have the opposite effect of intensifying and strengthening it. When the couple feels rejected by parents, each partner may gravitate all the more to the other as the primary source of attachment and support. Conversely, parental support can also strengthen the sense that "we are a couple," as is the case with Gary and Jay. Third, objectification of the relationship is formalized by a public announcement that positions it within the larger sociocultural framework of society, either by "going steady," "being pinned," "getting engaged," or becoming monogomous.

Defining the Other as Marriageable

A second outcome produced by escalators is the perception of the relationship as marriageable or permanent. Premarital interaction can be viewed largely as a process of impression formation. Each person presents an image of himself or herself to the other, and each forms impressions based on the other's self-presentation. When the image of the other's character falls within the range of what is considered desirable in a mate, the probability of establishing firmer commitments is enhanced. There is an important distinction to be made between the image of the other and the other's "real" character. Courtship promotes idealized images if for no other reason than the fact that each person tends to put his or her best foot forward. The image each projects is not so much false as incomplete. Newlyweds are often startled to discover how much they did not know about each other before they got married. This discovery should not be surprising; the range of premarital experiences is relatively limited and knowledge of each other is based largely on what the person says or does within the relationship. Rarely does one have an opportunity to form a moral image of the other based on observations of the other's independent actions toward persons outside the relationship.

What does it mean to construe another person as "marriage material"? While some variability undoubtedly exists, there are certain widely shared perceptions of an ideal marriage partner regarding the behavior, character, or personality of the other. These include the following: (1) a person who is a good listener, (2) an "open" person, one who shares feelings freely, (3) a person who would make a good parent, (4) a person with high moral and ethical standards, and (5) a secure and stable person.

There is a second dimension to the process of achieving the perception of marriageability that involves attributions about the relationship. Once the relationship is objectified, it takes on a personality of its own. The individuals then can stand back and consider whether the relationship is sound enough to justify thoughts about marriage. It is common to hear individuals justify the perception of their relationship in one or more of the following ways:

1. We are always comfortable and relaxed around each other.
2. There are certain feelings or thoughts that we can express only to each other; no one else knows me as well as he or she does.
3. We hardly ever quarrel.
4. We are extremely compatible; we hardly ever get on each other's nerves.
5. We've been through a lot together and our love has survived every crisis.
6. We make a good team.

These qualities are not necessarily characteristic of successful marriages. However, many individuals believe that the presence of these traits makes the relationship acceptable for marriage.

The Relationship as a Resolution to an Identity Crisis

A third function of escalators in some relationships is to provide a point of reference for resolving a person's identity crisis. Many persons are particularly concerned about finding a direction in life. For some people, the only structure in their lives is the one exerted through parental control, which they resent. They are troubled by the nagging questions, "Who am I?" and "What is the meaning of my life?" They want to be released from the domination of their parents, but they have not figured out how to escape. Some couples may enter a second marriage to regain lost self-esteem or to restore an image of themselves as loving and loveable. A close relationship offers an expedient solution to identity problems. Premarital interaction may focus on reappraising career goals in light of the opportunity to enter into a firm commitment with another person. The mate becomes a reference point for reconstructing one's identity outside the boundaries of previous experience. In the presence of the other, one feels secure and free. The more dependent these feelings are upon the relationship, the more necessary it becomes to secure a firm commitment from the other person.

TURNING POINTS

Relationships do not always progress logically and sequentially through the phases identified in the previous section. There are often dramatic episodes in the couple's life which either move the relationship forward or cause it to drift backward. When individuals look back on the history of their relationship, they can usually recall several explosive episodes that changed the course of the relationship (Baxter & Bullis, 1986). These decisive episodes in the relationship are called

turning points. Not all turning points lead to dramatic shifts in commitment; some merely cement feelings that existed already. In most cases, however, turning points are experienced either as breakthroughs, after which the relationship soars to higher levels of commitment, or as breakdowns, after which the relationship falls apart. When Anita and Carl weathered the storm of their separation and cooling off period, they reached a breakthrough which propelled them toward increasing commitment and a decision to marry.

We have described the development of a relationship as a communicative achievement that requires partners to work through certain obstacles that stand in the way of commitment to marriage. The major problem of premarital interaction is commitment. Turning points are the decisive moments when perceptions about self, other, and the relationship between self and other materialize or diminish. Although some individuals consider practically every major event to be a turning point (Baxter & Bullis, 1986), there probably are only a few such moments regardless of whether the courtship is brief or prolonged.

Braiker and Kelley's (1979) research on conflict in the development of close relationships reinforces some of our earlier observations about how the **perception of marriageability** is achieved. They identify three sets of perceptions that are associated with increased closeness and greater interdependence. The first set involves *self-perceptions*. Self is perceived as being increasingly connected to the other by virtue of feeling "in love," and being affected by the other's feelings, experiences, and behaviors. The second set concerns *perceptions about the other*. The partner is viewed as a person who is worth spending a lifetime with. The third set of perceptions focuses on *perceptions of the relationship*. The relationship is marriageable because it is special and different in positive respects from less meaningful relationships experienced in the past. Anita and Carl think their relationship has matured because they have worked through their earlier conflicts. This experience gives them confidence that they can survive future difficulties.

As these perceptions mount, so do feelings of dependence on the relationship; the individuals become more attached to and more in need of each other. These feelings of dependence are bolstered by the decision to make the relationship more exclusive. The **norm of exclusivity** is a relationship rule in which each partner agrees to seek sexual and emotional intimacy within their relationship only. Until the norm of exclusivity emerges, there is some ambivalence about the direction in which the relationship is moving. In fact, Braiker and Kelley (1979) found that most of the serious conflicts experienced during premarital interaction occurred early in the relationship, before the individuals agreed to make their relationship exclusive. An agreement to make the relationship exclusive removes a major source of conflict by clarifying the definition of the relationship.

The development of a relationship, then, hinges on three types of turning points. Each turning point has the potential to turn the relationship forward or backward. *First, commitments can turn on experiences that define the feelings of love that exist between self and other.* This is the affective dimension of experiencing feelings of being in love, feeling attached and close, caring about the other, and becoming sexually intimate. Each person must recognize and define the feelings he or she is experiencing toward the other, as well as the extent to which those feelings are shared or reciprocated by the other. One of the most widely shared beliefs in our culture is that people get married because they are in love. But the experience of being "in love" is extremely difficult to define. Erotic feelings and sexual excitement can easily be confused with feeling in love, especially during courtship when, as Lederer and Jackson observe, "individuals lose most of their judgment" (1968, p. 42). Nevertheless, amorous feelings undoubtedly play a large part in the development of commitments.

In their descriptive study of turning points, Baxter and Bullis (1986) reported that "passion" was one of the episodes associated with the largest increases in commitment. Passion episodes ranged from the first kiss to the first sexual encounter and included the first time each said "I love you" to the other. It is not difficult to understand how amorous expression can build momentum in a relationship. The statement "I love you" is not a deniable message. Once these words are expressed, they cannot easily be retracted. Similarly, when a relationship becomes sexually intimate a baseline of affectionate expression is established.

Second, commitments can turn on the basis of experiences that define the other person's character. Each person must determine whether the other is a sufficiently moral and virtuous person to justify a firmer commitment. In our culture, it is presumed that one should take the time to get to know the other person as well as possible. This premise is underscored by Baxter and Bullis's (1986) subjects. They emphasized the importance of episodes that helped them to get to know each other and showed them that they could enjoy doing things together. These subjects also indicated that their commitment increased when the partner made a personal sacrifice in their behalf. In a moment of crisis, the partner was there to help, or one person's reluctant request for a favor received a generous and benevolent response from the other. Apparently, sacrifices contribute positively to the momentum of the relationship by embellishing the image of one's character in the eyes of the other. What emerges is a perception of the partner as a helpful and self-sacrificing person who is worth the commitment of a lifetime.

Third, commitments can turn on the basis of experiences that define the marriageability of the relationship. This dimension of relational experience involves some of the most widely shared assumptions about marriage: (1) Effective communication is essential to a good marriage. The partners should be able to talk about their feelings and work out their problems together. They should function as a good team. (2) Conflicts will arise in the course of a marriage. The ability to resolve conflicts is essential to a good marriage. The individuals must be able to weather a storm. (3) Marriage is a monogamous relationship. The marital bond normally excludes close and/or amorous relationships with others. Baxter and Bullis (1986) found that these assumptions were pervasive in the reports their subjects gave about turning points. They also found that making up after a serious fight or period of disengagement was second only to living together or getting engaged in increasing commitment to the relationship. The ability to make up shows that the couple can weather a storm. The relationship is strong enough to withstand and rebound from painful conflicts. These subjects also reported that exclusivity increased their commitment to the relationship markedly. Exclusivity is a joint decision that publicly certifies the unit, removing all competitors from the scene. It is interesting to note that the partners reportedly engaged in the most talk about their relationship when they were making up and deciding to become exclusive. We can surmise that this relationship talk resulted in the perception that the individuals could communicate effectively, resolve a serious conflict, and establish a monogamous relationship.

Table 4.2 summarizes our discussion of turning points. The escalation of commitments hinges on experiences that provide answers to three fundamental questions: (1) Do I feel in love and is my love shared by my partner? (2) Is the

TABLE 4.2   Turning points as decisive moments of relational development.

DEFINITION IN QUESTION	TURNING POINTS	CONCLUSION
Feelings of love (Do I feel "in love"? and is my love reciprocated?)	Kissing. Making love	We're in love/ we're not in love.
Character of the other (Is my partner a moral and virtuous person?)	Getting to know each other. Doing things together. Making sacrifices. Doing favors.	The partner is worth spending a lifetime with/the partner is not worth spending a lifetime with.
Marriageable relationship (Can this relationship withstand the pressures of marriage?)	Making up after conflict. Developing exclusivity.	We act and feel married/we do not act and feel married.

character of my partner sufficiently moral and virtuous to justify a lifetime commitment? and (3) Is this relationship stable, strong, and close enough to survive the perils of marriage? The measures that are taken to answer these questions come in the form of amorous interactional episodes, tests of character, and challenges to the wholeness and efficacy of the relationship. The rise and fall of commitments rests largely on the outcomes of these encounters.

PATTERNS OF PREMARITAL COURTSHIP

In addition to the fact that couples can experience dramatic turning points in their relationship which influence the course of the relationship, couples also differ in their particular styles of courtship. We have repeatedly emphasized that there is no one path that leads to marriage. The processes that culminate in the decision to marry are pluralistic—different patterns can lead to the same result.

Short and Long Courtships

The most obvious difference is the length of courtship. Some courtships accelerate very quickly. In this type of courtship, the individuals "fall" for each other quickly,

APPLICATION 4.3

TURNING POINTS IN RELATIONSHIPS

Again, consider your media couple. Identify the turning points in their relationship. Identify the effects that each turning point had on the relationship and the communication that accompanied these turning points.

experience few setbacks, and develop a high probability of marriage within two or three months of their initial encounter (Huston, Surra, Fitzgerald, & Cate, 1981). Marriage is consummated within twelve to eighteen months. At the other extreme are the prolonged courtships that follow a long and winding road to marriage. Prolonged courtships suffer numerous setbacks and changes of heart; commitment to marriage may take as long as three years to achieve and the marriage may take up to five years to be effectuated (Huston, Surra, Fitzgerald, & Cate, 1981). Most courtships probably fall somewhere between these extremes.

Themes of Courtship

The most important dimensions that differentiate types of courtships are the themes of the relationship to which interactional episodes are directed. The **themes of a relationship** are the core issues or ideals that form the basis for prolonged commitment. In this respect, the length of a courtship is a consequence of interaction patterns rather than a cause.

The simplest way to describe different types of courtships is to examine some hypothetical cases. This section describes several uniquely different patterns of premarital interaction that culminate in the decision to marry. These include the following themes of courtship: (1) romantic ideal, (2) identity clarification, (3) relationship viability, and (4) tactical maneuvering.

Case I: We Were Made for Each Other (Romantic Ideal)

Tony and Maria grew up in the same South Philadelphia neighborhood. Although Tony was five years older than Maria and hung out with a different crowd, he had seen her around the neighborhood from time to time as he was growing up. When he was home on leave from the service, a mutual friend introduced him to Maria while they were shopping at the Italian Market. Several months later, when Tony got out of the service, he called Maria and asked her for a date. He was twenty-three years old at the time; she was eighteen. Tony and Maria immediately felt strongly attracted to each other. He was tall, dark, and handsome; she was dark, slender, and beautiful. They were a striking couple. Tony was physically strong and aggressive; Maria was more introverted but she felt comfortable around Tony. They seemed to fit together extremely well. During their brief courtship, they talked a lot about the traditions of the neighborhood and their desire to have a big family. They became sexually intimate quickly. Each viewed the other as a romantic ideal. It did not take them long to express their love for each other openly. Tony's parents became good friends with Maria's parents and the relationship received the blessing of both families. Tony and Maria were married one year after their first date.

This pattern of courtship reflects the meshing of personalities and conforms closely to a romantic ideal. Tony and Maria had very similar backgrounds and shared a rich ethnic heritage. They did not have to spell things out for each other. Indeed, they had an uncanny knack of reading each other's mind. They seemed perfectly matched: physically, temperamentally, and ethnically. Each fit the other's image of the ideal mate. They did not feel a need for a long courtship, because they knew they were right for each other.

Case II: Now I Know Who I Am (Identity Clarification)

Jim met Kathy in an English course at the University of Kentucky. Initially, they talked mainly about the books they were reading for the course. On several occasions, Jim walked Kathy to her car after class, and they stood and talked for long periods of time. Gradually, they started seeing each other more frequently, going out for dinner, studying together, and occasionally going to movies. Their conversations became more and more philosophical. They talked about the purpose and meaning of life, about moral and ethical conduct, and about the future of the world. Initially, they disagreed about many things, but gradually their viewpoints seemed to merge.

During this period, Jim was living at home with his parents. They watched over him closely and were opposed to his relationship with Kathy from the beginning. He resented their interference. The more conflict with his family that Jim experienced, the closer he became to Kathy. Jim and Kathy developed an isolated relationship. They did not mix with others and they even withdrew from their families. Each felt most secure in the presence of the other. They treated each other as equals and felt very compatible. The relationship seemed to rescue them from anonymity and gave meaning and purpose to their lives.

This pattern of courtship serves the function of clarifying the identities of one or both persons. The individuals become comfortable with each other quickly. Although they may have strong differences of opinion at first, their interactions bring increasing agreement on values. Conflict with parents pushes the individuals closer together. Endless intimate conversation is a major ingredient of the relationship. Their bond is very deep and they become very dependent upon each other as they withdraw from outside influences and confine their sphere of activity to each other. As each individual's identity becomes clarified, the relationship progresses slowly toward marriage.

Case III: Nobody Said It Would Be Easy (Relationship Viability)

Linda met Phil at an office party. Their mutual attraction was spontaneous and they fell quickly for each other. The relationship was dominated from the beginning by sexual intimacy. Consumed and absorbed by this overwhelming erotic experience, Linda and Phil were seduced into believing their relationship was viable for marriage. Their initial commitment to each other proved superficial. Linda began having serious questions about what she really meant to Phil and whether the relationship had any depth to it. Phil was uncomfortable about Linda's constant pressure to talk about the relationship. The relationship became a roller coaster. They would fight, break up, and then reunite. When they were apart, they would experience a lot of jealousy. Every time they got back together, they would feel closer than ever. But the feelings would not last. Phil and Linda were strongly connected to friends and colleagues at work. They experienced considerable outside pressure to maintain their relationship.

The central theme of this pattern of courtship is the viability of the relationship. This is the stormiest type of courtship. Commitments are superficial and tentative. Numerous breakups and makeups occur. The relationship is not grounded on shared understandings and agreements. Yet, there is a strong amorous identification cementing the relationship, and the pressure from outside forces makes it difficult for them to give up on each other. There is more talk about the relationship and more conflict than in any other pattern of courtship.

Case IV: We'd Be Happier If We Were Married (Tactical Maneuvering)

Fred and Amy were raised in traditional families. The members of Fred's family got along well with each other. There was never much conflict among them. Amy's mother and father did not get along well. They frequently yelled and screamed at each other. Occasionally, Amy's father would become violent. Amy was afraid of violence, and she was easily intimidated by loud and aggressive individuals. When Fred and Amy met, the main thing they shared was a dislike of conflict. They were gentle and kind to each other, but they did not express their feelings openly. Most of Amy's friends were married already and she had become increasingly concerned about whether she would ever find someone to marry. Amy fell in love with Fred quickly and was eager to secure a firm commitment from him. She raised the question of marriage on numerous occasions, but would back down when Fred expressed resistance. Fred had not had much experience in close relationships and had very little confidence in his attractiveness to women. Amy bolstered his confidence and fed his ego. As time passed her subtle attempts to secure firmer commitments paid off. He did not want to lose her.

This is a tactical courtship. Backgrounds may be similar but personalities do not mesh. One of the individuals feels a greater attraction than the other and cautiously presses for commitment. The individuals are not as dependent upon each other as they are upon the relationship. One needs the relationship to fulfill a fantasy, the other to resolve an identity problem. The lack of similarity in their definitions of the relationship makes it necessary to employ tactical maneuvers and friendly persuasion. Their preference for avoiding conflict heightens the probability of a marital commitment.

CONCLUSIONS ABOUT COURTSHIP

Theories of relationship development often leave the mistaken impression that all relationships follow the same general trajectory. From our examples we can see that different relationships take different paths. Courtship patterns might also differ depending upon the cultural conventions or age of one or both partners or whether either partner has been married before. Our purpose in presenting these fictitious cases is to indicate that the themes of courtship can be diverse. These cases may seem like stereotypes and to a certain extent they are. However, each case represents one of the types of courtship patterns described by Bolton (1961) on the basis of extensive interviews with recently married couples.

From Bolton's research and our own analysis, we draw the following four conclusions about courtship:

1. Love does not always precede the desire to marry. Some individuals find marriage to be expedient and desirable in comparison to other available alternatives.
2. Relationships with family and friendship networks can have a significant effect on attachment to the relationship. Rejection from outsiders can

increase attachment to the relationship; when the attractiveness of the relationship is lessening, support for the relationship from outsiders can strengthen it.

3. Subtle forms of persuasion and manipulation are often used to induce greater commitment, particularly when attractions are not equal.

4. The knowledge on which individuals base their decision to marry is necessarily incomplete and imperfect. It is as if they are looking at each other through a crack in the wall that distorts the image. The image of the person is "real," but the picture is not placed in the proper perspective. An idealized image is not so much false as it is incomplete.

It is very difficult to predict the course a marriage will take. Individuals are forced to make a decision about an uncertain future (marriage) on the basis of a rather superficial past (courtship). There is no way to avoid this problem. Even cohabitation (living together) prior to marriage does not improve one's chances for success (Macklin, 1983). The decision to marry is a calculated risk. There is no way to simulate the experience, no way to guarantee a positive outcome. Does this mean that we are opposed to marriage? Not at all. Marriage offers the potential for expanding the meaning of our lives and heightening our sense of significance. Our purpose is not to question the validity of marriage but to increase your understanding of how individuals develop a relationship they perceive as marriageable.

Commonly it is assumed that people get married because they are in love. Lederer and Jackson (1968) point out that this is a false assumption. They suggest that many people mistake romance for love and are swept away by a tidal wave of passion and lust. Nevertheless, people do think that they get married because they are in love; it is easy to forget about other factors that may affect decisions to marry. Our observation of the ways that individuals develop and strengthen their commitments to each other indicates that people decide to get married for many reasons, including: (1) that individuals in our society are expected to marry; (2) that as we grow up, many of the books, television shows, and movies to which we are exposed romanticize marriage; (3) that parents can unintentionally increase a son's or daughter's commitment to a relationship by opposing it; (4) that loneliness and insecurity can make a person feel desperate for companionship; and (5) that low self-esteem can make marriage seem like the best way to improve one's lot in life.

SUMMARY

This chapter has argued that the process of selecting a marriage partner involves a significant amount of decision making and persuasion. Mate selection is not so much a matter of whether we choose partners who are similar to us or who complement our personalities and needs, but it is more likely an outcome of interpersonal processes. Once two people express an interest in each other, their relationship tends to progress through various developmental stages. We describe six factors that influence the development of a relationship: (1) ambiguity, (2) momentum, (3) escalation, (4) objectification of the relationship, (5) defining the other as marriageable, and (6) the relationship as a resolution to an identity crisis. Several phases were identified in the escalation of a relationship: (1) involvement, (2) commitment, (3) addiction, (4) fantasy, and (5) idealization.

We have discussed the importance of turning points as decisive events that either move the relationship forward or cause it to move backward. Three types of experiences seem to characterize turning points: those that (1) define feelings of love that exist between self and other, (2) define the other's character, and (3) define the marriageability of the relationship. In describing patterns of premarital courtship, we identify differences between short and long courtships and discuss several themes of courtship. Themes in four different patterns of courtship include: (1) romantic ideal, (2) identity clarification, (3) relationship viability, and (4) tactical maneuvering. Finally, we caution the reader against assuming that people get married simply (or only) because they love each other. It is somewhat sobering to recognize that a complex set of circumstances influences the decision to marry. Certainly, when it comes to "affairs of the heart," our emotional and intuitive responses are enormously significant. That is as it should be. But the rates of success for marriage in this country also suggest that one needs to be as informed as possible about the choice that he or she is making.

KEY TERMS

addiction	idealization
commitment	involvement
courtship as decision making	momentum
differential contact	norm of exclusivity
escalators	objectification
fantasy	perception of marriageability
filtering process	themes of a relationship
heterogamy	turning points
homogamy	

CHAPTER 5

MARITAL
REALITY
CONSTRUCTION

LISSA ADDINGTON

NINA'S STORY

Gail: Tell me about your family.

Nina: The family that I grew up in?

Gail: Start there. Then you might talk about the family you helped to create.

Nina: Okay. What do you want to hear?

Gail: Well, just tell me your story.

Nina: Okay. My parents are older. They are about seventy years old. They were married during World War II. Right after the war was over they moved to Texas. We have four children in our family. We lived there until I was about fifteen years old. I never really thought of my father as an alcoholic, but in looking at old pictures of my family, I see there was always alcohol in the pictures. And yet, I never realized as a child that that was going on. I wasn't aware of it. Anyway, at fifteen we moved back to Milwaukee (where we were originally from), and it was sort of like our family exploded at that point. Maybe that was just the last straw . . . I don't know. Maybe that would've happened anyway. I don't know.

Gail: The difficulties—the stress—of the move added to your problems.

Nina: Right. The stress added to everything else. My parents are still married. They've been married almost fifty years, but they really don't have any kind of relationship. I can see that I've had a lot of problems in my life, and my brothers have both led very unusual—what I would call unusual—lifestyles as a result of our upbringing.

Gail: Tell me something about each of your brothers—the different paths that your brothers have taken or that you've taken.

Nina: Okay. My oldest brother was very, very well liked

and popular. A lot of people thought of him as the "golden boy" in our family. He was very smart and very successful. He got a lot of praise. I have a brother who was just three years younger than him, who quit high school. He couldn't wait until he turned sixteen so he could quit. He's led a very bad life. He's been in prison. He's done drugs. He's dealt in drugs. He still lives that wow-wow lifestyle . . . "don't bring me down." It's that kind of stuff. And then there's me who I think has always tried to be the "peacemaker" of the family.

Gail: The good girl.

Nina: I try to keep everybody happy. Then I have a younger brother who is two years younger than me. He moved back to Texas when he was twenty-four. He's very determined to become financially successful. He's driven to prove that he's okay. There's a lot of extreme bitterness that I can see. He's doing a lot of things just to prove that he's okay.

Gail: How is your relationship with him?

Nina: My brothers and I sort of banded together against our mom, which probably wasn't terrifically healthy. But we took refuge in each other because my mother was very aggressive. She would slap . . . she slapped easily. She flew off the handle very easily. She is a very frustrated person, I would say.

Gail: She has a lot of anger?

Nina: She had a lot of anger, and she took it out on us. Not too long ago I tried to confront her about it. She is in complete denial over the whole thing. She just absolutely goes into this whole thing about how I must think she's just a terrible person, and the way I make her sound she must have been the worst mother in the world.

Gail: How did your father and mother get together?

Nina: How did they meet?

Gail: Yes. What are some of the details of their marriage? Do you know much about that?

Nina: Not to be bragging or anything, but both of my parents are very, very nice-looking people. Or they were. My father is an extremely handsome man—just gorgeous, really. People say, "Oh, wow," when they see my parents' pictures. My mother was just a beautiful, beautiful woman. I think that they strictly got together because they were both so good-looking. I really do.

Gail: There was a mutual attraction or admiration between them.

Nina: Yeah. My father was Italian and very unacceptable socially. I could tell you stories that you . . . that he felt unaccepted socially at the time. My mother was Algerian, so she was blond with blue eyes. He was very dark with brown eyes. They were kind of opposites. They were striking together. We have pictures of them. They look just like they could be from Hollywood. They were just . . . my mother . . . my grandmother, my mother's mother, didn't talk to my mother for six months after they were married because she knew he was Italian. She accorded him with the lower class.

Gail: Your grandmother didn't speak to your parents after they were married?

Nina: Yes. Yes. The rest of their relationship has been sad. . . . I know that my father has had affairs. Not lots and lots of them, which I think would be easier for my mother to accept, but he has had two long-running affairs that I know of. I mean that have lasted for more than ten years. My father's affairs made my mother very bitter. I see it as the old Italian thing where the husband can have his women on the side and have home and children, too. I think that he thought that that was okay. And yet, we were just neglected emotionally.

Gail: And your mother became very angry?

Nina: Yes. And in the meantime, my mother is frustrated and mad and angry and taking it out on us when he's not there. And who knows . . . I started thinking about this not too long ago. I was thinking that I've always just been mad at my mother. I funneled that energy toward her behavior. What I really see as an older person, I see why she felt all that. It's because of what he was doing. She just didn't do anything to stop it. She didn't have enough courage to leave or stand up or whatever it was going to take to stop it.

Gail: You think she should have left or stood up to your father even though you don't like what she did?

Nina: Right. Right.

Gail: How do you see your place in your family? You said you were the "peace-maker"? Do you still have that role?

Nina: Yes. Although I began to resent it.

Gail: That's understandable.

Nina: Yes, I basically, still . . . the thing is all three of my brothers moved. We all came back to Milwaukee and then they moved back to Texas. My oldest brother tried for years to get me to come out to Texas. He promised me . . . he even came out to get me one time in his truck to move me. I couldn't go. I just couldn't leave my parents. I know it's pathetic, but I felt that I was abandoning them. I worried about leaving them. They needed me to keep their relationship intact because without the kids between them it was terrible. That's all they do is fight. After all these years, it's still that way, I think. Although they are peaceful around us. So one of the children needed to stay. I couldn't just leave them.

Gail: So you felt that if you left and went to Texas they would really destroy each other?

Nina: Right. Right. Right. I guess in the long run I'm glad that I didn't go. Ten years ago I moved about 200 miles from where they live, which was just far enough to be able to go back for birthdays and holidays and any time of the year. That has helped me a lot.

Gail: When you talk about your parents and siblings, I have some sense that you've done some reading, or that you seem to understand what's going on—understand the problems in your family. Have you done some reading in the literature about alcoholism? Or done some things for yourself that have helped to heal some things that have been painful for you?

Nina: I've done a number of things. I've done some reading, but I've also been involved in some twelve-step programs, which I don't participate in. I did for a while, and I found the information in the literature helpful, but I did not feel that attending the meetings was particularly helpful. Something that really changed was that I began to take my religion seriously. I have a different perspective on things now. I am trying—it's like a process—to forgive things that have happened in the past and to see them as they happened—not hide from them—and why they happened. I can change, because I don't want to repeat. I don't want to repeat with my daughter what happened to me.

Gail: What about your present situation? Do you have a family at home?

Nina: Uh-huh. I was married very young and divorced. I married someone who I thought, because he came from the same culture—he came from a half-Italian, half-something-else family—I thought we had many, many things in common. Yet, I couldn't be married to him. It just didn't work. I was miserable. But, anyway . . . so then I was single for, like, seven years, and I remarried ten years ago to a person who is the complete opposite personality of my first husband. So I went from one extreme to the other trying to make up. The man I'm married to now is much more reserved, less aggressive. It's only been really—we've been married about ten years, and it's only been in, like, the last five years that we've really started to function well. So, we're on the road.

Gail: What is his family like?

Nina: His mother is widowed. His father died when he was six. He comes from not a good situation either. His mother is very German. She is very staunch, unemotional, and task-oriented. He did not have a good relationship with her.

Gail: Was she stern?

Nina: Yes, yes. Very stern.

Gail: How do they get along now?

Nina: They don't. Derek has no relationship with her at all. I've tried to encourage him to spend some time with her and make comments and stuff, but he says he doesn't have the energy. He says it is just not worth the effort. I can understand, kinda. He has tried before and it just doesn't work.

Gail: It's just too much for him.

Nina: Yeah. So he keeps his distance. They don't have much contact.

Gail: Do you have any children, the two of you?

Nina: No, we don't have any children together. I think that if we were where we are now, if we were younger—I'm almost forty and my husband is forty-four, and if we were younger we would have a lot of children, but I don't think that we will now, although over the last year or so we have been doing very well, and my husband has started to talk about it. Before that he was completely and totally against it. The door is not closed on the matter yet. Like, I said, we're becoming a family and who knows?

Gail: Well, do you have a child?

Nina: I have a child.

Gail: You have a child from your first marriage.

Nina: Seventeen-year-old daughter. We do great together, I'm happy to say. We're very close.

Gail: How does your daughter get along with your second husband? Are they close?

Nina: Very close.

Gail: What do you think is the key to the success of that relationship?

Nina: Um [pause] well, when we were first married, I felt that I had to be the mediator in that relationship, and it didn't really go very well. And like I said, about five years ago I realized what I was doing, so I just took, like, a major step backwards and when one would come to me or another one would come to me to side with them in the usual conflict, I'd say inside that I really think that that could be worked out directly, and suddenly they started working things out themselves, and just everything changed.

Gail: Everything got much better.

Nina: Yes. Because when either one of them tried to work through me, it seemed like they were irrational. They were almost calmer with each other.

Gail: How do you see that your husband's family influenced him?

Nina: How? Well, his mother . . . I used to always say to him that (this was mean), but I used to sort of make fun of him and say that business came before pleasure because he couldn't do anything until—when he would come into the house he would put things away and start a load of laundry and do all this work around the house. He had to put away his good clothes and get into his other clothes and look at the mail and put things in order before he could even say hello. It was like—to me it was like a joke because I was not like that at all.

Gail: Attending to chores that need to get done before affection?

Nina: Yes. But that is exactly how his mother trained him. The minute he would come home from school—and she prided herself on this—but when he came home she had a list of things for him to do, and he had to do everything on the list first. When he got that done then she could talk to him or spend time with him or whatever. It has taken him a long time to break that terrible training.

Gail: To feel like the chores don't come first?

Nina: Uh-huh. [Pause] Another thing too is that when I met him, we moved here, and it was 200 miles. I had all my friends and family long distance. Well, they never made long-distance phone calls. His mom called him once a year on his birthday and that was it. He never, never, never made long-distance phone calls. It was just something they didn't do. After I moved here our phone bills were like well over a hundred dollars for a long, long time. He just hated it—we fought like cats and dogs over it. I tried to explain to him repeatedly that I couldn't completely sever all ties with everybody. I could write some letters, but I was not going to sever all my ties with everyone immediately just because he thought I shouldn't make long-distance phone calls. So we had a lot of serious fights about it, and then again all this sort of changed five years ago. He said, "Okay, I've come up with a budget. We are allowed to spend seventy-five dollars on the phone—on long-distance calls." This was quite reasonable.

Gail: Sort of a compromise that you worked out?

Nina: Right. Halfway in between over a hundred and nothing.

Gail: This sounds like the long-distance phone calls represented a struggle over the fact that he has this kind of distance in relating to his family and you are more emotionally expressive.

Nina: Oh, yes. Definitely. But, we are getting there. We're getting there.

Gail: Slowly, but surely, you're making progress.

Nina: That's right; we *are* making progress.

UNDERSTANDING NINA

In the conversation we have used to introduce this chapter, Nina briefly describes the family that she grew up in, her role in the family, her first and second marriage, and something about the differences that she and her second husband have struggled with in their relationship. She discusses the difficulty that she has with her husband's task-oriented behavior when they arrive home after work and describes a dispute over long-distance telephone calls. Both of these issues might be thought of as representative examples, or metaphors, for their different relationship orientations. Nina's outgoing, immediate, and emotionally expressive communication style can be contrasted to Derek's more reserved, "business-before-pleasure" orientation. We can see how the family that Nina and her second husband each grew up in has influenced their relationship. Even though Nina expresses more satisfaction with her second marriage than with her first, her story illustrates how challenging and complicated the task of integrating two lives into one relationship can be. As Beck (1969) suggests in his description of what lies ahead for any couple:

> Once the marriage rites have been celebrated, however, and the glow of the morning fades, the realities of the task ahead become clear in the bright light of noon. Somehow the two must integrate into a satisfying partnership and a conjoint career, plan two designs for family living, two sets of expectations for the relationship, and two dreams for the future (p. 584).

Partners carry "baggage" from their separate histories and families of origin to a marriage. The "baggage" can include such things as habits, preferences, anxieties, skills, and previous experiences. Some of Nina's previous experience, or "baggage," includes being the mediator or peacemaker in an alcoholic family; feelings of frustration with and understanding of her alcoholic father and embittered mother; a determination not to repeat the mistakes of the past; an awareness of and sensitivity to her own feelings, which she developed from her effort to heal the bruises of past family experiences; and a willingness to see compromise as a way to improve the quality of her relationships. Once a commitment to marry has been made, a couple begins the process of coordinating their different backgrounds into a manageable relationship. Through their communication, Nina and her husband reconstruct their lives as they build their relationship. They are confronted with a number of marital tasks in the taken-for-granted everyday activities and conversations of their life together. A good example of this includes Nina's description of interactions with her husband after the two arrive home from work or in her discussion of the conflict over the phone bill. This chapter examines five tasks involved in the process of building the marriage relationship: (1) integrating two sets of expectations into one relationship, (2) co-defining reality in the construction of the marriage relationship, (3) negotiating a communication code, (4) organizing the relationship, and (5) managing differentiation and integration in the marriage relationship.

EXPECTATIONS

Each individual brings to marriage a set of expectations relevant to the relationship. A set of **expectations** is a collection of images, unspoken assumptions, and attitudes about what a partner expects to give in return for what he or she expects to receive (Sager, 1976). Nina, for example, expects that Derek will be supportive and understanding of her emotional needs, something that she did not have when she was growing up. Derek expects Nina to supply the warmth and spontaneity that was missing in his family of origin, without sacrificing his need for order and fiscal responsibility.

Sources of Expectations

Where do expectations for marriage originate? There are three significant sources for expectations about marriage: (1) the families of origin, (2) the immediate culture, and (3) the mass media.

Parents provide a model of marriage for their children by the way they relate to each other as husband and wife: how they reach decisions, show affection, express their hopes and fears, interact with their children, disagree, and cope with stress. Children are taught what it means to be married not so much by what their parents say about marriage but by how they act in their marriage—by their deeds rather than by their words. Of course, some children openly reject their parents' marriage as a model for their own, though they may be unrealistic about how different they are or will be when compared to their parents (Laing, 1972). The formidable influence of parents may be too powerful to overcome merely by wishing to be different (Kramer, 1985; Boszormenyi-Nagy & Spark, 1984). In Nina's case, developing a marriage that was better than the one her parents had meant enduring an unhappy first marriage, participating in a twelve-step program for adult children of alcoholics, and spending a considerable amount of time reading and reflecting.

The myths, values, and assumptions about marriage that a person acquires from the surrounding culture also have a powerful effect on an individual's expectations about marriage (Lederer & Jackson, 1968). In the last century people tended to marry primarily for economic and social reasons. Now, we place much emphasis on companionship and the emotional compatibility of partners. Our culture reinforces the notion that marriage should help us stave off feelings of loneliness, provide friendship and emotional support, enhance personal growth and development, and provide sexual pleasure and gratification for the partners. For a satisfactory marriage in our culture, personal and emotional fulfillment are generally expected. Cultural values may lead to the expectation that one partner should not only like and appreciate how the other thinks and feels about almost everything, but also be capable of filling up the gaps and empty spaces that each partner experiences. As Napier (1988) writes:

> After years of anxiety about being alone, we finally *have* someone: here is a wonderful body to enjoy sexually (and we do a lot of that), to snuggle with hungrily in the night; and here is someone who is always ready to talk, always willing to help. It seems that a lifetime of loneliness is over (p. 250).

The mass media provide another powerful source of influence in the creation of expectations. As we grow up we are influenced by what we read, see, and hear about family relationships (Buerkel-Rothfuss, Greenberg, Atkin, & Neuendorf, 1982). Television often defines the ideal marriage as one in which "love conquers all," physical beauty is primary, conflict can be easily resolved, manipulation is a way to smooth over differences, and energy and money are endless resources.

It is also useful to note that, in general, women and men may bring different expectations to a marriage. Women often value connectedness, interdependence, and emotional expressiveness more than do men, who tend to place more value on autonomy and rational expressiveness (Gilligan, 1982; Walters, Carter, Papp, & Silverstein, 1988). These differences are values that are learned in the culture and may be changing. These differences may also create a disadvantage for women if women's "connectedness is equated with dependency" or if the emotional well-being of the family is left primarily to wives and mothers (Walters, Carter, Papp, & Silverstein, 1988, p. 19). In a culture that values individualism and personal freedom, connectedness may not be valued as much as autonomy. Similarly, the role of maintaining the emotional well-being of the family may be viewed as secondary to providing for the economic survival of the family. A rigid separation of roles in the family can also lead to husbands and fathers underparticipating in the emotional and intimate aspects of family life. Nevertheless, gender differences, reinforced by cultural patterns, can influence expectations.

Content of Expectations

Each spouse brings individual expectations about what life together will be like—the content of expectations for the marriage. Nina may see marriage as a way to heal her wounds, receive the kindness and consideration she deserves, and build an equal partnership with someone who is willing to support her personal growth and development. Carrie, who grew up in a large family in a small rural town, may see marriage as the route to raising a flock of children. In Carrie's case, marriage is seen as the way to have the economic support to create her life as a homemaker and mother. Harry, who always felt close to and cared for by his mother, has the expectation that he will marry someone who will nurture him in the way his mother did. He has the image of a marital partner as someone who will be emotionally and sexually responsive to him without his having to "try overly hard" to

TABLE 5.1   Expectations that Nina and Derek bring to their marriage.

Derek's Expectations	*Nina's Expectations*
Nina will give him the warmth, acceptance, and open expression of affection that was lacking in his relationship with his mother.	Derek will provide a sense of security, stability, maturity, and loyalty that was missing in previous relationships with her father and her first husband.
Nina will contribute to the family income so that he doesn't need to feel overburdened in the way that his mother did.	Derek will support her in her efforts to return to school and develop a new career for herself.
He and Nina will share responsibility for household maintenance tasks, but Derek will have primary responsibility for managing the family budget.	She and Derek will share responsibility for household maintenance tasks, and he will be open to her opinions and needs regarding their financial matters.
Nina will always be there for him and will not require frequent verbal confirmation in order to know that she is important to him.	Derek will be understanding and supportive of her need to maintain frequent contact with her family and friends.
Nina will be in charge of the couple's social activities and will not require him to initiate contacts with friends and family members.	Derek will accept her suggestions for their social activities.
Nina will provide the cheerfulness, good humor, and positive climate in their relationship so that he does not have to feel overwhelmed by the negative feelings and sober attitude that he sometimes displays.	Derek will validate her view of the world as a place that essentially rewards someone who is kind, cheerful, and a peacemaker. Derek will make an effort to love and nurture her daughter from her first marriage.

please her—a wife should be responsive, as his mother had been, because she loves him.

Couples develop expectations about a wide variety of behaviors and issues. Expectations can include how much time the couple will spend together and how they will manage household tasks and economic decisions, as well as sexuality and the decision to have or not to have children. Couples can also expect that the partner will help them to deal with loneliness, compensate for an unhappy childhood, and make them feel better about themselves.

Often expectations have a *reciprocal quality* to them. Harry may expect that, if he is not overly critical of his wife and works hard to contribute to the family income, his wife, in turn, will provide the kind of emotional and sexual responsiveness that he needs. Jules Henry has pointed out "If the marriage is to succeed, each partner must master the other's unconscious conception of what he wants in return for what he gives. . . . Love-in-our-time is supposed to arise and endure when the man and woman are able to give each other what each wants," (Henry, 1973, p. 196).

Sager (1976, 1981) has developed the concept of the marriage contract to describe the reciprocal quality of expectations. The **marriage contract** identifies what each partner expects to get in return for what he or she is expected to give or do for the partner. Suppose that Nina has the expectation that her husband should be willing to support her return to school and new career aspirations. She expects that she will, in turn, support her husband in his need to achieve financial security.

She may also expect that, in return for her sharing in the economic stability of the partnership, her husband will participate fully in the housekeeping. In forming an idea about what her role is likely to be in a marriage, Nina develops an image of the reciprocal behavior that she expects from Derek. Derek may have the expectation that Nina will be the one in their relationship to initiate social interactions with friends and family. Derek likes the comfort and relaxation of being with family and friends. However, he is also reserved and sometimes has trouble coming up with ideas for social activities or initiating new contacts. Nina's ease with people and willingness to plan the couple's social life gives Derek enjoyment. In return, Derek appreciates Nina's social skills and supports her suggestions in a good-natured way.

Relationship Dimensions of Expectations

Expectations also have relationship dimensions. The relationship dimensions of a couple's expectations about marriage describe how the two sets of expectations fit together. Two important relationship dimensions of expectations are (1) congruence and (2) salience.

The **congruence** of a couple's expectations about marriage has to do with the extent to which individual expectations are similar or compatible (Boss, 1983). Let's go back to the example of Nina and her husband. Nina and Derek each expect a marriage partner to share in housekeeping and home maintenance activities. Nina also expects that Derek will be emotionally faithful and loyal to her, be interested in contributing to the financial well-being of the family, and provide security and stability in their relationship. Derek expects Nina to contribute warmth, good humor, acceptance, and outward displays of affection to their relationship. In both cases, their expectations are congruent and build on qualities that were missing for them in previous relationships.

There are also areas where the expectations of Nina and Derek are not congruent. Nina feels that intimacy is related to being able to talk openly and freely to the person she loves. For her, being comfortable in marriage implies the freedom and willingness of each partner to talk about feelings and negotiate areas of conflict. For Derek, intimacy is related to the feeling that one can trust another person without "having" to tell the partner everything. In this sense, Nina and Derek may have expectations for marriage and for their relationship that are not congruent with one another. The extent to which a couple's expectations are congruent may be related to their satisfaction with the relationship (Craddock, 1984).

In the course of their relationship, a couple's expectations may be modified as they create a life together. **Salience** relates to the *importance* of the congruence or incongruence of a couple's expectations. The need for Nina to "talk about feelings" and for Derek to "keep some of his thoughts and feelings to himself" may become a difference that is relatively unimportant to their happiness together. On the other hand, as time evolves, events and episodes may unfold in their conversations and activities that could heighten the importance of this difference for them.

The conflict between Nina and Derek over long-distance phone calls described in our introductory narrative is an example. Nina wants Derek to understand how important it is for her to talk with family members periodically, to check up on them, to maintain an auditory, emotional connection. Derek is not interested in the "reasons why" Nina uses the phone; he just wants Nina to understand that they "cannot afford the financial burden." Nina gets hurt and angry by

Derek's "unwillingness" to be interested in her feelings; Derek gets irritated and impatient because he believes that Nina's "lengthy discussion" about her feelings only "avoids the reality" of facing up to the issue of their phone bills. In this case, the differences in their expectations may become an important issue for them in their marriage. The extent to which particular expectations are important to a couple is synonymous with the salience of the expectation for their relationship.

Incompatible expectations often manifest themselves as typical patterns in the couple's communication. For example, in the conflict over long-distance telephone calls, Nina expects Derek to understand her behavior in terms of relational and emotional needs; Derek expects Nina to understand what he believes are the factual or rational exigencies of the situation. The difference may be a recurring

APPLICATION 5.1

WHAT ARE YOUR EXPECTATIONS FOR MARRIAGE?

- What are some expectations that you have for your marriage?
- What expectations do you have about having children and the role of children in the marriage?
- What expectations do you have for how economic responsibilities will be managed?
- Will one or both of you pursue careers?
- How will you and your spouse handle housekeeping tasks?
- What will be your relationship with family and friends?
- What role, if any, will religion play in your marriage?
- How will you deal with intimacy, emotions, and the sharing of feelings? How will you expect your spouse to react if you are angry, sad, or have your feelings hurt?
- How will you manage dependence and independence in the relationship? Will you expect to spend as much time as possible with your spouse or will you expect to spend considerable time pursuing different interests or just being alone?
- To what extent are your expectations influenced by your family of origin, the culture in which you live or grew up, the mass media, or your history of experience?
- Are there some expectations that are more important to you than others?
- What do you expect to give your marriage partner in return for what you receive? What do you think marriage should do for the partners in the relationship?

pattern for the couple, a pattern that is reflected in Nina's description of Derek's need to "take care of chores" before he gives his wife an affectionate greeting after work. The issue over a couple's entry behavior after work can become related to how the couple maintains closeness and distance in the relationship (Napier, 1988).

Whether they are congruent or incongruent, expectations are part of the "baggage" that partners bring to the marriage from their family of origin and their history of experience. The "baggage" that each partner brings influences how the couple integrates their lives together and the significant problems that emerge for them in their relationship.

CO-DEFINING REALITY

Because their backgrounds are different, the expectations that partners bring to a marriage may differ. At the same time, even before a couple is married they become more similar in their beliefs, attitudes, and values (Stephen, 1985). As Stephen has written, communication functions "as a persuasive force which shapes an emergent 'couple reality' and bonds the couple in a framework of shared knowledge" (p. 961). As a couple converses and interacts, each partner influences the other partner in a variety of ways. Through their communication, partners reinterpret their separate histories, experiences, and views of the world from within the context of living and conversing with one another. A newly married couple is continually engaged in interpreting specific behaviors, words, events, mannerisms, movements, time, distance, and objects in the formation of their relationship. Marriage requires that each partner match, to some degree, his or her views of reality.

Elizabeth and Daryl are newly married. Elizabeth tells Daryl that she would like to buy a big house. Daryl is reluctant and nervous about the idea. He tells her that a house seems like an overwhelming responsibility to him and he complains about the expense of such a venture. Elizabeth begins to shape a more modest image of a house and explores the issue again with Daryl. Daryl becomes more receptive to the idea. They talk more seriously about what they might consider buying. They pay more attention to houses and talk about what they like and do not like as they drive around town. Every day is filled with events and conversations in which marriage partners shape each other's perceptions in a similar manner. In the process of modifying or clarifying beliefs, suggesting or rejecting ideas, reinforcing or discouraging interests, both partners begin to create a common set of experiences from which to view the world—shared experiences that mold and shape their perceptions over a wide range of issues.

Berger and Kellner (1974) have used the phrase **co-defining reality** to describe how marriage partners reconstruct their perceptions, identities, and beliefs through the management of everyday activities. The impression that one has of other people, the attitudes and feelings about oneself, and the values that provide the philosophical framework for establishing goals and for evaluating oneself and others, are subtly reshaped by marriage. This reshaping is accomplished through communication.

How does a couple do this? In this section we describe how marital communication facilitates a joint reconstruction of reality in four significant ways by (1) narrowing alternatives for the marriage partners, (2) focusing movement and energy in the system, (3) altering perceptions and changing relationships with others outside the marital dyad, and (4) supporting some aspects of each person's identity at the expense of others.

Narrowing Alternatives

Commitment to the marital relationship typically narrows alternatives for both partners. **Narrowing alternatives** describes the ways in which commitment to the marital relationship limits options for the partners. Margo, for instance, might fantasize about living in New Orleans, where she would work as a waitress during the day and write poetry at night or she might have the fantasy of borrowing some money to open up a bookstore in Maine or of going to New York to study dance at a famous dance theatre. After marriage, where she lives and what she does for a living is negotiated with her husband.

When Margo makes the choice to get married, she will begin to redefine alternatives for herself within the context of her relationship with her husband. If Margo is not going to be a Southern poet, or a New York dancer, or a Maine entrepreneur, then what is she going to be? This issue normally is worked through (either satisfactorily or unsatisfactorily) in collaboration with her spouse. As the couple talks, Margo's view of her future and, therefore, of reality is modified.

If Margo and her husband decide to accept jobs teaching at a state university in the Midwest, Margo's (as well as her husband's) alternatives will have been limited. If the couple buys an old farmhouse with the intention of restoring it, her alternatives will have been narrowed further. Every choice that the couple makes narrows alternatives by eliminating options that were not chosen. As alternatives are narrowed, perceptions, identities, and belief systems are affected. The way that Margo views the world will be structured by her commitment to a specific relationship, career, and environment.

Religious affiliation is another example of how alternatives become narrowed through marriage (Berger & Kellner, 1974). Before marriage, one or more partners may experiment with various religious systems. A woman may have grown up in a Catholic family but have an interest in different forms of Eastern religion. She may have roots in Jewish culture but feel detached from any religious commitment. Or, like her parents, she may have only a casual and philosophical interest in religion. He may be from a Protestant family where religion played an important part of the family's life. Through the mutual influence of daily conversations, the two individuals will integrate their orientations to religion. Their conversations may stabilize the degree of commitment which they make to a specific religious organization; they may sever their connections to any formal religious establishment entirely; or they may settle into a pattern of quarreling about religion.

Focusing Movement

Once the available range of alternatives is narrowed, energy and movement in the relationship become more focused (Berger & Kellner, 1974). **Focusing movement in the relationship** means that the couple's interactions and activities become more predictable and goal-oriented. More attention is given to working out the specific details of their lives together, to planning agendas and making decisions that will influence their future. After their marriage, Daryl and Elizabeth spend time negotiating schedules, deciding who will do the shopping, how the cars will be serviced, and planning to spend time with family members. They talk about where they would eventually like to live, whether or not they want to buy a house or have children, and their future dreams. As their alternatives are narrowed through marriage, the couple's interests become more intense and less diffuse. Activity and energy become more focused. The couple's attitudes and orientations toward their careers, for instance, are influenced by conversations that they have with one another. Daryl and Elizabeth spend less time socializing with friends than they did before marriage and more time developing their careers and managing their household. They may save for a summer vacation in New England, a new car, a washing machine and dryer, and, eventually, a down payment on a house. As Elizabeth settles into her home with Daryl, her attitudes toward a woman's family role crystallize as she undertakes tasks in her role as "wife." She will also formulate opinions about her career that will influence how she views herself at work. At the same time, Daryl is undergoing a similar experience.

The context of the relationship alters what is important for each partner. The couple begins to establish a hierarchy of priorities as they talk and engage one another in ordinary activities. The process influences each person's identity and his or her perceptions of marriage and of the world. As energy and movement in their relationship become more focused, the identities of the partners and their views of the world stabilize. Through the couple's daily interactions, each partner begins to develop, adapt, and integrate his or her identity and world view with that of the other partner—that is, they co-define reality as they communicate with one another.

Changing Relationships with Others

Relationships and interactions with other people also change through the couple's process of co-defining reality. Perceptions of others are affected by conversations with the partner. Such conversations alter the social support system (contacts with family, friendship attachments, neighborhood associations, etc.) of the partners and consequently affect the way the couple experiences their lives. In addition, the frequency of interaction with other people changes after a couple marries.

Berger and Kellner (1974) point out that "friendships that precede a marriage rarely survive it (p. 225)." How does this happen? Margo's husband may become jealous of the closeness that she shares with an old friend, Jenny, or he may just have a negative reaction to her. When they talk about Jenny from time to time, Margo's husband may point out negative features about this friend, which Margo never noticed before. Gradually, Margo's image of her friend may change. As Margo's image of her friend changes, she may begin to act less friendly toward her. Thus, the friendship becomes less important to Margo; it may even end. Berger and Kellner have called this the process of **conversational liquidation** since it is the talk of the marriage partners that is responsible for changing the definition of the friendship. The friend outside the marriage has little control over this process. This is another example of how conversation recreates reality (in this case the perceptions of a friendship). This same process works in family, neighborhood, and work relationships as well. As Minuchin (1974) suggests:

> A marriage must replace certain social arrangements that have been given up for the formation of the new unit. Creation of the new social system means

the creation or strengthening of a boundary around the couple. The couple is separated from certain former contacts and activities. The investment in the marriage is made at the expense of other relationships (p. 30).

Supporting Identities

As part of the process of co-defining reality, some aspects of each partner's identity are supported at the expense of others. Each partner makes comments about the habits, mannerisms, abilities, and preferences of the other partner. These comments can be met with openness, resistance, humor, or defensiveness. Each partner can also fail to notice or attend to other characteristics of his or her spouse. In subtle day-to-day discourse, aspects of each partner's image of himself or herself are supported, discouraged, and/or altered.

Consider the example of Daryl and Elizabeth. Elizabeth has never been interested in sports. Daryl participates frequently in sports activities, keeps himself in good physical condition, and enjoys being a spectator at sports events. After they were married, Daryl offered to teach Elizabeth how to play tennis. As a way to share some fun with Daryl, Elizabeth accepted her husband's offer. She soon found out that she really enjoyed the sport and began to be more actively involved in sports activities in general. Through her relationship with her husband, Elizabeth began to change an aspect of her image of herself. She became interested in physical fitness and began to see herself as athletic.

While Daryl felt confident when involved in some sports activity, he generally considered himself a little too reserved and awkward with people. He did not find social gatherings and large parties much fun. Elizabeth sometimes wished that she knew more about what Daryl was feeling, but she did see that he was a good listener. He made eye contact with people and looked friendly when other people talked to him. After a party one Friday evening, Elizabeth told Daryl that he was a good listener, that people relaxed in the presence of his easy-going manner, and that she enjoyed being with him in the company of other people. Daryl began to change his view of himself as a loner; he began to enjoy getting together with people and came to see himself as more socially oriented than he had previously.

Through daily interactions and conversations with each other, Elizabeth and Daryl influence each other's self-perceptions in various aspects of their lives. Daryl reinforces Elizabeth's interest in her work, but does not notice how well she cooks, and he tells her that she is incompetent when it comes to mechanical problems. Elizabeth appreciates the fact that Daryl does not seem to bring his work home and is grateful that he is only moderately ambitious. She also thinks of him as steady rather than reserved, ignores the fact that he can play the piano well, and is convinced that he has no real money sense. The perceptions that they have of one another carry over into talk and daily activities. Through their conversations and actions the couple reinforces some aspects of each partner's identity and discourages others.

One significant point needs to be made. The process of supporting identities in the construction of the couple's reality is not something that is done to one spouse by another. Supporting aspects of one another's identities is a process of mutual influence. As Elizabeth finds herself more involved in sports, she is also validating Daryl's interest in sports and his image of himself as someone who can handle himself well in sports activities. Elizabeth may also be validating Daryl's participation at social activities, which also validates Elizabeth's social orientation and need for people. As we have stressed in so many ways in this book, the process is interactive, circular rather than linear.

A couple does not deliberately set out to recreate their world. Yet they do abandon certain behaviors and goals and pursue others. The choices that they make are subsequently pursued with greater conviction and more intensity. Intense commitment to certain activities—work, household maintenance, saving for the future, and so on—influences the couple's view of the world and their reality. Through conversations and shared pursuits, the couple creates a reality that they inhabit together. Their reality includes what is important to them, the evaluations they make of others, and the meanings they attach to events. Their satisfaction in the relationship may depend upon how the couple manages to coordinate their two separate constructions of reality.

NEGOTIATING A COMMUNICATION CODE

Any two individuals entering an intimate relationship bring with them a style of communicating, a set of life experiences, self-perceptions, and needs which make up the identities of the partners. Each partner brings to the relationship a preferred and typical mode of expressing affection, exerting influence, making requests, managing problems, and so on.

As they build a marriage, a couple also goes through the process of negotiating communication in their interactions with one another. The way a couple constructs their relationship depends, in part, on how they develop a mutually understood communication code. Negotiating a communication code, then, is a primary task facing the marital dyad. In this section we discuss the process of creating meaning and coordinating communication codes in marriage.

Creating Meaning

As a couple engages in daily conversations and everyday activities, they develop the meanings that will regulate their lives together (Berger & Kellner, 1974). A couple undertakes the task of **creating meaning** through talk and action. Meaning-making occurs whenever interpretations, significance, and order are attached to actions and words. Interaction provides information to the participants about what is important and unimportant, what behaviors are acceptable and unacceptable, and how they view themselves, each other, their relationship, and reality.

Each partner brings conceptions and behaviors learned in the family of origin to the marriage. These transplanted images and behaviors influence and are modified by the marital relationship. Elizabeth grew up in a large family where there was physical contact among members, flamboyant emotional displays were accepted, and spontaneity was encouraged. When she married Daryl, who grew up in a more reserved family, the couple began to reconcile the differences in meanings attached to a wide range of expressive behaviors. How will she know when he is pleased, hurt, or angry? Will he feel uncomfortable if she demonstrates her affection for him in front of other people?

In another couple, one partner may have been born into a family where a typical response to a child crying over a broken toy was, "How did that happen, sweetheart? Maybe we can find out how to fix it." If the other partner grew up in a family where the typical response to the same behavior was, "Those things happen—big boys learn not to cry," the couple is confronted with the problem of integrating two different meaning systems that each response implies. And this is an example taken from only one event! The meaning-making histories of each of the two persons who make up the marital partnership are composed of a vast array of such episodes.

In negotiating the meanings of their words and gestures, a couple must learn how to interpret a wide range of behaviors. If the family of one partner, for instance, values gift giving and the other partner's family does not, some negotiating of the meaning of the act will very likely take place. A partner who grew up in a family where gift giving was especially important may long for a sentimental gift at Christmas time—a book of poetry or an antique rocker—and feel slightly cheated when he or she receives a power saw or an electric blender. For another couple, it may be necessary to negotiate the importance of verbal expressions of affection. A woman may have a strong need to have her husband state frequently "I love you." He, on the other hand, may feel that "words are cheap" and "actions are what count." Instead of saying "I love you" he may refinish an old desk for her or plan a camping trip for the two of them.

This negotiation of meaning pervades other areas of married life as well. A newly married couple has to negotiate the meanings that they attach to particular habits and sets of behaviors. What, for instance, does a disorderly household mean to each partner? For one partner, a disorderly household may mean that life is not controlled by objects.

Consider, as another example, the meaning of being on time. If Elizabeth is consistently late, Daryl may perceive her behavior as inconsiderate and become irritable. On the other hand, Elizabeth may have difficulty understanding why being on time could possibly be so important to her husband. As a consequence, she may experience Daryl's irritability as a lack of concern for her feelings.

Numerous other examples can be given that illustrate the necessity for a couple to negotiate the meanings of certain acts. A man may interpret his wife's casual grooming habits or her need to be alone during a crisis as a lack of caring for him. In a woman's family of origin the preparation and eating of food may have been associated with feelings of affection and conviviality. If her new mate fails to be enthusiastic about a specific eating occasion she may experience disappointment or resentment. Struggling over or negotiating issues such as these is part of the process of creating a relationship. As Sillars, Burggraf, Yost, and Zietlow (1992) write, "Symbolic interactionists have long pointed out that interpersonal relationships are not so much objective entities as collective fabrications made plausible by the exchange of suitable testimony" (p. 147). In Chapter 8 we will explore more specifically how relational themes are managed through the couple's communication (Sillars, et al., 1992).

Coordinating Communication Codes

A couple's **communication code** includes a set of unspoken principles used to translate words and behavior into meaning. Through the use of a communication code, a person interprets the meanings of gestures, words, and other symbols. A communication code determines the couple's choice of language and those nonverbal behaviors that will be selected to express feelings and ideas.

A newly married couple is confronted with the task of co-defining reality.

A man and a woman may enter marriage with very different codes. Henry may have heard his mother affectionately referred to by his father as "my old lady" and be surprised to learn that his wife is insulted by his use of the term in reference to her. Two people can use the same words and yet mean two different things. A partner who says, "pass the butter, please," may be making a polite request. The spouse might employ the same phrase in order to use formality as a way to indicate displeasure at some previous transgression of his or her partner.

Groups of words may be combined in different ways so that their content is subtly different. Consider the following ways of expressing a desire to leave a social gathering:

1. "I would like to leave now."
2. "I think we should leave now."
3. "We have to get up early in the morning."
4. "Aren't you getting tired?"
5. "Aren't you about ready to go?"
6. "I'm getting tired."
7. "I'm worried about the presentation I have to give tomorrow."
8. "We have a long drive home."
9. "Could we leave pretty soon?"
10. "This party certainly is dull."

Each of these ways of expressing the same desire presents the message a little differently. As the form of the message changes, so does the specific orientation toward the other person. In some of the examples, the request is stated directly, even forcefully ("I think we should leave now"). In others, the choice of words avoids expressing the request directly ("I'm getting tired"), but it is assumed that the message will be understood. The selection of language may present the desire directly but avoid making a demand ("Could we leave pretty soon?"). Another version only hints at the desire to leave—yet the message is clear ("We have to get up early in the morning"). Some requests are even phrased in language that suggests that it is a concern for the other person that underlies the message, whether or not that is the case ("We have a long drive home").

One of the most important tasks of newly married couples is to arrive at an understanding of how to interpret each other's messages. What is worth noting is not that misunderstandings occur, but that so often couples are able to read each other accurately. The spouse who says, "I am worried about the presentation I have to give tomorrow," is confident in assuming that his or her spouse knows that the statement means, "I would like to leave now." Couples often develop an abbreviated style of talking related to their ability to translate a brief communication. They develop a code for exchanging information.

The task of **coordinating a communication code**, then, involves acquiring mutually understood interpretations of the meaning of messages. Rabkin (1967) and Tannen (1986, 1990) have both made the point that marriage partners frequently have problems coordinating communication codes because of differences in their gender, cultural background, or family of origin.

Consider this example: a husband says to his wife, "This party certainly is dull," and his wife responds with, "Yeah, it sure is." Three hours later she then says to him, "I'm tired and would like to go home now." As they leave, the wife notices that her husband is somewhat cool toward her. On the way home he is silent. Finally, she asks him what is wrong. He indicates that he is irritated because they stayed at the party so late and he wanted to go home sooner in order to be alone. His wife's response is, "Well, why didn't you say you wanted to leave?" Angrily, he replies, "I did!" And she retorts with, "You did not!"

The husband's statement, "This party certainly is dull," was intended as a request to leave, but his wife did not interpret or decode the message that way. It may be difficult for the couple to straighten out their confused exchange of messages. It is probable that the quarrel will shift from the topic of "Here's what I meant and understood you to mean," to "You are not sensitive to my needs and my feelings." This example of "uncoordinated communication," as Rabkin calls it, illustrates the problems that develop when one spouse relies on a particular code for expressing preferences and the other spouse has expectations that a different code will be used in making requests.

Another example of uncoordinated communication is the following dialogue reported by Rabkin (1967) in which a husband's failure to respond appropriately to a wife's direct request leads to conflict:

Wife: Would you like to go to the movies? (asked in earnest, information-gathering voice)

Husband: No. (Ten-minute pause)

Wife: You never take me out! Why did you refuse to take me to the movies?

Husband: But you never asked me.

Wife: I never asked! I asked you ten minutes ago. You never listen to me. You don't care about me.

Husband: (to himself) She may be right. I don't remember her asking so I guess I really don't listen to her. Maybe I don't want to hear her (p. 11).

APPLICATION 5.2

PROBLEMS COORDINATING COMMUNICATION CODES

What problems in coordinating communication codes can you identify in the following dialogue?

Jeff: (At the breakfast table) What are you planning to do this weekend?

Rachael: I thought that I would take Patty (her daughter) out shopping on Saturday.

Jeff: What else do you have planned?

Rachael: I need to do some errands and I'd like to spend some time with Mom. I also need to do some laundry, take the dog to the vet, and I'd like to write a few letters this weekend.

Jeff: Okay, maybe I'll go to a ball game in Detroit with Steve.

Rachael: (She is silent for a moment and then speaks.) You spend more time with Steve than you do with me.

Jeff: What do you mean? You said that you were going to be busy this weekend. Would you like me to stay home?

Rachael: You don't seem very enthusiastic.

Jeff: Look, I'm the one who asked you what you were doing this weekend.

Rachael: But you didn't say that you had something in mind for *us* to do.

Jeff: (Frustrated) That's because I *didn't* have anything in mind. I was just trying to find out what your plans were.

Rachael: Oh, never mind. Go ahead and go to the ball game with Steve. (She leaves the room in disgust.)

In this example, the woman appears to be asking her husband if he would like to go to the movies. In actuality, she is making the statement, "I would like you to take me to the movies." The husband, however, responds literally to the first question because he has failed to identify the intended message. Failing to detect the husband's confusion, the wife makes a judgment about her husband— "You don't care about me."

Why do spouses have coding difficulties like this? One partner in a marriage may come from a family in which members could "read meaning" into each other's words; understanding involved reading each other's minds. Specific requests may have been perceived as aggressive acts or may even have been subtly punished. The other partner may have grown up in a family in which seeking an elaboration of what has been said would be a sign of caring (Bernstein, 1971) and requests or expressions of emotion were made directly. Coordinating a mutually understood code for such a couple would be likely to pose a problem. Yet most newly married couples learn, with surprising frequency, to recognize discrepancies between their own communication code and the codes of their mates. At the same time, they also achieve agreement about what certain messages say about the definition of their relationship.

If Elizabeth's preferred style of communicating is to send explicit, verbal messages in her interactions with Daryl, she may assume that Daryl will be direct in expressing his likes and dislikes. Consequently, she becomes confused or impatient whenever she discovers that he has not been. Daryl's preferred style of communicating is to be less verbally explicit and direct. He, therefore, perceives that he had communicated his enjoyment of a picnic they shared by fixing Elizabeth's broken hair dryer. As they become familiar with their styles of communication, several alternatives become available to them. Elizabeth and Daryl may find that they learn how to read each other more comfortably. They may also find that their differences tend to provoke conflict and turn into routine domestic dramas as each partner tries to change the other. In either case, what occurs in the process of their marriage is some shared understanding of how the behaviors and actions of the other are to be interpreted.

Our point is a simple but critically important one: creating meaning and coordinating a communication code are vital and complex processes for a newly married couple. Patterns of expressing affection, regulating closeness, and making demands or requests become clearly developed, even if the patterns result from an indirect mode of communication. The partners begin with the patterns and interpretations that they learned in their families of origin. Out of these separately developed codes, couples are confronted with the task of coordinating the meanings of the words they use and their nonverbal displays, as well as their interpretations of actions that have significance for one or both of them.

ORGANIZING THE RELATIONSHIP

The partners in any marriage have an almost infinite number of tasks and routines to work out. They must decide, for instance, how they are going to relate to their families of origin, whether or not they are going to have children, how they are going to spend their money, what leisure time activities they will engage in, what occupations they will pursue, and how they will present themselves in front of other people—to name only a few. As they work on these issues, the couple also establishes patterns that will govern how their relationship is organized (Krueger, 1985).

We have divided our discussion of the couple's task of organizing their relationship into three sections: (1) first, we explain what we mean by the concept of organization in a marriage relationship; (2) then, we examine control as a primary aspect of organizing the relationship; and (3) finally we describe competitive, complementary, and parallel relationship structures as alternative ways in which the relationship may be organized.

Organization

In nearly every social situation there are cues, some obvious, others subtle, that influence whether one person relates to another as an equal, as a subordinate, or as a superior. The cues prescribe a certain set of appropriate behaviors. We have no difficulty understanding that birds, insects, or other species behave in an organized and structured manner. Yet, the complexity and diversity of human activity and social arrangements make it difficult for us to see that human behavior is also organized or structured.

In his book, *Problem-Solving Therapy* (1976), Haley writes, "If there is any generalization that applies to men and other animals, it is that all creatures capable of learning are compelled to organize" (pp. 100–101). **Organization** can be defined as a description of the functions or role relationships that exist among interdependent parts. The organization of a system describes the structure of that system. How a couple has organized their relationship is revealed in their communication. In Chapter 10, we discuss the relationship of communication to family roles (Haley, 1976).

The concept of social organization can be easily understood in a nuclear family with children. Parents, who have responsibility for nurturing, teaching, and socializing their children, may be democratic in their orientation toward their children, but they are not peers with their children.

To suggest that families have structures and are, therefore, organized does not mean that parents do not include children in decision making, seek their children's opinions and perceptions, or integrate the children's preferences into the family. It does describe the fact that in social systems there is a structure that indicates how members of that system relate to each other as equals, subordinates, or superiors.

Marriage also involves a process of organization. In part, organization in the marriage relationship is related to the extent to which each partner functions as an equal, subordinate, or superior in various aspects of their relationship. Many couples do not accept a definition of the relationship in which one person, in general, has more status and power than the other (although that may be the case in some marriages). Organizing the marital relationship answers such questions as: How are the priorities and decisions of the couple achieved? What constraints do the couple agree to accept for themselves in their relationship with their partner? How has the couple managed issues related to individuality and dependence (or interdependence)? What are the limitations and boundaries of the relationship? That is, what is each partner allowed or not allowed to say and do as a partner in the marriage?

Control Patterns

The process of organizing the marital relationship describes to a significant degree a couple's maneuvers to control various aspects of their relationship (Haley, 1976). Control of the relationship is related to communication patterns that establish the distribution of authority in the relationship or in various aspects of the relationship (Lederer & Jackson, 1968; Millar & Rogers, 1976; Rogers & Farace, 1975). Simply stated, **control** refers to how each partner functions as an equal, subordinate, or superior in various dimensions of a couple's life together.

A newly married couple develops shared agreements dealing with numerous areas of their relationship (frequently without the agreements being discussed). For example, how does the couple handle who will do the cooking? Does the wife do most of the cooking? Does the husband? Do they cook together, or do they eat out most of the time? How is this decision made? Does one partner make a demand or request of another ("I don't cook") and the other accommodates (happily or resentfully)? How do decisions develop about who is to be the budget planner in the marriage? What social involvements, if any, will the couple establish? Will they go to social events together or will one spouse typically participate alone?

How each of these activities is managed reveals something about how the couple has defined authority in their relationship—that is, how the couple has organized their relationship. Organization is accomplished through the couple's communication. Elizabeth, for example, may exert control over the social activities of the couple. Suppose that she is interested in going to a movie that has come to the suburban theatre near where she and Daryl live. She calls up another couple and invites them to go to dinner at a nearby Mexican restaurant and suggests that they all go to the movie afterward. The couple accepts the invitation and Elizabeth tells Daryl when he gets home from a trip to the library that she has made arrangements to go to dinner and a movie with the Sharps on Saturday night. Daryl indicates that he is pleased and asks what time they will be leaving. Elizabeth initiates and Daryl accepts (rather than refuses or suggests that they do something else). Through their conversation, Elizabeth and Daryl have coordinated their agendas. They have also established that Elizabeth is "in charge" of planning the social activities of the couple—that is, she has control of this aspect of their relationship.

One spouse may have primary influence over certain aspects of the relationship and the other spouse may have primary influence over other aspects of the relationship. A couple can also compete for control in areas of their relationship. Elizabeth has primary control over the couple's social activities. Daryl has primary control over the research that goes into the purchase of a new appliance. He might, for instance, return home from the library on a Saturday afternoon and indicate to Elizabeth that he has read an article in a consumer magazine and decided which vacuum cleaner they should purchase. Elizabeth says, "Great!" She tells Daryl to go ahead and purchase the one that he thinks is best—and then she tells him about her plans for Saturday night. Another couple might negotiate almost every issue, including which vacuum cleaner to buy and what to do on Saturday night. Still another couple might argue repeatedly over whose influence will prevail in almost every situation. In any case, couples will develop patterns of communication for managing these issues that reveal the nature of the control in various aspects of their relationship.

Organizing the relationship is achieved through the establishment of generally unspoken rules that indicate who has control over various aspects of the relationship. The couple develops patterns for who is to control what is to take place in what areas of the relationship and thereby control the definition of their relationship in those areas (Haley, 1963). In Chapter 7 we will discuss at length the concept of rules as governing mechanisms in marital and family communication.

In addition to establishing rules, a couple also reaches agreements regarding who is to define the rules in each area of their marriage. In Chapter 2 we discussed the concept of metacommunication as a description of a couple's communication about their communication. Similarly, conscious or unconscious agreements that identify who has the right to establish certain rules are called **metarules**.

Suppose that Elizabeth has become concerned about how busy she and Daryl are pursuing their careers. She is interested in creating more time for them to be together. She might announce to Daryl, "I want us to agree to take Sunday afternoon off to be together." Daryl agrees. Not only is Daryl agreeing to make it a "rule" to take Sunday afternoon off to be together, but he is supporting a rule that suggests that it is acceptable for Elizabeth to propose a rule that they structure their time in a specific way. The rule suggesting that it is okay for Elizabeth to propose a rule concerning the couple's time allocation is a metarule. Daryl might have argued with Elizabeth; he might even have resisted her suggestion and indicated that it was impossible for him at this time to take Sunday afternoon off. He would not only be disagreeing with her suggestion, he would be challenging Elizabeth's "right" to make such a rule for the couple.

Negotiations over rules are accomplished through the couple's communication. In their conversations and interactions with each other, marital partners define the nature of control in their relationship. As Krueger (1985, p. 128) writes, "It is within the stream of communication that one discerns the obvious maneuvers and subtle nuances of control." Imagine a wife at a dinner table neutrally asking her husband to get her a napkin. Each of the following alternative responses reveals a different orientation toward the structure of the relationship:

"Honey, I'm just too tired to get up."

"Sure, I'll be glad to."

"Okay, that's fair since you made the dinner."

"You are closer to the kitchen than I am—get it yourself."

In Chapter 2 we discussed the difference between the content and relationship dimensions of a message (Watzlawick, Beavin, & Jackson, 1967). The relationship dimension of messages suggests how control in particular situations or in an aspect of the couple's relationship will be managed. Relationship dimensions of messages are usually governed by metarules—rules that indicate who has the right to establish particular rules and patterns for the couple. Metarules often reflect how a couple has managed control in their relationship.

In a program of research developed by Rogers and her colleagues (Millar & Rogers, 1976; Rogers, 1972; Rogers, 1983; Rogers, Courtwright, & Millar, 1980; Rogers & Farace, 1975), **control patterns** are described not as something which one person does to another but as descriptions of the nature of the relationship; that is, control is seen as a reciprocal process reflected in the communication transactions of the couple. How a couple manages control in their relationship is a function of how each partner responds to the other and the extent to which their relational patterns are rigid or flexible.

For example, in our opening story, Nina agrees to Derek's proposal for budgeting their long-distance telephone calls. In accepting his proposal, Nina has accepted Derek's right to control this aspect of their relationship. To the extent that their communication patterns are characterized by assertive moves on Derek's part, which are accepted by Nina, one might describe their relationship as complementary. We know, however, that this complementarity was not achieved without an earlier round of arguments and conflicts, episodes in which Derek's control moves were not accepted. These earlier conflict episodes were characterized by competitive patterns in which Derek's efforts at control were matched by similar moves from Nina. In this sense, one might describe the overall control patterns in their relationship as flexible rather than rigid.

Based on ideas developed by the Palo Alto Group of family therapists, the work of Rogers and her colleagues has provided empirical research that supports descriptions of how couples often organize their relationships (see also Rogers & Bagarozzi, 1983; Watzlawick, Beavin, & Jackson, 1967). Three types of relational organization are competitive, complementary, and parallel (see Figure 5.1).

Competitive, Complementary, and Parallel Relationships

How a couple has managed control over various aspects of their marriage describes its structure or organization. We use the terms *competitive, complementary,* and *parallel* to identify three alternative ways in which a relationship may be organized.

Competitive relationships are ones in which the partners continually struggle or compete for control of the relationship (Lederer & Jackson, 1968; Millar &

FIGURE 5.1   Competitive, complementary, and parallel relationships.

Connie and Stuart Have a Competitive Relationship

They frequently argue over whose views are to prevail in a situation. Connie, for instance, would like to remodel the bathroom and Stuart would like to buy a new car. They often try to "balance the scales" in their relationship. If Stuart has to work one weekend, then Connie will tell Stuart that she plans to work the next weekend so that it does not appear that Stuart's work is more important than her work. If Connie insists that they go out to dinner at O'Brien's (which Stuart does not like very much), then Stuart will insist the next time that they go to the Chinese Palace (which Connie does not like very much). Both take care not to let the other person get his or her way more often than the other. Equity is an important issue for them.

Robert and Carrie Have a Complementary Relationship

Carrie enjoys taking care of the children and running the household. Robert, however, makes most of the major decisions for the family. He decides where they will live, what they will do on weekends, and when the children will go to bed. He also makes most of the financial decisions and decides whether or not the family will visit friends and relatives on holidays. Carrie reinforces this arrangement by making it clear to the children that Robert has the final word about almost everything. Most of her decisions take into account Robert's response. If he does not want her to do something, she usually will not do it.

Elizabeth and Daryl Have a Parallel Relationship

Elizabeth balances the checkbook, but Daryl does the income tax. Daryl accepts Elizabeth's suggestions for social activities and Elizabeth accepts Daryl's advice about the purchase of new appliances. Elizabeth does most of the cooking. Daryl maintains the cars. Each partner is somewhat independent, but sometimes lets the other person make decisions for both of them. Elizabeth will visit her family when she wants to do so, knowing that Daryl will not object; Daryl makes an effort to keep in touch with his mother. Elizabeth encourages him to do what he feels he needs to do. They have separate agendas, but they can also do things together without feeling competitive.

Rogers, 1976; Rogers & Farace, 1975). It is possible for a couple to carry on a lengthy dialogue in a struggle over who has the right to define the relationship in particular situations. Imagine a situation in which a husband and wife argue for most of their married life over how to acknowledge each other's birthday. Every year the wife indicates that she would like a nice gift, flowers, and a card for her birthday. Every year the husband forgets his wife's birthday and tells her, when she reminds him that he forgot, to go out and buy something for herself and he will pay for it. She always refuses to buy a gift for herself and does not speak to her husband for several days. For decades the couple repeats this episode. The wife asserts her need to receive a gift acknowledging her birthday. The husband "forgets" his wife's birthday and then offers his own suggestion, thereby asserting his right to refuse to comply with his wife's request and, hence, to control the situation. In response to his refusal to perform the ritual as she prescribes, the wife punishes her husband by giving him the "silent treatment."

This couple is struggling over who is to define the relationship and, by defining it, control an aspect of their relationship. The wife attempts to influence her husband to behave in a specific way. He, in turn, refuses to comply. Neither one is willing to acknowledge the other's needs or to "give in." Each partner interprets the situation differently. After all, the husband did suggest that his wife should go out and buy herself a gift, even after she nagged him about his failure to remember her birthday; he does not deserve her "silent treatment." She, in turn, could say that he was insensitive to her feelings and provoked her behavior. Each partner *punctuates* this situation differently depending upon his or her point of view. The point is that both the act of his suggesting that the wife buy her own gift and the act of her refusing to speak to the husband are competitive acts aimed at winning the struggle over who has the right to set up the rules of the gift-giving ritual. The struggle for control becomes a kind of game that they play together.

In **complementary relationships** one partner does "give in" or relinquish control of the relationship, at least in certain significant areas (Lederer & Jackson, 1968; Millar & Rogers, 1976; Rogers & Farace, 1975). Complementary relationships exist when one partner continually submits to the directives offered by the other partner. By doing this, the one accepts the other's right to control the definition of the relationship. A wife who agrees to help out with the bookkeeping duties associated with her husband's business, in spite of the fact that she isn't happy doing the work, has allowed her husband control over this aspect of their relationship. When one partner, more frequently than not, acquiesces to the other person's plans, decisions, requests, or demands in most areas of their relationship, the relationship can be viewed as complementary. One difficulty with this type of relationship may be that one partner may lose his or her own sense of self by always relinquishing control of the relationship to the other person.

A couple that has agreed to allow one partner control of certain areas of the relationship and to allow the other partner control of other, equally important, areas of the relationship can be described as having a **parallel relationship** (Lederer & Jackson, 1968). For instance, a man may be willing to offer sympathy to his sick spouse provided she agrees to praise his career achievements. Another couple might decide to alternate years when each partner is responsible for paying bills, balancing the checkbook, and monitoring the budget so that both partners share in the control of the family finances. Lederer and Jackson (1968) make the point that, in the parallel relationship, a couple can shift between complementary and competitive patterns, depending upon what is most appropriate or most adaptive to the unique preferences and abilities of each partner.

Keep in mind that the process of organizing a relationship is subtle and complex. The rules that define the nature of control for the partners in the relationship are usually tacit and somewhat covert. They are often out of the conscious awareness of the partners. Neither the husband nor the wife in the gift-giving example may be aware that they are engaged in a struggle over how the relationship will be defined—they each feel "wronged."

Organizing the relationship is achieved, then, through rules and roles that specify both the structure of the relationship and the nature of control in the relationship. Rules that specify what each partner can and cannot do or say or that specify each partner's privileges and obligations also describe patterns of organization in the relationship.

MANAGING DIFFERENTIATION AND INTEGRATION IN THE MARRIAGE

In addition to the tasks of negotiating two sets of expectations, co-defining reality, coordinating a communication code, and organizing the relationship, a couple is also confronted with the need to manage differentiation and integration in their relationship. We introduced the concepts of differentiation and integration in Chapter 1 in our discussion of dialectical processes. Each partner in a marriage is differentiated from the other by unique needs, abilities, and preferences that require attention. The marriage relationship itself also has special needs that require attention. Sometimes meeting the needs of the relationship and meeting the needs of the individual can create competitive or contradictory demands for the couple.

Beth and Rob met when Beth was completing an internship in the University Counseling Center where Rob worked. They became good friends initially because they shared a common philosophy in their work. They appreciated the warmth and sense of playfulness that they each brought to their relationships with other people. In addition, both of them were going through painful divorces and they were drawn closer together as they began to share their feelings with one another.

After a long friendship and an intense romantic involvement, they lived together for a while. The arrangement worked out so well that a year-and-a-half later they decided to get married. Both of them felt that the other person made them happier than they had ever been before. Beth, for instance, felt that Rob brought out the best in her and appreciated aspects of her character and personality that she had suppressed because they had made her first husband uncomfortable. Rob was surprised and inwardly delighted by how sensitive Beth was to his feelings and how she discovered things about him that he thought no one would ever know.

As they began to settle into a life together, Rob began to focus his energies at work on some goals for himself. Now that he had begun to resolve some of his personal problems, other aspects of his life began to take on direction. He found himself committed to a research project that he had been considering for several years. He experienced a new burst of creativity. Beth also began to work on some goals for herself. She was completing her doctorate and instead of just "hanging in there" as she had done for the last two years, she really was making progress toward finishing. As she approached completion of her degree, she applied for a position that she really wanted. When she was offered the position, she was elated.

Their relationship was a motivating force in Beth's and Rob's life. Each partner was able to take pride in the other's achievements as well. As they pursued their goals, however, they began to discover that they had less and less time for each other. This did not happen all at once; the problem seemed to sneak up on them. Beth was also going through changes as she began to experience success. Sometimes she wanted to share this with Rob, but when they had some time together they used it to relax and have fun together. They seldom discussed serious issues. Furthermore, Rob's involvement in his work became so intense that he began working at night and on weekends; his long hours, in turn, gave Beth time alone to study.

The issue of making time for the relationship, however, seemed to get worse, not better. As a consequence, Beth and Rob found themselves barking at each other over little things. A bickering episode sometimes led to a more serious quarrel. Finally, knowing that summer was coming and that they would have some time together on their vacation, they decided to reassess their situation. During the three weeks while they were on their vacation they had a chance to get away from their work, to talk to each other about the changes they were going through, and to work out some plans for establishing priorities in their lives. There were difficult episodes the following year, but, overall, the couple felt that they were managing their lives much more comfortably.

The problem that evolved after Beth and Rob got married reflects one of the tasks that confronts a newly married couple and continues to be an issue in most marriages. The relationship had a positive effect on the identity of each spouse. Each partner's sense of self seemed to be confirmed and validated through the marriage. This new sense of validation gave both of their lives energy, creativity, and direction. Paradoxically, as Rob and Beth began to grow and change because of what the marriage had done for them, they began to pursue their own interests with more intensity. As a consequence, they found themselves wanting to pause and assess the needs of the relationship before they drifted too far from one another. The demand to attend simultaneously to personal needs, to family members, and to the relationship as a unit is an ongoing activity in marriage.

Beth and Rob were involved in the process of managing differentiation and integration in their relationship: differentiation in that each individual is developing a strong sense of identity through the relationship; integration in that the couple is faced with the task of integrating their separate identities into one relationship.

It is important to remember that negotiating differentiation and integration in the marriage relationship is achieved through and reflected in the couple's communication. Sillars and his colleagues (Sillars, Weisberg, Burggraf, & Wilson, 1987; Sillars, Burggraf, Yost, & Zietlow, 1992) have explored how the content of a couple's *conversational themes* can reveal how the couple has managed differentiation and integration in the relationship. For example, the conversation of couples who are more oriented toward integration tends to focus on communal themes, exhibits more "we" terms, and uses language suggestive of "cooperation" and "togetherness." On the other hand, the conversation of couples who are more differentiated tends to reflect themes related to personality differences, to aspects of "separateness" in the couple's relationship, and to individual role performance. In Chapter 9, we explore the topic of family themes in more detail. The point that we wish to make here is that how a couple negotiates differentiation and integration in their relationship can be revealed in conversations about their relationship.

In our opening story, for example, Nina describes her relationship with her husband as one in which her more expressive, affectionate, and affiliative personality can be differentiated from her husband's more reserved and taciturn personality. How Nina talks about her relationship suggests a particular focus in her relationship with her husband. Were Nina to discuss the couple's common religious beliefs or describe their mutual goals, she would focus more on the communal aspects of the differentiation/integration dialectic. Furthermore, Nina suggests that as differences in each spouse's personality needs and preferences achieve some degree of resolution, there is a greater tendency to experience integration in the relationship. Her final comments are "We're getting there . . . we're making progress." While indicating that issues of differentiation are significant in their relationship, Nina's account also illustrates the dynamic relationship between differentiation and integration.

THE IDENTITY–RELATIONSHIP DIALECTIC

In the process of building the marriage relationship, a couple is confronted with the need to simultaneously validate the individual identities of the partners and the integrity of the relationship. Validation of individual identities is related to differentiation in the marriage; validation of the integrity of the relationship is related to integration in the marriage. The **identity–relationship dialectic** refers to the simultaneous need for a couple to maintain personal identities and to maintain the integrity of the relationship. The assumption that couples pursue both a sense of identity and a sense of relationship integrity is a hypothesis explored and supported in the work of Askham (1976, 1984).

Failure to achieve both differentiation and integration in the relationship can lead to disruption or termination of the relationship. There is, however, a dialectical tension between the need for partners to pursue the development of their personal identities and the need to maintain the integrity of the relationship. The pursuit of individual identities and of the integrity of the relationship depend upon each other for their satisfaction; at the same time, fulfillment of one has the potential to undermine the other. Askham's (1976, 1984) term for the dialectical process between differentiation and integration in the marriage relationship is "the identity–stability didactic."

According to Askham (1976, 1984), individuals are attracted to stable relationships because of the opportunity to develop a sense of personal identity through conversations with a significant other. At the same time, the integrity of the relationship may be threatened by activities related to the pursuit of personal identities. Askham illustrates the potential for contradiction and paradox as couples negotiate differentiation and integration in their relationship.

Symbolic interactionists argue that individual identity can be created only as the individual interacts with others. It is through interactions with others that one learns not only the various social roles (wife, mother, husband, father, teacher, doctor) that make up identity but also how one perceives himself or herself as a unique human being. In developing the confidence that a person is who she thinks she is, one needs to interact with intimate others with whom one can discuss such things as fantasies, goals, needs, perceptions, ideas, values, complex feelings, important past experiences, and personal conflicts (Berger & Luckman, 1966). As Elizabeth and Daryl or Beth and Rob share complex feelings with each other, they each discover some things about themselves. Their discoveries, made through interactions with each other, help them to gain a clearer sense of their own identities.

Along with the confirmation acquired in conversations with a significant other, however, contacts outside the relationship are necessary in order to confirm one's perceptions of his or her partner and to give one something to converse about with the significant other. In addition, periods of privacy are required to enable one to reflect on the other's interpretation of reality and to integrate potentially conflicting information about the self. With reflection and privacy also come the potential for change, the impetus to seek new experiences, and the clarification of individual goals.

On the other hand, the conditions necessary for the development of identity are likely to be perceived as undermining the couple's stability. Conversation that highlights the uniqueness of the individual's needs, values, desires, and perceptions of reality may also underscore differences that are perceived as fragmenting the relationship. In the pursuit of stability, contact with others who may offer support for a sense of identity that is incompatible with that of the significant other or who may interfere with the integrity of the relationship are discouraged. As Askham (1976) argues:

> Thus, on the one hand, identity-maintenance requires open and wide-ranging conversation, a certain amount of privacy or independence, the possibility of new experiences and the development for each individual of a minimum of restricting objectification roles, and the chance for intimate interaction with other persons. On the other hand, stability-maintenance requires the inhibition of all these factors (pp. 538–539).

TABLE 5.2   Five tasks in building the marriage relationship.

	EXAMPLE
1. Integrating expectations	How will Nina and Derek integrate their different expectations about the management of the household budget?
2. Co-defining reality	Through conversations with her husband, Evan, Margo gradually changes her perceptions of her friend, Jenny. Likewise, Evan finds that he is more critical of his friend, Bobby, as a consequence of conversations with Margo about Bobby.
3. Negotiating a communication code	Stan gets frustrated with Liz because she does not make requests directly; Liz gets upset because she thinks that Stan is not sensitive to cues that she sends.
4. Organizing the relationship	Elizabeth functions as the leader in some areas and Daryl functions as the leader in other areas of their marriage.
5. Managing differentiation and integration	Now that their relationship is going so well, Stan and Liz are thinking of taking some risks with their careers, knowing that such risks will require them to focus more time and energy on their work.

Strategies for Managing the Identity–Relationship Dialectic

In her interviews with couples, Askham (1976, 1984) confirmed her hypothesis that both identity and relationship integrity are sought in intimate relationships. In exploring how couples manage the contradictory nature of the two activities, Askham identified some of the alternative strategies that couples develop for coping.

Each of the strategies identified in Askham's work may be viewed as an attempt by the couple to manage paradoxical or contradictory needs. One option is for the couple to attempt a **compromise** in the pursuit of the two activities in which a "certain amount of stability is attained while at the same time each partner is allowed a certain amount of independence, etc., so that their sense of identity is not totally crushed" (1976, p. 545).

APPLICATION 5.3

MANAGING THE IDENTITY–RELATIONSHIP DIALECTIC

How does the following situation illustrate the identity–relationship dialectic?

Margo and Evan were married while they were in graduate school. Margo completed her degree a year ahead of Evan and accepted a teaching position at a state university in New York. Margo worked hard establishing her career while Evan finished his dissertation. She gained confidence as a teacher and managed to get two research articles published.

After completing his degree, Evan accepted a temporary position in the area. At the end of the second year, however, Evan told Margo that he was depressed about his job. They both decided that Evan should search next year for a new position that was more satisfying for him. Although Margo was very happy where she was, she knew it was important for her marriage that Evan be moderately happy in his career.

Evan found a teaching position at a university in the Midwest. The teaching assignment was not quite what he had hoped for, but he really liked the people in the department and thought he could adjust. The situation was much better than what he had in New York and there were opportunities for Margo. Margo was hired to teach full-time as a temporary faculty member, with the possibility that she could apply for a permanent position should one become available. The couple seemed pleased with the arrangement and they made plans to move.

Would you say that Margo and Evan have managed the identity–relationship dialectic by using compromise, by alternating one need over the other, or by focusing energy at one end of the polarity at the expense of the other?

A second strategy is for the couple to **alternate** in stressing one need over the other. A couple may go through a phase where the integrity of the relationship is stressed and mutual exploration of identity remains relatively repressed. After some time there may be a push to risk the integrity of the relationship in order to achieve a greater sense of personal identity in the system.

Another option may be for both partners to **focus energy** at one end of the polarity at the expense of the other. A couple may subvert their personal identities in pursuit of the maintenance of the relationship or retain their independence and freedom to explore new experiences, risking the permanence of the relationship.

In the process of negotiating a solution to the identity–relationship dialectic, the couple will find themselves caught in a complex set of rules, all of which are compelling and operating at various levels in the system. At the same time that the couple navigates the identity–relationship dialectic, they also negotiate meaning and control in their relationship.

SUMMARY

This chapter discusses five tasks involved in the process of building the marriage relationship: (1) integrating two sets of expectations into one relationship, (2) co-defining reality in the construction of the marriage relationship, (3) negotiating a communication code, (4) organizing the relationship, and (5) managing differentiation and integration in the relationship.

Every individual brings a set of expectations to marriage that gets integrated to some extent (comfortably or uncomfortably) into the relationship through the couple's communication. Interests, goals, friendships, interpretations of behaviors, and other aspects of each partner's life are changed through conversation with one's spouse. In acquiring some understanding of what is meant by each partner's messages, the couple creates meaning in their relationship. Each couple is confronted with having to coordinate their communication codes as they negotiate meaning in the relationship. Through their conversations with each other, partners organize their relationship, assigning duties, rights, and privileges to each partner and developing the patterns that characterize their interaction.

A central concern of this chapter is the communication processes through which the couple manages the issue of differentiation and integration in the system—the fact that there exist two individuals and one relationship to be cared for and that sometimes these components in the system are in competition. It is these processes that establish the foundation for the nuclear family.

KEY TERMS

alternate

co-defining reality

communication code

competitive relationships

complementary relationships

compromise

congruence

control

control patterns

conversational liquidation

coordinating a communications code

creating meaning

expectations

focus energy

focusing movement in the relationship

identity–relationship dialectic

marriage contract

metarules

narrowing alternatives

organization

parallel relationships

salience

<small>CHAPTER 11</small>

CHANGE
AND
GROWTH

JANET YERBY

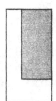

DIANE'S FAMILY

Diane speaks:

My parents, Gil and Sheila, are in their mid-forties and are self-employed insurance agents. I also have a brother, Mack, who is 19 and also sells insurance. My family unit is small, which has tended to make us closely knit. My father and mother seem to have a solid and successful marriage. They have never fought excessively or indicated to my brother and me that they are anything but happy with each other. They both work hard and share most of the responsibility for earning the money and caring for the family. My brother and father are also very close, and I would even go so far as to say that they are best friends. They hunt and fish together, and my father is teaching my brother the business. My brother and I have always been extremely close, too. In fact, I cannot recall ever arguing as children the way other siblings do. My brother gets along well with my mother. I feel close to both of my parents; however, there is considerable tension between my mother and me. Sometimes I have the feeling that our family unit is too close. We tend to get overinvolved with one another's lives and become frustrated and panicky when things do not go the way we want them to. This may be why the tension between my mother and me is difficult for the two of us and for the whole family to handle.

Since I left for college almost four years ago, a central theme has developed in conversations and interactions with my parents about separating from them and establishing my own identity. I will be graduating soon and I feel very concerned about my future. During my freshman year of college I was overwhelmed. I was exposed to different cultural experiences and points of view that were different from anything I had ever known. Sometimes this made me feel insecure and sometimes I questioned my parents' ideas and values. Growing up, I thought that my parents' beliefs about the world were the only way to view certain issues and cultures. I think that the process of developing one's own ideas and beliefs is interesting because as young adults, once we are away from our parents' protection, we tend to become more open and liberal. During the last two years, I have challenged my parents' beliefs and openly clashed with them. Sometimes they will make a comment about politics or some stereotyped perception they have, and I will disagree with them—even lash out at them—with an intensity that seems to catch all of us off guard. My impatience, frustration, and anger at something my parents will say surprises even me.

What I am realizing is that I am learning that I have a right to think and believe differently than they do. As children, my brother and I were raised to respect our parents and to believe that everything that they told us was the truth. Now, I tend to question almost everything they say. I am not speaking of disillusionment, but I am speaking of the identity stage of development when I am trying to become my own person and to separate from my parents' assumptions about me, about how I should think, and about what is good for me. It's not that what my parents taught me to believe is wrong, but as children my brother and I were like puppets who obeyed our parents and accepted their value system without question. They loved us; they took good care of us; they taught us their values; we trusted and believed in them. Specific political, religious, and social beliefs were ingrained in us—beliefs which, only until a couple of years ago, reflected what I considered to be the only way to view certain issues.

I do not blame my parents for any of this "brainwashing" and I do know that some of my behavior has been difficult for them to reconcile. However, as children, my brother and I respected and loved our parents and longed for their approval so much that we took on their ideas to avoid offending them. Over the last several years it has been difficult for me to define my own identity. I believe that it is important to let children know that there are ways of looking at the world other than through their parents' eyes. This is a concept that seems very difficult for my parents to accept.

At this point in our lives, the struggle between my parents and me seems to be the central theme in our family. I am beginning to view the struggle as an issue related to normal development and growth, but my parents cannot view it this way and object to my developing beliefs and goals that are different than their own. I find myself feeling upset every time I go home because, since I have moved out of their house, they seem to constantly disapprove of decisions I have made. Even my brother has difficulty understanding my feelings; he still lives at home and doesn't understand why I do not do more to try to keep the peace. Because I love my parents, I am confident that this period of conflict will eventually work itself out, but until then I know that the decisions I make will be under careful scrutiny. I wonder when my parents will realize that they cannot control me or my opinions anymore.

What makes the process of separating from my parents' protection and guidance especially hard is the fact that I must continue to rely on them for financial help. This gives my parents leverage to use against me, which makes me resentful. Some examples of these two central themes in my family involve recent incidents when I freely voiced my opinion and shared decisions that I had made about my living situation and my college career. I have recently decided to move in with my boyfriend. We have been thinking about getting married sometime in the future and since we spend so much time together anyway, we decided to find an apartment together. I have also decided to change my major from management to sociology. I feel uninspired by the business courses I've taken and have really enjoyed a couple of sociology courses that I took as electives. My parents let me know, in a not-so-subtle way, that they did not agree with either of these decisions and hinted that I might have to pay for my own tuition next year if I did not reconsider. They were shocked that I might consider living with my boyfriend before getting married and worried that I will not be able to find a job after college if I major in sociology. They seem to be genuinely concerned about my welfare, but it is almost impossible for them to understand how I feel about these two issues. I also have the feeling that they are asking themselves, "Where did we go wrong?" At first, their response made me doubt my own judgment and then it made me very angry.

I know there are risks in both of these decisions, but I did not make either of these decisions hastily and I feel betrayed and let down that they cannot support me. We have argued intensely—yelling and calling each other names—but have not been able to settle anything. I'm still not certain what I am going to do. The fights we have often leave me feeling guilty and bitter. Occasionally, I consider not telling my parents anything of importance about my life—or lying to them. Thoughts of withholding feelings from them, however, make me feel isolated, lonely, and depressed. I yearn for my parents' respect and approval—that may never change—but these confrontations wear me down. I also feel that I have to stand up for myself and begin to make some decisions on my own sometime. I hope that we can work out this separation/identity process eventually and that our struggle can be resolved.

I hang on to the hope that my family can continue to grow and become even closer and that my separation from the family will get easier. When I am calm, I realize that we are slowly improving our ability to confront each other, to listen to each other, and to work on our conflicts in a more functional way. I try to be optimistic about the future and accept the fact that even the healthiest family cannot avoid the kind of turmoil we are experiencing. Sometimes it is difficult, however—painfully difficult.

Sheila speaks:

Diane makes her father and me sound so unreasonable, but it is also difficult for her to see our point of view. My husband and I have worked very hard for what we have: we have a terrific family and are, generally, financially secure, and we live in a state that has suffered a 15-year depression with numerous economic ups and downs. We have raised our children to be thoughtful and caring, with strong moral values, in the best way that we could. Our family and our religion are important to us, and we believe in the work ethic. I don't feel like I should have to apologize for that. To some extent, we have shielded the children from the hardships of life: the bedroom fights that Gil and I have had about money, Gil's high blood pressure, or our worries about my elderly mother. We worry also about what the kids will do with their lives: will the business be able to support Mack? Will Diane find a career for herself?

Diane has always been independent, and sometimes she doesn't take our advice or listen to what we have to say. Lately, she "flies off the handle" when we least expect it and she seems to make impulsive decisions that worry her father and me. Even if she is at college and on her own, we are still her parents and we still want her to be okay. We do not want her to make decisions to suit us, but we would like her to be more open to our opinions—especially since we have an investment in her education also. I know of several young people who have had to move back in with their parents after college; that put a strain on the whole family.

We want her to prepare herself for the future—they say that her generation is likely to have a tough time of it—and we don't see how changing her major because she "enjoys" some courses more than others is going to help her in the years ahead.

As far as moving in with her boyfriend—that just doesn't make sense to me. He is a nice boy, but he is no more certain about his future than Diane is about hers. His parents recently got a divorce—after twenty-seven years of marriage—and he was so upset that he dropped out of school for a semester. I think he is using Diane right now for emotional support. I know that he has been engaged before. What if it doesn't work out between them? What if she gets hurt? Diane needs to focus on her education for now. If they are meant for each other, Diane and her boyfriend can move in together after they get married. Living together to see if you like each other does not fit my idea of a strong, loving relationship. I know I sound like a moralist, but that is what I believe—and I thought that is the way we raised Diane. Diane wants to make her own decisions and run her own life, but she doesn't always indicate to her father and me that she can exercise good judgment. Would we be responsible parents if we just supported everything she did, in spite of what we know is right? I would like some acknowledgment from her that independence brings with it responsibility as well as freedom.

The fights we have with Diane are no easier on us than on her. She accuses us of not listening to her or taking her feelings into account, but she does not seem very willing to listen to us and take *our* feelings into account. She didn't ask how we felt about these two decisions she has made—without warning, she just announced what she was going to do. We would have liked to have been consulted; we would have liked her to talk things over with us, to listen, at the very least, to our input rather than just declare her plans after the fact. In general, I find it very difficult to talk with Diane about almost anything these days—she argues with every opinion I express and sometimes I think that she says things just to shock me. She told me the other day that she doesn't know if she believes in God anymore. I wondered later if she said that just to hurt me or get a rise out of me. When she comes home for a visit, she spends half her time on the phone and the other half sleeping. I feel grateful if all four of us are able to squeeze in a nice dinner together without feeling tense and uncomfortable.

I have talked to other parents who have children in college, and they have expressed some of the same concerns that Gil and I have. I know that what we are going through is fairly normal, but when you have a twenty-two-year-old daughter screaming at you in the kitchen, it does not feel normal. It is easy to lose your perspective and sense of humor. We all love and care about one another in this family, but sometimes that's just not enough.

UNDERSTANDING DIANE'S FAMILY

Diane and Sheila each have very different stories to tell about how they are currently experiencing each other and the family. However, we can identify common themes in their stories. Both of their narratives reveal feelings of frustration, ambivalence, and uncertainty in the family's attempts to launch children into adulthood. Diane needs the approval and support of her parents, but she also wants to make decisions on her own—decisions that she knows might not always be consistent with her parents' values and views of the world. Sheila wants an independent, secure, and happy future for her daughter. Sheila also wants to be included in Diane's decision making and has difficulty supporting Diane when she believes that Diane's actions are not wise or consistent with the family's values. Diane and Sheila also share the belief that their conflicts are normal and have some faith that their love and caring for each other will see them through this trying period of change.

This chapter focuses on the processes of change and growth in families. One of the most common sources of stress in family life is the tension between stability and change. In previous chapters, we examined the ways in which families develop stable and relatively predictable patterns of relating. Although each family may develop a somewhat unique pattern of interaction, all families share the tendency to repeat certain routines and sequences of behavior over and over again. The sequences may be different in different families, but every family will have some recurrent and stable sequences of interaction. On the other hand, families also are systems in flux. Every family must confront the forces of change brought on by the forward movement of time.

At about the time a couple has become secure in their patterns of relating to each other as husband and wife, their first child is born. The new demands of parenting the child can challenge or interfere with their pattern of relating to each other as spouses. They must now learn how to function both as spouses and as parents. Another example is the case of parents of adolescents. As the children become teenagers, the parents discover that they are being asked to allow their children more independence and to relate to them more as peers than as parents. This adaptation requires a change in the interactional rules of the family. Moreover, the children seem to want more distance from their parents at about the same point in time that the parents want more closeness to their children. These apparent cross-pressures can make matters difficult, indeed. As children enter adulthood, they need to feel confident in making their own decisions, and yet, like Diane, they need the approval and support of their parents. Another common example of the requirement for change occurs when "the nest is emptied." After years of focusing on parenting and togetherness as a whole family under a single roof, parents must come to grips with being alone again.

In family life, the demand for change is matched against the demand for stability. Sometimes change is welcomed; often it is resisted. Haley (1963) refers to resistance to change as "the first law of human relationships." According to Haley, whenever change in the definition of relationship is attempted, it is resisted. If Haley is correct, then all of us must sooner or later face a troubling dilemma. The forces of biological, social, and cultural change mandate that we must change—one cannot not change; yet when change is attempted, it will probably be resisted. Change is also related to issues of differentiation and integration in the family. Periods of change provide opportunities for family members to differentiate themselves from the family, to redefine themselves, and to assert their identities. Differentiation can also lead to anxiety and fears of rejection and isolation. This dilemma may explain why change so often is experienced as disruptive, difficult, and/or disturbing. Change is inevitable and so is resistance to change!

The purpose of this chapter is to enlarge your understanding of how and why families change. Many of the changes that occur in families are predictable and can be anticipated; but some changes come with no forewarning and these unexpected developments can shock and disrupt even the most secure and stable families. How many of us are ever sufficiently prepared for the death of a parent, the loss of a job or stable income, the breakup of a marriage, or some similarly intense family crisis? In our opinion, the most truthful answer is that few of us are prepared to cope effectively with these blows of fate. Yet each of us is likely to be forced to face some kind of family crisis at some point in our lives.

Considering what is known about family dissolution, teenage childbirth, and violence in the home, it is probably a good idea to question any utopian images you may have about the "normal" or "average" American family. More than fifty percent of persons under seventy who have been married also have been divorced. Today, nearly twenty percent of all births in the United States are to unmarried women; many of these are children born to children. Another twenty percent are children of divorced parents who are raised by a single parent or in blended families where one of the parents is a stepparent. One of the most significant and distressing social problems of our time is family violence. Gelles (1979, p. 11) bluntly stated that "people are more likely to be hit, beat up, or even killed in their own homes by another family member than anywhere else, or by anyone else, in our society." Tragically, more than six million men, women, and children are subjected to some form of severe physical abuse at the hands of parents, spouses, or adult children each year (Gelles, 1979). These data suggest that, instead of being a place of love, warmth, and security, the family context too often becomes a source of pain, fear, and disappointment.

The developmental perspective discussed in this chapter encompasses the predictable historical changes that most families experience as they grow older together and the unpredictable and/or unexpected blows of fate. This developmental perspective presents a focus on the family ecosystem. The chapter is divided into four sections. The first section describes the family life cycle and discusses transitions between stages that may require changes in rules and roles. The second section distinguishes between the family life cycle and processes of family development. This distinction has been advanced by Wynne (1984), who emphasizes the relational processes associated with functional adaptability to new stages in the family life cycle. What we like most about Wynne's developmental approach is his emphasis on the interpersonal skills associated with successful adaptation to changes in the family's stage of life. In the third section, we discuss the irony and tragedy of family violence. The topic of family violence draws attention to the crucial importance of understanding how stable patterns of communication can turn into vicious cycles of self-reinforcing, destructive communication. The final section of the chapter reviews the contradictions of family life that form the foundations of personal growth and summarizes what we have learned about optimal family functioning.

SOURCES OF CHANGE IN THE FAMILY LIFE CYCLE

Many social scientists have described families as social systems that change over time (Carter & McGoldrick, 1980; Haley, 1973; Hill & Rodgers, 1964; Hill, 1970; Duvall, 1977; Olson, et al., 1983). The term **family life cycle** is used to describe a sequence of developmental stages associated with the passage of time during which members of the nuclear family enter, exit, and mature, and the performance of important life tasks that accompany each stage of development. One of the main advantages of a life cycle perspective is that it helps us to understand the demands placed upon families and the problems they can expect to face at particular points in time.

Individuals normally become members of a family through birth, adoption, marriage, or blending (as in stepfamilies). The family is unique insofar as it is the only organization into which some of its members are born (McGoldrick & Carter, 1982). You do not choose to be a member of the family into which you are born.

Exit from a family occurs when children grow and establish lives apart from their family of origin or when a family member dies. Family members mature as they age and pass through various biological, physical, cognitive, and moral stages of development. As each member of the family changes, the family as a whole changes too. Sometimes these changes are too small or subtle to notice; at other times, they are too obvious to miss. As a family adjusts to the birth of a new child, adapts to the departure of a young adult, or tries to cope with parents in "midlife crisis," changes in family rules and role relationships occur.

Family life tasks provide the primary focus for goals, energy, and activity in the family at various stages in the family's life cycle. In a family with young children, for example, life tasks normally revolve around the socialization and nurturance of the children, the advancement of careers for the adults, and the management of the economic and emotional stability of the family. Life tasks for a family in which the parents are much older and the children about to finish college would be different than for a family with young children. Life tasks for two divorced households, whose parents are entering new spousal relationships and whose children and stepchildren are defining their relationships to one another, present still a different challenge to the family.

All families do not experience stages in the life cycle in the same way or at the same point in biological time. For example, dual-career couples often have their first children in their late thirties or early forties, after their careers have been established. Married couples who blend children from previous marriages sometimes decide to wait until these children are almost grown to have children of their own. Men and women frequently launch new careers in midlife; grandparents may take on the responsibility of helping to raise grandchildren; and some children return to live at home after finishing college or experiencing a marital separation. These variations in the sequences of family experience make it very difficult to generalize about "normal" or "natural" patterns of family development.

A focus on stages in the life cycle helps to highlight the ways in which communication functions and changes as a family evolves over time. For example, when Diane was younger she says that she accepted, without question, her parents' values and beliefs about the world. She felt protected and cared for by her parents and seldom disagreed or fought with family members. Once she entered college, she became exposed to new ideas and cultural views that challenged her parents' ideas. As she began to develop opinions and ideas of her own, she found herself arguing with her parents more frequently and displaying feelings of impatience, anger, and irritation during some of their conversations. Sheila expresses her frustration and discomfort with Diane's style of communicating and with the changes in Diane's behavior. The transition to adulthood in this family is characterized by interaction that tends to be tense, unpredictable, and modestly confrontational.

The communicative problems experienced by Diane and Sheila may be seen as one of the natural outcomes of intergenerational influences in the family (Carter

& McGoldrick, 1980; Kramer, 1985; Pillari, 1986). **Intergenerational influences** can be defined as communication between the generations, the influences of one generation on the next, or the transmission of patterns of relating from one generation to the next. To a significant degree, Diane is going through a process of constructing her own beliefs and value system by contrasting the new ideas to which she has become exposed with those of her parents.

Intergenerational influences also include relationships between the family of origin and the extended family, as we discussed in Chapter 6. Many important questions come to mind. How do the parents' experiences in their families of origin influence the way that they respond to a noncompliant young adult child? How does the family of origin communicate with the nuclear family when a grandchild is born? How do in-laws influence the marital relationship at various stages in the family's life cycle? How do midlife parents relate to or care for older parents while, simultaneously, launching children into independent lives of their own? Clearly, relationships inside the family can be strongly influenced by transactions across these generational boundaries.

Our discussion of family tasks centers on five stages in the family life cycle: the newly married couple; the family with young children; the family with adolescents; the launching family; and the empty-nest and retirement family.

STAGES IN THE FAMILY LIFE CYCLE

The Newly Married Couple

In Chapter 5 we discussed some of the relationship tasks that a newly married couple must face as they co-define two realities into one relationship. They must work through many new rules about who can say and do what to whom under what conditions (Haley, 1973) and they must develop a satisfactory connection to both spouses' families of origin. The life cycle perspective focuses particular attention on the relationship of the couple's family of origin in the process of the

APPLICATION 11.1 ──────────────────

INTERGENERATIONAL ISSUES

Interview your family or a family that you know and ask them the following questions:

- How is communication between parents and children different than it was five years ago (or when the children were younger)?
- What is the relationship between the parents and grandparents of the family? How have these relationships influenced the nuclear family system?
- How have the parents' patterns of communication influenced the children's patterns of communication?

transition to marriage. The "baggage from the family of origin," which individuals bring into marriage, is so important that McGoldrick and Carter (1982) have referred to tying the marital knot as "the joining of families through marriage." According to these writers, the crucial issue may boil down to how effectively each spouse has managed the separation from his or her family of origin. This issue was discussed as an important aspect of courtship and commitment in Chapter 4.

The Family with Young Children

As you learned in Chapter 5, communication for the newly married couple focuses primarily on the processes involved in co-defining reality and building the marriage relationship. For families with young children, however, the focus shifts to how effectively the spouses can balance the pressures of parenting against the pressures of maintaining an intimate relationship with each other. Nurturing and caring for children, managing authority relations between parents and children, and sustaining affection for each other and a satisfactory sexual relationship are crucial life tasks during this cycle of family history. Patterns of relating established at the previous stage of the family life cycle—before the couple had children—will influence what occurs, just as unresolved issues from the family of origin continue to influence the marriage relationship. This shift becomes most intense, perhaps, during the transition to parenthood, when parents need to adjust their role expectations and support each other in the performance of parental roles (Stamp, 1994). The patterns established at one stage change but, even as they change, they influence communication at a later stage.

The Family with Adolescents

Families with adolescents are confronted with the task of preparing their children for roles of adulthood. This involves adapting old rules and forming new ones that reflect the need for more responsibility and independence normally associated with adolescent development. Children begin to reach out for independence while still needing clear messages about authority in the family. As McGoldrick and Carter (1982) indicate, the goal is for families to "make the appropriate transformation of their view of themselves to allow for the increasing independence of the new generation, while maintaining appropriate boundaries and structure to foster continued family development" (p. 183).

Max and Tim Wiley are a case in point. These two sixteen-year-old twin brothers have developed a small lawn-mowing business. Though they argue frequently, they do work well together. Their mother, Annette, who is a single parent, used to intervene; now she tries not to unless the twins begin to "drive everyone crazy." She also does not exert control over how the boys manage the money that they make. Annette does, however, make it clear that certain chores are their responsibility—for instance, the twins usually do the grocery shopping for her every other Saturday morning so that Annette can visit with her married daughter and see her grandson. Annette also tries to keep a sense of humor about the mood swings of her sons and what she calls their "back talk." None of this is easy, for as Minuchin (1974) suggests, and we concur, few parents are able to escape the perils of parenting unscathed.

The Launching Family

The primary life task of launching families is to help young adults to establish independent lives for themselves and to help parents redefine their personal goals after children leave. The difficulties that this stage may bring often depend upon the family's experience in the previous stage. For some families, it is the adolescent stage that is most challenging. For Diane's family, the conflicts and assertions of independence that are often the hallmarks of adolescence have become pronounced in the launching stage, as Diane enters adulthood. New experiences outside the family have caused her to differentiate her own beliefs from those of her family. Rather than seeing these challenges to their belief system as appropriate, Diane's parents respond with resistance, which makes the process of Diane's separating from her parents tense and strained. If Sheila were able and willing to communicate her confidence that Diane could make decisions on her own and that any mistakes that Diane makes would not likely be fatal (and are necessary to Diane's learning and growth), perhaps Diane could feel less defensive. Then she could experience the support she needs to forge a life on her own and become more accepting of her parents.

The Empty-Nest and Retirement Families

The primary issue for empty-nest and retirement families is to attend to marriage issues and develop goals that no longer focus centrally on children. A couple who has directed most of their attention toward the needs of their children or their own careers may need to reestablish their importance to each other and redefine their relationship. Once the children are launched, the couple may find themselves struggling with significant relationship issues that were never addressed when their attention was primarily directed to working and parenting. There is now more pressure to relate one-to-one, and face-to-face. Conversations that previously involved the children may seem awkward and unnatural. On the other hand, there may be more time and opportunity for sharing recreational activities or for getting to know each other in new ways. This stage simultaneously presents communication difficulties and opportunities. As the couple ages, financial problems and deteriorating health may have to be confronted or one member may be left alone after the other dies. As they experience the deaths of friends and relatives, separation from children and careers, and/or disassociation from old landmarks such as their place of residence and neighborhood, elderly spouses face new and sometimes terrifying changes and challenges. Often they want or require involvement with their children; sometimes children must become parents to their parents. This change in family patterns often can be full of growth and also stressful for family members of both generations.

FAMILY CHANGE: POINTS OF IMPASSE

Transitions in Family Development

We have already made the point that families develop predictable patterns of relating at particular points in time. As a family moves from one stage of the family life cycle to another, changes in rules and roles may be necessary. The period

FIGURE 11.1   Stages in the family life cycle.

The Newly Married Couple

- co-define reality
- establish relationship rules
- join two family histories

The Family with Young Children

- nurture and care for children
- manage authority relations with young children
- sustain affection
- maintain a satisfactory sexual relationship in the marriage

The Family with Adolescents

- balance responsibility, authority, and independence in parent–child relations

The Launching Family

- help young adults establish independent lives
- help parents redefine their personal goals when children leave

The Empty-Nest and Retirement Families

- attend to marriage issues
- develop goals that no longer focus on children

---

marked by changes from one stage in the family life cycle to another is called a **transition**. Diane's family is having a difficult time launching children into adulthood. The parents' concern about the consequences of their children's decisions and the children's need for approval from their parents make the transition to adulthood conflictual for the family. Transitions can be relatively natural and the shift from one stage to another may occur without any direct awareness of change on the part of family members. More often than not, however, transitions bring difficulties. Family members may begin to sense that their stability as a family is threatened or that the family is somehow regressing. For instance, LaRossa (1986), in his work on the transition to parenthood, found that egalitarian marriages tend to regress toward a more traditional division of roles after the birth of the first child. Families with children in the early stages of adolescence may find it difficult to redefine parental authority to provide increased freedom and control for the teenaged children. Ironically, about the time a family reaches some degree of security and stability within a particular stage in its life cycle development, the security and stability is threatened by new demands for changes in rules and roles.

For example, since her children were babies, Charlene and her two children have lived with her mother in the house where Charlene grew up. In more recent years, their neighborhood has become threatened by the invasion of drugs, gangs, and random acts of violence. When the children were small, in order to combat some of the negative influences of the neighborhood, Charlene and her mother developed a set of strict rules about where the children could go and with whom they could play. The children went everywhere with the two adults or were looked after by one of them. These rules worked well—they gave the family a sense of security and cohesion—primarily because Charlene and her mother had forged a formidable alliance. As the children have gotten older, however, it has become more difficult to keep them at home. Charlene knows that she must "loosen the leash" a little, but she spends sleepless nights worrying about her children and quizzes them incessantly about their friends, what they are doing, and the need to "stay out of trouble."

Adapting communication and relationship structures that are appropriate at one stage of development to the current stage of development is the primary challenge of family life cycle transitions. Even simple patterns can present difficulties. Penny and Jeff were the parents of a six-year-old daughter, Anna, to whom they gave a new bicycle as a birthday present. It was the first two-wheel bicycle Anna had received and, with her father's help, she worked hard to learn how to ride it. Once she learned how to ride her bicycle, Anna's view of the world changed. She wanted to go exploring beyond the front yard and her immediate street. One evening after supper, Penny and Jeff told Anna that she could ride around the block alone on her bicycle. Both parents sat on the lawn as they watched their daughter heading down the street. They waited until Anna appeared around the corner as she completed her short journey. As Anna reached the driveway, Penny and Jeff realized that all three of them had entered a new stage and that Anna would continue to push the boundaries of their neighborhood (and their parental authority). It was wonderful, exciting, and a little frightening too. The old rule was that Anna stayed within one or two houses of their yard. How would the new boundary be defined? How would they decide? How would they talk about it?

Family Crisis

A significant number of family therapists view family problems as outcomes of life-cycle adjustments. Strategic and structural family therapists (Minuchin, 1974; Haley, 1973, 1976; Madanes, 1983; Palazzoli, et al., 1978) perceive families seeking help as caught in communication patterns and role relationships potentially relevant to one stage of development but inappropriate for the family's current stage in the life cycle. Unable to make the transition to the next stage of development, the family experiences itself as "being stuck" in dysfunctional patterns, often resorting to scapegoating or blaming particular family members. A family may not be able to launch their late-adolescent child into adulthood because the parents, who have an unhappy marriage, will be left alone to confront their marital relationship. Struggling with a rebellious adolescent helps the family to avoid "saying good-bye" to a particular kind of companionship provided by the adolescent and to avoid confronting serious issues and grievances that were never adequately communicated in the marriage (see, for example, Napier & Whitaker, 1978). In Diane's family, Diane's need to question her parents' values and views of the world threatens the family's identity and creates conflict.

Families may become stuck in patterns appropriate for a previous stage of development in several different ways. Penny and Jeff, who became parents in their early forties, always wished for more children. They went through a difficult period when they argued about their parenting styles, worried excessively about their daughter, Anna, and found that letting Anna become more independent was painful. A family therapist helped them to mourn the fact that they would not have any more children. They acknowledged their decision to have only one child, felt sad for a brief time, and began to realize that they needed to enjoy Anna's development instead of try to hang on to her as if she were still a baby and needed protection. Once they were able to finish and leave behind the babyhood stage of family development, everyone seemed to relax somewhat. They began to develop patterns that would accommodate Anna's slow but inevitable maturing and to discover how to have fun with each new stage in Anna's growth rather than panic at how fast she seemed to be reaching out to the world and away from them.

When families are unable to let go of previous stages in their lives together, the family can reach a point of impasse that inhibits its ability to change. Families that are confronted with unpredictable change must also overcome points of impasse in their development. A point of **impasse** is represented by the experience of being stuck in a cycle of destructive conflict, pain, or anxiety because the family is not ready to leave behind previous patterns of functioning and relating to one another that may no longer be appropriate. Family members may argue with one another without resolving issues or changing patterns. Patterns that provide stability for the family at one stage in their lives may be very difficult to change even though circumstances and individuals in the family have changed. Family systems are continually seeking stability and, at the same time, continually changing. Understanding the family from a developmental perspective helps to give us additional insight into the evolving and reflexive nature of family communication and experience.

RELATIONAL PROCESSES AND FAMILY DEVELOPMENT

Wynne (1984) makes a distinction between family life cycles and family development that has important implications for understanding family communication. Stages in the life cycle do not wait for us to prepare for them. Children are sometimes born into the family before parents are ready for them; a child may leave home before she or her parents have been readied for the separation; and few people ever adequately anticipate how they will react to the death of a parent, grandparent, or sibling. Life cycle events move inexorably forward through time without regard for the preparedness or skills of family members.

Wynne argues that family development, in contrast to family life cycles, does not progress with the same forward inevitability. Family development is qualitative movement in the family. *Developmental stages* are identified by qualitative changes in the interaction of family members rather than by life cycle events. A couple, for example, who spent their early married years negotiating work schedules and making time for social life with each other finds that their world is turned upside down when they have a child. Their relationship seems to be terribly strained for a time by the demands of parenthood. And then, as if giving in to their exhaustion, they find themselves sharing more of their feelings with one another, making more concessions to one another, and quietly talking about things that they never before discussed. Their relationship, from Wynne's perspective, takes a developmental leap.

Developmental leaps can be thought of as qualitative shifts in family communication patterns. Changes in the family life cycle often are associated with specific events: a baby is born; a child enters school or acquires a driver's license; children leave home, marry, and begin their own careers; a grandmother moves to the same town where her middle-aged children are living. Qualitative movement in the family's communication patterns, however, does not always move forward logically through time; it often has its own inner logic. It is possible that Diane will graduate, marry, and continue to experience tension when she is around her parents. Gil and Sheila may be unable to accept Diane's views on religion, politics, and relationships. Diane may continue to be frustrated with her parents' inability to support her unique beliefs and values, and yet she may also feel a need for their closeness and support.

Wynne's definition of family development as qualitative movement calls attention to some of the emotional or irrational aspects of communication in families. Sometimes relational processes associated with change can be identified even when specific events leading to change cannot be identified. The couple for whom qualitative changes in their relationship have occurred may be able to describe how their relationship is different than it used to be, though they may not be able to describe any sequence of events that brought them to where they are. Understanding and recognizing the importance of these relational processes provides additional insights into the functions of communication in the family.

Four Features of Wynne's Model

We will emphasize four features of Wynne's (1984) model of family development:

1. the distinction between the family life cycle and family development stages
2. the idea that stages of family development are sequential, with each one building on a previous stage
3. the qualitative progression of relational processes at each stage of family development
4. the identification of dysfunctional, as well as functional, aspects of relational processes at each stage of development

Family development is seen as a sequence of different stages of relating among family members. Family life cycle events, on the other hand, sometimes bring changes in the way members relate to one another; sometimes they do not. The term **epigenesis** is used by Wynne to describe the sequential movement of developmental stages in which each stage builds on the skills acquired or on ways of relating achieved at the previous stage. Developmental stages have a hierarchical quality in that each stage is more complex than the previous stage; each stage incorporates behaviors and ways of relating achieved at the previous level. Wynne uses the term "epigenesis" in the same way that we have used the concept of levels in a system. Each level in a system incorporates the characteristics of components at previous levels but the system as a whole is more than the sum of its parts. A family system has particular characteristics such as rules and role structures that integrate the needs, expectations, and histories of individuals. The system functions, however, are more than the sum of these individual attributes.

Epigenesis describes communication patterns as evolving qualitatively, with each level incorporating more complex and sophisticated behaviors and ways of relating than the previous level. Wynne emphasizes changes in the nature or quality of the relational processes at each stage of development. He also indicates that there are dysfunctional or negative aspects of behavior at each developmental stage. An example is communication that maintains an exaggerated overinvolvement, detachment, or rejection between or among family members.

Five Stages of Family Development

Wynne identifies five stages of family development, each of which is defined by a particular relational process: (1) attachment/caregiving, (2) communicating, (3) joint problem solving, (4) mutuality, and (5) intimacy. The label for each of the five stages is descriptive of a "positive side of a domain of relatedness." Negative forms of relatedness for each of the developmental stages are also identified. The chart in Table 11.1 summarizes negative and positive aspects of relating for each of the five stages.

Attachment/caregiving. Wynne describes **attachment and caregiving** as complementary functions. The growth of parental love for an infant, the reciprocal tie of infant to parent, and the care that a parent administers to an infant are examples of attachment and caregiving. Attachment refers to the bond that develops between family members. Bonding is a fundamental and essential process in the development of strong parent–child relationships and in establishing a child's sense of self-worth and ability to care for others. In a parent–infant relationship, attachment/caregiving is established primarily through nonverbal communication—through embrace, touch, tone of voice, and facial expression.

In his review of the research literature on attachment, Wynne identifies three characteristics of attachment: the need to be close to the attached person in times of distress, the sense of heightened comfort and reduced anxiety in the presence of an attachment figure, and the increase in discomfort and anxiety when accessibility or availability of the attached person is threatened. "Falling in love" is an experience that is associated with attachment. Caregiving is related to the ability to attend to the survival and comfort needs of the attached person.

Attachment/caregiving is the most basic relational process. Without the ability to attach and give care appropriately, it is doubtful that one could even begin to establish a personal relationship with another human being. When a relationship terminates, participants in the relationship may suffer from loss of attachment, in spite of the fact that more complex levels of relational development were never achieved. Negative aspects of attachment/caregiving are emotional overinvolvement (in which family members experience extreme anxiety in the absence of the other person or experience an inability to function as separate individuals), detachment, excessive criticism, and withdrawal.

Communicating. According to Wynne, **communicating** involves the ability to develop shared meaning among family members. The capacity to communicate builds upon the attachment/caregiving capacity of family members. Without some degree of attachment/caregiving, concern for the other would not be possible. At this stage of development, family members have the ability to understand how other members of the family feel and think. They develop shared codes of communicating and of interpreting behaviors. Negative aspects of the communicating stage of relational development involve communication pathologies (such as double-bind communication), guarded communication (in which family members must be "overcareful" about their communication with one another so as not to provoke each other), and fragmented communication (where communication between family members is indirect and unclear).

Joint problem solving. Wynne makes the point that "when attachment/caregiving has not taken place, a shared cognitive and affective perspective cannot be well

TABLE 11.1   Wynne's five stages of relational development.

STAGES CHARACTERISTICS	EXAMPLES	DYSFUNCTIONAL ALTERNATIVES
Attachment/Caregiving • development of bonds between family members; the need to be close in times of distress; sense of comfort and reduced anxiety in the presence of the attachment figure; discomfort or anxiety when faced with lack of availability of the attached person; ability to attend to the survival and comfort needs of the attached person	• falling in love; parental care of a child; basic caring of one spouse for another	• emotional over-involvement; extreme anxiety in the absence of the other; inability to be involved with family members
Communicating • ability to develop shared meanings; ability to decenter and take the point of view of the other person; developing coordinated communication code	• attending to what others say with interest in understanding them; direct and clear requests and inquiries that are not emotionally laden; empathic understanding	• guarded communication so as not to be provocative; fragmented communication where messages are indirect and unclear
Joint Problem Solving • flexible role structures; comfortable coordination of tasks; managing differences and conflicts; successful movement from one life cycle stage to another	• negotiation; shared decision making; testing solutions; provisionalism; behavioral flexibility	• cyclical repetitions of conflicts; avoidance of problem solving; disruptive and emotional disagreements; blaming and scapegoating
Mutuality • ability to develop and try new forms of relating that will lead to relational renewal or termination (if appropriate); requires members to stand back from the relationship temporarily to observe the relationship; often motivated by a sense of dissatisfaction with the current relationship	• a couple assessing their relationship and making changes; deciding to terminate a marriage; planning a new lifestyle; children and parents relating as adults when children are grown	• pseudomutuality or preserving a fixed and stable but painful pattern at the expense of individual needs; repeating old conflicts with no commitment to take relational risks in order to change
Intimacy • intense emotional sharing; reciprocal self-disclosure that could make the speaker vulnerable and that assumes total trust of the listener; high relational risk taking; knowing the other person as one knows oneself	• a couple deeply in love and who share aspects of themselves in an intensely revealing way	• fixation on the relationship; inability to balance the intimate relationship with other relationships and responsibilities; over-reliance on intimacy in order to give meaning to one's life

established. However, when communication processes build upon attachment/ caregiving, the participants draw upon abundant information that can be taken for granted" (p. 307). In a similar way, the **joint problem-solving** stage of family development builds upon the previous stages of relating and on skills established in the attachment/caregiving and communicating stages. Through joint problem solving family members are able to develop informal role structures, coordinate task activities, and manage differences and conflicts in the family.

Wynne sees the joint problem-solving stage as essential to facilitating the successful progression of families from one important life cycle stage to another. For instance, imagine a family that has not been able to resolve attachment/ caregiving issues and achieve some degree of shared meaning and understanding (or empathy) in their communication with one another. They will have difficulty managing the transition from being a family with young children to being a family with adolescent children who require new, and less formal or socially prescribed, family role functions. Negative patterns associated with the joint problem-solving stage of development include such behaviors as cyclical repetitions of solutions that do not work, avoidance of problem solving about important issues, and disruptive disagreement (which, in the case of violent families, may become dangerous). Wynne makes the point that joint problem solving requires sufficient emotional attachment and the ability to communicate: "Without a background of attachment/caregiving and communication skills, joint problem solving is doomed to be muddled and dysfunctional" (p. 307).

Mutuality. The **mutuality stage** involves negotiations associated with long-term relational renewal, reengagement, and, in some cases, termination. At this stage of development, there is the recognition that previous forms of relating are no longer adequate and new patterns must be developed. Diane and Sheila, in our opening story, express the difficulties they are having in negotiating and redefining their relationship. In another family, successful launching of their children may mean that parents need to make changes in the spousal relationship. A couple that has launched four children into adulthood may, for instance, find themselves rattling around the house and bumping into each other until they begin to redefine their relationship in terms of their new childlessness. Mutuality can also mean that two partners in a relationship no longer wish to stay married. Whether mutuality involves redefining and revitalizing a relationship or terminating a relationship, the processes involved at this stage build on joint problem-solving skills.

Mutuality differs from joint problem solving. Not every family attains a high level of mutuality; nor is a high level of mutuality necessary to the experience of a rewarding and satisfying family life for everyone. It requires partners or family members to stand back from the relationship temporarily and observe the functioning of the relationship. This is often the function of marital counselors who are asked to help couples achieve more rewarding ways of relating to one another. The therapist can describe what he or she observes about the marriage and, thereby, provide the opportunity for the participants to step outside their adversarial roles and take on participant–observer roles in order to make their own evaluation, assessment, and commitment to new patterns of relating. Renegotiation of old patterns may involve global reevaluations of the relationship or smaller, more specific concerns. One couple may be planning a new lifestyle for themselves in New Mexico after retirement; another may be negotiating the reorganization of household management tasks when one of them begins a photography business after the children are grown.

The process of mutuality is related to the family's ability to separate their identities from a relationship problem and to externalize or objectify the problem as outside of themselves and between or among family members (Friedman, 1993; Gilligan & Price, 1993; White & Epston, 1990). In becoming observers of their interactions rather than defenders of their identities, family members can gain the detachment necessary to develop a new perspective of their situation and explore alternative versions of the story that they tell about the situation. Diane and Sheila might talk about how difficult the process of moving from adolescence to adulthood can be for families (which they have already begun to do). They could verbalize their awareness that each of them has different and sometimes contradictory needs at this stage in their lives: Diane would like to feel free to take some risks and make decisions on her own; Sheila would like to be included in Diane's decision making and would like to have the family's values validated. In conversing about the problem in this way, Diane and Sheila free themselves "from being defined by the problem" and open the door for change and mutual resolution of the problem (Freeman & Lobovits, 1993, p. 190).

Intimacy. Of all the relational processes that we have described, intimacy is the most difficult to define. Intimacy involves intense emotional sharing distinct from sexual passion. Wynne describes the **intimacy stage** as requiring more significant degrees of personal disclosure and trust than sexual passion. Intimacy can give one a sense of connectedness and transcendence that is exhilarating—in a sense, a way of escaping the boundaries of our private, mortal existence. But intimacy is not only difficult to attain, it also is risky. As Wynne (1984) writes:

> I believe that intimacy is best characterized as the inconstant, subjective side of relatedness, the sharing of personal feelings, fantasies, and effectively meaningful experience associated with each of the stages that have been described. These processes are relational, between persons, but are not necessarily symmetrical. They include emotionally charged verbal or nonverbal self-disclosures of a kind that connote an acceptance of the listener, who could betray or exploit the speaker but is trusted not to do so. This definition suggests that intimacy can be a deeply powerful, meaningful, humanizing experience, subtly and emotionally complicated, seductive but frightening. . . . Erotic elements, joint inspiration, and reciprocal self-disclosure are some of the more obvious elements that surely contribute to intimacy beyond the elemental starting point of attachment/caregiving. . . . Paradoxically, preoccupation with intimacy as a goal, as with simultaneous orgasm, interferes with its attainment and also distracts, at the very least, from attention to other forms of relatedness (p. 310).

Wynne's model describes family communication as a hierarchy of relational skills. At the most elementary level is the sense of attachment and caregiving that family members give and communicate to one another. By building on a foundation of mutual attachment and caring for one another, individuals are able to understand how other family members perceive experiences, and they can then create the shared meanings and sense of mutual understanding that makes joint problem solving possible. Joint problem solving enables family members to coordinate agendas, negotiate tasks, resolve differences, and adapt roles to meet

Attachment and caregiving are fundamental to the qualitative development of family relationships.

PEGGY BRISBANE

life-cycle changes. Mutuality in family relationships requires skills in joint problem solving as well as the ability to step outside of the relationship in order to assess the potential of the relationship. Intimacy is characterized by intense personal sharing and requires the use of relational skills achieved at each of the previous stages of development. It is, perhaps, the most emotionally rewarding and infrequently achieved stage of relational growth and the stage most fraught with risks to the participants.

Wynne's developmental model describes a hierarchy of relational skills which provides a repertoire of responses to the changing goals of the family and the changing demands of the life cycle.

FAMILY DEVELOPMENT AND FAMILY VIOLENCE

In this section, we apply Wynne's stages of relational development to a specific form of family crisis—family violence. There are many important forms of family problems that could be discussed here, including families characterized by drug or alcohol abuse (Stanton, 1981a), families having members with eating disorders (Minuchin & Fishman, 1981), and families manifesting a variety of other problem behaviors (Palazzoli, Cirillo, Selvini, & Sorrentino, 1989). We have chosen family violence as our case in point for two reasons. The first reason is the extremely high incidence of family violence. The fact that each year millions of people are victims of some form of physical abuse by other family members indicates that family violence is not rare, occasional, and confined only to "sick families" (Gelles, 1979, 1980; Straus, Gelles, & Steinmetz, 1980; Steinmetz, 1977; Lystad, 1986; Pagelow, 1984). None of us can hide from the stark reality that, instead of being an individual aberration, violence "is a pattern of family relations in millions of American families" (Gelles, 1979, p. 11). The second reason for focusing on family violence is its emergent and developmental quality. Families do not normally start out with a pattern of violence and abuse. More likely, a pattern of violence develops, is perpetuated, and escalates over time. Moreover, violence and abuse can interfere with healthy developmental progress and growth in the family, creating a crisis environment and an impasse in the family so severe that the lives and self-worth of family members are threatened, a circumstance especially painful and tragic for its most vulnerable members.

Our discussion of family violence will be limited and focused. By **family violence** we mean the spirals of family conflict that escalate into physical attacks upon family members. This broad definition of family violence does not distinguish among the various specific forms of family violence such as wife-battering and spouse abuse, child abuse and neglect, sexual abuse of children and marital rape, sibling abuse, abuse of elderly relatives, psychological abuse of family members, and violence by children. Family violence can include any member of the family and a wide range of behaviors. The severity of violence in the family can also vary, as can the vulnerability of the victims of family violence. Considerations of the specific types, forms, and patterns of family violence is beyond the scope of this chapter's narrower focus on change.

Violence in families is the most profound and devastating irony of human relationships. "Love and violence," writes R. D. Laing (1967, p. 58), "properly speaking, are supposed to be polar opposites. Love lets the other be, but with affection and concern. Violence attempts to constrain the other's freedom, to force him to act in the way we desire, but with ultimate lack of concern, with indifference to the other's existence or humanity." The profound irony of family violence is that in the one social unit where members have the highest potential for supreme joy, they often inflict tremendous pain. As anthropologist Jules Henry (1973) stated so poetically, "life lures us with small favors to commit great crimes."

Following Giles-Sims's (1983) application of systems theory to the problem of wife-battering, we distinguish between the question of *why* family violence occurs and *how* it occurs. Discussions of why family violence occurs requires that we identify the causes of family violence. There is evidence to suggest, for instance, that unemployment, rigid sex-role orientations, social isolation, cultural approval of violence, use of corporal punishment in disciplining children, and the use of violence in one or both of the spouses' families of origin may contribute to family violence (Gelles, 1979). It is important to acknowledge that family violence is most often a consequence of **power inequities** in the family which are embedded in cultural attitudes. Those with the least power, women and children, are most likely to be the victims of family abuse and violence (Gelles & Straus, 1988). A concern for why family violence occurs calls for a systematic analysis of the family ecosystem.

Focus on the interaction processes associated with family violence will help to determine whether episodes of repetitive patterns that erupt into violence can be identified, understood, and changed. Consistent with the developmental and systematic orientation of this book, we center our attention on how family violence occurs rather than why it occurs, specifically sequences in the cycle of violent episodes in families, characteristic dysfunctions in the structure of rules, and role relationships in families prone to violence. We then apply Wynne's developmental model for understanding family violence.

Stages in the Cycle of Violent Episodes

Families that respond violently to each other or to their more vulnerable members often progress through interaction stages that culminate in violence. Giles-Sims (1983) has identified the following interactional sequence characteristic of episodic violence in families:

1. an equilibrium or precompetition stage
2. a stage of competition and increasing tension

3. a crisis event in which emotions escalate and violence erupts
4. contrition or withdrawal leading toward a renewal of equilibrium

The **equilibrium or precompetition** stage is characterized by moderate levels of temporary stability in which family members maintain enough detachment from one another to avoid provoking each other. The **competition and increasing tension** stage is marked by an accumulation of unexpressed grievances among family members. The **crisis event** stage involves an escalation of emotions that erupt into violence. The **contrition and/or withdrawal** stage is characterized by conciliation after a period of emotional and physical distance.

Tom Gilchrist feels angry, frustrated, suspicious, and depressed by the circumstances of his recent job loss. He and his wife have recently spent time apart, allowing the couple to create some distance in what has become a tense relationship. Tom spends the day doing what he can to find work and completing mechanical repairs on a car so that the couple will have two functioning automobiles available to them. Their two children are at school most of the day. Janine, Tom's wife, is employed on a part-time basis. On this particular day, Janine brings home fried chicken; everyone eats dinner, watches a little television, and then goes to bed tired. For today, at least, some degree of quiet association has been maintained. The family is in the equilibrium or precompetition stage.

The next afternoon and evening are different. During the stage of competition and increasing tension, family members begin to experience their relationships as an accumulation of grievances. Janine has the day off and becomes increasingly frustrated by Tom's lack of interest and concern about the condition of the house. Tom does not express his feelings. He says little in response to Janine's requests and complaints, which he perceives as nagging. The less responsive Tom is, the more frustrated Janine feels and the more intensely she expresses her frustrations. Tension between the couple builds. Janine begins complaining about Tom to the oldest child in the family, who is torn between his alliances to both parents.

During the third stage of the cycle, the tension increases until a crisis event produces an escalation of emotions that erupts into a violent episode. Sometimes the triggering behavior can be a trivial issue. The previous night Tom Gilcrist had told Janine that he was going out to have a few beers with some friends. Tom felt that he had to get away from Janine's nagging. Janine felt resentful about spending the night alone.

Tom came home late—long after Janine had gone to bed—and collapsed on the couch. The next day, he got up late and spent most of the afternoon working on the car he was repairing. During the early evening hours, he fell asleep on the couch while he was watching television. Janine, who was still irritated about being left at home the previous night, told the children not to wake him for dinner. That evening when he woke up, the children had eaten and were upstairs and Janine was reading in the bedroom. Tom was furious that no one had tried to wake him for dinner. When he found the youngest child in the kitchen, he grabbed her arm in a painful grip and yelled, "Why the hell didn't you get me up for dinner?" Terrified, the child ran to her mother in the bedroom. Tom followed. Holding the child in her arms, Janine told Tom to control his temper; she indicated that she thought Tom had wanted to sleep and that he would only be "ugly" if she or one of the children tried to get him up. Tom's fury increased. He yelled at Janine, "You want to see ugly? I'll show you ugly!" Janine got up off the bed and Tom grabbed her

FIGURE 11.2   Stages in the cycle of violent episodes.

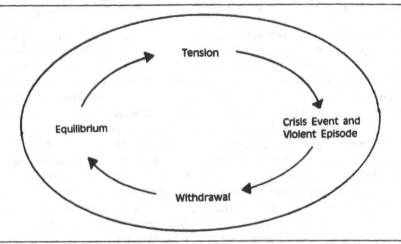

by the shoulders and shoved her against the wall. Janine called him "a son of a bitch" and Tom punched her in the face. Janine worked herself free and ran to the kitchen, threatening him with a butcher knife. Both children ran to the kitchen crying and screaming at their parents to stop. Tom stormed out of the house and did not return that evening. Janine cried all night. The next day she went to work.

Tom returned two days later with a gift. They sat on the couch in the living room. Tom cried and promised not to hit Janine again. Janine did not say much, but she was touched by Tom's efforts at conciliation. In this fourth stage in the cycle of violence, family members may experience some degree of contrition or, at least, establish a safer emotional distance. A degree of stability is temporarily achieved until competition and tension in the system is triggered by some new incident and escalates again.

In describing the stages of family violence, we do not mean to sanction Tom Gilcrist's behavior or to define his behavior as "provoked." In discussing family violence, there is always the chance that identifying one member's behavior as "provoking" another's may be misleading or suggest that the violent behavior of a stronger family member against a weaker one can be rationalized or justified. This certainly is not our view. Indeed, we cannot think of any nonviolent behavior that can be considered as legitimate provocation for the violent physical assault of one family member against another. The cycle of violence depicted in this example is intended to illustrate how violent families can find themselves caught up in family patterns that tend to repeat and escalate.

Application of Wynne's Developmental Model

Wynne's model can be used to examine violence in families as a developmental crisis in relational processes. At the attachment/caregiving level, violent families may vacillate between severe criticism of each other's behaviors and withdrawal from accepting responsibility for influencing other family members. Rather than sustaining basic complementary bonds of affection, attachments among family members prone to violence are more likely to be characterized by emotional over-involvement in which minor behaviors evoke intense emotional responses; small signals provoke large responses.

Because of their inability to develop functional levels of attachment and caregiving, the violent family may have difficulty communicating adequately (Chandler, 1986; Whitchurch, 1987). Members of violent families rely less on argumentative skills in resolving conflicts and more on verbal aggressiveness or verbal abuse (Sabourin, Infante, & Rudd, 1990). Moreover, in violent families, there is an unwillingness or an inability to understand the other's perspective and subsequently to develop shared meanings. Understanding the other's perspective requires more individuation than members of these families are able to achieve. Developing shared meanings requires an ability to exchange information about needs, feelings, and perceptions and to understand "where the other is coming from." Without a sense of what it means to share another's perspective, family members are unable to exchange messages that take into account the point of view and probable response of the other person.

We see this communicative difficulty in the Gilcrist family. Tom does not share his feelings of inadequacy and helplessness over his unemployment situation with Janine. In an attempt to get Tom involved in the family, Janine complains about his thoughtlessness around the house. Tom is unable to understand how Janine might experience his silence as isolating himself from her and how she might be using her "nagging" as a way to get him to connect with the family. As a consequence, each person experiences the other's behavior as a source of provocation.

In Chapter 7, we discussed "communication as metaphor." The influence of actions and behaviors is a function of the meanings they are assigned as messages. People respond according to what they think others are trying to do to them; that is, what others "mean" by what they say or how they act. Family members who behave violently often see their behavior as a fitting response to being "provoked." Messages do not necessarily have unambiguous and unequivocal meanings. A problem in violent families is that family members are prepared to respond to each other's actions as threatening and provocative. Consider what stands for provocation for the Gilcrists. Tom's lack of concern for things around the house "provokes" Janine into nagging him. The failure of Janine and the kids to wake up Tom for dinner is sufficient to provoke his rage because he views it as a purposeful attempt to agitate him. The inability to view the situation from the other's perspective may distort the other's intentions and provide all the justification one requires to fly into uncontrollable rage.

Without a foundation of adequate caregiving and shared understanding about each other's experience, joint problem solving is impossible. Violent families often seem unable to coordinate basic tasks and negotiate agendas. Even more importantly, there may be an "evasion of problem solving," to use Wynne's phrase (1984). Important issues are not addressed; instead, accusations are exchanged. And, of course, without adequate ability to attach, communicate, and jointly solve problems, mutuality cannot be sustained. Connections and interaction patterns among family members become rigid (Gelles & Maynard, 1987). There is little acknowledgment and tolerance for divergent self-interests of other members of the family. Family members, especially parents, also have little ability to step back from the system in order to analyze the needs of relationships in the family. Lacking this ability, members of violence-prone families too often view differences among them as a threat to the survival of the family or themselves. They fight when they ought to resist (Henry, 1973).

Moreover, families inclined toward violence find it extremely difficult to break their destructive cycle of anger and pain, a circumstance that is influenced by social constraints and opportunities (Goodrich, Rampage, Ellman, & Halstead, 1988; Gouldner, 1985). Women find it difficult, sometimes next to impossible, to overcome their economic and emotional dependency upon their husbands and, given the wage discrepancies between men and women, to support themselves and their children on their own should they choose to leave an abusive situation. Children seldom get help from persons outside the family who are willing or legally authorized to intrude on parental rights and the family's privacy in order to intervene on the children's behalf. Male socialization makes it relatively easy for men to avoid taking responsibility for their lack of empathy for the pain they inflict and for their use of family members as *objects* of their frustration and rage. Reconciliation, which often completes a cycle of family violence, offers false hope and reinforcement for staying in the relationship (Walker, 1979; Giles-Sims, 1983). This reinforcement makes it more difficult to contemplate or discuss separating or terminating the marriage. Members of violent families have not developed skills to distance themselves from their cycle of destructive interaction and to talk about their family relationships in objective ways that could lead to radical change or termination. Consequently, they are inclined to repeat their cycle of projected blame, provocation, violence, and reconciliation.

In the previous sections of this chapter we have discussed various ideas that explore how life stages, developmental phases, and repetitive cycles can facilitate or inhibit change and growth in the family. Families develop ways of relating as members are born into, enter, mature, develop new loyalties, exit, and die. How families cope with the changes that accompany natural life processes depends to a significant degree on the quality of their communication. In spite of the difficulties confronting them, some families are able to achieve a degree of joint problem solving, mutuality, and detachment which supports every member's integrity. Other families seem to repeat painful episodes that leave all or most of its members diminished and depleted. Diane feels crowded by her parents' expectations and simultaneously feels dependent upon them for love and nurturance. Sheila feels pushed away by her daughter and anxious about her daughter's future. And yet, in both of their stories, Diane and Sheila can find spaces to breathe, to grow, and to accept each other's different perspectives, even if they do not converge conveniently. They can talk about their feelings, acknowledge positive aspects of their relationship, discuss their problems with some degree of objectivity, and express their caring for each other and their hope for the future. In the following section we discuss more specifically our views of the characteristics of optimally functioning families.

OPTIMAL FAMILY FUNCTIONING

In this book we have purposely avoided such value-laden terms as "healthy," "normal," and "adjusted" families. It would be so comforting to be able to conclude our book by presenting a set of techniques or behaviors that would guarantee everyone a healthy and fulfilling family life. But we realize that it can be dangerous and presumptuous to give advice about how to be a family, primarily because there are so many different ways to be a family and so many different beliefs and values about what constitutes a "healthy family." All of us have to struggle with the paradoxes and contradictions of relational life discussed in this book. If there is a secret, it is that there is no secret. We can only cope with the confusion and uncertainty; we cannot resolve it.

Nevertheless, the topic of change provides an inspiration for considering what is better and what is worse for families. Many of us want to do better, and think we can, than our parents did with us; families that pay to get help from therapists usually expect to change for the better rather than for the worse. But what is better and what is worse and how big is the difference? The main difference between "them" and "us," according to Jules Henry (1973), is that they (extremely disturbed families) "seem to go to extremes and do too many things that are upsetting." Yet even in these "very disturbed" families, there is usually some alleviating health that makes family life seem tolerable and "normal." Our awareness of cultural diversity and history has also heightened our sensitivity to being judgmental about what is normal family functioning (Ho, 1987; Sue & Sue, 1990; McGoldrick, Pearce, & Giordano, 1982; Stephen, 1994; Stephen & Harrison, 1993).

This paradox—that is, the need to be cautious in making prescriptions about effective family functioning and the need also to identify the processes that "make things better" rather than "make things worse"—raises the question of precisely what is meant by the term *normal family*. Too often, normality merely represents the absence of some clinical definition of abnormality. What is "normal" then becomes confused with what is conventionally acceptable, which is not necessarily the same as what is "good" or "right." Indeed, the famous psychiatrist Don Jackson (1977) suggested many years ago that the concept of a normal family is a myth:

> As a student of the family for many years, I think it is *safer* to say there is no such thing as a normal family any more than there is a normal individual. There are parents who appear to live in extreme harmony together but who have nervous children, and parents who get along miserably but whose children appear to be functioning well. When one hears the expression, "Gee, they're a normal family," the speaker is usually referring to some facet of family living and not to the total family interaction, which is unknown to the casual observer. Such statements are usually made by persons who value conformity and see this family as one that lives up to all the ideals of the ladies' magazines, including the cardinal principle of "togetherness." Truly, such behavior has little to do with mental health. There are cultures and families within our own culture in which the family structure is very different from what is commonly considered normal. Yet the individuals therein are creative and productive (p. 161).

In more recent years, researchers, clinicians, feminists, and writers have demonstrated that particular conceptions of the "normal family" can in fact be viewed as "dysfunctional," depending upon one's perspective. Family roles that assign women to expressive, social-emotional roles and men to instrumental, task roles in the family have the tendency to reduce women's economic and decision-making power in the family and in society and to diminish men's capacity for intimacy. The tendency to view women as too often "overinvolved" in the family can be viewed as a tendency for men to be "underinvolved" and emotionally distant.

The Western cultural emphasis on individual autonomy, achievement, and expressiveness in the family can be viewed as "dysfunctional" in a culture that values family cohesion, connectedness to nature, intergenerational ties, and a sense of community above individual identity. It is our view that any description of the "normal family" can benefit from understanding that defining normality involves a selection process among competing perspectives of the family and should be presented tentatively, primarily as a way to begin a dialogue. Given these cautionary observations, can we make some generalizations as a starting point for a conversation about potential goals for optimal family functioning? In recent years, researchers and clinicians have identified several characteristics of optimal family functioning. Our discussion draws heavily from Beavers and Hampson's (1990) synthesis of the literature and their study of "successful families," the work of Hauser and his associates with adolescents and their families (1991), and from other articles by Bochner and Eisenberg (1987) and Walsh (1982, 1993). In the following section, we identify ten characteristics of optimally functioning families:

1. *Optimally functioning families tend to be more egalitarian than chaotic or authoritarian.* Egalitarianism is related to issues of power and leadership in the family (Beavers & Hampson, 1990). In chaotic families, no one seems to be in charge, attempts at directing family members may be covert or manipulative, and there is a lack of clarity about the responsibilities of each generation. For instance, the oldest child in an alcoholic family may take on child-care responsibilities usually assigned to a parent. In authoritarian families, leadership is characterized by dominance, rigidity, and the efforts of certain family members to control other family members. Beavers and Hampson state that less-than-successful families often vacillate between authoritarian and chaotic leadership. A rigidly authoritarian family may not be able to sustain the efforts of some members to dominate others; rigidity may mask an underlying insecurity and attachment to stereotyped family roles, provoking resistance and rebellion. In contrast, families characterized by **egalitarian leadership** provide opportunities for all family members to influence family decisions and to legitimately get their needs met in ways that promote everyone's self-worth. Children's opinions are not discounted because they come from children, and there is enough provisionalism about what is considered "right" and "wrong" to give the family the flexibility to handle different situations as they arise. Egalitarianism does not prescribe equality in every area of family functioning, but there is enough freedom for all family members to feel that their point of view is respected and valued.

2. *Optimally functioning families exhibit a congruence between the family's mythology and its actions.* In optimally functioning families there is a general agreement between the images that family members have of themselves and how they act. For example, a family does not maintain the myth that "we are a happy family" when it is apparent to everyone in the family that several members are angry and depressed. Alcoholic families that are "in denial" often maintain the myth that "everything is fine," even when the drinking of one or more members of the family causes considerable pain and despair for other family members. To some extent, we can see a lack of congruence between the family myth and the actions of family members in our opening story. Diane refers to the family myth that "we are a close family." At the same time, she describes how difficult it is for her parents to understand her needs and to support her efforts to launch herself into adulthood. Sheila also complains that Diane does not understand her parents'

point of view. Would a "close" family be more understanding of the needs of a young adult? If the family were "close," would Sheila be better able to share her feelings with her daughter without making Diane feel that she is judging or controlling her?

3. *Optimally functioning families develop strong dyadic relationships without excluding members or forming coalitions against one another.* In healthy families parents do not consistently exclude children by being preoccupied with each other, nor does a parent and a child form a coalition against another parent. Beavers and Hampson (1990) observe that "Parents may undermine each other's authority at times, and even solicit some support from the children, but the consistent parent–child coalition is not evident, nor is there evidence of unresolved love relationships between parents and children" (p. 17). The family, instead, provides the opportunity for dyadic relationships to develop among family members that do not provoke consistent anxiety and distress among other family members. A mother helps to facilitate a positive relationship between her daughter and her husband. Mother and father are able to parent in ways that do not strangle their marital relationship. Father and son are able to bond without forming a coalition against mother.

4. *Optimally functioning families develop emotional closeness and bonds of attachment while also maintaining personal boundaries and individuation.* In optimally functioning families, closeness is a consequence of the appreciation of the uniqueness of each member's needs, preferences, personality, and identity. Family members respect one another's differences (Hauser, 1991; Wynne, Ryckoff, Day, & Hirsch, 1958). They do not assume that they can speak for one another's feelings ("You're not angry; you're just tired"), pressure each other to conform to a unified world view represented by the family's ideology ("We can't trust anyone outside the family"), or relate to each other almost entirely as role performers ("Husbands are supposed to control their feelings"). Family members can engage in activities that may not interest other family members, maintain strong friendships outside the family, and have political views that differ from the rest of the family without endangering their acceptance and participation in the family's group life. A family that is functioning optimally somehow finds a way for its members to achieve satisfactory separateness without damaging the family's sense of wholeness. This issue is related to our earlier discussion of negotiating the dialectic of differentiation and integration, and it is part of Diane's struggle in our opening story. Diane wants to maintain a sense of closeness with her family without feeling that she has to sacrifice her own feelings, opinions, and decision-making power in order to do so. In fact, she experiences the inability of her parents to let her become her own person as a threat to the closeness that she wants and needs in the family.

5. *Optimally functioning families encourage every family member to participate in the problem-solving process and can stay focused on the task.* In optimally functioning families there is a tendency for everyone to be involved in identifying problems, negotiating solutions, and making decisions. Once a decision is made everyone is able to commit to following through and assessing the outcomes. This process requires a willingness of family members to discuss their own issues and concerns or those of other family members, to make known their reservations about proposed solutions, and to carry out a contract with other family members. Beavers and Hampson (1990) write, "The husband who accedes to his wife about

a marital issue but then passively grumbles or sabotages, the sullen adolescent who refuses to discuss disciplinary problems with parents, and the dictator-like spokesperson who assumes all responsibility for family negotiation—all produce or contribute to ineffective negotiation processes" (p. 21). Families that function well tend not to have members who remain consistently disengaged, distant, and aloof from the problem-solving processes of the whole family.

6. *Optimally functioning families tend to be more empathic, affiliative, and warm than oppositional.* They do not use their communication intentionally and regularly to hurt, intimidate, or control one another. Family members do not make "enemies" of other family members; they do not feel that they have to "defend themselves" against one another or believe that they have the "right to punish" and "destroy" one another (Henry, 1973, p. 448). They are not looking to blame the others or to find a scapegoat for their problems. They do not behave "coldly" among themselves. In optimally functioning families there is an effort to understand everyone's point of view, an awareness that one's perspective is related to his or her developmental stage, and a tendency to be receptive rather than resistant to appreciating the struggles of all family members. As Stafford and Bayer (1993) indicate in their review of parent–child interaction, "In all the variables studies, from all frames and theories, the expression of interpersonal warmth and responsiveness appears beneficial to the child and to the family" (p. 168).

Diane and Sheila are each seeking, longing for, some empathic understanding of their respective perceptions and struggles as a young adult and as a parent. We sense in each of their accounts some hope for common ground in achieving mutual acceptance and warm feelings of regard that have not been crowded out by their feelings of disappointment and frustration. They each express a desire for reconciliation rather than a desire to retaliate against or punish the other.

7. *Optimally functioning families give all family members the opportunity to find and express their own feelings and stories.* These families actively solicit the feelings of individual family members and are "respectfully responsive" when members do express themselves (Beavers & Hampson, p. 22). For the most part they can listen to one another, acknowledge their individual experiences, and do not attempt to block one another. Optimally functioning families recognize that each member has ambivalent feelings, experiences divided loyalties, and must struggle and come to terms with the contradictions and dialectical processes of life. These families experience and can tolerate a wide *range* of emotions. For example, they do more than go through repetitive cycles of calm, anger, depression, and remorse; they can sometimes laugh at their problems, feel compassion for one another, acknowledge their frustrations, experience resignation, mourn, celebrate their successes, share their neediness as well as withdraw from one another, and so forth. Hauser and his colleagues (1991) have described with sensitivity the importance of tolerating ambiguity and enduring uncomfortable emotions in the families of adolescents who have been able to nurture rather than interfere with the growth and positive ego development of their children:

> Enduring and even making authentic attempts to engage with an abusive or rejecting son or daughter may be one of the most meaningful acts a parent can perform during these adolescent years. . . . Being willing and able to weather storms of disruptive and at times deeply offensive feelings, such as intense anger and rejection, is an important general family strength, one especially called upon during the adolescence of one of its members (p. 242).

In the successful families of Hauser's study, parents endure intense and complex emotions and accept the expression of a wide range of emotions as a way of helping their children find their own voices and come to terms with the problems and possibilities of life.

8. *Optimally functioning families encourage family members to take personal responsibility for their actions and do not punish them for acknowledging their mistakes.* Family members acknowledge the effects of their behaviors rather than avoid, minimize, or scapegoat one another for their errors, weaknesses, or inadequacies. Mistakes can include minor problems, such as getting a speeding ticket or hurting a relative's feelings. Mistakes can also inflict major damage and pain on others in the family, such as having an affair, or verbally abusing or physically harming someone. Accepting responsibility for one's mistakes requires honesty and trust in the family. In optimally functioning families, family members do not blame others for their actions ("Your brother deserved it"; "You have not been very exciting lately"; "She provoked me"), lie about their actions ("I didn't have anything to drink this afternoon"), or dismiss the problem as unimportant ("Why are you making such a big deal out of this?"). In some families, withdrawal of love and affection, overdramatization ("I can't believe that you would do such a thing—this will destroy me!"), or fear of retaliation may make family members fearful of accepting responsibility for their actions. In other families, ownership of one's actions tends to make the situation "better" rather than "worse" because members are not punished for their forthrightness. In optimally functioning families, family members are encouraged to accept the consequences of their actions ("Your father and I want you to help pay for your speeding ticket"), but they are not belittled for having been honest ("How could any responsible person daydream while driving a car?"). Being able to take responsibility for one's mistakes without fear of family reprisals is related to role modeling and to habits of relating in the parents' families of origin. If a parent was made to feel guilty and ashamed as a child whenever she or he made a mistake, the tendency will be to discount or blame others for mistakes as an adult. That parent, in turn, will not be an effective role model for the children. Supporting family members in acknowledging their mistakes is strongly related to intergenerational patterns and rules in the family.

9. *Optimally functioning families are more spontaneous, playful, and optimistic than introspective.* These families are more energized and emotionally connected. They have fun together; they are humorous and witty. They can laugh at their problems and be playful. They do not take life too seriously, nor do they "have a compulsion to murder pleasure" (Henry, 1973, p. 452). They notice their successes and can acknowledge the times that they overcame problems. The climate of less healthy families feels heavier; interactions are often tense, abbreviated, and confused; family members may experience feelings of depression, discouragement, and hopelessness about their ability to function as a family. In contrast, optimally functioning families are able to keep things in perspective, rejuvenate and nourish themselves even in "the worst of times," and tend not to be obsessive about their problems. The pleasure and comfort that they take in one another's company has more significance for them than do the difficulties that they experience. We are aware of the difficulties in Diane and Sheila's family in part because there are no references in their story to any fun times or to the times they manage to shift the focus away from their struggles and take a break from the

"tug-of-war" in the family. Moments of fun, play, and spontaneity provide spaces for family members to experience aspects of their life together in positive ways and to distance themselves from day-to-day negotiations.

10. *Optimally functioning families are able to negotiate conflicts and move forward rather than repeat the same conflicts without resolving issues.* These families are flexible and adaptable enough to change when they are confronted with problems. Successful families are able to make the transitions from one developmental stage to the next without developing coping strategies that damage its members or become problematic. Unlike the violent families we have described, optimally functioning families tend not to get caught in typical cycles of avoidance and confrontation which produce only "more of the same" (Dailey, 1992; Yelsma, 1984). They tend to be confident that differences that cannot be endured can be discussed and alternatives can be explored. Conflicts between family members do not become "life and death" struggles without room for some degree of a mutually satisfying outcome.

It is important to keep several thoughts in mind when you consider our description of the characteristics of optimally functioning families. The presence of a struggle or "inadequacy" in one or even several areas does not mean that your family or any family is "dysfunctional." It is also apparent that the presence of intense emotions is not a sign that a family is "falling apart" or has failed in some way. Notice the significance that enduring engagement, the coming to terms with the uniqueness of each person's experience, and the willingness to navigate opposing forces in the family (stability and change; differentiation and integration) has for the family. It is, perhaps, most useful to view these ten characteristics of optimally functioning families not as end states, which your family has either achieved or not achieved, but as processes that are constantly changing or *goals* that can be periodically renewed.

In our example of Diane and Sheila, it is possible to identify the ways that their different perspectives represent both problems and strengths in the family.

TABLE 11.2   Characteristics of optimally functioning families.

OPTIMALLY FUNCTIONING FAMILIES

1. tend to be more egalitarian than chaotic or authoritarian
2. exhibit a congruence between the family's mythology and its actions
3. develop strong dyadic relationships without excluding members or forming coalitions against one another
4. develop emotional closeness and bonds of attachment while also maintaining personal boundaries and individuation
5. encourage every family member to participate in the problem-solving process and to stay focused on the task
6. tend to be more empathic and affiliative than oppositional
7. give each family member the opportunity to find and express his or her own feelings and story
8. encourage members to take personal responsibility for their actions and do not punish them for acknowledging their mistakes
9. are more spontaneous, playful, and optimistic than introspective
10. are able to negotiate conflicts and move forward rather than repeat the same conflicts without resolving issues

APPLICATION 11.2 ——————————————————

OPTIMALLY FUNCTIONING FAMILIES

- Select several characteristics of optimally functioning families which seem to be difficult for your family. For each characteristic think of a particular episode that seems to illustrate a problem related to the characteristic you have identified.
- Then, think about situations when each of these same issues was not a problem. For example, if you are concerned that leadership in your family tends to be more authoritarian or chaotic than egalitarian, can you think of a time when that was not the case? What helped the family function in a more egalitarian way? How did you feel and how did everyone react when that happened?
- Finally, identify at least one characteristic of optimally functioning families that your family does relatively well. Think of a situation that illustrates your assessment. Are there other areas where your family seems to function in ways that make family life "better" rather than "worse"? Can you relate these to any of the characteristics of optimally functioning families?

Diane describes her family as "perhaps too close" and her assessment may be accurate; the family seems to be having trouble allowing Diane to have her own opinions and make her own decisions. But it is also "true" that the closeness of which she speaks has the potential to motivate the family to work on their problems and to accept one another's different perceptions and points of view more comfortably. Both Diane and Sheila indicate their frustrations about not feeling understood, and yet it is to their credit that neither is ready to scapegoat or punish the other person.

SUMMARY

This chapter discusses family change from a developmental perspective. We briefly describe family life tasks and potential intergenerational interfaces that may influence communication in newly married couples, families with young children, families with adolescents, launching families, and empty-nest and retirement families. Sometimes families have difficulties making transitions from one stage in the life cycle to the next. We describe the family crisis that may emerge if the family reaches a point of impasse at some stage in the life cycle.

Qualitative changes in the family do not always progress chronologically. This is one of the points that Wynne makes in his model of family development. Wynne discusses family development as qualitative changes in the interaction of family members. Using the term *epigenesis* to describe the sequential nature of developmental changes, Wynne identifies five epigenetic stages of family development: (1) attachment/caregiving, (2) communicating, (3) joint problem solving, (4) mutuality, and (5) intimacy. As a case in point we have applied Wynne's model of family development to the problems of violent families. First we discuss stages in the cycle of violent episodes and then examine violence in families as developmental dysfunction in relational processes. In the final section of the chapter we explore family change as it relates to optimal family functioning and identify several generalizations that can be made about optimal family functioning.

Optimally functioning families tend to foster a sense of equity among members; their beliefs about themselves as a family typically fit how they behave; they can be connected while being respectful of the integrity of individual family members; they are able to share responsibility for problems; they try to understand rather than blame each other; they encourage family members to express their feelings and take responsibility for themselves; they are not punitive when family members own up to their mistakes; they can enjoy one another and are able to live with or resolve their differences.

We believe that the future is not unalterably constrained by the past, and the possibility for achieving a satisfying (if not happy) "ending" to a family story may depend upon the extent to which a family can grieve over its failures, laugh at its mistakes, and acknowledge its resources. Perhaps in the years ahead, Diane and Sheila will have a different story to tell about the comforts, complexities, and frustrations of their relationship.

As you conclude this text we suggest that you reflect upon some of the ideas you have explored and discussions you have had while reading this book that have affected how you think and feel about families in general and about your family in particular. Some of your reflections could also be formulated into assertions about optimally functioning families or goals for the future. Has thinking about some of the issues presented in this book changed how you communicate with your family or influenced the kind of family relationships that you might help to create? As the future unfolds, what new narratives might you be able to tell about your family life? We hope that this book can influence your own family stories—just as the experience of writing and living has influenced ours.

KEY TERMS

attachment/caregiving stage	family life cycle
communicating stage	family life tasks
competition and increasing tensions stage	family violence
	impasse
contrition and/or withdrawal stage	intergenerational influences
crisis event stage	intimacy stage
developmental leaps	joint problem-solving stage
epigenesis	mutuality stage
egalitarian leadership	power inequities
equilibrium or precompetition stage	transition

Section II

The following Sections are taken from:

Family Communication, Nurturing and Control in a Changing World
by Beth A. Le Poire

Why Communication Is Central to Families

Because families are primarily composed of involuntary relationships (besides the primary couple unit), family communication can be fairly intense. Power struggles frequently occur as members struggle to attain different goals. Spouses argue over how to spend money, the best way to discipline the children, and whether to switch jobs or move to another house. Adolescents struggle against their parents' conceptions of them as children as they strive to develop their own unique sense of self as separate from their parents. The warmth and affection experienced in families can also be a source of great sustenance as individual family members go out into the world to do the business of their daily lives. Furthermore, the push and pull between warm nurturing behaviors and disciplinary or controlling behaviors can put communicators in complex dilemmas regarding the best way to communicate with their family members.

On a day-to-day basis, and to facilitate task completion, family communication can be quite mundane. Much of the morning communication between parents or marital partners often revolves around coordination of child care, transportation of the children to and from school and to various activities, preparation of the evening meal, and organizing necessary activities around the house (who will call the "bug man" or the apartment supervisor?). At the same time, communication can be affectionate to hostile (verbally or nonverbally). Each message contains both content (the verbal "stuff" of the interaction) and relational (implied messages about the nature of the relationship) dimensions (Watzlawick, Beavin, & Jackson, 1969). I can discuss the daily tasks with warmth and good humor or with coolness and seriousness and communicate very different messages regarding how I am feeling about my spouse and the relationship on any particular day.

Introduction of Theory

At this point, we have a full understanding of the definitions of *family, communication,* and *family communication.* We also have more understanding of the complexities of families in the 21st century through our exploration in Chapter 2 of the various family forms and their potential impacts on family communication. To most fully understand the nature of families and the communication dynamics within them, however, we must fully understand the nature of **theory**. Before you turn off completely at the abstractness of this concept in the face of the concreteness of the types of families we have just discussed, let me try to persuade you that theories will be concretely useful to us in our application to families. By focusing on families, theories can be socially meaningful and applied.

Theories give us a mechanism for understanding phenomena, and families are one such phenomenon. Theories provide us with several functions that will be highly useful as we go about the business of understanding families. First, theories can **describe** phenomenon (Littlejohn & Foss, 2005). In other words, theories can answer the "what?" question. To be more specific, understanding *what* single-parent families, binuclear families, and gay families are is all the work of description. Description can also allow us to delineate the similarities and differences of families (and their accompanying definitions). Families are all the same because they all exhibit the characteristics of relatedness, nurturing, and control, as we described these concepts in Chapter 1. In addition, they are all different in that single-parent families have a single head of household, and binuclear families have a biological mother and stepfather in one home and a biological father and stepmother in another home. Gay families have parents who are homosexual and live in a committed relationship with their partner. This offers a nice understanding of the *types* of families that are out there, but it does little to help us understand the complex differences and outcomes associated with each family type. The second function of theories can help us on this front.

Second, theories can help **predict** concrete outcomes (Littlejohn & Foss, 2005), or in other words, they help enumerate *how* something will occur. This is especially important with families because governmental agencies, religious groups, and concerned parents are all interested in the potential effects of communication among family members. Specifically, governmental agencies and religious groups frequently form theories that allow them to predict that traditional nuclear families produce different outcomes than do single-parent homes in terms of better academic performance and less delinquency among the children in those homes (e.g., McLanahan & Sandefur, 1994). Alternatively, parents with teenagers may be interested in predicting the best form of communicating with their teens about risky sexual behavior and the potential outcomes associated with it. They might want to know, for instance, that parent-child closeness is associated with reduced adolescent pregnancy risk through teens remaining sexually abstinent, postponing intercourse, having fewer sexual partners, and using contraception more consistently (e.g., Miller, Benson, & Galbraith, 2001). Regardless of *why* these outcomes are occurring, simply knowing that closeness predicts these outcomes is good enough to encourage mothers and fathers to try to be closer to their adolescent children. However, theories can offer us much more than simply description and prediction.

Most important, theories can provide **explanations** for phenomenon (Littlejohn & Foss, 2005). In this way, theories can help us understand the "why?" question. In other words, theories can not only help us differentiate among various family forms and their predicted outcomes but can also help us understand *why* these differences exist. In other words, knowing that nuclear families are traditionally from higher-income and lower-risk situations can help explain why they provide kids with the stability and guidance necessary to perform well in school and perform socially acceptable behaviors. In addition, theories can help us understand why parents who are closer to their kids are probably more likely to talk to them about more "risky" topics such as safe sex and therefore provide much-needed information to help their children choose to perform less risky sexual behaviors (*explanation*). The outcomes associated with those risky behaviors (e.g., pregnancy, sexually transmitted diseases) are therefore less likely to accrue (*prediction*). As you can see, theories that provide explanations are stronger than theories that only predict in that they also provide predictions for outcomes. Therefore, understanding the *why* necessarily informs the *how*. Closeness with parents leading to more talk about sexually risky behavior and its consequence is the why, and less negative sexual outcomes is the how (i.e., more talk leads to less negative sexual outcomes).

Finally, theories can help us **control** the outcomes in question (Littlejohn & Foss, 2005). Knowing that kids who are closer to their parents are less likely to engage in risky sexual behavior, for instance, allows us to make policy recommendations. Theories allow us to draw socially meaningful implications with the strength to explain why. To be more specific, if parents are encouraged to be closer to their teens and, further, encouraged to talk more openly with their kids about sex and its potential risks, then it is possible that sexually risky outcomes among adolescents can be diminished. We see, then, that strong theories can *describe, predict, explain,* and *control* phenomena and the outcomes associated with them. Instead of providing esoteric and abstract conceptualizations with very little real-world meaning, theories can provide us with the very vehicles that make it possible to describe, predict, explain, and control socially meaningful outcomes with regard to families and the communication that occurs within them.

Rules Theory

SOURCE: *Stone Soup* © 2001 Jan Eliot. Reprinted with permission of Universal Press Syndicate. All rights reserved.

Just as roles guide our behavior, rules of communication shape how we communicate with various family members. According to Shimanoff (1980), a *rule* is "a followable prescription that indicates what behavior is obligated, preferred, and prohibited" (p. 57). Applying this to families, rules inform us regarding the best way to verbally talk to, or nonverbally communicate with, other members of our family. In this way, rules help us know that we are *obligated* to tell our mothers what time we will be home and with whom we are going out. Rules also help us know that within families, it is *preferred* that we communicate in pleasant (as opposed to unpleasant and hostile) ways. Finally, rules help us know that swearing at our mothers or sharing the most intimate details regarding our sex lives is strictly *prohibited*. Rules theory has a long-standing tradition within communication (e.g., Cushman, 1977) and will be highly useful to consider in its application to family communication.

Verbal Rules of Communication

Rules regarding verbal communication within the family can prescribe appropriate behavior and prohibit others. These rules can be either explicit or implicit (Smith, 1982). *Explicit rules* are openly discussed and agreed on. In most families, there are well-stated rules about communicating whereabouts with adolescent children who are gaining independence. My two adolescent stepsons, for instance, know that they must communicate where they are going, who they are going with, and what time they can be expected home. After verbally communicating this information, they are also well aware that if any of these plans change, they are to inform one of their parents immediately. These explicit rules are clearly stated and well-understood. *Implicit rules*, however, are more subtle and are understood in unstated ways. For example, my husband and I never ever say anything remotely negative about their mother in front of the children. Nowhere is this rule explicitly communicated or documented. However, this rule is well understood; in fact, my eldest stepson complained to me about it as he was talking about the painful process of disentangling himself from his mother as he emotionally prepares to go to college in the fall. In turn, my stepchildren rarely talk about their mother or stepfather in derogatory terms in my house. This again was never stated explicitly; however, we all understand that loyalty among coparents and between parents and children prescribes such behavior.

Although verbal rules in families are extensive and cannot be covered in their entirety here, two examples bear mentioning. First, explicit and implicit rules are most highly apparent between adolescent children and their parents. As adolescents strive for autonomy from their parents, explicit rules regarding territorial markers become more evident, with many early teens resorting to hand-scrawled signs reading "Keep Out!" or "Enter at your own risk!" posted clearly on bedroom doors (Guerrero & Afifi, 1995). Implicit rules also abound with well-understood and unstated prescriptions regarding taboo topics with adults. For instance, although gender of parent and gender of child can have a significant influence, in general, adolescents avoid talking about sex and dangerous situations with their parents (Guerrero & Afifi, 1995). However, if adolescents do talk with their parents about sexual matters, they are more likely to do so with mothers than with fathers, and mothers are generally more effective at getting their kids to actually reduce their sexually risky behavior (e.g., Miller et al., 2001). Thus, while explicit and implicit rules abound throughout the developmental life span of the family, they are especially apparent during adolescence.

Nonverbal Rules of Communication

Nonverbal communication may be similarly dictated by explicit and implicit rules. Nonverbal communication includes **kinesics,** or overall use of the body, including gestures and posture. For instance, insulting hand gestures and slumping postures may be explicitly prohibited within a family, whereas animated facial expressions may be implicitly encouraged. **Vocalics,** or communication through the use of voice, can similarly be dictated by explicit or implicit rules of communication. How many times, for instance, have you heard a mother say explicitly to a loud child, "Indoor voice!" Still other mothers, however, try to communicate this message through the more subtle means of implicitly teaching the rule by using a lowered, quieter voice herself in hopes that the errant child will match her tone. **Proximity,** or communication through the use of space, is another type of nonverbal communication in the family that will be dictated by explicit and implicit rules. Standing too close, for instance, may be subtlely discouraged through compensatory steps backward and not entering your parents' bedroom when the door is shut may be explicitly stated and understood. **Haptics,** or communication through the use of touch, may be similarly prescribed explicitly and implicitly. One parent may be highly affectionate, whereas the other is less affectionate. Over time, children implicitly learn which parent is more receptive to hugs and kisses. Alternatively, parents no doubt spend time explicitly teaching close-talking, highly intimately touching 3-year-olds not to touch there! Finally, parents can implicitly or explicitly communicate rules regarding **chronemics,** or communication through the use of time, and **artifacts,** or communication through the use of physical objects. In other words, parents may have explicit rules about time limitations on television or computer usage, but they may also have implicit rules about the extent to which sexually explicit depictions are allowed on the walls of their house.

R egardless of the ways in which your family of origin added children (through birth, adoption, surrogacy, stepfamilies, extended families), it is likely that the parental figures in the family concerned themselves greatly with your well-being. Parents, stepparents, and grandparents all want the children in the family to grow up healthy. This overarching concern for health and well-being translates into communication styles and practices designed to influence several domains of development. To ensure their children's health and safety, parents and caregivers communicate in ways designed to help children develop *intellectually, physically, emotionally,* and *socially* in ways that promote their best health and well-being. To ensure their children's success in life, they also communicate in ways that help children develop intellectually and *academically* in line with their peers. To ensure that their children thrive and survive, parents attempt to communicate in ways that help their children develop *physically* in ways that enhance their health, well-being, and safety. Parents and other caregivers might also communicate in ways that ensure that their children mature emotionally in line with the current cultural trends for boys and girls: Will sons be strong? Will daughters be happy? Furthermore, and not unrelatedly, parents almost certainly communicate in ways that ensure their children's development of friendships and other social relationships. To help us understand how parents facilitate these academic, physical, emotional, and social developmental milestones in their children, parental communication strategies of both *nurturing* and *control* are examined here. What communicative strategies of control and discipline do parents, stepparents, and residential grandparents use to ensure these outcomes? Furthermore, to what extent does parental communication of warmth and affection promote intellectual, physical, emotional, and social competencies? Such developmental milestones and the ways in which parents can affect them through their communication is the focus of this chapter.

Control: Providing Discipline and Guidance Through Communication

Parenting Styles: Communication Strategies

Much work has examined the ways in which parents discipline their children and the various effects those **parenting styles** have on outcomes relevant to the socialization of children. Consistent with the perspective of this textbook, parents frequently vary their communication with their children along the dimensions of *responsiveness* (warmth/nurturing) and *demandingness* (control) in their attempts to guide their children's behavior. Parents who are *responsive* invoke **parenting practices** and communication that are warm and that provide reciprocal responses to their children's communicative behavior, clear communication and person-centered discourse, and the atmosphere for secure attachments with their children (Baumrind, 1996). Parents who are nonresponsive are at the opposite ends of these continua. *Highly demanding* parents use the parenting practices and communication strategies of confrontation, monitoring, and consistent and contingent discipline. Less demanding parents do not attempt to exercise much impulse control over their children's behavior. The examination of the effects of parenting styles and their communication can be facilitated by an examination of the responsiveness (nurturing and warmth) dimension and demandingness (controlling) dimension (Baumrind, 1996; Maccoby & Martin, 1983).

Authoritarian Parenting: The Communication of High Demandingness and Low Responsiveness

Baumrind (1966) delineates three types of parental control: *authoritarian, permissive,* and *authoritative.* The **authoritarian parent** is positioned at the intersection of *high demandingness* and *low responsiveness* (Maccoby & Martin, 1983). This parent overtly attempts to shape, control, and evaluate the behavior of the child in accordance with an absolute standard of conduct from some higher authority (e.g., religion). An authoritarian parent arbitrarily enforces restrictive directives (Baumrind, 1996). This parent seeks obedience from a child and uses punitive and forceful measures and communication to curb self-willed behavior. The authoritarian parent keeps the child in a subordinate nonautonomous role and does not encourage communicative give and take (Baumrind, 1978). Because this parent is most concerned with impulse control of the child at the expense of a loving and accepting environment, he or she is less concerned with warmth than with control. A student from my family communication class provided an example of an authoritarian parent. During her self-proclaimed willful stage, she was sent to live with her father. Following a particularly willful night out on the town, he provided her with a firm beating and forbade her from leaving the house for 3 months (other than to go to school or church). Not surprisingly, this response was met with greater obedience but also a lesser sense of affection toward her father.

The developmental outcomes associated with authoritarian parenting (communication of high demandingness and low responsiveness) have been less than optimal. In terms of communication outcomes, preschoolers with authoritarian parents were more discontent, withdrawn, and distrustful, as well as more insecure and apprehensive, less affiliative toward peers, and more likely to become hostile or regressive under stress (Baumrind, 1967). Furthermore, children with authoritarian parents report greater school-related conflict with parents because of demandingly high levels of expectations (Eskilson, Wiley, Muehlbauer, & Dodder, 1986). This continues into adolescence; adolescents with authoritarian parents report greater discord with parents (Baumrind, 1967, 1971). Academically, these same adolescents exhibit poorer grades, lower academic adjustment, and lower self-esteem (Lamborn, Mounts, Steinberg, & Dornbusch, 1991). Consistently, students designated as underachievers tend to provide descriptions of parents as overly strict, punitive, and highly demanding (i.e., authoritarian; see, e.g., Dornbusch, Ritter, Mont-Reynaud, & Chen, 1990).

Given these communicative and academic outcomes, it comes as no surprise that authoritarian parents have children with lower self-esteem (Buri, Louiselle, Misukanis, & Mueller, 1988). For instance, parents who are overprotective and use external or negative punishment and deprivation of privileges (i.e., authoritarian parenting) have children with markedly lower self-esteem (Halpin, Halpin, & Whiddon, 1980). Children also reported lower self-esteem if their parents used psychological control, demanded submissiveness, and suppressed autonomy (i.e., authoritarian parenting; Amanat & Butler, 1984). Authoritarian parenting is clearly associated with poorer communication, greater conflict, poorer academic performance, and lower self-esteem.

Permissive Parenting: The Communication of Low Demandingness and High Responsiveness

Courtesy of Don Tremain/Getty Images.

Figure 6.1   Permissive parents allow their children to explore and set very few limits on the behavior of the child.

In contrast, a **permissive parent** is positioned at the intersection of *high responsiveness/warmth* and *low demandingness/control* (Maccoby & Martin, 1983). This parent attempts to behave in nonpunitive, accepting, and affirmative ways toward his or her child's actions, impulses, and desires. This parent allows the child to regulate his or her own behavior and avoids extrinsic motivators and externally imposed rules and structure (Baumrind, 1996). To this end, the permissive parent uses reason and manipulation to affect the child's behavior and can be seen as highly nurturing and less controlling. Another student told of her single mom who attempted to be her friend and hang out with her friends. Although she enjoyed the greater degree of autonomy this less controlling environment provided her with, she often found herself wondering about the true concern her mother had for her when she showed up at 4 in the morning to no parent waiting tearfully by the phone and no punishment. She actually wished her parent would exercise *more* control. Thus, a permissive parent might communicate acceptance at the expense of communicating a concern for the well-being of the child.

Outcomes associated with permissive parenting (communication of low demandingness and low responsiveness) have also been less than optimal. For instance, preschoolers with permissive parents lacked self-control and self-reliance (Baumrind, 1967). Communicationally, children with permissive parents report higher school-related conflict due to exceedingly low expectations (Eskilson et al., 1986). Furthermore, students designated as underachievers tended to provide descriptions of parents as lax in their disciplinary techniques (i.e., permissive; e.g., Dornbusch et al., 1990). Academically, adolescent children with permissive parents have poorer grades, lower academic adjustment, and lower self-esteem (Lamborn et al., 1991). Consistent with children of authoritarian parents, children of permissive parents exhibit higher conflict, poorer academic adjustment, and lower self-esteem.

Authoritative Parenting: The Communication of High Demandingness and High Responsiveness

Authoritative parents attempt to be both nurturing and warm (*responsive*) and highly controlling *(demanding)* of their children's behavior (Maccoby & Martin, 1983). These parents direct their child's activities in a rational, issue-oriented manner. In contrast with the authoritarian parent's reliance on rules and regulations as the standard, the authoritative parent encourages verbal give and take, explicitly delineates the reasoning behind a particular rule, and solicits a child's objections to a rule. The authoritative parent values both the development of autonomous self-will and disciplined conformity (Baumrind, 1966). This parent is able to provide an accepting environment as well as a highly structured one. Authoritative parents, then, explain the logic behind a restriction on a car's use as being related to the lack of the child's ability to actually financially support the use of such a car (i.e., logical consequences). These parents also listen carefully to their child's tearful explanation regarding losing a job and the need for a car for school-related activities. In the end of the day, however, the child is driven to school and other activities but also knows that his or her point of view was taken seriously and that if the child alters the logically linked behavior (i.e., gets a job), he or she will regain car privileges.

The authoritative parenting style has been associated with the most positive socialization and communication outcomes. Communicationally, preschool children with authoritative parents were the most socially responsible and independent, self-controlled, affiliative, self-reliant, explorative, and self-assertive. They were also realistic, competent, and content. This finding of authoritative parents having more socially responsible and independent children was constant across studies (Baumrind, 1971) in that authoritative parental behavior was associated with independent, purposive behavior for girls. Authoritative parenting was also associated with more social responsibility in boys and greater achievement in girls.

Academically, authoritative parenting has also been associated with better competence among primary school children. Specifically, high parental support and high parental control were associated with better competence outcomes for primary school children (Amato, 1986). Interestingly, higher competence was also associated with higher allocations of household responsibility and low levels of parental punishment. Authoritative parents who are responsive and demanding both in terms of support and control, but who are not overly punishing and provide children with clear expectations for performance on household tasks, have children with the highest competence.

Authoritative parenting has also been associated with better academic outcomes in adolescents. Authoritative parents affect an adolescent's self-efficacy and self-esteem and enhance scholastic performance by creating situations in which their child can be effective and by sending positive messages about their child's qualities and competencies (Steinberg, Elmen, & Mounts, 1989). Also, the ways in which authoritative parents assist their children in managing their homework creates greater perseverance, time management, self-reliance, and planfulness, as well as self-regulatory skills (Strage, 1998). In particular, authoritative parents tend to use scaffolding (i.e., modeling the desired learning strategy or task followed by shifting the responsibility to the child) as they supervise homework, and this scaffolding has been associated positively with their child's performance on math achievement tests and gains in academic achievement (Pratt, Green, MacVicar, & Bountrogianni, 1993). Furthermore, children of authoritative parents were the most cognitively motivated, competent, and achievement oriented (Baumrind, 1991) and were the most intrinsically motivated (Ginsburg & Bronstein, 1993). They also attained the highest math and verbal achievement (Baumrind, 1991). This is consistent with the finding that adolescents with authoritative parents earn better grades than adolescents with authoritarian or permissive parents (e.g., Dornbusch, Ritter, Leiderman, Roberts, & Fraleigh, 1987) and demonstrate greater levels of academic adjustment and competence (Lamborn et al., 1991).

Although the authoritative style of parenting has been firmly associated with student's academic achievement, it is the child's self-esteem that predicts social, personal-emotional, goal commitment, institutional, academic, and overall adjustment of college freshmen (Hickman, Bartholomae, & McKenry, 2000). Furthermore, a child's self-esteem has been associated with social adjustment, academic achievement, and vocational aspirations (Rice, 1992). Parents with authoritative styles of parenting have children with higher self-esteem (Buri et al., 1988) and self-actualization (Dominguez & Carton, 1997). Consistently, parents with positive and functional child-rearing techniques and relations during adolescence had children with higher self-esteem (e.g., Bell, Allen, Hauser, & O'Connor, 1996; Kashubeck & Christensen, 1995). Parents who reported stronger companionship with their children and used nurturing, rewards, and positive punishment with their children (i.e., authoritative parenting) had children with higher self-esteem (Halpin et al., 1980). In addition, African American parents who were more supportive toward their children and African American and Euro-American parents with higher behavioral control had children with higher self-esteem and academic achievement (Bean, Bush, McKenry, & Wilson, 2003).

It is likely that differing parenting styles communicate differential beliefs in children's abilities and promote mastery orientations or learned help-lessness. For instance, it is likely that authoritative parents who are highly demanding through the use of confrontation, monitoring, and consistent and contingent discipline (Baumrind, 1996) are more likely to have children with a higher sense of mastery orientation. Such children should internalize goals, such as academic ones, and begin to experience some measure of competence over them. In addition, because authoritative parents communicate higher expectations for their children, these children should set higher expectations for themselves. In fact, the research in this area supports the relationship between authoritative parenting and mastery orientations toward academic life. College students with parents with authoritative styles of parenting (i.e., more autonomy, demands, and supports provided to children) had greater mastery orientations toward their academic work compared with students whose parents were authoritarian or permissive (Strage & Brandt, 1999). Specifically, students with authoritative parents were more confident, persistent, and positively oriented toward their teachers.

Encouraging Emotional Adjustment Through Communication

Social competence is often linked to the ability of the child to be emotionally competent as well. The way that parents communicate with their children can be associated with the child's ability to both express and be responsive to emotions in others. Both expression of and responsiveness to emotions are related to social skills.

Whereas some studies link parenting style to academic success and adjustment (e.g., Brooks, 1996), others argue that emotional intelligence, as measured through social adjustment, may be as important as other more cognitive factors (Hickman et al., 2000; Mohr, Eiche, & Sedlacek, 1998). Emotional intelligence refers to the ability to guide one's actions through understanding, monitoring, and regulating feelings and emotions (one's own and others; Mayer & Salovey, 1997). So important is this emotional intelligence that some have claimed it may be more important than IQ in determining the ability to learn tacitly (e.g., Gibbs, 1995; Goleman, 1995), the ability to persevere to succeed in college life (Hickman et al., 2000), and the ability to be promoted (Gibbs, 1995).

If emotional intelligence is as important as intellectual abilities in predicting life's successes, what factors promote this emotional intelligence? Some have argued that parenting styles of discipline and warmth are actually rooted in the emotions that parents display to their children (Darling & Steinberg, 1993). More specifically, Darling and Steinberg argue that parenting styles are composed of a whole host of attitudes communicated to the child through an *emotional* climate.

Encouraging Sex Differences in the Expression of Emotion

Besides providing an emotional climate for our children through our overall disciplinary style of responsiveness and demandingness, it is also likely that we socialize our children differently with regard to emotional expressions and emotional responsivity. Females, for instance, are more expected to display positive emotions and are more likely to smile (a major component of pleasant emotional expression) compared with males (Hall & Briton, 1993). In addition, we also teach our females to be more emotionally expressive than males (e.g., Wagner, Buck, & Winterbotham, 1993), and this emotional expressiveness is more acceptable from women than it is from men. Although very young children express emotions similarly regardless of gender, girls become both more expressive and more accurate at expressing emotions than boys (Buck, 1975). Boys, in contrast, are taught that it is more acceptable for them to display stronger emotions (e.g., anger, frustration, and disgust) than weaker ones (e.g., sadness, fear, surprise) or to be unemotional (e.g., Mulac, Studley, Weimann, & Bradac, 1987; Shields, 1987). In fact, gender differences are greatest in the expression of fear and sadness (Allen & Haccoun, 1976). Consequently, men may be evaluated more harshly when they display such emotions, whereas women tend to express both strong and weak (or positive and negative) emotions without restraint or fear of negative evaluations (Hess & Kirouac, 2000). These differences in emotional expressiveness and responsivity may be part and parcel of the sex role socialization of children discussed earlier.

Encouraging Academic Development Through Communication

Courtesy of Geostock/Getty Images.

Figure 6.5   Parents continue to encourage educational development through early reading, which has been linked to better academic outcomes later in life.

Besides physical and socioemotional development, a parent may be similarly concerned that their child masters the skills required of them in schools. The majority of us attended public schools, although a growing trend toward home schooling currently exists with up to 1.5% of all children (around 1.5 million) home schooled each year (Houston & Toma, 2003). Within these settings, parents want to ensure that their children excel intellectually to develop their reading, writing, and arithmetic skills to be in line with their peers (at a minimum). To this end, education has historically been considered the responsibility of the family (Stafford, 2004). In fact, children entering school with the basic learning capabilities already mastered have better peer relations and do better in school on measures of retention and graduation rates (Kagan & Cohen, 1995). It would seem that academic and social development go hand in hand. This is borne out by the literature showing that children who do better in school have fewer behavioral and social problems and get along better with their friends (Kagan & Cohen, 1995). Other outcomes are associated with better academic performance as well in that children who do better in school also tend to use fewer illegal substances, have better psychological well-being, and have lower rates of delinquency compared with kids who do more poorly in school. Children with poorer academic performances tend to act out, become delinquent, use drugs, get along poorly with friends, have greater rates of pregnancy, and have increased dropout rates (Durlak, 2001).

Given the relationship between poor academic performance and social outcomes, it is not surprising that parents devote much time to ensuring that their children do well in school. In fact, parents seem to have almost intuitive abilities to stimulate their children's learning (Papousek, Papousek, & Haekel, 1987), and most caregiver behaviors provide teaching to their infants (Van Egeren & Barratt, 2004). For instance, most caregivers frame their communication to infants in "infant-directed speech," or speech that is carefully constructed to attract the attention of the infant (Van Egeren & Barratt, 2004); they also use "motherese," which is specialized speech addressed to infants (Yingling, 1995). Characteristics of infant-directed speech include higher pitch, short emphatic words, exclamations, and gasps (e.g., Cooper & Aslin, 1989), as well as musicality and rhythm (Ochs & Schieffelin, 1984) and appear to be cross-cultural (Papousek, Papousek, & Symmes, 1991). Regardless of culture, parents appear to be intuitively aware of the needs of their infants as they attempt to stimulate and facilitate their child's future language acquisition through their own communication.

Furthermore, parents' communicative involvement with their children has been related to achievement in school. Specifically, parents who are more involved in their child's day-to-day lives have children with a greater internal locus of control in academic domains (Grolnick & Ryan, 1989). In addition, children's perceptions of their parents' expectations (Patrikako, 1997), aspirations, and support (Marjoribanks, 1997) were related to their own educational and career aspirations. This is consistent with all the earlier literature indicating that parental responsiveness and demandingness (i.e., *authoritative parenting*) relate to greater academic achievement.

Maintaining Closeness in Marital Relationships _____

There are many reasons for researchers' conclusion that marriages with greater communication of closeness tend to be more satisfying. One piece of evidence comes from examining the connection between self-disclosure (how much personal information a person shares with someone else) and marital satisfaction. People who disclose more intimate information with their spouse are generally more satisfied with their marriage (Hendrick, 1981; Hendrick, Hendrick, & Adler, 1988). Furthermore, when both people prefer the same level of intimacy as their partners, they tend to be happier (Sanderson & Cantor, 2001). This is true not only for married couples but also for dating couples (Sanderson & Evans, 2001). Not surprisingly, the opposite is also true. Partners who want different levels of intimacy are typically less satisfied than couples who want the same level of intimacy. People who want more intimacy than their spouse are often frustrated by their partner's lack of comfort with intimacy and their partner's lack of self-disclosure (Miller, 1990; Miller & Read, 1991).

Assuming that marital satisfaction is related to the communication of closeness in the marital relationship, it is useful to differentiate between **stable marriages** (i.e., marriages that endure and do not end in divorce) and **satisfying marriages** (i.e., marriages that partners evaluate positively). Many marriages may not have closeness and high marital satisfaction, but they are stable and enduring. Specifically, one landmark study revealed that stable marriages differ from the ideal happy marriage (Cuber & Haroff, 1965). Their research revealed five types of enduring (stable) marriages—only two of which included high levels of marital closeness and marital satisfaction. *Vital marriages* represent the ideal marriage in that spouses share true intimacy and find their greatest satisfaction in life with each other. *Total marriages* are similar to vital marriages in that the spouses share true intimacy and find their greatest satisfaction with each other, but they are also highly involved in each other's activities (including outside work). The final three types of enduring marriages do not include closeness or marital satisfaction. *Conflict habituated marriages* center on tensions and disagreements that manifest in the communicative behaviors of nagging, quarrelling, sarcasm, condescension, and, potentially, physical violence. *Devitalized marriages* center on duty and maintenance of the relationship despite the loss of romantic love. Finally, *passive congenial marriages* provide stability for the couple whose members do not expect love but use the marriage base to direct their energies elsewhere (e.g., toward work or relationships external to the marriage). This research reveals that closeness is related to marital satisfaction in that the two couple types that share closeness are satisfied. This research also illustrates, however, that marriages can survive without closeness. In other words, marriages do not need to include the communication of closeness to avoid divorce. However, marriages that do include the communication of closeness can be *both* satisfying and stable. Therefore, the communication of closeness is essential to have the winning combination of marital stability *and* marital satisfaction.

Offering even more support for the relationship between closeness and marital satisfaction and marital stability, the circumplex model describes family functioning in terms of family cohesion and family adaptability (Olsen, Russell, & Sprenkle, 1989). This model posits that families are well functioning to the extent that they are cohesive (i.e., have emotional bonding) and adaptable (are responsive to situational and developmental demands with changes in power structures, roles, and rules). The authors argue that evidence exists supporting a linear relationship between cohesion and marital stability and satisfaction and between adaptability and stability and satisfaction (Olsen & Tiesel, 1991). Therefore, cohesiveness (i.e., closeness) and adaptability are both key to the long-term functioning of the family unit as a whole.

Dialectic Models of Relationship Maintenance: The Autonomy-Closeness Dialectic

Once individuals have established their primary relationship, entered marriage, and started to have children, many are concerned with how to balance their own and their partner's needs for *closeness* and *autonomy* in the family. These needs for closeness and autonomy create a dialectic tension in any relationship whereby one person's need for the communication of closeness can be in direct opposition to their partner's needs for self-directed behavior. The demands of **closeness** (e.g., intimate conversations, cuddling, sexual activity) often come head-to-head with time constraints imposed by the household and child care tasks inherent in the family (e.g., organizing the house, preparing the meals, and overseeing homework, the demands of children, and their activities) and the needs of both partners to maintain **autonomy** (e.g., having independent senses of self, directing their own behavior, controlling their own activities). For instance, you may want to spend long moments in delicious and well-deserved adult conversation with your partner when he or she gets home from work, but the toddler's demands for attention combined with your partner's need to drive the 10-year-old to soccer practice may make this impossible. Consistently, you desire the sexual activity that you were promised three times a week (just like all the books said), but you're so tired from managing the children and coping with little 18-month-old Johnny's demands for cuddling all day through his 17th cold that you feel like any more demands for touching are out of the question. Thus, your needs for intimate conversation (i.e., self-disclosure), physical affection, and sexual intimacy take a backseat to the time constraints of family life with all the tasks required. In addition, by the time you get to have the time for closeness, you or your partner may have lost the desire for intimacy and want that precious 15 minutes at the end of the day before bedtime to unwind, chill out, and basically be on your own for awhile. Therein lies the tension between closeness and autonomy needs in the family.

In these ways, the demands of daily family life interfere with marital closeness and make it difficult to maintain. Assuming that marital closeness is directly related to marital satisfaction, it is not that surprising then that marital satisfaction declines over the first 10 years of marriage (e.g., Cowan & Cowan, 1988; Glenn, 1998; Karney & Bradbury, 1997; Kurdek, 1993; MacDermid, Huston, & McHale, 1990; McHale & Huston, 1985). As we observed in Chapter 5, this is especially the case for married couples who add children, where marital satisfaction is highest in the preparental and postparental stages (Benin & Robinson, 1997). Thus, the age-old advice and wisdom suggesting that couples wait to have children appears to be supported once again in that the primary couple has time to devote to their relationship and its success *before* jumping on the wild ride of activity that is family life. However, because nearly half of all marriages in the United States are remarriages, many marital couples jump into the intimacies of married life with children already to hand. These families may not experience a preparental stage and thus may have their intimacy affected by the influence of children early on. You might remember that my husband came with a full complement of children as a free added benefit of marriage. I moved from a one-bedroom condo in sunny Santa Barbara's downtown district (complete with a yard attended to by the communal gardener) to a five-bedroom house in the suburbs (with a fair commute to work and a large piece of land) complete with a husband, two kids, and a dog. The demands of household and child care came as quite a shock and immediately had an impact on when and how my husband and I could express closeness.

Every relationship has dialectic tensions between competing needs, and marital relationships are no exception. Marital couples need expressions of closeness and nurturing, but the individual members also need autonomy to have time alone and the ability to engage in self-directed behavior. The need for autonomy, or self-directed behavior, interferes with the ability to be close. Conversely, the need for closeness and intimacy takes away an individual's ability to be self-directed and autonomous. In other words, engaging in individual goal-directed behavior (e.g., working out in the yard) takes away the ability to use that time to cuddle, nurture your partner through a crisis, or whisper sweet nothings in your partner's ear. At the same time, the demands to be close through conversations (e.g., self-disclosure and debriefing), physical affection, and sexual intimacy take time away from an individual's ability to be self-directed and independent in his or her activities (e.g., run to the mall, play sports, go out with the guys). In this way, the needs for autonomy and closeness compete with each other. This section of the chapter explores the dialectic tensions between autonomy and intimacy in the marital relationship and its effect on marital satisfaction and marital stability.

Although several dialectic models exist, communication researcher Leslie Baxter's (1990; Baxter & Montgomery, 1996) dialectic approach to relationship maintenance is highlighted here because it emphasizes the ongoing tensions between contradictory impulses that exist in already developed *family* and *marital* relationships. Central to the notion of dialectics in relationships is the idea of contradiction. A **contradiction** refers to the unity of opposites in that two concepts are wed together at the same time that they compete with, or diminish, one another (Baxter & West, 2003). The qualities of relationships that compete with one another form the anchors for the same idea, where, for instance, total closeness—that is, no autonomy can exist—is at one end of a continuum and total autonomy—where it is impossible for closeness to exist—is at the opposite end of the continuum. Although autonomy and closeness are opposing concepts, they are both necessary within relationships. Therein lies the dialectic tension between autonomy and closeness. Ideally, marital couples provide at the same time a safe haven in which nurturing and closeness can occur (e.g., cuddling, self-disclosing, comforting, emoting) and a secure base from which the individual members of the couple can emerge and act independently in their day-to-day activities (i.e., autonomy). Thus, in their purest forms, closeness exists to allow autonomy, but closeness and autonomy rarely exist simultaneously.

Autonomy and closeness are not the only dialectic contradictions in marital relationships, however. Many communicative dialectic tensions have been delineated, but the four that are the most relevant to discussions of marital satisfaction, marital stability, and family life in general are these:

1. Autonomy and closeness (connectedness)

2. Openness and protection (closedness)

3. Novelty and predictability

4. Positivity and negativity (Baxter, 1990)

In support of a greater attention to autonomy and closeness needs, autonomy-connectedness and openness-closedness are both given the greatest importance in terms of predicting relational turning points (Baxter & Ebert, 1999). As discussed previously, *autonomy* refers to desires to be independent from our families, whereas *intimacy* refers to our desire to be close to our families. As we have seen above, much research exists linking goals for intimacy and matching of intimacy between partners and marital satisfaction. *Openness* refers to our desire to be emotionally vulnerable while revealing personal information to our families, whereas *protection* (or closedness) refers to our strategic attempts to protect ourselves from our families by not revealing potentially risky information to them. Protection is especially apparent to the extent that marital partners desire privacy or maintain secrets from one another, other family members, or from nonfamily members. This will become more apparent through our review of communication privacy management (CPM) theory below. *Novelty* refers to our desire for excitement and change, whereas *predictability* refers to the comfort of stability. Below, we will refer to research showing that those with highly idealized notions of what it means to be, and have, a partner in early courtship exhibit greater disillusionment following marriage. Part of the disillusionment can be explained through the distinction between the early and *novel* first months of relating compared with the boring but *stable* days of patterned marriage and stability. *Positivity* refers to our desire for evaluating our family members in positive ways, whereas *negativity* refers to the inevitability of our evaluating some things about our family members negatively. The dialectic tension between positivity and negativity is especially relevant to marital satisfaction in that, as we have seen previously, positive and negative communication patterns in marriage affect both marital satisfaction and stability. Thus, *closeness-autonomy, openness-protection, novelty-predictability*, and *positivity-negativity* are particularly relevant communication dimensions in the maintenance of marital and family stability and satisfaction.

Protectedness in Marriage: Communication Privacy Management (CPM) Theory

The openness-protection communication dialectic provides an especially rich forum for considering the relationship between privacy and secrets and closeness between marital partners. Communication privacy management (CPM) theory argues that individuals desire to control private information because they have ownership over it and because revealing the private information might make them vulnerable (see Caughlin & Petronio, 2004, for a review). Control over private information is achieved through rules about regulation of (a) *boundary permeability* (i.e., the degree of access given to private information), (b) *linkages* (i.e., connections formed through allowing others inside of a privacy boundary), and (c) *ownership* (i.e., individuals with access to the private information). Intuitively, it would seem that privacy in marital relationships might detract from the overall closeness of the couple. This is in fact the case in marital relationships where marital partners maintain privacy and secrets *from* the other marital partner. In this case, one marital partner is surrounded by the boundary, has no linkage to the partner, and has sole ownership over the information, and decreased closeness should result. This might be the case if one partner hides a drinking or gambling problem from the other partner. However, it is also possible that privacy and secrets may be held by the marital couple as a unit. In this situation, privacy and secrets may enhance the bonding between the marital couple. Collective boundaries are constructed through the linkages created through the sharing of the personal information between the marital couple. Marital partners are surrounded by the boundary, partners are linked to one another, and the couple "co-owns" the private information. They become comrades in adversity, as it were, both working to protect the secret information from exposure. This co-ownership can create greater bonds and closeness between the couple. This might be the case, for instance, if marital partners try to keep one partner's drinking and gambling from other family members and from outside family members. Thus, privacy maintenance may actually enhance closeness for a marital couple. Although this model is considered here with regard to marital couples and ensuing closeness, it is possible that the CPM has implications for sibling relationships and whole family secrets as well (see Vangelisti, 1994a; Vangelisti, Caughlin, & Timmerman, 2001). This model may be especially useful for families that include gay heads of households while maintaining privacy and for other families who maintain privacy surrounding drinking behavior or other secrets within the family. Regardless, privacy may enhance or detract from the communication of marital closeness and may affect marital satisfaction and stability.

Sexual Intimacy and Communication

Closeness in marriage can also be enhanced through *sexual intimacy* and associated communication (e.g. Greeff, 2000). Although the early stages of romantic life included high levels of eroticism and a high frequency of sexual relations, the same household and behavioral routines that interfere with other types of intimacy also interfere with sexual activity as well. Prepare yourselves, because many of my students find this section of the course highly disappointing. I consider it to be a valuable service in terms of having what Pearson (1992) calls *lowered and realistic expectations*. Many of you will be in the earliest throes of the most exciting romance (i.e., high levels of novelty), but remember that family life and all it entails in terms of household labor and children's demands interferes with intimacy at all levels (i.e., high levels of stability). In what is considered the most scientific study to date of sexual activity in America, Laumann, Gagnon, Michael, and Michaels (1994) completed 3,500 face-to-face interviews with a random sample of men and women between 18 and 59. Surprisingly, married individuals have more sex than nonmarrieds; nearly 40% of marrieds have sex at least twice a week compared with 25% of singles. To break this down a bit more, for the married people sampled, a small percentage of both men

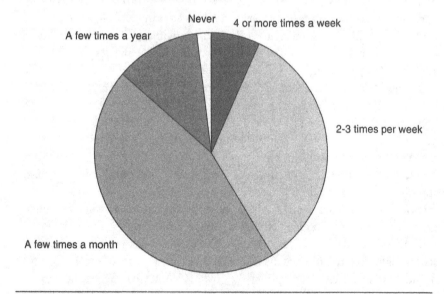

Figure 7.2   Frequency of Sex in Married Couples' Lives

SOURCE: Laumann, Gagnon, Michael, and Michaels (1994).

and women reported having sex four or more times a week (7%), about a third reported having sex two to three times a week (32% of women and 36% of men), the greatest majority reported having sex a few times a month (47% of women and 43% of men), another small percentage reported having sex a few times a year (12% of women and 13% of men), and a small minority reported never having sex (3% of women and 1% of men).

Thus, the most frequently occurring amount of sexual activity among married couples is at least twice a week. On the positive side, the researchers also found that compared with singles (who are rumored to have the most interesting and varied sex lives—can you say *Sex in the City*?), married individuals had the most sex and the most orgasms, and 40% of both married men and women describe their sex lives as extremely satisfying both emotionally and physically. So although you thought you might be having sex more than twice a week when you were married, the good news is that you will be having more sex than if you were single *and* it will be more satisfying.

If the largest number of married couples are having sex twice a week (40%) *and* the same number of married individuals are highly satisfied with their sex lives (40%), you might be wondering about the nature of their sexual activity. Laumann et al. (1994) found that men and women are fairly traditional in their sexual behavior in that nearly everyone reported that vaginal intercourse was their preferred and most common sexual activity. Not surprisingly, men think more about sex every day (54%) than women (19%), and more men have orgasms every time they have sex (75%) than women (29%). Men also find receiving (50%) and giving (37%) oral sex more appealing than women (33%; 19%; Mackay, 2000). Males also request sex more frequently than females and are the initiators of sexual activity in marriages. Wives most often accommodate their husbands' preferences.

Both interpersonal communication and sexual communication can enhance sexual satisfaction. Specifically, the better a man understands his partner's sexual preferences and the more the partners' preferences match, the more sexually satisfied both married partners are (Purnine & Carey, 1997). Thus, communicating about preferences and reaching an understanding about those preferences seems essential to increasing sexual satisfaction for both partners. In addition, sexual communication satisfaction mediated the role of sexual attitude similarity in terms of predicting sexual satisfaction (Cupach & Metts, 1995). Once again, sexual communication seems highly related to sexual satisfaction. Lawrance and Byers (1995) also found that social exchange principles (from Chapter 4) can predict sexual satisfaction in that when relationship rewards exceed costs, relative reward levels exceed relative cost levels and perceived equality of rewards and costs exist across relationship partners, sexual partners are more sexually satisfied. Relationship satisfaction also added to the model.

Compared with many nonscientific reports of extramarital affairs reporting higher figures, the Laumann et al. (1994) study found that only 25% of men and 15% of women reported extramarital affairs. This is consistent with the attitudes of those surveyed; the researchers found three patterns of beliefs about sexuality inside and outside of marriage. About half of the sample was described as *relational* in that they believed that sex should be part of a loving relationship but that it does not necessarily need to be in a marriage. They were also highly disapproving of extramarital sex. About one third of the sample was described as *traditionals*. Traditionals disapproved of premarital sex, teenage sex, extramarital sex, and homosexuality. Traditionals also reported that their sexual behavior is guided by their religion. Finally, about one quarter of the sample were described as *recreational* in that they believed that sex need not have anything to do with love.

In general, then, most people believe sex should be within marriage, and most married couples report having sex twice a week. This form of closeness and the communication surrounding it can add to the marital satisfaction and stability of the couple.

The Nature of Conflict

As alluded to in the introduction, **conflict** can be defined as "an expressed struggle between at least two interdependent parties who perceive incompatible goals, scarce rewards, and interference from the other parties in achieving their goals" (Hocker & Wilmot, 2000, p. 9). This definition can help us understand why marital satisfaction is higher for couples who have greater similarity in terms of ethnic homogamy, educational similarity, religious similarity, and so forth. Because they come into the relationship already agreeing on fundamental goals such as whether or not to have children and how to raise them, couples who are more similar initially may be more satisfied in family and marital relationships because they may have a tendency to have less conflict. For example, couples who are more traditional (i.e., the wife fulfills the nurturer role while the husband primarily fulfills the resource provider role) may have less conflict because they have agree *beforehand* that the wife will fulfill most of the household responsibilities and the husband will fulfill the provider role. This may help explain the seeming inequities in these roles and why traditional women accept more inequities in household responsibilities compared with traditional husbands. They have already agreed that the family would function in this way, and conflicts are less likely to accrue because goal interference is less likely to happen or be perceived. Thus, greater similarity may enhance smoother family functioning in that conflict, or goal interruptions, is less likely to result because the goals of the couple are more likely to be similar.

In our society, most individuals are conflict aversive; that is, most of us report that we dislike conflict and even fear its potential destructive outcomes. Regardless, the nature of intimacy and closeness is such that it makes it more likely that goal interference and ensuing conflicts will occur. More specifically, high levels of investment in a relationship or family (i.e., more loving, caring, and concern) actually make it *more* likely that conflicts will occur (e.g., Braiker & Kelley, 1979; Shantz & Hobart, 1989). Having closer relationships increases the frequency of interaction and our level of concern, which ultimately enhances the likelihood that members of close familial relationships will interfere with each other's goals (Sillars, Canary, & Tafoya, 2004). This is the heart of the paradox of conflict; we don't want to hurt the ones we love, yet these same loving familial relationships provide a rich forum in which conflict is more likely to occur.

The answer seems straightforward: If conflict is inevitable in close relationships characterized by high levels of concern for others, engage in conflicts that create positive outcomes and then conflict seems consistent with loving relationships. Unfortunately, not all of us have the communication skills necessary to engage in **constructive conflict**, or conflict that builds on the strengths of the relationship (i.e., enhances closeness, increases understanding, results in a net gain in positive feelings). Even those of us with the best communication skills can engage in **destructive conflict**, or conflict that is damaging to the relationship (e.g., results in hurt, reduces closeness, damages trust). Thus, the nature of the conflict can be drastically different depending on whether the processes and outcomes are constructive or destructive. This chapter attempts to delineate the differences between destructive and constructive conflict and the individual and interpersonal factors that make it more or less likely that destructive or constructive conflict occurs within families.

Given the assumption that family life provides a rich forum for goal interference, it might be useful to investigate how often conflict occurs in families (for a review see Sillars et al., 2004). Sillars et al. report that 80% of married couples say that they have conflict once a month, while 6% report disagreements once per week (McGonagle, Kessler, & Schilling, 1992). This is fairly consistent with another study, which reports disagreements between married individuals two to three times per month (Kirchler, Rodler, Hölzl, & Meier, 2001). Parents and adolescents report more conflict than in marital relationships—about two conflicts per week (Montemayor, 1986), which is consistent with Laursen's (1993) report that adolescents report 7.4 conflicts per day across a variety of relationships. Finally, sibling relationships are the most conflictual, with siblings observed or estimated to have conflict six (Lollis, Ross, & Leroux, 1996) or seven times (Perlman & Ross, 1997) *per hour.* (My youngest stepson, Jake, assures me that this number is accurate). Given this review, it is apparent that family life is rife with conflict in that conflictual episodes in families occur hourly for siblings, weekly for parents and adolescents, and at least monthly for marital couples.

Although these estimates are useful at painting an overall picture of family life, it may be that conflict frequency is higher in families who are experiencing greater developmental stress or distress (i.e., less satisfaction and stability). Specifically, newlyweds and those adjusting to marriage

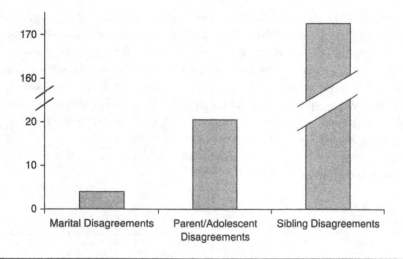

Figure 8.1   Family Disagreements (number per month)

typically have more conflict (e.g., Crohan, 1986); couples who are married longer report fewer disagreements (e.g., McGonagle et al., 1992). Thus, conflict is higher in couples who are adjusting to marriage and adding children. In addition, distressed couples (couples low in marital satisfaction) spend more time in conflict, have more frequent conflicts, and spend more time avoiding conflicts than nondistressed couples (e.g., Schaap, Buunk, &

Kerkstra, 1988). What is unclear from these types of studies is whether conflict predicts marital distress or marital distress predicts greater conflict. In other words, do unhappy couples fight more or does fighting make previously happy couples unhappy? The research on developmental stressors and conflict suggests that stressors *lead* to conflict. It is also possible that distressed couples have more conflicts that are *perpetual* (repetitive conflicts with no apparent resolution), as opposed to typical and minor conflicts, and may be more destructive than constructive. The following section presents models of conflict that help us understand destructive as opposed to constructive outcomes of conflict.

Inconsistent Nurturing as Control Theory

Most of you remember that the basic premise of this book is that all families, regardless of family form, consistently offer *nurturing* and *control* to their family members. What you may not know is that the idea that all families nurture and control their members was extended from a theory I've been developing called inconsistent nurturing as control (INC) theory (Le Poire, 1992, 1995). Basically, this theory argues that while all family members nurture and control each other simultaneously, families that include a member who is out of control in terms of some undesirable behavioral tendency or another (e.g., drinking, eating disorder, gambling, violence, sex addiction), use *nurturing as a way to control* their family members. The use of nurturing as control is argued to be paradoxical (i.e., logically inconsistent) and is expected to result in less than effective strategies being used in families with members who exhibit undesirable behavior. INC theory attempts to explain the communication dynamics underlying these families' nurturing and control mechanisms and how these dynamics ultimately affect how successful family members can be at curtailing their family members' undesirable behavior.[2]

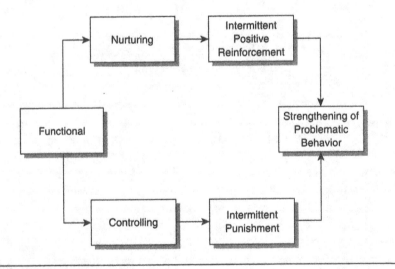

Figure 9.2   Inconsistent Nurturing as Control Theory

Paradoxes

The relational dynamics of this functional (i.e., no behavioral problem) but afflicted (i.e., behavioral compulsion) relationship produce a power structure that is paradoxical. A **paradox** contains two consistent premises that contradict the logical conclusion (Watzlawick, Beavin, & Jackson, 1967). Communicationally, this results in requests that are impossible to carry out. For instance, if I were to ask you not to read this sentence, it would be too late by the time you have read this for you to carry out my request. In other words, the communication makes a request that is impossible. My other favorite example of a paradoxical communication is the parent who says, "Stop obeying me." Obviously, recipients of this request are left in a conundrum because if they do not stop obeying, they have not obeyed the request. However, if they do stop obeying the parent, then they have obeyed the parent. In other words, it is impossible to carry out a paradoxical communication. The effects of these conundrums are evident in the functional-afflicted relationship. The first paradox is about *control*, the second paradox is about *sacrifice and dependency*, and the third paradox is about the *nurturing and control*. Although all three are relevant to the communication of nurturing and control in families including one member with problematic behavior, we focus on the last one here.

Nurturing and Control

The *nurturing and control paradox* concerns the nature of the relationship and is probably the most fundamental in terms of sabotaging functional partners' attempts to help their partners regain control over their behavioral compulsion. In general, the functional partner simultaneously desires to nurture and control his or her partner, two processes that unfortunately result in contradictory communication behavior. These fundamental needs are predicated on the assumption that the functional partner wants to maintain a nurturing relationship with the afflicted partner. There are a lot of reasons why this may be the case. First, the functional loves the afflicted and is committed to the relationship. Second, the functional partner has invested a lot of time and energy in helping the afflicted person regain his or her health. Third, while marital couples choose one another voluntarily, all other familial relationships are nonvoluntary. Fourth, the functional partner may self-identify as nurturing and caring and therefore may help meet this definition by maintaining this relationship with an afflicted who is in need of help and assistance.

At the same time, the functional desires to control or eliminate the substance abuse, eating disorder, or depression of the afflicted. At some point, it is highly likely that the functional gets fed up with the emotional crises surrounding the behavioral compulsion of the afflicted. In the case of substance abusers, the functional partner may get fed up with the afflicted partner's absences, tendency to spend money in pursuit of substances, tendency to commit crimes to get the substances, or lack of attention to the children. However, because the functional nurtures the afflicted during times of crisis, this caretaking behavior is very rewarding for the afflicted. In general, the caregiving behavior of the functional partner provides the support necessary for the afflicted to enact the behavioral compulsion. In other words, it is unlikely that the afflicted could enact the behavioral compulsion without a functional partner to pick up the slack (e.g., provide the money, organize the house, care for the children). If it is the case that the afflicted person actually stays with the functional partner because of this caregiving (and potentially enabling) behavior, then it is possible that extinguishing the afflicted's behavioral compulsions would result in an elimination of this rewarding caretaking behavior. In other words, the functional could not nurture the afflicted in times of crisis if the afflicted actually stopped the behavioral compulsion or tendency. As a result, this paradox suggests that by accomplishing the goal of stopping the substance abuse, the functional partner may actually destroy the relationship.

How You Think Is What
You Feel: Or Perception Is Reality

If we have learned one thing together throughout this textbook, it is that cognition plays a powerful role in terms of determining communication behavior and ultimately improving family satisfaction and family stability. The literature is replete with examples of how family members who cognitively frame their communication partners (e.g., marital partners, parents, children, siblings) in positive ways have more satisfying and more stable relationships. Perhaps one of the most striking examples is marital couples who have been married for more than 40 years. These couples were able to maintain marital satisfaction and stability partially because of their ability to *positively distort their perception* of their marital partner (emphasizing positive traits and abilities over negative ones; Pearson, 1992). Remember that they also had *realistic and lowered expectations*. In other words, if you *think* that your partner is wonderful, then you will feel more positively about him or her and feel more satisfied in the relationship. You might remember that this is consistent with research showing that married couples who were more globally satisfied had both positive *and* negative perceptions of their spouse but were more likely to *weight the positive perceptions as more important than the negative perceptions* (Neff & Karney, 2003). Consistently, married couples were more satisfied and had more stable marriages when their partners held *idealized notions* of them (Murray, Holmes, & Griffin, 1996a, 1996b). Thus, positive framing is related to greater satisfaction and stability in marriages.

Section III

The following chapters are taken from:

Family Communication, Theory and Research
by Lorin Basden Arnold

1

Communication and the Family

Chapter Outline

What Is Communication?
  Definition of Communication
Why Study Family Communication?
What Is a Family?
  Defining is Communicative
  Medical or Biological Definitions

Legal Definitions
Scholarly Definitions
Personal Definitions

Chapter Objectives

1. To develop a foundational awareness of the nature of communication and the importance of family communication

2. To understand the importance of family communication definitions and the communicative nature of defining

3. To understand some of the basic ways family has been defined in medical, legal, scholarly, and personal domains

4. To be able to critically approach a variety of definitions, seeing both strengths and weaknesses in each

5. To begin creating and understanding your own definition of family

> *What we have here is a failure to communicate.*
> —Captain (Strother Martin) in *Cool Hand Luke*, 1967

How many times have you heard someone blame a problem with a spouse, a child, a sibling, or a parent on communication? Even on sitcoms and in hit songs, communication takes the fall for relational problems. We know, from our daily experiences, that communication is important. We also know that when it "works," we feel more at ease than when there is a "breakdown." As important as communication is, however, we often don't stop to think about it until we feel there is a problem. Yet, consideration of how communication functions in our lives, both in the positive moments and in the negative ones, is an important part of understanding and critically analyzing our life experience as humans.

Communicating with others occurs across many types of relational settings, which results in the field of communication studies being extensive in both breadth and depth. In this book, we focus on the communication that occurs in family settings, as well as mediated messages about family. As a starting point, it is important to establish what is meant by *communication*.

What Is Communication?

> *Communication is talking to each other. Some ways you can communicate are: telephones, cell phones, talking, computers, and kind of TV if you are the President and you want to communicate with the country.*—Max, age 8
> *Communication is people talking together.*—Casey, age 11
> *Communication is when two people talk to each other and you can understand what each other is saying.*—KD, age 7
> *Communication is how people get along with each other and how they talk to each other.*—Abbi, age 11

As in these examples of how a group of children defined the word *communication*, we often tend to think of communication as talking. However, it actually encompasses

BOX 1.1 • *A Few "Communication" Songs*

INXS—*Communication*
Marianne Faithfull—*Eye Communication*
The Cardigans—*Communication*
Duran Duran—*Communication*
Led Zeppelin—*Communication Breakdown*
Black Eyed Peas—*Communication*
Naked Eyes—*Communication without Sound*
Bela Fleck—*Communication*
Ratt—*Lack of Communication*
Janet Jackson—*Communication*
The Von Bondies—*Lack of Communication*
Spandau Ballet—*Communication*

much more, including verbal elements (spoken and written language), nonverbal elements (such as gestures, facial expressions, and clothing), and the process of interpretation and meaning creation. Even scholars have had difficulty figuring out how to define simply a process that is so complex.

Definition of Communication

Some scholars have created definitions that focus primarily on how communication allows us to share meanings and understandings through the use of shared symbols (the transmission of information). Other scholars have focused more on the process through which communication creates symbols, meanings, and understandings.

We will use a definition that includes both the sharing of meaning or understanding and its creation. **Communication** is the process of creating, negotiating, and sharing meaning through verbal and nonverbal channels. Looking at the parts of this definition can clarify the nature of communication more fully.

- *Communication is a process.* Communication is not a "thing," it is a process. This is why most communication scholars use the word *communication* (a process verb) rather than *communications* (a plural noun) in their discussions. Considering communication as a process puts focus on the continual change that occurs in human encounters and the ways in which those exchanges unfold, rather than simply on the content of the exchange.
- *Communication includes the creation of meaning.* As we engage in interaction with others we develop meanings and understandings. When you were a child, you began to develop meanings for the word *friend* based on the interactions you had with others and what you saw around you.
- *Communication involves the negotiation of meaning.* The communication process is not always without struggle. Various individuals and groups have divergent understandings and meanings for concepts, objects, and so on; the emergence of meaning is a process of negotiation via those different meanings.
- *Communication is a way of sharing meaning.* By communicating with others, we attempt to share our own beliefs and understandings with them. It is not a simple transfer of meaning, but an attempt to influence others to share our meanings.
- *Communication includes both verbal and nonverbal elements.* Verbal elements (language) both oral and written are an important part of the communication process. However, equally important are the nonverbal aspects such as gestures, facial expressions, tone of voice, eye contact, clothing, time management, and even our surroundings.

The process of communication occurs all around us each day, in a variety of forms. The media communicates messages to us as we gaze at billboards, listen to the radio, watch TV, and read magazines. We chat with friends and kiss romantic partners. We hold business meetings and study sessions with classmates. And, we communicate in a variety of ways with and about family. It is that arena of communication that we turn our attention to in this text.

Why Study Family Communication?

There are a variety of reasons why the study of family communication is vital to understanding our human experience (see Vangelisti, 2004, for additional discussion). The importance of family communication in our lives lies both in the connection between communication and family, and in the connection between family communication and the larger culture.

The relationship between communication and family can be visualized (albeit in a simplified fashion) as a circle (see Figure 1.1).

As we communicate with our family members, we create and reflect understandings of the nature of family life, the expectations that go along with family roles, the rules and standards of family behavior, and who we are as a family. In this way, communication produces our understandings of family and our experiences (positive, negative, and in between) of family. But, that is only half of the circle. In addition to communication creating family, family is also a producer of our patterns of communication. In family settings, we learn how to communicate with those close to us. Family members teach us how to communicate in our earliest years. The patterns that we learn in the family are often then reproduced, to some degree, in other relationships throughout our lives. Thus, family is a product of communication, and communication is a product of family.

The impact of family communication is not limited to our individual family settings, or even to the close relationships we have in life. Family is also connected to the larger social structure. In family settings, we learn about the world, what it is like, what we can expect from it, and what it will expect from us. Families teach us about our "place" in the larger culture. Our parents and adult caregivers communicate to us lessons about what is acceptable behavior and what is not. Family is the first institution of socialization (though it is accompanied by other social institutions such as schools, churches, and media). Family is also connected to the larger social structure because the cultural messages we encounter impact our understandings of what families are and what they should be. When we see particular images of family in the media, or learn about family types in school, we develop understandings of family that impact our own experiences of family life. Thus, the connection between family and social structure is a part of communication *in* and *about* family.

For these reasons, studying family communication (including both communication in and about family) is an important part of social scholarship. Scholars from the field of communication—as well as others affiliated primarily with sociology, psychology, and family studies—have studied these important processes, developing a body of theory as well as research findings. (If you are unfamiliar with research studies, see Appendix A for

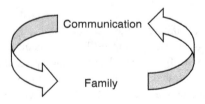

Communication

Family

FIGURE 1.1 *Communication and Family Reciprocal Creation*

BOX 1.2 • *Family in the News*

The "baby signs" program, springing from a desire to be able to "speak" to babies sooner than they acquire speaking skills, is a hot topic in the media, featured in magazines, on talk shows, in books, and online. You can read more about baby signs at www.babysigns.com.

a discussion of two prominent perspectives in family communication study and how to read research articles based on those perspectives.) In this text, we consider a variety of family communication issues, including theoretical claims and empirical research that has been conducted by family scholars. To begin, it is important to address how family has been, and continues to be, defined and delineated.

What Is a Family?

- If you were told that you could invite anyone you would like to your college graduation as long as they were family members, whom would you invite? How many people would the group include?
- If you decided to have a family picnic in the summer, whom would you ask? Would you need a lot of sandwiches, or only a few?
- If you won the lottery, and decided that you would share your winnings with your family, whom would that include? How would you decide who got the money?

Looking back on your answers to the previous questions, are all three groups of people you selected the same? For many people, they would not be. The number of people and types of relationships included in each set are also likely to vary widely from person to person. Some individuals would include only parents and siblings in the lottery beneficiaries. Others would also include grandparents, aunts, uncles, or cousins. Some might include close friends they think of as family. The picnic group might include immediate family, extended family, friends, and dating partners. The graduation invitees could be grandparents, siblings, and parents only, or maybe spouses and children, perhaps dating partners, and so on. For any person answering these questions, the composition of the groups is likely to differ from others' responses. All of these differences in what "family" might include point to the difficulty of defining the word *family*.

Defining Is Communicative

To define anything, including family, is a uniquely communicative phenomenon. The communication theory of **symbolic interactionism** states that it is through communication with others that we reach our understandings of any concept, thing, person, and so forth. Once we develop particular meanings, they then impact how we respond to the concepts, things, and people in our environment (Blumer, 1969; Mead, 1934). Thus, as we communicate together about family, and in families, we develop ways of understanding, or defining, family. Those definitions of family then impact how we enact and respond to families, both our own and

6   Chapter 1

those of other individuals. For this reason, before discussing the relational practices that occur within family settings, we should begin with thinking carefully about what family "is."

In the next section, we consider various ways of defining family used in four primary domains: medical or biological, legal, scholarly, and personal. We look at the benefits of definitions, as well as what the problematic aspects are (see Table 1.1 for a summary). The

TABLE 1.1   *Definitions of Communication*

Definition	*Characteristics*	*Benefits*	*Drawbacks*
Medical or biological	Defines family on the basis of genetic connection	Allows for study of genetic links to behavioral traits	Restricts family only to those related by blood—limiting
Legal, formal	Defines family on the bases of blood ties or legal ties (marriage/adoption)	Makes it easy to clearly establish family ties for legal issues	Fails to acknowledge familial role of individuals not related by blood or law
Legal, functional	Defines family on the basis of fulfillment of family functions	Places emphasis on familial behaviors rather than legal or genetic ties—broad definition	Creates ambiguity in legal settings; unclear which functions should be used as criteria
Scholarly, traditional	Defines family primarily on the basis of the parent–child unit	Places emphasis on the unit that many individuals view as the most important part of family	Limits consideration of the role of extended family and childfree couples, as well as other groupings
Scholarly, functional	Defines family based on primary functions families fulfill in society	Allows for more cross-cultural comparison and understanding through focus on essential functions	Makes it difficult to fully establish which functions of family are essential and may overemphasize families with children
Scholarly, behavioral or transactional	Defines family by the behaviors that are associated with family groups	Has relatively inclusive focus on behaviors and intimacy building	Makes it difficult to delineate what it means to behave like family, and different behaviors may build intimacy in different cultural settings
Personal	Defines family on the basis of our individual beliefs about who counts as family	Allows for the most variety of family forms—flexible and wide ranging	Makes study difficult as each individual will define family somewhat differently

definitions or types of definitions we consider here will not be exhaustive, merely representative of some of the common ways family is defined. In fact, you should note that these definitions primarily come from twentieth century understandings of family, arising mostly from European and U.S. culture, though some of these views are shared in other cultures. If we were to go back further in time, or delve more deeply into other cultural understandings, we would see many additional understandings of family. As you read this material, begin to develop your own working definition of what family is.

Medical or Biological Definitions

Probably the most restrictive or narrowest way to define family is to use solely biological or "blood" connections. A biological family can be defined by looking at a family tree and tracing the family back through its bloodline. **Biological definitions** of family are principally used in genetic tracing or other medical issues. Researchers and doctors look at how genetic links are implicated in increased risk of breast cancer, manic depression, attention deficit disorder, and other conditions. For physicians or geneticists considering how illnesses may be passed from family member to family member along with genetic material, the biological family is the natural focus.

For research in family communication processes, a biological definition is not the most common. However, some researchers do investigate how genetic traits are related to communication, and how these traits may be passed along family bloodlines. For example, Docherty and colleagues (Docherty, 1993, 2005; Docherty, Grosh, & Wexler, 1996) are interested in the connection between genetic predispositions for schizophrenia and the specific communication patterns that are exhibited by individuals with schizophrenia (for example, disorganized speech and poor sequencing). Other researchers have considered how heredity might be more generally related to communication styles for issues such as verbal aggressiveness, social adaptability, and communication apprehension (Beatty, 2005; Beatty, Marshall, & Rudd, 2001; Horvath, 1995). These scholars use a biological definition of family in order to address communication issues thought to be primarily related to the blood/genetic connection between family members. A scholar studying communication from this perspective might also be interested in the extent to which genetics influence an individual's ability, or desire, to interact with others (what we often call "shyness").

A positive aspect of using a biological definition to define family is the clarity that it has. From this view, it doesn't matter whether individuals perceive themselves, or others, as part of the family. The sole criterion is the blood relationship of the family members and therefore it is easy to define who is "in" a family and who is "out." In addition, for communication study, a biological definition of family allows researchers to focus on genetic influence in communication processes.

Although a biological family definition can be useful in understanding how health issues or communication tendencies follow genetic lines, it results in the omission from "the family" of adoptees, stepparents, and even marital partners who did not procreate within that family line. Biological definitions also may prevent a full consideration of the effects of environmental factors on communication phenomenon. If a study did find that communication reticence (shyness) seemed to be common in particular families, there could be a genetic connection. However, it is possible that family members who share this trait have learned it from each other, rather than passing it along genetically. Thus, biological definitions may seem too restrictive to many researchers.

Legal Definitions

Systems of law are generally quite complicated. Thus, it is probably no surprise that legal definitions of family are diverse and complex. Documents and legal bodies at varying levels have defined family in different ways, across different time periods. How family is defined legally can have serious implications for important family issues like custody of children, inheritance, public services, insurance, and so on. Because legal issues involving family definition vary widely across the world, we will focus on the legal system of the United States in this discussion. However, it is important to understand that legal decisions made in the United States are based on cultural heritage. This means that they are not necessarily any more or less accurate or better than those made in other systems.

Formal.   As discussed in the *Harvard Law Review* ("Looking for a Family Resemblance," 1991), the legal system in the United States has recently taken two primary approaches to the definition of family. The first approach is to use a formal, **traditional legal definition.** This typically means defining family in terms of biological and/or formalized legal connections. One example of this type of definition can be seen in how the U.S. federal government defines families in the census: "A group of two or more people who reside together and who are related by birth, marriage, or adoption" (www.census.gov/dmd/www/glossary/ glossary_ f.html). This definition requires the sharing of a household and either a blood (birth) or formal legal (marriage or adoption) connection between the individuals. In many cases, formal legal definitions do not include the stipulation of shared dwelling, but typically retain the aspects of a marital, adoptive, or blood relationship between the members. This definition is based on a model of the nuclear family as including a married couple and their children.

Functional.   In other instances, the legal system has chosen to adopt a **functional legal definition** of family. Such an approach looks at the functions of a traditional family (economic cooperation, affection between family members, the maintenance of long-term relationships, the rearing of children, etc.) and then uses those functions as criteria for defining family units (Hickman, 1999). The focus is on how the members interact with each other, what they do for each other. Families are groups of people that do the things a family is supposed to do.

A functional approach to family is sometimes used in legal forums when making decisions about particular family groups. For example, if a widowed stepfather and a biological father were debating the custody of a child, this standard or definition might be applied. If the judge decided that the biological father had not "functioned" as a father to the child, whereas the stepfather had, the custody may be awarded to the stepfather. In the same situation, application of a formal traditional definition would result in custody being awarded to the biological parent. It should be noted that the functional approach is typically taken by individual judges or other members of the legal system, and is somewhat rare. At this time, this view of family has not become an extensive part of official legal code in the United States.

Both the formal and functional approaches have benefits and limitations that can impact the lives of families as they take part in legal processes. Formal definitions of family are relatively clear and can be applied with ease across cases and time periods. Additionally, this type of definition places a strong emphasis on the value of marriage, adoption, and blood relation, which is consistent with the moral and ethical beliefs of large segments of the U.S. population.

As indicated by Hickman (1999) and others, the most problematic aspects of formal legal definitions are that they marginalize those individuals who participate in nontraditional family groupings and prioritize the morals and ethics of one segment of society over others. By this definition, if a man lives with a woman and her children for many years, he would still not be considered a part of her family because there is no legal bond. If the couple decides to separate, the "parent" without legal or blood ties to the child may lose all opportunity to interact with that child again and will hold no further responsibility for the care or upbringing of the child.

In legal settings, the primary benefit of the functional approach is its inclusiveness. Individuals who act as a family, yet may not qualify under a formal approach, can be considered a family, with the legal rights and privileges, when a functional definition is applied. For example, a homosexual couple living together and co-raising children would be considered a family when applying a functional definition. They would likely not be considered a family if using a traditional formal definition. This means that those individuals who operate in nontraditional family forms can still receive the legal benefits of family status under a functional definition, which can be very important in issues such as child custody, inheritance, dwelling ordinances, adoption, and divorce settlement.

As noted in *Harvard Law Review* (1991), the difficulty of the functional definition lies in its vagueness. There are no clear guidelines as to which functions of traditional families should be applied to nontraditional groupings in order to define them as families. Individual courts or judicial agents may apply standards very differently, thus resulting in unfair or uneven application of law. Additionally, you need to know a lot about the day-to-day interactions of a family to understand what functions an individual is fulfilling.

As legal environments change, so too do the definitions of family in those settings. One example of this can be seen in the ongoing discussions of same-sex relationships and laws applying to them. As countries and other municipalities around the world respond to issues such as the question of sexuality in family law, formal definitions of family are likely to change.

BOX 1.3 • *Internet Connection*

The American Bar Association provides up-to-date information about family law in the United States on its Web site at www.abanet.org/family/familylaw/tables.html

Scholarly Definitions

Like those in the legal field, scholars who study family often face challenges in their attempts to define it. Anthropologists, sociologists, philosophers, family communication theorists, and others have defined families in various ways in an attempt to reach a definition that covers the essential elements of family.

Traditional.   Some scholars take a relatively **traditional definition** of family. One example of this is provided by Lévi-Strauss (1956), a French social anthropologist:

> Let us try to define the family. . . . It would seem that this word serves to designate a social group offering at least three characteristics: (1) it finds its origin in marriage; (2) it consists in husband, wife, and children born out of wedlock, though it can be conceived that other relatives may find their place close to that nuclear group; and (3) the family members are united together by a) legal bonds, b) economic, religious, and other kinds of rights and obligations; c) a precise network of sexual rights and prohibitions, and a varying and diversified amount of psychological feelings such as love, affection, respect, awe, etc. (pp. 266–267)

In his attempt to delineate what the term *family* means, Lévi-Strauss rooted the definition in the relationship between a married man and woman and their children. Thus, this definition is considered traditional. The bonds between the family members are legal, marital, and genetic.

Another, slightly expanded yet still traditional definition was provided by Murdock, an American anthropologist and sociologist, in 1949:

> The family is a social group characterized by common residence, economic cooperation, and reproduction. It includes adults of both sexes, at least two of whom maintain a socially approved sexual relationship, and one or more children, own or adopted, of the sexually cohabiting adults. (p. 1)

In this definition, Murdock attempts to account for the varying legal forms that may exist in different cultures. Thus, he does not indicate that the adults must be married: rather, he states that their relationship should be "socially approved." In cultures, like the United States, where marriage is the most socially approved type of sexual relationship, you might assume this to be a married couple. Additionally, Murdock allows for the possibility that there might be more than two adults involved in the relationship. This accounts for cultures where polygamy is practiced and families are composed of more than two adults. Although Murdock's definition does not rule out homosexual relationship per se (that is, he does not say that the two sexes need to have sex with one another), his definition does seem to imply that the sexual union is primarily heterosexual. And, the socially approved sexual relationship between the adults and the production or adoption of offspring are still key.

Traditional definitions primarily proceed from the idea of the union between man and woman as the root of family. Such definitions focus on the heterosexual nuclear family (parents and their biological children). They do not typically include others who may reside in or out of the household, such as grandparents, aunts, uncles, and so on. As such, this type of definition is relatively rare in family communication scholarship (Whitchurch, 1993).

In attempts to address the intergenerational nature of family, some scholars turn to other definitions. Beutler, Burr, Bahr, and Herrin (1989) use the term *family realm* to differentiate the family experience from other human endeavors. They define the family realm as

> the realm that is created by the birth process and the establishment of ties across generations. The irreducible parameter of this realm is the biological, emotional, social, and developmental processes that are inherent in the procreation and the nurturing of dependent children. (p. 806)

As you can see from this definition, Beutler et al. widen the scope of family somewhat from the definitions of Lévi-Strauss and Murdock. In defining a family realm, Beutler and colleagues focus primarily on the actions involved in the rearing of children. Therefore, in its focus on the blood or adoptive relationships implied by childrearing, this view does not completely depart from the more traditional definitions. However, this view does include more generations in the "family realm" than the nuclear family referred to by traditional definitions. Additionally, in its focus on the function families perform in the nurturing of dependent children, this definition begins to hint at a more functional view of families.

Functional.   Previously, we considered how the legal system sometimes relies on a functional view of families in attempting to define who and what "count" as family. Some family researchers also utilize **functional definitions** in the attempt to delineate family. Murdock (1949), whose traditional definition of family was mentioned previously, also argued that families performed four primary functions: Families act to socialize the young, represent the economic cooperation of members, fulfill the sexual needs of the adults, and result in the reproduction of the species. Murdock argued that, whereas families provide other functions, these four are universal across cultures. Additionally, he claimed that though other social institutions may participate in some of these functions (for example, schools act to socialize children), they are not as important as the family to those functions.

Not all scholars agree with Murdock's claims. In response to his work, Reiss (1965) states that "the family institution is a small kinship structured group with the key function of nurturant socialization of the newborn" (p. 449). "Nurturant socialization" refers to the process of caring for and raising a child and teaching him or her the socially accepted behaviors of the cultures in which he or she exists. Reiss argues that, although families may provide other functions as well (depending on the culture), this is the universal function that defines family. Thus, for Reiss, the family can principally be defined by social groupings that function to socialize children (see also Lerner & Spanier, 1978).

Functional views attempt to define the primary functions that all families perform. This allows the definitions to be more easily applied across cultures, because marriage arrangements, household structures, and so on. vary from culture to culture. However, to designate which functions of family are the most important or most crucial is quite difficult. Additionally, because functional definitions, like traditional definitions, often place a significant emphasis on childrearing, couples that do not have children seem to exist outside the framework of family provided by these views.

Behavioral or Transactional. In an attempt to avoid some of the pitfalls of both traditional and functional approaches to defining family, some scholars operate from a more **behavioral or transactional definition.** Wegar (2000) argues that a more appropriate way to consider family is to look at how individuals behave toward each other and impact each other. Being part of a family means behaving like a family member. Fitzpatrick and Caughlin (2002) state that transactional approaches consider how the interactions between family members over time stem from and create commitment, intimacy, and family identity. This type of definition allows for a much broader and more inclusive concept of family. Same-sex couples, childfree couples, and large groups of adults living communally with or without children could all be considered family in this approach. What becomes complex about this view is that it requires consideration of what it means to "behave" like family and how various types of communicative interaction may contribute to the establishment of family identity.

Some communication scholars blend together bits and pieces from functional, behavioral, and genetic definitions in an attempt to create an understanding that is more inclusive. An example of this can be seen in Baxter and Braithwaite (2006), where a family is defined as "a social group of two or more persons, characterized by ongoing interdependence with long-term commitments that stem from blood, law, or affection" (p. 3). This definition reaches into the legal realm, acknowledges the blood/genetic realm, considers the interdependent functions of family, reflects the notion of the commitments of behavior that family may include, and also approaches the idea of the highly personal dimension of affection and feelings in how we define family (for similar definitions, see DeGenova & Rice, 2002; Galvin, Bylund, & Brommel, 2004). This is important because, as other authors would argue, our beliefs about who is and is not family, and what family members should and should not do may be highly personal.

Personal Definitions

A variety of authors, including Jorgenson (1989), have noted that family members may define their families differently than theorists or researchers do. In fact, individuals may consider their families to be composed of others who are not related by blood or legal means. Weston (1991) discussed the concept of **families of choice** as applied to homosexual men and women. Weston argued that, often, homosexual men and women are separated from families of origin (the family in which an individual was raised) due to the social stigma of having a gay or lesbian relative. Additionally, they have been generally prohibited from marrying and thus creating a new family. Therefore, gay men and lesbian women select members of their friendship community to function as a sort of substitute family (see also Allen, 1997; Allen & Demo, 1995).

The same phenomenon has been noted in other situations as well. McRae (1992) considers how older men and women select **fictive kin** to replace family members who may not be accessible to them. In retirement communities and nursing homes, older adults form family-like relationships that offer support as well as the opportunity to express affection and provide comfort and care for another. Karner (1998) discusses how health care workers can adopt a family role for the older adults they attend. These workers may take on the role of son or daughter, grandson or granddaughter, to the older adults in their care. In exchange for the care and attention they provide, the older adult provides affection, advice, and encouragement.

The concept of fictive kin has also been applied to understanding the lives of individuals who are homeless. In their study of homeless adolescents, McCarthy, Hagan, and Martin (2002) found that "kin" groups are formed among the street population. These groupings, often designated by use of familial terms like *sister, uncle, mom,* or *dad,* become replacements for the absent family of the homeless youths. Such associations provide the youths with mechanisms for support, affection, a sense of responsibility, and even increased safety on the streets.

As homeless individuals or gay or lesbian persons may adopt fictive kin because they have been physically or emotionally separated from their families of origin, so too immigrants might form strong familial relationships with people who are not related by blood or legal ties. Ebaugh (2000) discusses the development of fictive kin relationships among immigrant populations. Individuals who immigrate find themselves facing the challenges of a new culture. In many cases, they may have few, if any, family members available to support and aid them through this acclimation process. Fictive kin may then provide that group cohesiveness that is needed.

In addition to the populations mentioned here, fictive kin can be found in many other situations. Perhaps you have a godparent (or more than one). Godparents are ritualized examples of fictive kin. In some cases, godparents may be related by blood to their godchildren, but in other cases they are not. However, once the ritual of godparenting is completed, they may assume a familial relationship to the child. Or, you might have a family friend that you call "Aunt" or "Uncle." That individual is not really related to you, but you have developed a relationship with him or her that seems more similar to a family relationship than friendship.

None of the types of personal families discussed in this section would be adequately accounted for by the many definitions we have discussed in this chapter. This points to the inherent difficulty in defining family. In order to study any social phenomenon, including family and family communication, it becomes necessary to reach some sort of definition of what that phenomenon is. The act of defining something, a truly communicative behavior, is at the root of how we understand and respond to that thing. However, family is not an easy phenomenon to define. Each definition we have studied here has its benefits and its drawbacks. This doesn't mean they don't have utility; it simply means that they aren't perfect. This is partly because of the multitude of family forms that exist throughout the world. And, how we understand what counts as family is deeply embedded in our cultural mores and expectations. Additionally, it is difficult for researchers, theorists, legal agents, and even students like you to separate personalized understandings of family from the attempt to define what family is.

Think back on your answers to the questions at the start of this section. Whom did you select to include in the three events mentioned? How did you make that selection? The answers likely indicate something about how you would define family. As you read the remainder of this text, you will encounter research being done from a variety of perspectives. As you do so, I encourage you to consider the ways in which each author seems to define and discuss family. Think about some of the ways family has been defined in this chapter as they apply to your life understandings and the readings you encounter here. Compare what you read with your own definitions of family and ponder where your definitions come from. Most people would agree that family is vitally important, but like other social concepts including love and friendship and trust, it is sometimes extremely hard to pin down. Perhaps in the end, you will find that a family is simply a group of people who consider themselves to be family and are somehow bound together by that belief.

Questions for Consideration and Discussion

1. What is your definition of family? Who is included and who is left out of your definition?
2. What is an example of how family communication impacted your understanding of the world?
3. Thinking about your most recent family communication encounters, how were both verbal and nonverbal elements important parts of the interaction?
4. How possible, or appropriate, do you think it is for definitions of family to be developed that apply across cultures worldwide? Why?
5. What do you see as the utility (usefulness) of attempting to clearly define family? What do you see as the drawbacks of such an attempt?

Key Terms and Concepts

behavioral or transactional definition (scholarly)
biological definition
communication
families of choice
family realm
fictive kin
functional definition (legal)
functional definition (scholarly)
symbolic interactionism
traditional definition (legal)
traditional definition (scholarly)

References

Allen, K. (1997). Lesbian and gay families. In T. Arrendell (Ed.), *Contemporary parenting: Challenges and issues* (pp. 196–218). Thousand Oaks, CA: Sage.

Allen, K., & Demo, D. H. (1995). The families of lesbians and gay men: A new frontier of family research. *Journal of Marriage and Family, 57*, 111–127.

Baxter, L. A., & Braithwaite, D. O. (2006). Introduction: Metatheory and theory in family communication research. In D. O. Braithwaite & L. A. Baxter (Eds.), *Engaging theories in family communication: Multiple perspectives.* Thousand Oaks, CA: Sage.

Beatty, M. J. (2005). Fallacies in the textual analysis of the communibiological literature. *Communication Theory, 15*(4), 456–467.

Beatty, M. J., Marshall, L. A., & Rudd, J. E. (2001). A twins study of communicative adaptability: Heritability of individual differences. *Quarterly Journal of Speech, 87*(4), 366–377.

Beutler, I. F., Burr, W. R., Bahr, K. S., & Herrin, D. A. (1989). The family realm: Theoretical contributions for understanding its uniqueness. *Journal of Marriage and Family, 51*(3), 805–816.

Blumer, H. (1969). *Symbolic interactionism: Perspective and method.* Englewood Cliffs, NJ: Prentice Hall.

DeGenova, M. K., & Rice, F. P. (2002). *Intimate relationships, marriages, & families* (5th ed.). Boston: McGraw-Hill.

Docherty, N. M. (1993). Communication deviance, attention, and schizotypy in parents of schizophrenic patients. *Journal of Nervous and Mental Disease, 181*, 750–756.

Docherty, N. M. (2005). Cognitive impairments and disordered speech in schizophrenia: Thought disorder, disorganization, and communication failure perspective. *Journal of Abnormal Psychology, 114*(2), 269–278.

Docherty, N. M., Grosh, E. S., & Wexler, B. E. (1996). Affective reactivity of cognitive functioning and family history in schizophrenia. *Biological Psychiatry, 39*, 59–64.

Ebaugh, H. R. (2000). Fictive kin as social capital in new immigrant communities. *Sociological Perspectives, 43*(2), 189–209.

Fitzpatrick, M. A., & Caughlin, J. P. (2002). Interpersonal communication in family relationships. In M. L. Knapp & J. A. Daly (Eds.), *Handbook of interpersonal communication*. Thousand Oaks, CA: Sage.

Galvin, K. M., Bylund, C. L., & Brommel, B. J. (2004). *Family communication: Cohesion and change (6th ed)*. New York: Allyn & Bacon.

Hickman, L. A. (1999). Making the family functional: The case for legalized same-sex domestic partnerships. *Philosophy of the Social Sciences, 29*(2), 231–247.

Horvath, C. W. (1995). Biological origins of communicator style. *Communication Quarterly, 43*(4), 394–407.

Jorgenson, J. (1989). Where is the "family" in family communication?: Exploring families' self-definitions. *Journal of Applied Communication Research, 17*(1–2), 27–41.

Karner, T. X. (1998). Professional caring: Homecare workers as fictive kin. *Journal of Aging Studies, 12*(1), 69–82.

Lerner, R. M., & Spanier, G. B. (Eds.). (1978). *Child influences on marital interaction: A lifespan perspective*. New York: Academic Press.

Lévi-Strauss, C. (1956). The family. In H. L. Shapiro (Ed.), *Man, culture and society* (pp. 278–286). New York: Oxford University Press.

Looking for a family resemblance: The limits of the functional approach to the legal definition of family. (1991). *Harvard Law Review, 104*(7), 1640–1659.

MacRae, H. (1992). Fictive kin as component of social networks of older people. *Research on Aging, 14*(2), 226–247.

McCarthy, B., Hagan, J., & Martin, M. J. (2002). In and out of harm's way: Violent victimization and the social capital of fictive street families. *Criminology, 40*(4), 831–865.

Mead, G. H. (1934). *Mind, self, and society*. Chicago: University of Chicago Press.

Murdock, G. P. (1949). *Social structure*. New York: Macmillan.

Reiss, I. L. (1965). The universality of the family: A conceptual analysis. *Journal of Marriage and Family, 27*(4), 443–453.

Vangelisti, A. L. (2004). Introduction. In A. L. Vangelisti (Ed.), *The handbook of family communication* (pp. xiii–xx). Mahwah, NJ: Erlbaum.

Wegar, K. (2000). Adoption, family ideology, and social stigma: Bias in community attitudes, adoption research, and practice. *Family Relations, 49*(4), 363–370.

Weston, K. (1991). *Families we choose: Lesbians, gays, kinship*. New York: Columbia University Press.

Whitchurch, C. G. (1993). Designing a course in family communication. *Communication Education, 42*, 255–267.

5

Communicating Intimacy, Affection, and Social Support

Chapter Outline _____

Chapter Objectives _____

1. To be able to define intimacy, affection and social support in families
2. To develop understanding of some of the factors that contribute to intimacy, affection, and social support patterns in families
3. To understand some of the outcomes that have been associated with intimacy, affection, and social support patterns in families
4. To be able to apply this material to assessing and planning your own family patterns

Section 1: Overview of Intimacy, Affection, and Social Support in Families _____

- If you had to explain your feelings for family members, what kind of words would you use?
- Pick two people in your family and imagine expressing your positive feelings about them (to them). How would you do it?
- If you needed help with a serious issue, whom would you turn to?

> *The best thing about having a family is that a family takes care of you and helps you out a lot . . . and even though you might get in fights with them, they will still try and be nice and love you.*
>
> —Response of a nine-year-old asked what the best thing about a family is

One of the things that often springs to mind as we think about family is the love we expect family members to feel for each other, and the ways that they express that love. Hopefully, one of your early memories of childhood is experiencing affection and support given to you by your family members. Responding to such positive displays starts soon after birth. We know from research and common experience that babies are soothed and comforted by affection, and by an early age, children learn to appreciate affection being shown to others as well. In their 1981 study, Cummings, Zahn-Waxler, and Radke-Yarrow concluded that children as young as one year old responded positively to displays of affection between others, and were likely to respond with signs of pleasure and their own displays of affection. Based on this study, others that we consider as the chapter proceeds, and our own experiences, it seems that affection, intimacy, and social support are an important part of the family system from birth throughout life.

Intimacy, Affection, and Social Support Defined

Let's begin by defining these three terms and considering the similarities and differences between them. **Intimacy,** a word originating from the Latin word *intimus*, meaning "inner", can be defined as the degree to which individuals feel a sense of closeness and connection to one another, a feeling that we can or have revealed our inner self to the other (Baumeister & Bratslavsky, 1999). The intimacy that we have with others is developed through the interactions in that system. Although in casual conversation we often use the word *intimate* to refer to sexual intimacy, intimacy can actually be divided into a variety of types (Kouneski & Olson, 2004; Schaefer & Olson, 1981). We use a typology developed by Schaefer and Olson that is commonly used both to understand intimacy and to evaluate it using methodological tools (see also Kouneski & Olson, 2004; Laurenceau, Barrett, & Rovine, 2005; Laurenceau, Rivera, Schaffer, & Pietromonaco, 2004). This typology classifies intimacy as emotional, intellectual, recreational, social, or physical intimacy (see Table 5.1).

TABLE 5.1　*Types of Intimacy*

Emotional intimacy	Shared sense of closeness and shared emotion
Intellectual intimacy	Shared ideas and worldview
Recreational intimacy	Enjoyment of shared leisure time
Social intimacy	Overlapping social networks
Physical intimacy	Comfort with physical expressiveness

Emotional intimacy is the sense of closeness that you have with others on an emotional level (Schaefer & Olson, 1981). It represents the extent to which you believe that you can tell other persons about your emotions, and he or she can do the same with you.

Intellectual intimacy is the degree to which you feel connected to another because you share a similar worldview and ideas about how things are or should be (Schaefer & Olson, 1981). You experience a sense of closeness because you share these ideas, and you find it easy to talk to each other about your thoughts.

Recreational intimacy refers to the extent to which you and another enjoy time together and participate in recreational activities together (Schaefer & Olson, 1981). For families, this could include watching television, going to a park, playing sports, and so on.

Social intimacy is sharing of social networks and doing things with others as a family; for example, a married couple going out to dinner with friends (Schaefer & Olson, 1981). The more your social networks overlap, the more opportunity you may have for engaging in social activities with both family members and others outside the family system.

Physical intimacy relates to how comfortable you feel being physically expressive with another (Schaefer & Olson, 1981). Types of physical intimacy can range from feeling okay about a pat on the back, to giving a hug, to sexual intercourse. In some relationships, physical expressions may be shown without indicating a great deal of intimacy (e.g., the social kiss on the cheek), whereas in other relationships, the same behavior indicates more closeness (e.g., kissing a grandmother on the cheek). The behavior itself isn't necessarily indicative of the level of intimacy felt; it is how that behavior is understood and interpreted by the members of the relationship that indicates the importance of that behavior in establishing, maintaining, and reflecting intimacy.

These five types of intimacy don't necessarily correspond in a relationship. In some relationships we have a high degree of emotional intimacy, but a low degree of physical intimacy.

BOX 5.1 • *Did You Know?*

Physical affection is not only enjoyable for babies, but also good for them! Studies have indicated that caring touch has a positive impact on the physical and psychological development of babies (Caulfield, 2000).

Chapter 5

In other relationships we may have a high degree of physical intimacy, but little or no emotional intimacy. Intimacy is a feeling experienced by family members and degrees of intimacy are negotiated in relational systems. Thus, each family will experience and negotiate intimacy in its own way. Likewise, the individual members of the family may feel differently about the amount of intimacy they experience in the system.

Affection is similar to emotional intimacy in that it refers to the degree of caring, closeness, and positive regard that individuals have for one another (Floyd & Morman, 1998). Generally, we can consider affection to be the positive feelings (i.e., love, caring) that we have for those we are close to. Because affection is a feeling that we have, it is experienced differently by different people, even within one family. This makes it somewhat difficult to define. In research, however, the focus is often on how that affection is displayed, rather than how it is felt (Floyd & Morman, 1998; Floyd & Morr, 2003; Floyd & Ray, 2003), because it is very difficult to accurately assess a complex feeling like affection or love. Affection can be displayed verbally (saying "I love you"), and nonverbally (a hug, a kiss, a favor done) in ways that are very similar to the types of social support we consider next.

Social support can generally be defined as communication that makes people feel that they are valued and cared for within their particular group as the members of that group offer them assistance in some way (Burleson & MacGeorge, 2002; Cobb, 1976). There are various types of social support that can be offered within families and other social systems. Some of the types that have been identified by scholars include instrumental support, emotional support, and informational support (House, 1981) (see Table 5.2).

Instrumental support is doing something practical to help someone (Braithwaite & Eckstein, 2003; House, 1981). When you carry boxes for family members as they move from one house to another, give them a ride to the airport for a trip, or loan them a car if theirs is broken down, you are engaging in instrumental support.

Informational support is providing someone with additional knowledge about a topic in order to help out him or her (House, 1981; MacGeorge, Samter, & Gillihan, 2005). If you've ever explained something to a child you care for, given a family member directions to get somewhere, or warned a friend about a particular computer virus, you've offered informational support.

Finally, **emotional support** is the way that we caretake others with regard to their feelings (MacGeorge, et al., House, 1981). When family members are particularly unhappy or stressed, we may offer a sympathetic ear, give a hug, or just spend time with them. These are all forms of emotional support. Some studies have indicated that emotional support messages are seen as more helpful by receivers than other types of support (Burleson & MacGeorge, 2002).

TABLE 5.2 *Types of Social Support*

Instrumental support	Providing practical help for others
Informational support	Supplying needed information to others
Emotional support	Caretaking the feelings of others

From these various examples, we can see that social support amounts to providing some sort of "aid" to those we care about. In family settings, social support is both common and important.

Although intimacy, affection, and social support are theoretically somewhat distinct, in our daily lives they are expressed in similar ways and experienced as interwoven aspects of our relationships. They are developed through our communication with family members; they impact how we feel about and understand our relationships; they create our family cultures; and then, through our communication, they reflect those cultures. Thus, in this chapter we address these three factors of family communication simultaneously.

Factors Affecting the Expression of Intimacy, Affection, and Social Support

At the start of this chapter, you were asked to think about how you might express your affection to different members of your family. Let's continue to investigate the expression of positive regard here. As you grew up, was there a difference between how your female and male caregivers expressed their affection and support for you? How do you show affection and support for your romantic partners? Do you see similarities or differences from the way your parents or other adult caregivers expressed emotion to their romantic partners?

Sex and Gender Differences

Our life experiences suggest that not everyone shows their affection and intimacy for others in the same way. At one time or another, we have probably all been surprised by how someone else indicated his or her feelings of intimacy and affection for us. There are a variety of factors that may influence how family members express their caring. Research indicates that one thing that affects our expression of emotions is the sex (being male or female) of the communicators.

In a study of the families of college students at Brigham Young University, Barber and Thomas (1986) found that fathers were more likely to display physical affection (hugging and kissing) with their daughters than with their sons. Mothers tended to display affection in a physical manner equally with both sons and daughters. But, both mothers and fathers tended to pick up, or hold on their lap, girls more than boys. In addition to their findings with regard to physical displays of affection, Barber and Thomas concluded that mothers and fathers were more likely to show companionship affection (time spent together doing things) with children of the same sex.

Gender differences can be seen in the behavior of marital partners as well. Aylor and Dainton (2004), in a study of relational maintenance behaviors, found that feminine people are more likely to engage in more routine openness (being open as a matter of course, not for a particular purpose), whereas masculine people are more likely to engage in strategic openness (openness to reach a particular end goal). Other scholars have also found that the sex or gender of the affection recipient, and the affection giver, has an impact on how much and in what ways these positive emotional messages are provided (see, for example, Lytton & Romney, 1991; Stafford, 2003; Tucker, McHale, and Crouter, 2003).

It is likely that some of these differences can be attributed to cultural expectations about men and women and their behavior (Brody, 1997). Men in U.S. culture are generally discouraged from showing a lot of physical affection for others, except within the confines of heterosexual romantic relationships. Thus, fathers may feel more discomfort showing physical affection for sons. With regard to companionship affection, our cultural expectation in the United States is largely that women have more in common with other women, and the same is true for men. Therefore, it is probably not surprising that companionship affection between parents and children tends to align along sex lines. Likewise, in the United States femininity is associated with open expression of positive emotion, whereas masculinity is not. Thus, it seems reasonable that masculine people would be less likely to routinely engage in openness, without a goal in mind.

Other scholars would likely suggest that there are "inherent" (or natural) tendencies for men and women to behave in certain ways. **Evolutionary psychologists** argue that our ancestral history from thousands of years ago and the evolution that followed have impacted how we interact with one another today, and have influenced behavioral and psychological differences between men and women (Kenrick & Luce, 2000). These scholars would argue that, because of these evolutionary differences, men and women have an innate tendency toward different relational behaviors and expressions, such as the expressions of affection considered here.

Whether the differences in affection/intimacy behavior are biologically based or culturally developed (or some combination of the two), research seems to clearly suggest that within most family settings there are differences between how men and women (and boys and girls) express their affection and support. This does not suggest that all men or women show their intimacy in these ways or that this pattern will be represented fully in your individual family experience; rather, these are tendencies that seem to be common for men and women.

Position or Role in the Family

Research has indicated that a person's position or role in the family can also affect how he or she shows affection (or receives it) (Taylor, Chatters, & Jackson, 1993; Vogl-Bauer, 2003). Not surprisingly, these scholars found that children often receive the most social support in families, and that support frequently comes in the form of advice, encouragement, or financial assistance from parents and grandparents. Grandparents also receive support from family members, and common forms of support they receive are companionship,

BOX 5.2 • *Family in the News*

Recent news reports, television programs, and even movies have focused on the fact that adult children in their 20s and 30s seem to be more likely to live at home than in the past, in the United States. Media reports suggest that this is because of an increased comfort with that situation. Read a news example at www.usatoday.com/printedition/life/20060316/d_cover16.art.htm.

services (picking up groceries, housecleaning, etc.), transportation, and help when sick. Parents indicated that they receive support from extended family members, including grandparents, and some common types of support they receive are child care help and assistance during illness.

Here, too, we can see the effects of cultural expectations, as well as pragmatic factors, on how social support is exhibited. In the United States, we expect support between parents and children to primarily be provided from parent to child, rather than the reverse. This is partly pragmatic when children are young, because their access to resources is limited and they are in more need of financial and emotional assistance. Additionally, our cultural expectation is that parents will care for and provide guidance to children until they become adults, and even beyond formal adulthood until the children establish homes of their own.

As children become adults, parents often continue to serve a supporting function by providing babysitting services or advice for their adult children. At this point, the child and parent may have relatively equal access to monetary resources, so financial assistance is less needed by either party. Culturally, adulthood is also thought of as the time when we more completely "strike out on our own" and establish ourselves, which is the final stage of a process of gaining independence that begins in adolescence. This, too, may explain why less support is provided to the parental generation.

When an adult reaches his or her elder years, the pragmatic need for assistance may return as health becomes less robust and mobility more inhibited. Additionally, to some extent we have a cultural expectation that family members will help care for the elderly in their midst (though this is less the case in the United States than in some other cultures). Thus, it is not particularly surprising that the grandparent generation in the family experiences increased social support.

Relationships between Members

In addition to the sex or gender of communicators and family roles, the relationships that develop between family members, including the behavior of the recipient of affection, impact how much and what type of affection is shown. Russell (1997) found that when children behaved toward their parents in a way that was warm and affectionate, both mothers and fathers were more likely to also behave in such a way. This is somewhat like the question of the chicken and the egg, because causal direction cannot be claimed (that is, are children warmer and more affectionate because parents are, or is it the other way around?). However, what is apparent from this study is that reciprocity is active in the parent–child relationship in terms of warmth and affection. When we receive warmth and affection from a family member, we are more likely to reciprocate that behavior. Similarly, Brody, Stoneman, and McCoy (1992) found that when children had a more difficult temperament, parents were less likely to be affectionate toward them. Tucker, McHale, and Crouter (2003) note that, in their study, children who were particularly emotional received less affection than children who were less emotional. Additionally, they indicate that when children displayed the characteristics commonly associated with their position in the family (for example, firstborns being more independent, the youngest child being less brave), they were likely to receive more affection than if they did not display such characteristics, or displayed characteristics that seemed counter to their role. From these examples, we can see that the relationships and patterns of behavior developed between the partners affect how intimacy is shown in the family.

Not only does the relationship between the two individuals (affection giver and affection receiver) affect that process, but so too do the other family relationships that exist in the family system. White (1999) found that a parent's affection for a child was not only correlated with his or her relationship to the child, but also with the other parent's relationship to the child and to the marital relationship of the parents or stepparents. Similarly, in this study White discovered that a child's affection toward one parent was related to his or her feelings toward the other parent. This isn't surprising when we consider the argument of family systems scholars that all relationships within the family are interconnected.

From these studies, we can see that there are many factors (not limited to those discussed here) that impact how and to whom support, affection, and intimacy are directed. The outcomes of those communicative behaviors also proceed in a variety of ways.

Outcomes Related to Intimacy, Affection, and Social Support

How others treat us leaves an impression and affects both us and our relationships. Thus, it isn't surprising that the ways in which family members treat each other with regard to affection, intimacy, and social support can have an impact on how they feel about and assess their relationships.

Parental/Romantic Relationship Outcomes

The parental/romantic relationship that often is a part of family life can be affected by the way these communicative elements are displayed. Xu and Burleson (2004) found that emotional support from a spouse was correlated to marital satisfaction for both men and women, in both Chinese and American marriages (see also Gardner & Cutrona, 2004; Wan, Jaccard, & Ramey, 1996). Similarly, in a study of young dating and married couples, Gulledge, Gulledge, and Stahmann (2003) concluded that displays of physical affection between young couples (not including sexual intimacy) were connected to more relational satisfaction and better ability to manage conflict.

Other Family Relationship Outcomes

But, it is not only the parental relationship in the family that is affected by how closeness is exhibited. This same finding has been seen in other family relationships. For example, Floyd and Morr (2003) considered displays of affection in the relationships of siblings, spouses, and siblings-in-law (see also Gardner & Cutrona, 2004). Not surprisingly, they found that affection in these relationships was correlated positively to satisfaction. Similar results have been obtained relating to how children and parents understand and evaluate their relationships with each other (Gardner & Cutrona, 2004; Morman & Floyd, 2002; Punyanunt-Carter, 2005). For example, Lang and Schütze (2002) found that the relational satisfaction of elderly parents was increased when their children showed more affection and emotional support.

It isn't always clear which factor is affecting the other (that is, do we express more social support when we are satisfied, or are we more satisfied when we express more social support?). But, the correlation between these elements and relational satisfaction is clear. It is likely that these two aspects (how we show intimacy, affection, and support and how satisfied we are with the relationship) have some sort of reciprocal effect on each other.

Individual Outcomes

The benefits from these positive communication phenomena can be individual as well as relational. Support from family members has been found to be correlated with better mental health (Burleson & MacGeorge, 2002; Gardner & Cutrona, 2004). Bal, Crombez, Van Oost, and Debourdeaudhuij (2003) studied the role of family support in adolescent well-being after a stressful and traumatic life event. They found that, generally, increased family support was correlated to less trauma-related symptoms for these adolescents. Barber and Thomas's (1986) study found a connection between parental displays of affection in childhood and the self-esteem of young adults. As parents' displays of various types of affection for their son or daughter in childhood increased, there was a correspondent increase in the positive self-esteem that child had when he or she became a young adult. Social support also affects the mental functioning of adults. Postpartum depression is a common occurrence for new mothers. It affects the mother, impacts her relationship with the new child, and also has outcomes for other familial relationships. Cutrona and Troutman (1986) concluded that social support helped reduce postpartum depression by helping new mothers feel more capable about their parenting. Similarly, Arnold (2003, 2005) found that supportive interactions contributed to positive and empowered feelings about parenting for pregnant women and parents of large families. Thus, such support can improve the lives of parents, children, and other family members.

In addition to positive impacts on mental health, social support has also been associated with physical health benefits, or helping people cope with health issues (Berkman, Glass, Brissette, & Seeman, 2000; Burleson & MacGeorge, 2002; Gardner & Cutrona, 2004). There are far too many such studies to detail here, so a few examples will suffice. Some studies have focused on cancer patients and how they deal with the disease and the associated

BOX 5.3 • *Internet Connection*

Studies have indicated the value of social support for individuals with medical conditions. In the absence of (or in addition to) support from family and friends, online discussion forums may provide a venue for advice and support. You can find many health related bulletin boards at www.healthboards.com.

medical interventions. For instance, Manne et al. (2003) concluded that, particularly when the husband was unsupportive, social support from family and friends helped women with breast cancer more effectively cope with the disease. Other medical issues have been considered as well. Holtzman, Newth, and Delongis's (2004) study of adults with rheumatoid arthritis revealed that increased social support had an impact on pain levels and pain management. Similarly, scholars have found an association between heart health and social support, particularly for individuals who have had a heart attack (see, for example, Janevic et al., 2004; Pedersen, Van Domburg, & Larsen, 2004).

Factors Affecting Outcomes

Although findings such as these suggest that displays of social support, intimacy, and affection have very real effects in the lives of family members, those effects can vary depending on how the messages are constructed and understood, as well as the sender (and the receiver) of the positive messages. Some communication scholars have focused their attention on the effectiveness of positive relational messages, with respect to the elements of the message itself. Applegate, Burleson, and colleagues (for a review see Burleson & MacGeorge, 2002) argue that messages intended to offer emotional support and comforting are most effective when they are person centered. **Person centeredness** is the extent to which a message communicates both an understanding of and adaptation to the perspective of the message receiver. Burleson and colleagues state that comforting messages that are highly person centered (explicitly recognize the emotions of the other, indicate the legitimacy of those emotions, discuss the reasons for the emotions, and offer new ways to understand the emotions) are most effective. Messages that reject or ignore the perspective of the other are the least effective and can be problematic for the recipient, the sender, and their relationship. Holmstrom, Burleson, and Jones (2005) found, in a study of undergraduate students, that senders who offered low person-centered support messages were evaluated more negatively and liked less than those who offered highly person-centered messages (see also Goldsmith, McDermott, & Alexander, 2000). They found this to be even truer for women comforting other women, and the authors suggest that this may be because of cultural expectations that women are good at supporting others.

In outcomes, as well as in factors contributing to affection, there are sometimes gender differences. According to Lawton, Silverstein, and Bengtson (1994), greater affection for the mother tends to lead to more frequent contact between adult children and their parents. In relation to the father, however, greater affection is not associated with increased contact. This could be because fathers are less likely to initiate contact, perhaps due to their social role having less of an expectation of being relationship experts (Lawton et al., 1994). Or, it could be that children feel less compelled to contact their father than they do their mother, perhaps because of childhood relational patterns. In a similar finding, Jorm, Dear, Rodgers, and Christensen (2003) argue that, in their sample of adults, individuals whose parents had shown more affection had fewer mental health problems. However, when fathers showed more affection and mothers showed less, there were increased family interaction problems and also increased mental health problems for the adult children. The authors contend that this could be because family problems cause fathers to show more affection and mothers to show less. Alternately, it may be that, because mothers are expected to be more affectionate in behavior than fathers, when that role is reversed it is problematic for the family system. Thus, we can see that the sex or gender of the family members may impact how affection, support, and intimacy affect members (see also Gardner & Cutrona, 2004).

In addition to gender or sex effects, the culture in which the family exists can impact how these communicative elements impact family members. Some research suggests that in families where members are overly "attached" to one another (enmeshed), problems for the children may result (Olson, 2000). Additionally, as noted previously, research often finds that in Western cultures, affection and support displays are important to satisfaction in a marital relationship. However, it is likely that the impact of these family aspects varies based on the culture in which the family lives. Rothbaum, Rosen, Ujiie, and Uchida (2002) argue that in Japanese culture extremely close relationships exist between mother and child, and less affectionate marital relationships are expected and common. Thus, this type of pattern does not have negative impacts on the family members or the family system in Japanese culture.

Whereas social support has generally been found to have positive impacts on physical and psychological health, as discussed earlier in this section, Dressler, Balieiro, and Dos Santos (1997) found that these effects are also impacted by cultural expectations. In their study, participants who were receiving social support most closely resembling that expected in the culture had the biggest health benefits. Similarly, Burleson and Mortenson (2003) and Mortenson (2006) found that support needs, expectations, and outcomes showed both similarities and differences for undergraduate students from the United States and undergraduate students from China. Thus, in different cultures different amounts or types of social support may be needed to see the positive benefits of support.

From these examples, we can see that as culture and gender affect how social support, affection, and intimacy are displayed, they also are related to how these aspects of relational communication impact the family members. Additionally, the construction of such messages impacts their outcomes. All of these factors point to the complexity of these aspects of family life.

In this section, we have considered definitions of social support, intimacy, and affection. We've also addressed some of the research on factors that impact how these phenomena are displayed and how they affect participants. Section 2 discusses a study using conversational analysis (a common methodology of family studies in communication) to understand how intimacy is cocreated in a mother–daughter relationship. It also addresses the use of positive relational messages and gender differences in marital relationships, and looks at social support and family communication patterns. Finally, in Section 3, I address how what you have learned in the chapter might be applied in your own life experiences.

References

Arnold, L. B. (2003). Delivering empowerment: Women's narratives about the role of pregnancy bulletin boards. *Qualitative Research Reports in Communication, 4*, 45–52.

Arnold, L. B. (2005). Don't you know what causes that?: Advice, celebration, and justification in a large families bulletin board. *Communication Studies, 56*(4), 331–351.

Aylor, B., & Dainton, M. (2004). Biological sex and psychological gender as predictors of routine and strategic relational maintenance. *Sex Roles, 50*(9/10), 689–697.

Bal, S., Crombez, G., Van Oost, P., & Debourdeaudhuij, I. (2003). The role of social support in well-being and coping with self-reported stressful events in adolescents. *Child Abuse & Neglect, 27*(12), 1377–1395.

Barber, B. K., & Thomas, D. L. (1986). Dimensions of fathers' and mothers' supportive behavior: The case for physical affection. *Journal of Marriage and Family, 48*, 783–794.

Baumeister, R. F., & Bratslavsky, E. (1999). Passion, intimacy, and time: Passionate love as a function of change in intimacy. *Personality and Social Psychology Review, 3*, 49–67.

Berkman, L. F., Glass, T., Brissette, I., & Seeman, T. E. (2000). From social integration to health: Durkheim in the new millennium. *Social Science and Medicine, 51*, 843–857.

Braithwaite, D. O., & Eckstein, N. J. (2003). How people with disabilities communicatively manage assistance: Helping as instrumental social support. *Journal of Applied Communication Research, 31*(1), 1–25.

Brody, G. H., Stoneman, Z., & McCoy, J. K. (1992). Parental differential treatment of siblings and sibling differences in negative emotionality. *Journal of Marriage and Family, 54*, 643–651.

Brody, L. (1997). Gender and emotions: Beyond stereotypes. *Journal of Social Issues, 53*(2), 369–393.

Burleson, B. R., & MacGeorge, E. L. (2002). Supportive communication. In M. L. Knapp & J. A. Daly (Eds.), *Handbook of interpersonal communication* (3rd ed., pp. 374–422). Thousand Oaks, CA: Sage.

Burleson, B. R., & Mortenson, S. R. (2003). Exploring cultural differences in evaluations of emotional support behaviors: Exploring the mediating influences value systems and interaction goals. *Communication Research, 30*, 113–146.

Caulfield, R. (2000). Beneficial effects of tactile stimulation on early development. *Early Childhood Education Journal, 27*(4), 255–257.

Cobb, S. (1976). Social support as a moderator of life stress. *Psychosomatic Medicine, 5*, 300–314.

Cummings, E. M., Zahn-Waxler, C., & Radke-Yarrow, M. (1981). Young children's responses to expressions of anger and affection by others in the family. *Child Development, 52*(4), 1274–1282.

Cutrona, C. E., & Troutman, B. R. (1986). Social support, infant temperament, and parenting self-efficacy: A mediational model of postpartum depression. *Child Development, 57*, 1507–1518.

Dressler, W. W., Balieiro, M. C., & Dos Santos, J. E. (1997). The cultural construction of social support in Brazil: Associations with health outcomes. *Culture, Medicine and Psychiatry, 21*(3), 303–335.

Floyd, K., & Morr, M. C. (2003). Human affection exchange: VII. Affectionate communication in the sibling/spouse/sibling-in-law triad. *Communication Quarterly, 51*(3), 247–251.

Floyd, K., & Morman, M. T. (1998). The measurement of affectionate communication. *Communication Quarterly, 46*(2), 144–162.

Floyd, K., & Ray, G. B. (2003). Human affection exchange: IV. Vocalic predictors of perceived affection in initial interactions. *Western Journal of Communication, 67*(1), 56–73.

Gardner, K. A., & Cutrona, C. E. (2004). Social support communication in families. In A. L. Vangelisti (Ed.), *Handbook of family communication* (pp. 495–512). Mahwah, NJ: Erlbaum.

Goldsmith, D. J., McDermott, V. M., & Alexander, S. C. (2000). Helpful, supportive and sensitive: Measuring the evaluation of enacted social support in personal relationships. *Journal of Social and Personal Relationships, 17*, 369–391.

Gulledge, A. K., Gulledge, M. H., & Stahmann, R. F. (2003). Romantic physical affection types and relationship satisfaction. *American Journal of Family Therapy, 31*, 233–242.

Holmstrom, A. J., Burleson, B. R., & Jones, S. M. (2005). Some consequences for helpers who deliver "cold comfort": Why it's worse for women than men to be inept when providing emotional support. *Sex Roles: A Journal of Research, 53*(3/4), 153–172.

Holtzman, S., Newth, S., & Delongis, A. (2004). The role of social support in coping with daily pain among patients with rheumatoid arthritis. *Journal of Health Psychology, 9*(5), 677–695.

House, J. S. (1981). *Work stress and social support*. Reading, MA: Addison-Wesley.

Janevic, M. R., Janz, N. K., Dodge, J. A., Wang, Y., Lin, X., & Clark, N. M. (2004). Longitudinal effects of social support on the health and functioning of older women with heart disease. *International Journal of Aging and Human Development, 59*(2), 153–175.

Jorm, A. F., Dear, K. B. G., Rodgers, B., & Christensen, H. (2003). Interaction between mother's and father's affection as a risk factor for anxiety and depression symptoms: Evidence for increased risk in adults who rate their father as having been more affectionate than their mother. *Social Psychiatry and Psychiatric Epidemiology, 38*(4), 173–179.

Kenrick, D. T., & Luce, K. L. (2000). An evolutionary life-history model of gender differences and similarities. In T. Eckes & H. M. Trautner (Eds.), *The developmental social psychology of gender* (pp. 35–63). Mahwah, NJ: Erlbaum.

Kouneski, E. F., & Olson, D. H. (2004). A practical look at intimacy: ENRICH couple typology. In D. J. Mashek & A. Aron (Eds.), *Handbook of closeness and intimacy* (pp. 117–135). Mahwah, NJ: Erlbaum.

Lang, F. R., & Schütze, Y. (2002). Adult children's supportive behaviors and older parents' subjective well-being: A developmental perspective on intergenerational relationships. *Journal of Social Issues, 58*(4), 661–680.

Laurenceau, J.-P., Barrett, L. F., & Rovine, M. J. (2005). The interpersonal process model of intimacy in marriage: A daily-diary and multilevel modeling approach. *Journal of Family Psychology, 19*(2), 314–323.

Laurenceau, J.-P., Rivera, L. M., Schaffer, A. R., & Pietromonaco, P. R. (2004). Intimacy as an interpersonal process: Current status and future directions. In D. Mashek & A. Aron (Eds.), *Handbook of closeness and intimacy* (pp. 61–78). Mahwah, NJ: Erlbaum.

Lawton, L., Silverstein, M., & Bengston, V. (1994). Affection, social contact, and geographic distance between adult children and their parents. *Journal of Marriage and Family, 56*, 57–68.

Lytton, H., & Romney, D. M. (1991). Parents' differential socialization of boys and girls: A meta-analysis. *Psychological Bulletin, 109*, 267–296.

MacGeorge, E. L., Samter, W., & Gillihan, S. J. (2005). Academic stress, supportive communication, and health. *Communication Education, 54*(4), 365–372.

Manne, S., Ostroff, J., Sherman, M., Glassman, M., Ross, S., Goldstein, L., et al. (2003). Buffering effects of family and friend support on associations between partner unsupportive behaviors and coping among women with breast cancer. *Journal of Social and Personal Relationships, 20*(6), 771–792.

Mormon, M. T., & Floyd, K. (2002). A "changing culture of fatherhood": Effects on affectionate communication, closeness, and satisfaction in men's relationships with their fathers and their sons. *Western Journal of Communication, 66*(4), 395–411.

Mortenson, S. (2006). Cultural differences and similarities in seeking social support as a response to academic failure: A comparison of American and Chinese college students. *Communication Education, 55*(2), 127–146.

Olson, D. H. (2000). Circumplex model of marital and family systems. *Journal of Family Therapy, 22*, 144–167.

Pederson, S. S., Van Domburg, R. T., & Larsen, M. L. (2004). The effect of low social support on short-term prognosis in patients following a first myocardial infarction. *Scandinavian Journal of Psychology, 45*(4), 313–318.

Punyanunt-Carter, N. M. (2005). Father and daughter motives and satisfaction. *Communication Research Reports, 22*(4), 293–301.

Rothbaum, F., Rosen, K., Ujiie, T., & Uchida, N. (2002). Family systems theory, attachment theory, and culture. *Family Process, 41*(3), 328–350.

Russell, A. (1997). Individual and family factors contributing to mothers' and fathers' positive parenting. *International Journal of Behavioral Development, 21*(1), 111–132.

Schaefer, M. T., & Olson, D. H. (1981). Assessing intimacy: The PAIR Inventory. *Journal of Marital and Family Therapy, 7*, 47–60.

Stafford, L. (2003). Maintaining romantic relationships: A summary and analysis of one research program. In D. J. Canary & M. Dainton (Eds.), *Maintaining relationships through communication: Relational, contextual, and cultural variations* (pp. 51–78). Mahwah, NJ: Erlbaum.

Taylor, R. J., Chatters, L. M., and Jackson, J. S. (1993). A profile of familial relations among three generation Black families. *Family Relations, 42*, 332–341.

Tucker, C. J, McHale, S. M., & Crouter, A. C. (2003). Dimensions of mothers' and fathers' differential treatment of siblings: Links with adolescents' sex-typed personal qualities. *Family Relations, 52*, 82–89.

Vogl-Bauer, S. (2003). Maintaining family relationships. In D. J. Canary & M. Dainton (Eds.), *Maintaining relationships through communication: Relational, contextual, and cultural variations* (pp. 31–50). Mahwah, NJ: Erlbaum.

Wan, C. K., Jaccard, J., & Ramey, S. L. (1996). The relationship between social support and life satisfaction as a function of family structure. *Journal of Marriage and Family, 58*, 502–513.

White, L. (1999). Contagion in family affection: Mothers, fathers, and young adult children. *Journal of Marriage and Family, 61*, 284–294.

Xu, Y., & Burleson, B. R. (2004). The association of experienced spousal support with marital satisfaction: Evaluating the moderating effects of sex, ethnic culture, and type of support. *Journal of Family Communication, 4*(2), 123–145.

Section 2: Research Examples

Negotiating Intimate Family Ties in Ordinary Family Interaction

Shirley A. Staske-Bell

Intimacy is a relational creation, developed through interaction. In this work, Staske-Bell uses conversational analysis, which is a prominent methodological tool in interpersonal and family study, to look at how intimacy is negotiated in the everyday interactions of a mother and daughter. Although this example is about a particular dyad, it points to how conversations that are not explicitly about relationships can carry messages about relational factors such as intimacy. As you read, consider the last few conversations you have had with family members and what they may have "said," without necessarily ever speaking it, about your relationships.

L.B.A.

If you don't- (0.3) ↑te:ll me: (0.9) those things. . . .
the:n (0.3) ↑guess wha:t. There becomes a little stagnant
↑part in our re↑la↓tionship. (1.5) >Know wha' I mean?<

—Mother to her young adult daughter

Mommy hates you.

—Snookie, a stuffed animal, speaking *for* one adult sister, his "mommy," to her twin sister

That's all you've been saying since the day I was ↓born.

—Young adult daughter to her father

These utterances come from ordinary, naturally occurring conversations between members of three families who are at the launching stage in the family lifecycle (Fitzpatrick & Badzinski, 1994). The speakers of the utterances are involved in rather different conversational activities—a mother–daughter relationship talk, a sibling advice episode, and a heated father–daughter conflict. However, that they are talking with an intimate conversational partner is evident even without the speaker identification provided at the end of each quotation. Clearly, these interactants know their conversational partner well, they share a significant relational history, and the conversations from which these utterances were taken contribute to their ongoing negotiation of intimate relational bonds. Intimacy and distance, like other relational properties, are coconstructed by conversational partners' verbal and nonverbal actions in their ordinary, everyday interaction. It is in the doing of conversation that relational partners negotiate a power distribution of some sort (e.g., by making, confirming, and challenging claims of authority), affectionate and hostile relational ties (e.g., by using terms of endearment and insult), and intimacy and distance. The construction and reconstruction of these relational properties is an ongoing, interactional task to which close relational partners attend whenever they interact (Staske, 2002a). Although we often speak of "having" or "being in" an intimate relationship, these phrases are but a shorthand or gloss for the interactional work collaboratively accomplished by close relational partners across multiple conversations over some period of time.

This conceptualization of intimacy is fundamentally social in that it locates this relational property in the interactive communicative behavior of two (or more) people in an interpersonal encounter (see Baxter, 1998; Tracy & Haspel, 2004). As such, investigating intimate family relationships requires the close analysis of family members' everyday, naturally occurring conversations (i.e., both partners' sequentially organized conversational actions must be examined if we are to explain how they go about coconstructing intimate [or distant] relational bonds). The particular social approach taken in my investigations of interpersonal relationships begins with Conversation Analysis (CA) of close partners' ordinary interaction, and then theory and research findings from the more traditional, psychological study of interpersonal communication are utilized to explore how conversational actions work to address relational concerns (see Staske, 2002a, on this approach and Metts & Planalp, 2002, and Tracy & Haspel, 2004, for discussion of it).

Data collection for this study of family intimacy therefore began with the collection of naturally occurring conversations between family members and was accomplished with the help of students who completed my Family Communication course. The major paper assignment for that course requires students to audiotape four hours of ordinary conversation between themselves and one or more family members, transcribe four minutes of that using Jefferson's (1984) transcript notation system, and then analyze the conversation. Students are advised to tape the ordinary, everyday things families do together (e.g., eating meals, traveling, working on projects or hobbies, "catching up" since their last visit home). At the end of the course, I ask students if they want to contribute their tapes to my Conversation Analytic Family Communication database and the students who choose to do so are assured of anonymity, obtain signed research release forms from all family members on the tapes, and provide ethnographic information about their family. Thus, the mother–college-aged daughter conversation analyzed in this study was selected after listening to and analyzing hundreds of ordinary family conversations between parents or stepparents and their adult and younger children, siblings, and, sometimes, husbands and wives or extended family members.

Connecting across Miles and Milestones: Mother and Daughter Negotiating Changing Relational Boundaries

The conversation examined in this study occurred during the launching stage of the family lifecycle and Mother and adult Daughter are negotiating changes in what has been, according to Daughter, a very close mother–daughter relationship. Being an adult child and being the parent of one can be challenging as mothers, fathers, sons, and daughters reconstruct relational bonds to achieve a more equal, voluntary, adult relationship than the one they have coconstructed over two decades of shared interactional history (Staske, 2002b). Being an adult means fulfilling one's obligations as one sees fit, and constructing a more equal adult relationship requires that both relational partners acknowledge and act upon one another's rights to determine its nature and conduct. That is what is being negotiated in the conversation investigated here and, as will be seen, although sharing intimate information (including "problems") is the mother's method of maintaining intimate ties with her daughter, as an adult, the daughter has the right to decide whether and to what extent she will employ similar practices.

The conversation discussed here was audiotaped during the spring semester of 1999. Mother, Daughter, and Don, the man the mother has lived with for the last three years, are traveling home from a restaurant where they had dinner. They have stopped at a gas station, Don has exited the car, and Mother and Daughter converse during the 21 minutes before his return. According to the ethnographic data obtained from the daughter, her mother and father are separated and her mother and two younger siblings have been living with Don for the last three years while she lived with her father and attended a community college close to home. Daughter is now enrolled in her second semester at a university far enough away to require on-campus residence, and so has been home during the previous eight months only during the main college break times. Before reading the analysis to follow, please review the transcript notation conventions and mother–adult daughter conversations in the text boxes that follow. Note that, in the talk between Mother and Daughter, each conversational turn is numbered, to make following the analysis easier.

TEXT BOX 5.1 • *Transcript Notation Conventions Adapted from Jefferson's (1984) Notation System*

The purpose of transcribing conversation is to obtain a detailed description of the talk as it is actually said and heard by the interactants, so utterances are transcribed as they are heard, up to the point of unrecognizability or presumed reader confusion. Turns of talk are numbered consecutively and speakers are identified by their family relational identity (e.g., M = Mother).

[ ] Brackets mark simultaneous utterances (overlaps) at the start and end of the overlap.
= Equal sign marks contiguous utterances—no pause between turns.
(·) Micropause marks pauses, which are timed in tenths of a second—for example, a pause less than three-tenths of a second is marked (0.3)
- Hyphen marks a short, abrupt stop at the end of a word.
: Colon following a sound marks the speaker's extension of that sound.
· Period indicates a stopping fall in tone.
, Comma indicates a continuing intonation.
? Question mark indicates the rising inflection typically accompanying yes/no questions.
↑ Up arrow marks raised pitch on the syllable or word following it.
↓ Down arrow marks lowered pitch on the syllable or word following it.

underline marks stress.

CAPITALS mark the talk as louder than surrounding talk.

° ° Degree symbols enclose talk that is lower in volume than surrounding talk.

(( )) Double parentheses mark sounds where they occur (e.g., laughs).

> < Greater than and less than symbols enclose speech that is spoken at a faster rate than surrounding speech.

( ) Parenthesis mark transcriptionist uncertainty due to auditory difficulties.

. . . Ellipses indicate that part of an utterance has been left out.

TEXT BOX 5.2 • *Mother–Daughter Conversation*

M: Mother; *D*: Daughter, 21 years old; Eric, Daughter's boyfriend of six years; Aunt Wanda, her great-aunt; Dotty, her grandmother; both on her father's side of the family. The radio is playing Rock Oldies in the background throughout the conversation.

(14-second pause prior to first transcribed utterance)

1 M: Oh. (0.6) ↑I know:. There was somethin' I wanted ta tell ya.

2 D: Ye:ah.

3 M: U:m (2.4) rememer when you ↑ca:lled me:?

4 D: °(Uh huh   too)° ((laughs))

5 M: And um (1.2) I talked ta ya 'bout (2.3) u:m (3.9) you know my ↑heart.

6 D: Y:[eah.]

7 M: [(An:)] that deal. (1.6) Well (0.6) I just wanchu ta know: that- (2.1) I'm just gonna have that looked into: an (everything).

8 D: Mm hm.

9 M: An um: (2.3) but- (1.6) I din't- (0.3) tell ya tha:t (1.2) the only reason- I don't know why: I told you that. (1.3) Huh- (0.9) Just because I was ↑tal↓kin' to you. (0.5) You kno::w an (1.7) >lettin- ya kno:w everything.< (1.1) Okay? (1.3) And (0.7) the ↑po:int i:s tha:t (1.4) if you have a ↑problem at scho:ol? (3.1) or you have a- (0.9) ↑problem with Er:ic (1.1) or: some: body or some↑thing:,

10 D: ([ )]

11 M: [Tea]cher- whatever- (0.8) ya know: ah (1.0) if you don't- (0.3) ↑te:ll me: (0.9) those things,

12 D: Ye:ah?

13 M: U:m (0.5) the:n (0.3) ↑guess wha:t. There becomes a little stagnant ↑part in our re↑la↓tionship. (1.5) >Know wha' I me:an?<=

14 D: =Mm hm.=

15 M: =There becomes kind of like a: (2.4) It gets <u>wo:rse.</u> (0.7) Like. (0.6) Like I did that with Aunt Wanda?

16 D: [Yeah]

17 M: [Becau]se I ↑thou:ght (.) that- >she didn't-< (.) cause at one time she ↑sa:ys (0.5) she ↑sa:id- <u>I</u> didn't wanna ↑<u>he:ar</u> anything about- (.) what ↑Do:tty's (0.5) I didn't wanna hear ↑Dot↓ty's ↑pro↓blems cause it up<u>set</u> me too much an (besides) (0.5) yaknow: (0.5) I have hea:rt problems an this:, that, an >the other-.< (0.6) But what ↑happened wa:s, then ↑I stopped ↑talkin' to her. (1.0) About any problems? (2.3) Well you know life- (0.4) isn't a bowl of ↑cherries. (2.3) (So) if you don't discuss the ↑pro:↓blems, (1.3) well ↑<u>wha:t</u>- (0.4) you're just <u>ma:sking.</u> (0.4) >Yaknow an then:< (.) even the ↑happy part's unre:al. (1.0) °Ya understa::nd?°

          (1.5)

18 D: °Ye:ah.°

19 M: So: um: (1.1) °ya know > (tellin' to think about that, what you think about that)°<

20 D: °(Whadaya mean.)°

21 M: ↑Kinda ↑think↓ing that a liddle? (0.8) Didn't wanna ↑bo:ther ↑<u>Mo::m:.</u> (1.5) You know,=

22 D: =°No[:]°

23 M: [Sh]e has these ↑pro::blems, she's

24 D: I just wantedju ta go: an ↑<u>check</u> it.

25 M: Okay:. (0.6) We:ll (0.4) I have an appointment, twenty ninth, (to check it). (0.5) Ka:y?

26 D: Cool.

27 M: °>Okay.<°

28 D: °(I don't have a) problem.°

29 M: °But- I <u>do</u> wantcha to tell ↑me:. (.) I don't care: if it's twelveaclock at night. (1.3) Ya can't ↓sleep.

30 D: M↓mm.

31 M: You have a ↑pro:↓blem. (2.2) You know, you can ↑ca:ll me. (4.1) You: are my ↑<u>daughter</u>.

32 D: I ↑<u>kno:w</u>: I am- (0.3) I haven't- (0.6) °(well)° (0.5) [thought different.]

33 M: [(You don't-)] If you: like- (0.9) if you feel like crying all night, 'er somethin'. (0.5) I mean (0.8) ↑why: would you feel like °crying all night.° We:ll, (.) I don't know, we can ↑TALK ↑ABOUT ↑I:T. Yaknow I might not be able ta (1.7) ↑<u>SOLVE</u> your ↑<u>PRO</u>:↓blems. (0.5) 'Er whatever:, (.) or: whatever but- (.) yaknow, (.) jus' talkin' about it's ↓great. (1.6) Oka:y:? (4.5)

34 D: °(Yeah)°

          (36-second pause during which a new song, "Little Diana," comes on the radio)

Twenty-one Minutes of Mother–Daughter Time

Transcribing the entire 21-minute episode made it possible to locate the relationship talk contained in turns 1–34 in the real time of Mother–Daughter interaction. Turn 1 begins 5 minutes and 15 seconds after Don exited the car and, during this time, Mother and Daughter have engaged in three very brief exchanges of talk. The transcribed conversation is not the first topic discussed in the 21-minute episode nor is it the last because Daughter's turn 34, which closes this topic, is followed by a 36-second pause and then the introduction of a new topic about the song playing on the radio. Thus, this mother–daughter relationship talk is clearly demarcated from their other talk. It is preceded and followed by unrelated topics and by extended (many seconds or minutes) pauses. It is also unlike the prior and subsequent topics in that it is fully developed and both Mother and Daughter make multiple contributions to it.

As the transcript also makes evident, Mother not only initiates this topic, her contributions to it are longer and more substantive than Daughter's. Seven of Daughter's 17 turns consist solely of acknowledgment tokens (*Yeah, Mm hmm, Mmm*) and only two (turns 4 and 32) of her other 10 contain more than one conversational action. This is the case despite (1) the many pauses within Mother's turns that provide an opportunity for Daughter to respond; (2) three turns (9, 17, and 21) Mother makes with questions within them; and (3) the six turns (3, 13, 15, 17, 25, 33) Mother completes with questions or question intonation that overtly solicit a response from her daughter. Mother does much more of the interactional "work" (Fishman, 1983) of this conversation—initiating topic, elaborating topic, directly and indirectly soliciting Daughter's response—and although Daughter does participate in the conversation in important ways, development of the mother-initiated topic is largely dependent upon Mother's conversational actions. At any rate, afforded a 21-minute unplanned (but perhaps not unforeseen) opportunity for private, two-party talk, Mother and Daughter close out talk about the dinner they shared with Don, mark their immediate shared context with talk about that context (gas station activities, radio content), and, after another extended pause, make entry into what will become a 3-minute, 17-second conversation about the vitality and intimacy of their relationship. Importantly, addressing concerns about intimacy in this particular interactional space works, in part, to redress them because private, two-party talk about closeness in a relationship can be taken to be evidence of closeness in that relationship.

Mother begins turn 1 with "Oh." which, as Heritage (1984) demonstrates, marks a change in the speaker's state of knowledge or awareness—in this case, a remembrance of "somethin'" Mother wanted to tell her daughter. After a short pause this is followed with "↑I know:.", a claim of existing knowledge that is routinely employed as a responsive action, often to a prior speaker's informing, assessment, or offering of advice (Gornick, 2004). This claim, however, is clearly not a response to prior talk because it follows an extended pause in interaction. Although arguable, this "↑I know:." can be seen to mark Mother's orientation to an interactional difficulty that her upcoming utterance will remedy. Recall that Mother and Daughter have been alone in the car now for more than 5 minutes and they have engaged in only brief exchanges of talk about matters that neither acted to elaborate in any depth. Fishman (1983) has demonstrated that "making conversation" can be problematic because for an initiated topic to become a topic of conversation, one's partner must provide uptake on it and the brief exchanges preceding and following this conversation suggest that uptake alone may not be enough. Without multiple contributions by both interactional partners, a proffered topic can be quickly exhausted and when interactants remain in one another's presence following such an eventuality, they confront what can be a problematic pause in activities (i.e., an "awkward silence," until a new topic is located). The Mother's "Oh. (0.6) ↑I know:." can, therefore, be seen to mark both her remembrance of "somethin'" she wanted to tell her daughter and the locating of a topic that is likely to enjoy full development and so resolve the problematic silence preceding it. This analysis is supported by the finding by Duck, Rutt, Hurst, and Strejc (1991) that the mere presence of talk, regardless of content, is taken by relational partners as a sign of the healthy continuation of their relationship. The Mother has, then, with the first three words of her first utterance marked both the lack of conversation with Daughter as problematic and, with the higher pitch on "I," underscored her part in resolving the difficulty.

The third item in Mother's first turn, "There was somethin' I wanted ta tell ya," is a "pre"—the first in a sequence of utterances that project a future action, an announcement in this case, by the speaker of the "pre" (Levinson, 1983; Terasaki, 1976). The standard, full pre-announcement format consists of four positions that are often, not always, performed in four consecutive turns where turns 1 and 3 are performed by the initiator of the sequence and turns 2 and 4 are performed by the other speaker; for example, A: "Guess what."; B: "What."; A: "I got the job."; B: "Terrific." Position 1 turns prefigure the action to be performed in position 3 by serving notice to the hearer of the upcoming action and checking the hearer's ability or willingness to respond to that action. Position 2 in the standard format is slotted for the second speaker to provide either a "go-ahead" (i.e., perform the action) or to discourage performance of the action. Daughter's turn 2, "Ye:ah," is a go-ahead, whereas discouragements (or outright blocks) would include utterances like "Wait a minute, I can't hear," or "I don't wanna hear about it." Position 2, then, fully involves the second speaker in his or her partner's projected action: "Forewarned is forearmed"; and if speaker B is disinclined to participate in the action speaker A has projected, he or she has, in position 2, the opportunity to decline to do so.

Thus, "There was somethin' I wanted ta tell ya" projects the telling of a particular but as yet unspecified item and, prefaced as it is with the change-of-state token ("Oh") and the locating of a topic to repair the most recent silence, Mother projects an announcement of some import. It is important to note that the format of this first turn significantly influences conversational development. Mother could have told Daughter the things she eventually does tell her and made the request she eventually does make of her by simply continuing her talk in turn 1 with these actions; for example, she could have said, "I'm concerned because you haven't been talking to me about your problems and I'm asking you to tell me about what's going on in your life." Such an utterance is clear and efficient; however, it also places tighter constraints on Daughter's response. That is, a direct request creates an immediate and expectable "slot" for a grant or refusal of the request (see Sacks, Schegloff, & Jefferson, 1978). Consequently, Daughter's alignment on this issue, or lack thereof, would be quite visible. Moreover, Daughter's response to this kind of utterance would not provide for her collaboration in the upcoming action in the way that the position 2, go-ahead slot of a preannouncement sequence does. Mother's "Oh. (0.6) ↑I know:. There was somethin' I wanted ta tell ya." therefore not only serves to mark her solution to the problematic silence Mother and Daughter have experienced, but it also makes the achievement of that solution a shared activity. Importantly, then, despite Daughter's clear go-ahead in turn 2, in neither of the mother's next *two* turns does she offer the announcement she prefigured (i.e., turns 3 and 5 are done in question and quasi-question form and they concern additional background information about the "somethin'" rather than the "somethin'" itself). Both also receive go aheads from Daughter. Consequently, in six turns and a few seconds of mother–daughter time, barring recourse to direct refusals to engage (e.g., "I don't want to talk about it") the daughter in this conversation has collaborated in the construction of a conversation about a topic whose nature is not yet clear and which her mother has prefigured as relationally important and troublesome.

Turn 7 is, therefore, an ideal location for delivery of the announcement because mutual tracking of the conversation has been established with the go-aheads in turns 4 and 6 (i.e., Daughter does recall the phone call Mother is referencing and she does recall the discussion about her mother's heart problem). The announcement projected in turn 1 could, then, be delivered here and Mother does report in this turn her intention to have her heart problem "looked into." However, if this report is the announcement, the construction of the turn makes recognizing it as such problematic. The turn begins with And-Prefacing (Heritage & Sorjonen, 1994)—"(An:) that deal."—and it interrupts Daughter's third go-ahead. It's constructed, then, as a continuation of Mother's turn 5 (she's still backgrounding) and the report of her intention to have her heart problem "looked into:" is positioned at the end of the turn after three short pauses, a "Well," and the beginning of an utterance that is aborted ("I just wanchu ta know: that-"). Consequently, although this report could be the announcement Mother projected in turn 1, it may not be that and Daughter's "Mm hm." in turn 8 treats it accordingly ("Mm hm" is routinely used as a "continuer" which acknowledges and invites continuation of the prior speaker's talk [see Schegloff, 1982], unlike a news receipt [Maynard, 1997], which receipts the news and may comment on it, such as "Oh" or "That's good.")

Like her two prior turns, Mother begins turn 9 with And-Prefacing, so Mother and Daughter have now coconstructed turn 7 as not the "somethin'" Mother wanted to tell her daughter. This "An" is followed, after a short pause, with a stressed "but-" and the account that follows is interesting in multiple respects. First, it is an unsolicited account of Mother's reasons for discussing her heart problem with her daughter which is (again) located in an interactional space where the important and troublesome announcement could be told. Second, the account follows (1) multiple brief pauses; (2) two clear restarts following the "but-" which concern something that was not the reason she discussed the heart problem with her daughter; (3) a claim of insufficient knowledge (Beach & Metzger, 1997) about her own actual motivation; and (4) the very interesting "Huh-" that, as a responsive action, appears to mark Mother's "just found" discovery of that which actually did motivate her disclosure. Finally, this account of Mother's reasons for discussing her heart problem with her daughter—"Just because I was ↑tal↓kin' to you. (0.5) You kno::w an (1.7) >let-tin- ya kno:w everything.<"—references the phone call previously mentioned such that it can be seen and treated as an instance where Mother disclosed (">lettin- ya kno:w") or "shared" her concerns about her heart problem with her daughter. This is important because, as it turns out, it is this kind of mother—daughter interaction that becomes the primary topic for the remainder of this conversation.

The rest of turn 9 and Mother's next four turns are devoted to the explication of a theory, of sorts, about intimacy and distance in family relationships. Mother's "And (0.7) the ↑po:int i:s tha:t" is heavily marked (note the sound extensions, pitch change, and stress) and it directly claims that the upcoming utterance is what her prior turns have been "leading up to," so the delayed announcement appears about to be delivered. This is followed by a series of utterances, completed in Mother's turn 13, which are constructed as an "if-then" narrative that outlines multiple potential problems Daughter could be having and might not be telling her mother about. Importantly, the daughter does not receipt Mother's explanation, which creates the one and a half second pause that follows the "then" part of the narrative (i.e., "There becomes a little <u>stag</u>nant ↑part in our re↑la↓tionship.") In fact, Daughter provides no uptake at all until Mother directly solicits a response by asking ">Know wha' I me:an?<."

Daughter's "Mmhm" in turn 14 acknowledges understanding of her mother's explanation without taking a position (agreement or disagreement) on it and this is responded to by Mother with renewed efforts to explain and support her theory of intimacy. She begins, in turn 15, with an emotion narrative (a narrative where a character's emotional experience is the point of the telling—Staske, 1994, 1998) that is completed in turn 17. This narrative illustrates the intimacy theory outlined in turns 9–13, supports the account Mother offered for telling Daughter her concerns about her heart, and it legitimates that telling. The gist of the story is that Mother once "stopped ↑talkin'" to her sister-in-law about the problems in her life and, as a result, they lost genuine closeness in their relationship (they were "just <u>ma:king</u>" and even the happy times became "unre:al"). Goodwin (1993) has described young girls' tactical use of stories as "a preliminary stage" (p. 129) in the accomplishment of larger conversational activities and this story appears to function similarly in that it sets the stage for Mother's upcoming request (the larger action) that her daughter talk to her about her problems.

As in the previous set of mother—daughter turns, Daughter does not respond to the story and so Mother again directly solicits a response with "°Ya understa::nd?°" which, after another significant pause, Daughter affirms with "°Ye:ah.°" Goodwin (1993) notes that in conflict interactions between young girls, taking up alignments to story characters' actions can be "interpreted as commitments to undertake future action for which parties may be held responsible by others" (p. 127). Daughter's turn 18 can, then, also be seen as tactical: "°Ye:ah.°" claims understanding of the distance created when her mother and Aunt Wanda stopped talking about problems, but it does not take up an alignment to their actions and so does not commit Daughter to sharing her own problems with her mother. Mother's turn 19 is not entirely recoverable; however, it appears to be the first open-ended (as opposed to yes/no questions) solicitation of her daughter's response made in this conversation, so, Daughter is free to address Mother's prior talk as she sees fit. It's interesting then that her response "Whadaya mean." is a clarification question and repair initiator (Schegloff, 1992) which work to narrow her options for appropriate response. In turn 21, Mother responds accordingly by offering a candidate answer (Pomerantz, 1988) to her own query which is immediately (note the equal sign) disconfirmed by Daughter first with "°No:°" (i.e., she was not avoiding discussing her problems with her mother because of the heart problem), and then with a statement asserting what she did think about that (i.e., she wanted her mother to go and "↑check it").

This is important in that it redirects the conversation to what should be done about that problem rather than following the topic Mother identified as "the ↑poi:nt" of this conversation and the one she asked about (i.e., Daughter telling her mother about her problems). Mother's turn 25 aligns with the topic shift (with the "Okay") and then continues with an utterance that is unambiguously an announcement of news: She has made an appointment on the twenty-ninth to have her heart problem "checked." This is met with a pause, so Mother (again) solicits Daughter's response with "Ka:y?" whereupon the daughter issues a clear and positive news receipt: "Cool." Mother's following "Okay" completes the news report and, perhaps, the presequence with which Mother initiated this conversation.

Daughter's "(I don't have a) problem." in turn 28 is, again, ambiguous due to auditory difficulties for me but apparently not the interactants, and it apparently claims a current lack of problems in Daughter's life. Mother does not address this seemingly positive state of affairs in turns 29 and the continuing 31 and, instead, requests her daughter to tell her about her problems ("I do wantcha to tell ↑me:.") and offers to hear them regardless of sleep needs and distance ("You know, you can ↑ca:ll me"). The pause following this utterance is important because it's long (4.1 seconds is much longer than the typical few tenths of a second gap between speakers' turns) and because it follows an offer; thus, it constitutes the slot for Daughter's acceptance or declination of that offer. Mother herself ends this long pause with an utterance that deserves more analysis than can be here provided: "You are my ↑daughter." is interesting in many respects. First, it violates a conversational rule that one not tell one's partner things one has reason to believe he or she already knows. Clearly, Daughter already knows she is her mother's daughter and the relevance of those identities has been referenced in prior talk—see, especially, turns 13 and 21—and so informing or reminding are not good explanations of the work the utterance accomplishes.

"You are my ↑daughter." is located in this conversation after (1) Mother's discussion of intimacy and the role that talking about problems plays in maintaining it, (2) her request that Daughter tell her about her problems, and (3) her offer to talk about such problems even in the middle of the night (i.e., "I don't care: if it's twelveaclock at night."). Importantly, Daughter has not taken up any kind of alignment to any of these actions. The heavily stressed "You are my ↑daughter." underscores the importance of this relationship in Mother's life and, located after Mother's report of her concerns, her request, and her offer, it works to summarize these actions such that Mother's relationship with her daughter can be seen as one where, despite time, geographical distance, and significant changes in family life, Mother remains ever-available and talking about Daughter's problems is not only acceptable, but it is expected and desired.

Daughter's response to this utterance is her longest in the entire conversation; it contains the most substance (two complete actions—"I ↑know." and "I haven't- (0.6) °well° (0.5) [thought different.]"), and it was not overtly solicited by a question. It is, then, unlike nearly all of her prior utterances and constitutes an unqualified agreement—daughter claims existing knowledge of her mother's ongoing interest in her life and reports not having thought otherwise. Mother overlaps the last part of the utterance to, again, restate her willingness and desire to talk about her daughter's problems even if she cannot solve them. And, again, given no immediate uptake, she issues a question to which, after another significant pause, Daughter apparently responds with another acknowledging "°(Yeah)°." This mother–daughter relationship talk is then jointly terminated with the 36-second pause that follows and the introduction of an unrelated topic, derived from the new song playing on the radio.

Discussion

The findings of this study demonstrate that explaining the construction, maintenance, and change in relational processes over the many years of the family lifecycle requires examination of the conversational practices family members employ in the natural interactional settings that constitute family life. That is where and how family relationships and the relational identities appropriate to them are made, negotiated, and renegotiated. Mother's use of the conventional presequence format and her delay of the announcement projected by that action made it possible for her to develop a "theory" of intimacy in family relationships and to tell an emotion narrative that legitimated the disclosure of her problem to her daughter and supported the request she eventually makes that her daughter reciprocate such disclosures. The presequence, repeated pauses within turns, and overt requests for response, actively solicited Daughter's involvement in the relationship talk and, thus in the coconstruction of their changing relational boundaries. Daughter's repeated use of continuers and acknowledgment tokens made it possible for her to claim understanding of her mother's concerns and desires without committing herself to as yet unperformed and, perhaps, undecided future actions.

Sharing intimate information (including "problems") is one index of an intimate relationship, but it is only one and it is not an unproblematic one (Bochner, 1982). Consequently, the relatively indirect and preliminary conversational practices employed here are a good fit for the emerging and ongoing (it's not a done deal) relational changes that mother and daughter are addressing in this launching stage conversation. As the parent in this conversation, one could hardly lay claim to having settled an important relational problem and, as the adult daughter, one could hardly consider the matter one that will not come up again. Mother did tell her daughter some things she was concerned about and she did make a request of and offer to her daughter. Daughter did listen to and claim understanding of her mother's talk; however, plans and promises regarding future action on this issue were not proffered and they were not interactionally pursued. Clearly, passing up a 21-minute opportunity to address and perhaps redress a problematic distance between mother and daughter would count as a lost opportunity; at the same time, "pushing too hard" in that 21 minutes would compromise, rather than facilitate, the achievement of intimacy between this mother and her adult daughter. Hence, the presequence, pauses, and soliciting questions; stories and theories about family relationships and continuers; withholding uptake; and claims of understanding but not agreement can be seen as useful conversational resources in the ongoing negotiation of intimate ties in a more equal, voluntary, adult relationship between this mother and the young woman who is, as they both affirm, her "↑daughter."

Questions for Consideration and Discussion

1. Staske-Bell's work presented here is based on the idea that intimacy is primarily created and negotiated in everyday conversation. What other relational factors are created or negotiated in the same way?
2. This analysis focuses on a mother–daughter pair, where the daughter is in college. Why does the shift from high school to college tend to call for a renegotiation of intimacy? What examples of this renegotiation can you see in your own relationships?
3. In addition to the shift from an adult/child to an adult/adult relationship, what other life changes might call for a renegotiation of intimacy in the parent–child relationship? How so?
4. What are the advantages of studying intimacy through an examination of everyday talk?
5. Conversational analysis considers not only the verbal element of conversation, but also the nonverbal vocal elements, such as pauses and vocal inflection. What do you see as the benefits and drawbacks of this approach?

References

Baxter, L. A. (1998). Locating the social in interpersonal communication. In J. Trent (Ed.), *Communication: Views from the helm* (pp. 60–64). Boston: Allyn & Bacon.

Beach, W., & Metzger, T. (1997). Claiming insufficient knowledge. *Human Communication Research, 23,* 562–588.

Bochner, A. (1982). On the efficacy of openness in close relationships. In M. Burgoon (Ed.), *Communication yearbook* (Vol. 5, pp. 109–124). New Brunswick, NJ: Transaction Press.

Duck, S., Rutt, D., Hurst, M., & Strejc, H. (1991). Some evident truths about conversation in everyday relationships: All communications are not created equal. *Human Communication Research, 18,* 228–267.

Fishman, P. (1983). Interaction: The work women do. In B. Thorne, C. Kramarae, & N. Henley (Eds.), *Language, gender, and society* (pp. 89–101). Rowley, MA: Newbury House.

Fitzpatrick, M. A., & Badzinski, D. M. (1994). All in the family: Interpersonal communication in kin relationships. In M. L. Knapp & G. R. Miller (Eds.), *Handbook of interpersonal communication* (2nd ed. pp. 726–771). Thousand Oaks, CA: Sage.

Goodwin, M. (1993). Tactical uses of stories: Participation frameworks within girls' and boys' disputes. In D. Tannen (Ed.), *Gender and conversational interaction* (pp. 110–143.). New York: Oxford University Press.

Gornick, M. (2005). *Sibling interaction: Sisters' use of advice episodes in the construction of relational identities.* Unpublished master's thesis, Eastern Illinois University, Charleston, IL.

Heritage, J. (1984). A change-of-state token and aspects of its sequential placement. In J. Atkinson & J. Heritage (Eds.), *Structures of social action* (pp. 1–16). Cambridge, England: Cambridge University Press.

Heritage, J., & Sorjonen, M.-L. (1994). Constituting and maintaining activities across sequences: *And*-prefacing as a feature of question design. *Language in Society, 23,* 1–29.

Jefferson, G. (1984). Transcript notation. In J. Atkinson & J. Heritage (Eds.), *Structures of social action* (pp. ix–xvi). Cambridge, England: Cambridge University Press.

Levinson, S. (1983). *Pragmatics.* Cambridge, England: Cambridge University Press.

Maynard, D. W. (1997). The news delivery sequence: Bad news and good news in conversational interaction. *Research on Language and Social Interaction, 30*(2), 93–130.

Metts, S., & Planalp, S. (2002). Emotional communication. In M. L. Knapp & J. A. Daly (Eds.), *Handbook of interpersonal communication* (3rd ed., pp. 339–373). Thousand Oaks, CA: Sage.

Pomerantz, A. (1988). Offering a candidate answer: An information seeking strategy. *Communication Monographs, 55,* 360–373.

Sacks, H., Schegloff, E., & Jefferson, G. (1978). A simplest systematics for the organization of turn taking for conversation. In J. Schenkein (Ed.), *Studies in the organization of conversational interaction* (pp. 7–55). New York: Academic Press.

Schegloff, E. (1982). Discourse as an interactional achievement: Some uses of "uh huh" and other things that come between sentences. In D. Tannen (Ed.),

Analyzing discourse: Text and talk (pp. 71–93). Washington, DC: Georgetown University Press.

Schegloff, E. (1992). Repair after next turn: The last structurally provided defense of intersubjectivity in conversation. *American Journal of Sociology, 97,* 1295–1345.

Staske, S. (1994). *The instantiation of emotion in conversations between romantic partners, male friends, female friends, and cross-sex friends.* Unpublished doctoral dissertation, University of Illinois at Urbana–Champaign, Department of Speech Communication.

Staske, S. (1998). The normalization of problematic emotion in conversations between close relational partners: *Inter*personal emotion work. *Symbolic Interaction, 21,* 59–86.

Staske, S. (2002a). Claiming individualized knowledge of a conversational partner. *Research on Language and Social Interaction, 35*(3), 245–276.

Staske, S. A. (2002b). *Multi-party "family conflict": Now, again, and (ever?) after.* Paper presented at the annual meeting of the National Communication Association, Atlanta, GA.

Terasaki, A. (1976). *Pre-announcement sequences in conversation* (Social Science Working Paper No. 99). Irvine: School of Social Science, University of California.

Tracy, K., Haspel, K. (2004). Language and social interaction: Its institutional identity, intellectual landscape, and discipline-shifting agenda. *Journal of Communication, 54*(4), 788–816.

Sex and Gender in Relational Maintenance

Marianne Dainton

As discussed in the Section 1, research has indicated that there are sex or gender effects at work in how intimacy, affection, and social support are expressed, and those sex/gender effects are thought primarily to be cultural, though some theorists also argue a biological cause. In this article, Dainton looks at relational maintenance behaviors, communicative practices that help increase feelings of affection, intimacy, and satisfaction, and the gender/sex influence on those behaviors. Consider your own relational maintenance behaviors while reading, and the extent to which they do, or do not, fit with Dainton's findings.

L.B.A.

In the 1990s, for every two marriages in the United States one ended in divorce (Hughes, 2004). In fact, 40% of people born in the 1970s can expect to get divorced during their life span (Hughes, 2004). Given the high divorce rate in the United States, it is surprising that relatively little research centers on answering the question of which communication strategies work to keep relationships together. The research spotlighted in this chapter focuses specifically on relationship maintenance, which is defined as communicative efforts to keep a relationship satisfactory (Dindia & Canary, 1993).

A series of research studies has identified seven behaviors that people use to maintain a satisfying relationship (Stafford & Canary, 1991; Stafford, Dainton, & Haas, 2000). The techniques include *openness*, which means self-disclosure and direct discussions of the relationship (e.g., "I tell my partner what I want or need from the relationship"); *assurances*, which refer to verbal and nonverbal reassurances of commitment to the relationship and to the partner ("I say I love you"); *positivity*, which means being optimistic and pleasant ("I am cheerful and positive around him or her"); *social networks*, which means relying on common friends and family members for support ("I spend time with our same friends"); *shared tasks*, which means engaging in housework, child care, and other joint responsibilities ("I do my fair share of the work we have to do"); *conflict management*, which includes proactive and positive ways to resolve conflict ("I apologize when I am wrong"); and *advice*, which means counseling the partner ("I give him/her my opinion about things going on in his life").

Research indicates that these techniques are consistent and strong predictors of relationship satisfaction, commitment, love, and liking (e.g., Dainton, Stafford, & Canary, 1994; Stafford & Canary, 1991). Positivity and assurances seem to be of particular importance in relationship maintenance, as they are more strongly related to satisfaction, commitment, and love than other strategies. Surprisingly, openness does not seem to be very important; in virtually every study using these seven maintenance strategies, openness is a negative predictor of satisfaction, meaning the more open you are, the less satisfied you are with your relationship (e.g., Dainton, 2000). Of course, there are many reasons for this, including the possibility that people are more likely to talk about the relationship when they are unhappy. Nevertheless, the importance placed on self-disclosure in the popular press might be overstated.

The two studies reported in this chapter focus on why people choose particular maintenance techniques. Previous research has focused on sex differences as the explanation for the type and amount of maintenance activity performed. Results are fairly consistent, with women performing more maintenance than men (e.g., Canary & Stafford, 1992; Dainton & Stafford, 1993; Ragsdale, 1996). The fact that women use more maintenance strategies than men is probably not surprising to you. However, the issue is a fairly complex one that taps into the classic "nature versus nurture" debate. Do women perform more maintenance because they are biologically programmed to do so? Or are the differences based on the way that people are raised to behave?

The first study reported in this chapter asks whether the differences are really based on biology (e.g., sex differences) or whether differences are based on gender role (e.g., differences due to the way people are raised). Note that although the terms *sex* and *gender* are often used interchangeably, scholars have precise meanings for the terms. As alluded to previously, sex is biological (male vs. female) and gender is the way people are raised to behave (masculine vs. feminine).

Popular treatment of the topic emphasizes a biological explanation (Gray's 1992 book argues that men are from Mars and women are from Venus), treating men and women as different species. However, a growing body of scholarly research seems to indicate that biology alone explains very little about why people communicate in particular ways (Canary & Hause, 1993). The researchers in the following study hypothesized that femininity would be a stronger predictor of the frequency of using maintenance behavior than would be masculinity or biological sex.

Study One

Stafford and colleagues (2000) had 520 married people fill out a survey that asked them how frequently they performed the seven maintenance behaviors described earlier in this article. Each of the measurement scales was reliable as assessed by Chronbach's alpha. Reliability means the consistency of the measurement. If a measurement is not reliable, you should not trust the results of the study. Chronbach's alpha is a particular statistical tool that assesses reliability. Scores range between 0 (meaning no consistency) and 1.0 (meaning perfect consistency). In general, researchers look for a reliability score between .70 and 1.0. Think of these numbers as percentages on an exam—typically you want to score above 70%, and the closer to 100% you get the happier you will be. In this study, the lowest reliability score was for advice, with .70, and the highest was for assurances, with .92.

In addition to filling out the maintenance measures, the participants also filled out Bem's (1974) Sex-Role Inventory (SRI), which measures gender (masculinity and femininity). The SRI asks people to assess their own personality characteristics on a Likert-type scale (with 1 = never true and 7 = always true). For example, personality characteristics that are used to measure masculinity include *independent*, *ambitious*, and *competitive*. Personality characteristics that are used to measure femininity include *affectionate*, *sensitive*, and *sin-*

cere. Note that all people filling out the survey receive both a masculinity score and a femininity score. The average masculinity score (regardless of sex) was 5.75 on the seven-point scale, and the average femininity score (regardless of sex) was 5.70 on that scale.

To determine whether males were more likely to have higher masculinity scores and females were more likely to have higher femininity scores, the researchers ran a point biserial correlation between sex and gender. A point biserial correlation is a statistical technique that is used to determine the strength of the relationship between two variables. A correlation of 0 would indicate absolutely no relationship between the two variables (meaning that being female bears no relationship to being feminine). A correlation of 1.0 would indicate a perfect relationship between the two variables (meaning that being female and being feminine are exactly the same thing). In this study the correlation was .13, which indicates a relatively small relationship between sex and gender; men were not necessarily masculine and women were not necessarily feminine.

The major purpose of this study was to find out the relative importance of sex and gender in relationship maintenance. Do people perform more or less maintenance because of biology (sex), or do they perform more or less maintenance because of the way they are raised (gender), or is it some combination of the two? To answer these questions, the researchers ran a series of multiple regression equations. Multiple regression is a statistical technique that allows a researcher to use a set of variables to predict another variable. For example, college admissions officers use things like high school class rank, high school grade point average, and SAT scores to predict the likelihood of success in college. In this study, the researchers ran seven different equations, each predicting a different maintenance technique. The variables used to make the predictions were sex (male or female) and gender (masculinity and femininity). Results are reported in Table 5.3, p. 176.

To understand these results, look at the numbers for each of the maintenance strategies. Two statistics help us answer the research questions: *beta* and *adjusted R^2*. The beta score indicates how important a variable is relative to other variables in that same equation—the bigger the number the more important it is for the prediction (whether the score is positive or negative doesn't matter in terms of importance). If you look at assurances, femininity got a .46 and masculinity got a .14. That indicates that femininity is a stronger predictor of assurances than masculinity—feminine people are more likely to use assurances than masculine people. The beta for sex is zero, which means that the sex of the person (whether they are male or female) isn't important at all in determining if a person is going to use assurances or not.

Adjusted R^2 indicates how strong the prediction is overall. Once again, scores range from 0 to 1.0, with 1.0 being a perfect prediction. Low scores mean that it is something other than sex and gender that predicts maintenance enactment, and higher scores indicate that sex and gender provide a lot of information when predicting maintenance enactment. In this study, the strongest prediction is for conflict management, with an adjusted R^2 of .33. This means that knowing someone is feminine gives you about 33% of the information you need to predict exactly how much conflict management a person will use. The weakest prediction is for social networks; in this case, knowing someone is feminine explains only 8% of the information you need to predict how much the person will rely on social networks.

The most important thing for you to understand related to these results is the overall pattern. As the researchers hypothesized, femininity was the best predictor for every equation. That means that people high in femininity are most likely to use all seven of the

TABLE 5.3 *Results of Regression of Sex and Gender on Each Maintenance Behavior*

Advice	Assurances	Conflict Management
Feminine beta = .26 Masculine beta = .26 Sex beta = .00 *Adjusted R² = .13*	Feminine beta = .46 Masculine beta = .14 Sex beta = .00 *Adjusted R² = .24*	Feminine beta = .58 Masculine beta = .00 Sex beta = .00 *Adjusted R² = .33*

Networks

Feminine beta = .28
Masculine beta = .00
Sex beta = .00

Adjusted R² = .08

Openness	Positivity	Tasks
Feminine beta = .46 Masculine beta = .17 Sex beta = −.18 *Adjusted R² = .23*	Feminine beta = .37 Masculine beta = .20 Sex beta = .00 *Adjusted R² = .17*	Feminine beta = .23 Masculine beta = .00 Sex beta = −.22 *Adjusted R² = .11*

relationship maintenance behaviors (and therefore have a more satisfying marriage). This isn't surprising, because femininity is defined as being sensitive and affectionate. Being masculine was a less powerful predictor, but also appeared in several of the equations. Accordingly, things like independence and assertiveness also facilitate maintenance activities (especially giving advice and being positive).

Biological sex appeared in only two of the equations, however. This means that sex is relatively unimportant in predicting the use of relational maintenance communication. In both cases where sex appeared in the equation, being female predicted the use of the maintenance behavior. Earlier I indicated that whether the beta score was positive or negative didn't matter for importance; it is important for what is known as "dummy coding." Because sex is a single variable with two possible responses (male or female), the statistical procedures require you to mathematically indicate being male or female. In this study, being female was a negative score and being male was a positive score. The fact that the beta scores were negative both times that sex appeared indicates that the prediction is for women. It seems that being a female makes you slightly more likely to pursue open discussions about the relationship, and also makes you slightly more likely to do household chores. However, when looking at the betas, sex is not as important as gender in predicting these behaviors. And, recall that sex appears in only two of the seven predictions, meaning that it is not very important overall in predicting maintenance communication.

The results of Stafford and colleagues' (2000) study have profound implications for stereotypes about who does what in marriage. The results indicate that relationship maintenance is not biologically driven; women are not "programmed" to use more maintenance than men, it is a learned behavior. Despite Gray's assertions, men are not from Mars and women are not from Venus. As such, advice for married people should shift from a focus on what men can or should do and what women can or should do, and instead should focus on how developing feminine qualities—regardless of whether you are a man or a woman—can enhance marital success.

The notion that both gender roles and relationship maintenance can be learned leads to a second study linking sex, gender, and relationship maintenance. One of the central controversies in maintenance research is the extent to which maintenance is performed strategically versus routinely. According to Dainton and Stafford (1993), strategic maintenance refers to behaviors performed at a high level of consciousness, and for the explicit purpose of relationship maintenance. Routine maintenance refers to behaviors performed at a low level of consciousness (perhaps because they are overlearned), and without the specific intention of relationship maintenance (i.e., the married person does not think "I should do this for the sake of my marriage"). Dainton and Aylor (2002) found that both strategic and routine maintenance are important for relationship satisfaction, but that routine maintenance is slightly more important.

At issue is whether there are sex or gender variations in the extent to which maintenance is performed strategically or routinely, and what such variations might mean. Aylor and Dainton (2004) asked three research questions:

RQ1: Are there sex differences in the use of strategic and routine maintenance behaviors?

RQ2: Are there gender differences in the use of strategic and routine maintenance behaviors?

RQ3: Is biological sex or psychological gender a better predictor of routine and strategic maintenance?

Study Two

Aylor and Dainton (2004) collected survey data from 189 individuals in romantic relationships. The measurements were exactly the same as those described under study one, and the Chronbach alpha scores were all above .80, indicating the measurements are reliable. In this study, participants filled out the maintenance questions twice. First, they reported how frequently they had used each behavior strategically during the past two weeks, and then they reported how frequently they had used each behavior routinely during the past two weeks.

The first research question, which asked about sex differences in the use of routine and strategic maintenance, was assessed using a statistical technique known as multivariate analysis of variance, or MANOVA. This tool allows you to calculate the average scores for groups (males and females) and determine the likelihood that differences between the groups are due to chance, or whether they reflect real ("significant") differences. The result of the MANOVA indicated only one sex difference; women reported using openness more routinely than did men. Notice that this result supports and builds upon the results of study one, which found that one of the few sex differences in maintenance is related to openness. Aylor and Dainton's (2004) findings indicate that the difference between men and women when it comes to self-disclosure is not one of conscious intent, but that self-disclosure seems to be a part of women's interaction routines, whereas it doesn't seem to be a part of men's interaction routines.

The second research question asked about gender differences in routine and strategic maintenance. This requires a different statistical test because there are no groups to compare—every individual has both a masculinity and a femininity score. In this case, a multivariate multiple regression (MMR) was used. The MMR combines multiple regression, which was described in study one, and MANOVA, described previously. Two MMRs were run, one for routine maintenance and the other for strategic maintenance.

The first analysis found that femininity was significantly related to routine maintenance; feminine individuals were more likely than masculine individuals to use openness, positive conflict management, and advice as part of their interaction routines. The second analysis found that masculinity was significantly related to strategic maintenance; masculine individuals were more likely than feminine individuals to strategically use openness and tasks to maintain their relationship.

Aylor and Dainton's (2004) final research question asked whether sex or gender was more important when considering routine and strategic maintenance. Because there was only one sex difference found in this study, the clear answer is that gender is more important than sex. More important, the results of this study indicate that masculine people perform maintenance strategically and feminine people perform maintenance routinely.

The results are consistent with explanations of gender that suggest that masculine individuals tend to be more task-oriented when confronted by problems—they recognize a problem and then consciously decide on a course of action to "fix" the problem (Huston & Houts, 1998). Such an orientation would lead masculine individuals to treat relationship maintenance as a task that needs to be accomplished. Feminine individuals, on the other hand, are more likely to be relationally oriented, and so are more likely to incorporate relational maintenance into their everyday communication routines. The behavior happens more naturally and without great effort for them.

The results of the Aylor and Dainton (2004) study also allow us to explain the Stafford et al. (2000) study presented as study one in this article. Recall that the authors found that a combination of femininity and masculinity predicted four of the seven maintenance techniques. It may be that feminine people are performing the behavior routinely and masculine people are performing the same behavior strategically—which is why both masculinity and femininity predicted the behavior.

In the end, however, it doesn't matter whether the behavior is performed routinely or strategically; it matters only that the behavior is performed. And it seems that gender, rather than sex, provides the ultimate explanation for what is done and how it is done within a marriage. Combined, the two studies presented in this article suggest that there are dangers associated with the stereotypes of sex differences that appear so often in the popular press. As Aylor and Dainton (2004) argue, the more an individual believes that "men are like this and women are like that" the more likely that person is going to be disappointed and disillusioned when such stereotypes do not hold true. Instead, people interested in maintaining

their marriage should learn and reinforce both feminine and masculine gender roles in their relational partners, because femininity would encourage the routine use of maintenance and masculinity would encourage the strategic use of maintenance.

Questions for Consideration and Discussion

1. Studies have indicated that increased openness in marital relationships is not associated with increased satisfaction. Dainton suggests that one explanation may be that we are more open when we are unhappy. What other explanations might there be for this finding?
2. Do you think that more advice giving in a relationship would be associated with more satisfaction? Why or why not?
3. Dainton notes that sex and gender are not the same concept. However, the two are somewhat difficult to separate in our actual experience. Why is that the case?
4. Are you surprised that Dainton found femininity to be associated with greater use of maintenance behaviors? Why or why not?
5. All of the research reported here is self-report. That is, participants filled out questionnaires regarding their relational behavior. What are the benefits and drawbacks of this technique?

References

Aylor, B., & Dainton, M. (2004). Biological sex and psychological gender as predictors of routine and strategic relational maintenance. *Sex Roles, 50,* 689–697.

Bem, S. L. (1974). The measurement of psychological androgyny. *Journal of Consulting and Clinical Psychology, 45,* 195–205.

Canary, D. J., & Hause, K. S. (1993). Is there any reason to study sex differences in communication? *Communication Quarterly, 41,* 129–144.

Canary, D. J., & Stafford, L. (1992). Relational maintenance strategies and equity in marriage. *Communication Monographs, 59,* 243–267.

Dainton, M. (2000). Maintenance behaviors, expectations, and satisfaction: Linking the comparison level to relational maintenance. *Journal of Social and Personal Relationships, 17,* 827–842.

Dainton, M., & Aylor, B. (2002). Routine and strategic maintenance efforts: Behavioral patterns, variations associated with relational length, and the prediction of relational characteristics. *Communication Monographs, 69,* 52–66.

Dainton, M., & Stafford, L. (1993). Routine maintenance behaviors: A comparison of relationship type, partner similarity, and sex differences. *Journal of Social and Personal Relationships, 10,* 255–272.

Dainton, M., Stafford, L., & Canary, D. J. (1994). Maintenance strategies and physical affection as predictors of love, liking, and satisfaction in marriage. *Communication Reports, 7,* 88–98.

Dindia, K., & Canary, D. J. (1993). Definitions and theoretical perspectives on maintaining relationships. *Journal of Social and Personal Relationships, 10,* 163–173.

Gray, J. (1992). *Men are from Mars, women are from Venus: A practical guide for improving communication and getting what you want in your relationships.* New York: HarperCollins.

Hughes, R., Jr. (2004, April 5). The demographics of divorce—United States and Missouri. Retrieved November 24, 2004, from the University of Missouri Extension Web Site: http://missourifamilies .org/features/divorcearticles/divorcefeature17.htm

Huston, T., & Houts, R. (1998). The psychological infrastructure of courtship and marriage: The role of personality and compatibility in romantic relationships. In T. Bradbury (Ed.), *The developmental course of marital dysfunction* (pp. 114–151). New York: Cambridge University Press.

Ragsdale, J. D. (1996). Gender, satisfaction level, and the use of relational maintenance strategies in marriage. *Communication Monographs, 63,* 354–369.

Stafford, L., & Canary, D. J. (1991). Maintenance strategies and romantic relationship type, gender, and relational characteristics. *Journal of Social and Personal Relationships, 8,* 217–242.

Stafford, L., Dainton, M., & Haas, S. (2000). Measuring routine and strategic relational maintenance: Scale revision, sex versus gender roles, and the prediction of relational characteristics. *Communication Monographs, 67,* 306–323.

Family Communication Patterns and the Socialization of Support Skills

Ascan F. Koerner

Laura Maki

In this chapter, we have considered how displays of affection, intimacy, and social support are influenced by both family practices and the larger culture. Here, Koerner and Maki present the results of research investigating how family communication patterns impact the development of support skills. Reflecting on your own family experiences as you read the article may provide you insight with your support behaviors and skills.

L.B.A.

During your interactions with friends and romantic partners, you have probably noticed differences in the way individuals communicate. These differences arise in part because of the different ways in which families communicate. How parents communicate with their children influences the communication skills children acquire and later use in their own interpersonal relationships with friends and romantic partners. More formally, it can be said that family communication is the primary means by which children are socialized to communicate; that is, to interpret their own and others' behaviors, to experience emotions, and to develop and maintain their interpersonal relationships (Koerner & Fitzpatrick, 2002a, 2004; Noller, 1995). One important communication behavior affected by family communication is social support. In this article, we discuss two studies that investigated how family communication patterns affect social support in families and how family social support affects the social support children experience in their romantic relationships as adults.

Social Support

Social support refers to interpersonal behaviors that have positive outcomes for the targets of such behaviors and is best defined in terms of these positive outcomes. Cutrona and Russell (1987) identified six such outcomes: guidance, reliable alliance, attachment, reassurance of worth, social integration, and opportunity for nurturance. *Guidance* refers to receiving advice or information from the other on how to think or behave. *Reliable alliance* refers to receiving assurance that others can be counted on for tangible assistance, such as money or shelter. *Attachment* refers to a sense of emotional closeness to others from which one derives a sense of security. *Reassurance of worth* refers to others' recognition of one's competence, skills, and values. *Social integration* refers to a sense of belonging to a group that shares similar interests, concerns, and recreational activities. Finally, *opportunity for nurturance* refers to the sense that others rely upon one for their own well-being. This final outcome of social support differs from the other five outcomes of social support in that it places the individual in the provider role as opposed to the receiver role.

Family Communication Patterns and Social Support

Family communication patterns are consistent and pervasive ways in which families communicate and, as discussed in Chapter 2, can be defined by two underlying dimensions, conversation orientation and conformity orientation (Fitzpatrick & Ritchie, 1994; Koerner & Fitzpatrick, 2002b, 2002c, 2004). Conversation orientation is the extent to which family members engage in frequent, open, and spontaneous interactions with each other, unconstrained by topics discussed or time spent communicating. Conformity orientation is characterized by a uniformity of beliefs and attitudes within the family. Interactions focus on maintaining harmonious relationships that reflect obedience to the parents (Koerner & Fitzpatrick, 1997, 2002b, 2002c).

Previous research supports the idea that different family communication patterns are associated with different interpersonal communication skills and that children acquire those skills that they experience in their own families. For example, Koesten and Anderson (2004) examined the role of family communication patterns in fostering the development of emotional support. They found that conversation orientation was positively correlated with emotional support in same-sex friendships and adult children's romantic relationships, whereas conformity orientation was negatively correlated with emotional support, but only in same-sex friendships.

Similarly, Koerner and Cvancara's (2002) investigation of specific speech acts suggesting a speaker's orientation toward another's thoughts and feelings found that high-conformity orientation is associated with speech acts that are less concerned with the feelings and thoughts of others. Low-conformity orientation, by contrast, is associated with the validation of others' attitudes and beliefs. Being able to take another person's perspective, however, is a necessary condition for providing social support to them (Burleson & Kunkel, 1996). Consequently, Koerner and Cvancara's research suggests that conformity orientation in families is negatively associated with children's learning of social support skills.

To better understand the effects of family communication patterns on family social support and children's learning of social support skills, we conducted two studies that examined the influence of families on children's social support skills. Based on existing research, we predicted that family conversation orientation would result in higher levels of social support in both the family of origin and in children's romantic relationship as adults. A second prediction was that family conformity orientation would result in lower levels of social support in the family of origin and in adult children's romantic relationships.

Study 1—Method

Participants and Procedure

Participants were 268 undergraduate students at the University of Minnesota in romantic relationships that on average had lasted 2.2 years. Participants completed a Web-based questionnaire asking for demographic information, information about communication in their current romantic relationships and in their families during childhood and adolescence.

Instruments

Family Communication Patterns. Ritchie and Fitzpatrick's (1990) Revised Family Communication Patterns (RFCP) instrument was used to measure the two dimensions of family communication: conversation orientation and conformity orientation. The RFCP asks participants to rate their agreement on five-point scales (1 = completely disagree; 5 = completely agree) with 26 statements such as "My parents encourage me to express my feelings" (for conversation orientation) and "My parents often say things like 'My ideas are right and you should not question them'" (for conformity orientation).

Social Support. Cutrona and Russell's (1987) social provisions scale (SPS) was used to measure social support in families of origin and in adult children's current romantic relationships with two relationship-specific versions of the SPS (i.e., for participants' relationships with parents and for participants' romantic relationships). The SPS consists of 24 items asking respondents to agree or disagree on five-point scales (1 = completely disagree; 5 = completely agree) with statements regarding the six types of social support discussed earlier. Each type of social support was measured with 4 items, whose averages were used as scores for each type of social support. The average of all 24 items was used as a score for overall social support.

Study 1—Results

We used linear regression analysis to test the prediction that family communication patterns affect social support in the family. The result of the analysis was that family communication patterns explained 68% of the variance in overall family social support. Specifically, conversation orientation ($\beta = .73$, $p < .001$) had a strong influence on family social support, whereas conformity orientation ($\beta = -.03$, *ns*) had no measurable influence. The interaction between conversation orientation and conformity orientation, however, was significant ($\beta = .18$, $p < .001$). This means that for participants from high conversation orientation families, level of conformity orientation did not affect social support, which was uniformly high. For participants from low conversation orientation families, however, increased conformity orientation was associated with a decrease in social support. Results for the six social provision subscales essentially replicated the findings for the overall score, with the exception of reassurance of worth. Here, in addition to the significant effects of conversation orientation and the interaction, conformity orientation had a significant negative association with social support ($\beta = -.16, p < .01$).

Thus, the data collected in study 1 provided strong support for the hypothesis that conversation orientation is positively associated with social support in families. Support for the second hypothesis, that conformity orientation is negatively associated with social support, was supported only for families low in conversation orientation. In regard to our prediction that family communication patterns predict social support in adult children's romantic relationships, in this study we did not find any consistent correlations between family communication patterns and social support in adult children's romantic relationships. Thus, the idea that social support is learned in families was not supported in this study.

Study 2

The results of study 1 supported our prediction that family communication patterns affect social support in families, but not our prediction that family communication patterns affect social support in adult children's romantic relationships. One possible explanation for why we failed to support the second prediction is that how much social support adult children receive in their romantic relationships is not just determined by what they have experienced in their own families, but also by what their partners have experienced in their families. Thus, we decided to conduct a second study involving both partners in a couple to further examine the association between family communication patterns and social support in adult children's romantic relationships. We predict that family communication patterns will affect social support in adult children's romantic relationships in two different ways. First, family communication patterns will affect the social support experienced in families of origin and subsequently, how social support is experienced in adult children's romantic relationship. In addition, rather than having an effect only on participant's own perceptions of social support in their romantic relationships, we predict that family social support also affects partners' reports of social support. The reason for this prediction is that if social support is a communication skill learned in the family, than the person benefiting from that skill is the partner of the child and not only the child herself, because it is the child that is using the skill in the relationship with the partner. Finally, because social support should affect relationship satisfaction, we also predict that social support in adult children's romantic relationships will be associated with relationship satisfaction of both child and partner.

Study 2—Method

Participants and Procedure

Participants were 54 undergraduate students from the University of Minnesota and their romantic partners. The procedure for study 2 was identical to that of study 1; participants completed a Web-based questionnaire with the same instruments along with a relationship satisfaction instrument.

Instruments

The instruments for study 2 included the RFCP and the SPS as described previously and a measure of relationship satisfaction—Huston, McHale, and Crouter's (1986) version of the Marital Opinion Questionnaire. The measure consists of 10 semantic differential items (e.g., miserable-enjoyable) that asks respondents to rate how they feel about their relationship, as well as one overall indicator ranging from "completely satisfied" to "completely dissatisfied."

Study 2—Results

We collected data from romantic couples in study 2 to test the associations between family social support, social support in adult children's romantic relationships, and relationship satisfaction in adult children's romantic relationships. A path analysis was used to test all of our predictions simultaneously in one causal model (see Figure 5.1). The path analysis also allowed us to investigate gender differences, which was appropriate because past research has established some gender differences in perceived social support and relationship satisfaction.

The first interesting outcome of the path model analysis was that when separated into gender groups, the interaction between conversation orientation and conformity orientation no longer predicted family social support. Instead, we found different effects of family communication patterns on social support for men and for women. For men,

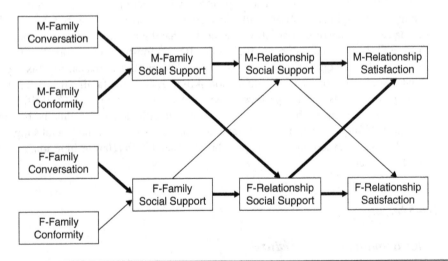

FIGURE 5.1   Associations between Family Communication, Social Support, and Relationship Satisfaction for Couples in Romantic Relationships.

Note: Statistically significant paths are indicated by thick arrows; hypothesized but statistically nonsignificant paths are indicated by thin arrows; M = males; F = females.

conversation orientation was positively correlated and conformity orientation was negatively correlated with perceived social support in families, as we predicted. For women, however, there was only one significant main effect for conversation orientation, whereas conformity orientation had no correlation with perceived social support. In other words, for males, greater conformity orientation leads them to perceive their families as less supportive, whereas females' perceptions of family social support are not affected by their families' conformity orientation. This is consistent with a society in which independence from parents is more important for males than for females, and consequently males, but not females, react negatively to parental pressures to conform (Fitzpatrick & Ritchie, 1994).

Our analysis also showed some significant gender differences between family social support and social support in adult children's romantic relationships. For both men and women, their own families' social support was associated with the social support they reported receiving in their own subsequent romantic relationships. As far as the social support of their partners' family is concerned, however, only the link between male partners' perceived family social support and females' perceived social support was statistically significant. The link between females' family social support and male partners' social support in their subsequent romantic relationship, however, was not. In other words, how supportive females are in their romantic relationships is independent of how much support they received in their own families, whereas how supportive men are in their romantic relationships depends on how much support they received in their own families.

A similar pattern emerged for the association between social support in adult children's romantic relationships and relationship satisfaction. For both men and women, we observed a large direct effect for social support and their own relationship satisfaction. The more social support they reported, the more satisfied they were. At the same time, men's relationship satisfaction, but not women's, was also affected by the social support their partners reported receiving in their relationships. In other words, men were happier if their partners reported more social support in their romantic relationship. Women's satisfaction, however, was not affected by how supportive they were perceived by their partners.

It is important to note that these interesting gender differences were observed only for associations among variables. As far as variable means are concerned, there were no differences between men and women regarding how they perceived their families and their own romantic relationships (see Table 5.4).

TABLE 5.4 *Summary of Variable Means for Couples Data from Study 2 (N = 54)*

Variables	Men	Women
Conversation orientation	4.8	5.1
Conformity orientation	4.0	3.9
Family social support	5.7	6.0
Relationship social support	6.1	6.3

General Discussion

Family Communication Patterns and Perceived Social Support in the Family

Results of both studies were consistent with the prediction that family communication patterns are associated with family social support. In both studies, conversation orientation was positively associated with all aspects of social support in families. Families that value open communication and the free exchange of ideas are more supportive than families that place less value on open communication. The predicted negative association of conformity orientation on family social support was more complicated. In study 1, it was supported as a direct effect only for one dimension of social support, reassurance of worth. Statistically significant interactions, however, revealed that conformity orientation had the predicted negative effect on the other dimensions of social support when conversation orientation was low. In study 2, we observed the negative correlation between conformity orientation and family social support for men, but not for women. Thus, the results showed that family communication patterns overall affect social support in families. The effect of conversation orientation is consistently positive, whereas the effect of conformity orientation is generally negative, but less consistent.

Family Social Support and Support in Adult Children's Romantic Relationships

In study 2, we investigated a sophisticated causal model linking family communication patterns to adult children's social support in subsequent adult children's romantic relationships and their satisfaction in those relationships. The finding that family social support affects how supportive adult children's romantic relationships are is consistent with a dyadic definition of social support. In a dyadic definition, social support refers to two interrelated interpersonal skills: (1) the ability to provide social support to others and (2) the ability to recognize and utilize the social support others provide. The ability to provide social support includes perspective taking, empathizing with the distressed person's situation, and providing symbolic and instrumental support. The ability to utilize social support includes acceptance of what others say and the assistance they offer. Thus, the ability and motivation to provide social support in a relationship is a necessary but insufficient condition to guarantee its benefits; recipients must also possess the ability and the desire to utilize social support by others if the need arises (Coble, Gantt, & Mallinckrodt, 1996). Our results suggest that experiencing social support in families allows adult children to experience it in their subsequent adult relationships as well.

Another very interesting finding was that only men's ability to provide social support is affected by how supportive their families are. We expected both partners' reports of how supportive their partner is to be a function of that partner's family social support. Instead, only women's perceptions of their male partner's supportiveness were correlated to the male partner's family social support. Men's perceptions of their female partners' supportiveness did not correlate with females' reports of their families' supportiveness.

This finding cannot be explained by gender differences in how supportive partners are, because participants of both genders perceived their partners to be equally supportive.

This suggests that the family is a more important socialization agent for social support for boys than for girls. Women seem to be able to acquire social support skills independently from how supportive their own families are, potentially from their female friends or from a culture that often defines being female in terms of being supportive. In contrast, men are more dependent upon their families of origin for these important interpersonal skills. If they do not acquire these skills in their families, in a culture that does not value social support in males, they do not acquire them at all before entering into romantic relationships as adults. Given that our sample consisted of predominantly young couples, our data do not address the issue of whether men are able to learn to be more socially supportive in their romantic relationships. Future research will have to address this important question.

Gender Differences in Social Support and Relationship Satisfaction

A final interesting gender difference we observed was that only men's relationship satisfaction was affected by how supportive their female partners perceived them to be, but not women's relationship satisfaction. A possible explanation is that women care more about having supportive partners and somehow communicate their satisfaction or dissatisfaction with their male partners to them in a way that affects the male partners' relationship satisfaction. As a result, men who are more supportive are more satisfied than men who are not as supportive. Because we did not observe actual communication between partners, this explanation is very speculative and needs to be investigated in a further study.

Conclusion

Our research has demonstrated the importance of family communication patterns for children's experience of social support in families and their acquisition of this important interpersonal communication skill. Results of both studies show that conversation orientation in families is strongly associated with family social support for children. We also observed a number of negative correlations between conformity orientation and social support. These correlations, however, were never entirely consistent and appeared to be limited to children of families low in conversation-oriented families (study 1) or to boys (study 2). Still, even if the results for conformity orientation are not always consistent, it is clear that when conformity orientation has an effect, it is always a negative correlation with social support, never a positive one.

In addition to creating family environments that differ in the social support they provide for children, family communication patterns also play an important role in socializing children to be supportive in their own romantic relationships. For both men and women, growing up in a supportive family leads them to identify supportive partners and to elicit supportive behaviors from them. In regard to their own behaviors of supporting their partners, men are much more affected by their families than are women, whereas women seem able to learn supportive behaviors outside their families, men do not. Thus, it is particularly important for families with boys to provide them with social support because they are unlikely to acquire this important interpersonal skill outside the family. Both boys and girls, however, are happier in supportive families and this happiness translates into healthier and more supportive relationships as adults.

Questions for Consideration and Discussion

1. Koerner and Maki note the connection between parental (or other adult caregivers) social support expression and how children express support. What examples of this do you see in your experiences?
2. This article discussed six outcomes of social support (drawing from the work of Cutrona and Russell). What outcomes of social support have featured most prominently in your experiences, and how has that changed over time?
3. These scholars used the Revised Family Communication Patterns instrument that requires participants to rate statements about family communication. What are the benefits and drawbacks you see in this research design?
4. The studies here found conversation orientation to be more important in explaining later social support than conformity orientation. What might be the reason behind this relationship?
5. Koerner and Maki looked at how family communication patterns (conformity and conversation orientation) related to social support. What larger cultural effects may be in operation here?

References

Burleson, B. R., & Kunkel, A. W. (1996). The socialization of emotional support skills in childhood. In G. R. Pierce, B. R. Sarason, & I. G. Sarason (Eds.), *Handbook of social support and the family* (pp. 105–140). New York: Plenum Press.

Coble, H. M., Gantt, D. L., & Mallinckrodt, B. (1996). Attachment, social competency, and the capacity to use social support. In G. R. Pierce, B. R. Sarason, & I. G. Sarason (Eds.), *Handbook of social support and the family* (pp. 141–172). New York: Plenum Press.

Cutrona, C. E., & Russell, D. W. (1987). The provisions of social support and adaptation to stress. In W. H. Jones & D. Perlman (Eds.), *Advances in personal relationships* (pp. 37–67). Greenwich, CT: JAI Press.

Fitzpatrick, M. A., & Ritchie, L. D. (1994). Communication schemata within the family: Multiple perspectives on family interaction. *Human Communication Research, 20,* 275–301.

Huston, T. C., McHale, S. M., & Crouter, A. C. (1986). When the honeymoon's over: Changes in the marriage relationship over the first year. In R. Gilman & S. Duck (Eds.), *The emerging field of personal relationships* (pp. 109–132). Hillsdale, NJ: Erlbaum.

Koerner, A. F., & Cvancara, K. E. (2002). The influence of conformity orientation on communication patterns in family conversations. *Journal of Family Communication, 2,* 133–152.

Koerner, A. F., & Fitzpatrick, M. A. (1997). Family type and conflict: The impact of conversation orientation and conformity orientation on conflict in the family. *Communication Studies, 48,* 59–75.

Koerner, A. F., & Fitzpatrick, M. A. (2002a). Toward a theory of family communication. *Communication Theory, 12*(1), 70–91.

Koerner, A. F., & Fitzpatrick, M. A. (2002b). Understanding family communication patterns and family functioning: The roles of conversation orientation and conformity orientation. *Communication Yearbook, 26,* 37–69.

Koerner, A. F., & Fitzpatrick, M. A. (2002c). You never leave your family in a fight: The impact of family of origin on conflict behavior in adult children's romantic relationships. *Communication Studies, 53,* 234–251.

Koerner, A. F., & Fitzpatrick, M. A. (2004). Communication in intact families. In A. Vangelisti (Ed.), *Handbook of family communication* (pp. 177–195). Mahwah, NJ: Erlbaum.

Koesten, J., & Anderson, K. (2004). Exploring the influence of family communication patterns, cognitive complexity, and interpersonal competence on adolescent risk behaviors. *Journal of Family Communication, 4,* 99–121.

Noller, P. (1995). Parent–adolescent relationships. In M. A. Fitzpatrick & A. Vangelisti (Eds.), *Explaining family interactions* (pp. 77–111). Thousand Oaks, CA: Sage.

Ritchie, L. D., & Fitzpatrick, M. A. (1990). Family communication patterns: Measuring intrapersonal perceptions of interpersonal relationships. *Communication Research, 17,* 523–544.

Section 3: Conclusions and Application— Intimacy, Affection, and Social Support in Your Life _____

We all experience aspects of intimacy, affection, and social support in our relationships. Whether the material you read here seemed very like your experiences, or very divergent, you can apply the understandings gained here to your family experiences: assessing patterns of intimacy, affection, and social support; considering how those patterns relate to the relationships and the culture in which they are embedded; and planning for the future of your relationships.

Assessing Your Family Patterns

There are many dimensions of intimacy, affection, and social support that you might consider as you assess the patterns present in your own family (or families). As you read in this chapter, families and family members express affection in varying ways. The readings and research reported here suggest that mothers tend to be more physical in expressing affection to their children, whereas fathers tend to show less physical affection. However, both mothers and fathers show affection more to their daughters than to their sons. Dainton's writing also argued that women tend to do more routine maintenance of relationships, whereas men tend to do more strategic maintenance. How are these patterns reflected in your family setting? If they are not reflected in your family setting, you might consider why that is the case. If they are reflected in your family, knowing that these patterns are common may provide you some idea of why your parents or adult caregivers may have related to you and/or your siblings in these ways.

You also read in this chapter that social support provided in family settings tends to vary by the roles occupied by family members. Children tend to receive the most support. Grandparents get less support than children. Parents are the least likely to be provided with social support, but are the most likely to provide it to the other two groups. Does this seem similar to your experiences of family? What types of social support do your parents or adult caregivers provide you? What types do you provide them? If you provide less, why? How much social support do you provide to your grandparents or other older relatives? How much do they provide you? Are the types similar or different?

Staske-Bell argued that intimacy is something that is negotiated in communication with family members. As you consider your own family relationships, think about some times that you have recently engaged in the negotiation and creation of intimacy with family members. Do the ways that you negotiate intimacy vary from family member to family member? As you have grown up and developed more autonomy in your familial relationships, has this impacted the ways that intimacy is negotiated?

These questions are just a few that you might consider as you assess intimacy, social support, and affection in your family (or families). Thinking about and analyzing your family patterns may provide you with a new window of understanding for the family inter-action patterns you have experienced.

Thinking about How Your Family Patterns Relate to Your Relationships and Culture

In addition to analyzing the patterns of behavior your family has in relation to intimacy, affection, and social support, you may also wish to consider how those patterns relate to the relationships in that family and the larger cultural settings in which your family is embedded.

Koerner and Maki argued that many of our family communication patterns are passed down from parent to child, and then continue on into future romantic relationships, potentially resulting in a new family of procreation, where those patterns will be learned anew by a new generation. After you have assessed the patterns displayed in your family, consider how those patterns may have developed. One way to do this is to look at the inter-generational transmission of patterns within your family settings. Are the ways that your parents communicate with you similar to the ways that their parents communicated these positive emotions to them? You might also wish to take time to think about how you have replicated the patterns you learned from your parents in your own romantic relationships.

In addition to the intergenerational transmission of communication patterns, the readings in this chapter considered the impact of culture on how we show affection, inti-macy, and social support. Dainton's work indicated that the patterns she saw with relations to maintenance behaviors were not sex based—that is, they did not occur because women naturally behave one way and men naturally behave another way. Instead, these aspects related to the gendered expectations of men and women (masculinity and femininity). In terms of the expression of social support, the fact that children receive the most support is probably at least partly due to culture. In U.S. culture, we place a high value on children, and have low expectations of them providing support to others (even as they get older). We tend to see adults as very self-sufficient, and thus do not necessarily view them as needing much support from either their parents or their children. These are cultural beliefs that are likely impacting our relationships. How can you apply these cultural understandings to how your family members interact? If your family patterns do not seem to represent what is being discussed in this chapter, consider the possibility that other cultural settings than the mainstream (racial culture, ethnic culture) are impacting your family patterns.

As we interact with others, we often think of the way that we do things as the natural way that interaction should happen. "Of course," we might say, "women are more affec-tionate, because that is how women are." "The way my family interacts and shows affection is the normal way to do so." "Children get more social support because they just need it, and parents don't." Considering how intergenerational transmission and cultural expecta-tions impact the way these elements of family interaction are created allows us to engage in critical analysis of our own behaviors and the behaviors of others. It helps us stop taking for granted the patterns that have become so normal to us and consider the possibility of other options (or to celebrate our own patterns for what they are).

Planning for Your Future and Making Changes(?)

Engaging in assessment of our relational patterns and critical analysis as to how and why we have developed those patterns provides us with the information we need to think about our relational futures. At times, this may mean planning to attempt changes in our interactions. At other times, it may mean feeling comfortable that the way we are doing things is a good way and we should just stick to the same path.

As you saw throughout this chapter, research has suggested a positive relationship between affection, intimacy, social support, and the relational and individual health of family members. Affection in marital and other family relationships has been associated with satisfaction in those relationships. Likewise, emotional and other forms of social support have been shown to be correlated with satisfaction for particular family dyads and members. Although it isn't clear which element causes the other, it seems clear that these aspects of family relationships are connected.

Similarly, social support has been shown again and again to be positively correlated to better mental health for parents and children. The effects of social support on physical health have also been widely supported by research in communication, health fields, sociology, and so on. So, what do we do with this knowledge?

I think we would probably all like to have more relational satisfaction, have better mental health, and have increased physical health. Even if the causality of these relationships is not always clear, it stands to reason that increasing the extent to which we offer affection and social support to family members is probably a good idea. If, by doing so, we can increase the positive outcomes for loved ones, that's a good thing. Additionally, reciprocity is at work in family affection displays and negotiation of intimacy. If we exhibit more affection and social support to family members, they are likely to do so for us, and this may increase our own relational satisfaction, mental health, and physical health.

Of course, this process is not always easy. We need to carefully think about the analyses we have made of our family patterns, and where they come from (including both cultural and intergenerational elements). Bucking the trend is difficult to do. Care must be taken to not alienate family members or suggest that their ways of showing affection, intimacy, and support are wrong or bad. We need to remember that these patterns are processes of negotiation between family members.

Thinking about how we want to respond to (and replicate or not) cultural expectations of us as men and women is another part of how we can plan for our familial future in terms of affection, intimacy, and social support. The patterns of expectation in culture do shift and change over time, but change is slow and comes from the changes that individuals make in their own interactions. After considering the extent to which culture has impacted our displays of these positive family elements, we are better prepared to address whether we want to support gendered patterns of behavior in our relationships, or if we would like to move in the direction of considering what is most helpful to the relationship, and engaging in those behaviors regardless of our sex and the expectations thereof.

Although changing our current family patterns may be difficult and slow, it can be rewarding. Our future relationships can be impacted by these considerations. Additionally, because the transmission of these patterns is intergenerational, changes we make in our own lives can have long-term impacts on future generations, and that deserves some attention.

Questions for Consideration and Discussion

1. As you have grown from a child, to an adolescent, to an adult, how have your intimacy, affection, and social support been renegotiated in the relationships you have with your family members?
2. In your family of origin, what types of affectionate displays were most common? How do you think that has affected your own affection behaviors?
3. Were there differences between how men and women (or boys and girls) in your family showed affection? How can the work presented in this chapter help you understand those differences (or the lack thereof)?
4. What type of role models did you have for romantic affection when you were a child? How do you think those models affected your behavior in your own relationships as an adult?
5. Most researchers argue that person-centered support messages are more effective than those which are not person centered. Can you think of any situation in which a person-centered message may not be most effective?

Key Terms and Concepts

affection
emotional intimacy
emotional support
evolutionary psychologists
informational support

instrumental support
intellectual intimacy
intimacy
person centeredness
physical intimacy

recreational intimacy
social intimacy
social support

6

Power and Conflict in the Family

Chapter Outline

Chapter Objectives

1. To understand the nature of conflict
2. To understand the nature of power and its sources
3. To become aware of familial and cultural roots of family conflict and power processes
4. To see the outcomes of family conflict and power processes
5. To apply the material to your own understandings of conflict and family interactions

Section 1: Overview of Power and Conflict
in Family Life _____

- When you hear the word *conflict*, what is the image that comes to your mind?
- If you envision a "perfect" family, how much conflict is there?
- How do you think your family experiences have shaped the way you think about and respond to conflict?

As a child, I vividly remember hearing my mother say "I am *sick* and *tired* of hearing you two argue!" Now, as a mother of six children, I know exactly what she meant. Hearing the arguments or squabbling of others isn't particularly enjoyable. And yet, conflict is an inevitable and even beneficial part of family life. In this chapter, we consider what conflict is, its relationship to power, the factors that affect how family members engage in conflict with one another, and the outcomes of conflict. Additionally, we address what happens when conflict becomes violent or otherwise abusive.

What Is Conflict?

Often, our conflicts with others stem from what we perceive as difference. It might be difference of opinion, difference in desires, difference in plans or goals, and so on (Koerner & Fitzpatrick, 2002). However, conflict is not simply about two people wanting different things, or one person being right and the other being wrong. Instead, **conflict** is a perception of difference developed in the interaction between relational partners as they discursively create positions and realities to which the other interactants respond (Sinclair & Monk, 2004). As we engage in communication with others, we cooperatively participate in creating our own position or reality about a point of disagreement, and we interact with others to do the same. This is why conflicts and the positions of the participants shift in the course of the interaction. At times, we may start a conflict about one issue, only to have it shift to something else. Or, we may believe that we know how we feel about a particular problem, only to realize that our position has changed in the course of a conflict. This is the interactive nature of the creation of conflict.

Every relationship has conflict (Sillars, Canary, & Tafoya, 2004). Conflict may occur in the form of argument, but it may not. Sometimes conflict goes unstated, yet it is still there in the interaction. Even when we don't acknowledge the conflict explicitly, it nonetheless exists. Conflicts can vary in their intensity and length, as well as in the number of relational members who participate. They can also have varying levels of impact on the participants and other members of the relational system. Family relationships are certainly no exception to these ideas.

Though we often think of conflict as a "bad" thing, it can actually be beneficial for the family system when it is managed constructively (Deutsch, 1973; Sillars et al., 2004). It is frequently through discussing our disagreements that we stimulate needed change in the family. If parents have established a 9:00 P.M. curfew for their child, and don't change that curfew as the child grows older, a conflict may prompt a reassessment of the age appropriateness of the time and possibly a change that is beneficial to family members. Conflict between family members can also serve to help members understand each other better. Although we tend to think that we know what our family members think about things (and this, in itself, sometimes produces conflict), at times it takes an argument to learn that a family member has an opinion or view that is surprising to us. And, as we have conflict with others, it often helps us understand our own ideas and beliefs more clearly (and to create those ideas and beliefs). While we talk to others about what we believe, and listen to and think about their responses, we clarify for ourselves what our own positions and opinions are. Thus, conflict should not be seen as something to be squashed in a family environment. Rather, we need to appreciate that conflict is as normal as (maybe even more normal than) peaceful agreement, and is an important part of family process.

How Is Power Related to Conflict?

Power can be defined as one's ability to influence others to act in a desired manner. Like other family phenomenon, power is relational. This means that an individual in a family has power to the extent that other family members grant or enable that power. Power is also not a unitary concept. There are different "sources" of power (but remember that regardless of source, power is only power if others grant it). Power can be based on "official" position in a system; this is called **legitimate power** (French & Raven, 1959). Power can stem from knowledge or things that a person knows how to do; this is called **expert power** (French & Raven, 1959). Power can be related to a person's attractiveness, whether that is physical, emotional, or otherwise, and how much we like that person; this is **referent power** (French & Raven, 1959). Power can also be related to ability to reward or punish others; these power bases are **reward power** and **coercive power** (French & Raven, 1959). So, different people can have power from different bases at different times. Generally, most people in a family system have some sort of power, even the people we might think of as being the "weaker" members.

Think about your family relationships. When you were just a baby, though you were ostensibly the weakest person in the family, you had power over your parents or adult caregivers because you could reward or punish them with your cries and coos. You also had power because of your baby cuteness (awwwww!). On the other hand, they had power over you because they had legitimate power (as parents), and also power based on knowledge and expertise. As you grew, power may have shifted. You gained some knowledge and expertise, so that provided an additional base of power to you. Your parents wanted your love and affection, so that too gave you a base of power. Your parents gained more ways to reward and punish you. (It's hard to really influence a newborn with rewards, but as a child ages, he or she becomes much more susceptible to reward offers.) When you became an adult, your parents lost some of their power over you (they can't ground you, or send you to your room: you've gained knowledge and expertise in some areas, and you have some of your own resources), yet, they can still affect you through rewards (gifts, affection, etc.), or punishment (withholding money, ignoring you, being upset with you). And, in your particular situation, your parents may have expertise or knowledge in specific areas that you don't have. Finally, parents maintain some sort of power because of their culturally defined position as parents. So, given the different bases on which power can rest, power is a negotiable concept within a particular family. Who is seen as having the most power, and when he or she has that power, is created through the interaction between family members and the acceptance or rejection of power moves.

Although power is negotiated within a particular family, cultural expectations of family roles also impact who has power in a family. We expect that adults will be more powerful, and have more control of resources that can be used to reward or to punish, than children. Therefore, it is not surprising that studies tend to show that parents typically do have more relational power than children or adolescents (Barber & Haddock, 2003). However, age is not the only cultural expectation that affects power. In American culture, we still maintain an expectation that men are more powerful than women. Barber and Haddock's (2003) research suggests that this is also true in family settings, where husbands, grandfathers, and even sons feel relatively more powerful than mothers, grandmothers, and daughters. This does not, of course, mean that children do not have some power over parents or that women don't have any power in their relationships with men. At times, we gain power through what is seen as a weakness (if you've ever said "but I don't know how to . . ." and gotten someone to do something for you, you've seen this in action). However, this study, and others like it, suggest that, on the whole, men feel themselves to have more power than women, and parents believe themselves to have more power than children (and these beliefs are relatively culturally supported).

The impact of such cultural beliefs about power is extensive. Culturally, we restrict parents' ability to punish children in some ways, but parents can still engage in corporal punishment in the United States. In no other relationship is hitting or spanking another considered appropriate or acceptable, but in the parent–child relationship, this is still culturally supported to some degree. In male–female relationships, physical punishments are no longer legal (though that hasn't been the case for a particularly long time). However, some scholars argue that physical punishment of women by men is still tacitly approved, or at least overlooked unless it gets "too bad" in many parts of American culture (Bent-Goodley, 2004; Locke & Richman, 1999). Additionally, the relative power of men over women in our culture can be seen in issues such as the distribution of household work. Even in homes where both partners work, women are likely to be responsible for the majority of household tasks and child care (Davis & Greenstein, 2004; Kroska, 2004). This is related to the power of men in U.S. culture.

Given all of these many issues that affect who has power, how, and in what ways, it is important that we think about power when considering conflict. After all, it is the power that is granted to us within relationships that affects who is more (or less) likely to achieve his or her final goals in a conflict situation.

In addition to the power that family members hold, how particular members handle conflict (often called **conflict management**) also impacts the outcomes of conflict within the family. Different families exhibit different arguing styles and, even within one family, various members will manage conflict at different ways at different moments in the relationship.

What Factors Affect How Family Members Engage in Conflict?

As you might guess, some scholars believe that individual characteristics impact how conflict management strategies are selected and used. For example, Jensen-Campbell, Gleason, Adams, and Malcolm (2003) studied the role of the personality characteristic of agreeableness in children. They found that children who had more agreeable personalities were better able to handle conflict in a constructive manner. Lee-Baggley, Preece, and DeLongis (2005) also found agreeableness, in addition to other personality factors, to be associated with effective conflict coping styles for adult partners in stepfamily relationships.

Cognitive Complexity

Another factor that has been seen as related to conflict management is how complex an individual's cognitions are. Scholars who follow a **constructivist** viewpoint argue that different people are more or less cognitively complex. A **social construct** is a descriptor of a characteristic that we believe another to have (e.g., nice, tall, teacher). Our constructs about others can be more or less abstract (for example, to say someone is nice is a more abstract construct than to say he or she is tall), can vary in number (a young child may have only a few constructs about another individual, whereas an adult may have many), and can be more or less connected or integrated to one another (you know someone is a teacher because he or she likes children . . . you have connected two constructs). People who are more **cognitively complex** have constructs that are more differentiated (numerically more), more abstract, and more integrated than those who are less complex (see Delia, O'Keefe, & O'Keefe, 1982). As individuals become more complex, they are able to create person-centered messages that are specifically oriented to their relational partners (Burleson, 1989; Clark & Delia, 1977) and thus those messages should be more successful. Because of this, constructivist scholars argue that cognitively complex individuals are able to handle conflict more effectively (Applegate, Burke, Burleson, Delia, & Kline, 1985; Applegate, Burleson, & Delia, 1992; Samter, 1994). Although cognitive complexity does not guarantee that an individual will produce effective messages, these scholars argue that this individual factor means that a person is capable of doing so.

Attributions

How individuals attribute responsibility for behaviors is an additional arena of social judgment that may impact conflict management. **Attribution theories** involve the way in which we explain our own behavior and the behavior of others (Manusov, 2006). In general, when we observe someone engaging in a particular behavior, either ourselves or someone else, we are often motivated to think about why that person did what he or she did. At times, we may think that the cause of a behavior is external to the individual (he or she did it because of a situational force out of his or her control), whereas other times we may believe that the behavior was caused by internal factors (he or she did it because of his or her personality or desires). As you might guess, how attributions are made can be important in conflict situations. If my son behaves poorly (let's say he says something extremely rude to his brother), I can attribute that behavior to the situation (his brother provoked it; he isn't feeling well today) or I can attribute that behavior to him (he's just rude). Which of these attributions I make will impact the character of the conflict to follow. Some research has indicated that more satisfied couples tend to attribute negative events to external causes, rather than to their partners. More dissatisfied couples or couples with violent relationships, on the other hand, tend to attribute negative events to their partners (Henning, Jones, & Holdford, 2005; Manusov, 1995, 2006; Sillars, Leonard, Roberts, & Dun, 2002). Similar results have been found with relation to how parents and children evaluate each other's behaviors (Fincham, Beach, Arias, & Brody, 1998; Wilson & Whipple, 2001) and for siblings (Matthews & Conger, 2004). Tendencies toward assigning particular types of attributions under particular circumstances are individual traits; however, scholars argue that those traits may stem in part from learned cultural and family patterns (Bugental & Johnston, 2000; Fincham et al., 1998; Matthews & Conger, 2004).

Parent Modeling and Couple Types

Various authors argue that family culture and how parents model and respond to emotional displays impact how children deal with conflict (Dumlao & Botta, 2000; Koerner & Fitzpatrick, 2002; Ramsden & Hubbard, 2002). In one research example of this, Rinaldi and Howe (2003) found that parental conflict management styles seemed to impact both parent–child conflict management and sibling conflicts. This suggests that the parental relationship both sets a tone for and models conflict behavior in other family relationships.

Given the impact that marital conflict management can have on the partners and the children in the family, understandings of marital conflict patterns are important to family communication study. Thus, some communication scholars have conducted research about marital conflict specifically, and based on that research have developed typologies of marital types. The basic argument here is that couples develop particular relational cultures that impact and are impacted by communication, and conflict management is an important part of that communication process. Two such scholars are Fitzpatrick and Gottman.

Fitzpatrick (1988) argues that heterosexual married couples can generally be divided into three types, based on their relational culture. Those types are traditionals, independents, and separates. **Traditional couples** tend to have a high degree of conformity with traditional sex-role expectations in the relationship; they are very interdependent with one another, and although they dislike conflict, they will engage in it when necessary to produce agreement. **Independent couples** tend to be more flexible with regard to sex roles; they are more independent of one another, though they still share (in terms of time and communication). They do not fear conflict and expression of personal difference. **Separate couples** tend to be fairly conservative in their views about sex roles, but live somewhat separate lives with little sharing. They try to avoid conflict when possible. Fitzpatrick argues that some couples may be a combination of the three, with one partner expressing more of one style, and the other one another. The couple types designated by Fitzpatrick tend to respond to conflict in a way that corresponds to how they understand intimacy and roles in the marriage (Sillars et al., 2004).

Gottman's (1994) work focuses even more strongly on conflict in his classification of marital styles. Gottman argues that successful couples are those that tend to exhibit one of three types of conflict styles. He terms these validating, volatile, and conflict avoiding. **Validating couples** are couples that "fight nice." These couples tend to have medium levels of both conflict and passion in their relationships. When they argue, they do so with respectfulness and strong attention to the relationship over personal needs (this type of conflict style might be expected from Fitzpatrick's traditional type). **Volatile couples** are those that have high levels of conflict, but also high levels of passion. They hold strong personal opinions and like to "win" an argument, but they also express high levels of affection for their partners at nonconflict times (this is parallel to Fitzpatrick's independent type). **Conflict avoiding couples** do not like conflict and prefer to ignore areas of disagreement. They often have low levels of both conflict and passion (this would be like Fitzpatrick's separate type). Gottman argues that it doesn't matter what style of conflict management is used; they can all be successful. What is important, he claims, is that the two partners are both using the same style, and that overall the positive communication moments in the relationship far outweigh the negative ones. Table 6.1 summarizes Fitzpatrick and Gottman Couple types.

The conflict styles parents develop may have far-reaching effects in the family system. As noted previously, when children observe their parents arguing in a certain fashion, they may understand this to be the way that people, or at least people in their family, deal with conflict (Sillars et al., 2004). And, the impact of this learning goes even further Koerner and Fitzpatrick (2002) note that the patterns we develop in our family of origin, with regard to conflict management, are often carried into our later romantic relationships (see also Andrews, Foster, Capaldi, & Hops, 2000). This means that these patterns may

TABLE 6.1   *Couple Types and Conflict*

Fitzpatrick's Couple Types	*Gottman's Couple Types*
Traditional couples—conservative sex roles, very interdependent, will conflict when necessary	Validating couples—medium level of passion and conflict; fight nicely when needed
Independent couples—flexible sex roles, more independent but still sharing, not afraid to conflict	Volatile couples—high level of passion and conflict; fight more frequently and with high intensity
Separate couples—conservative sex roles, very independent, avoid conflict	Conflict avoiding couples—lower levels of passion and conflict; avoid fighting if possible

then be reproduced for our own children, and so on. At times, the patterns we learn in the family may be constructive patterns that will help us in our future relationships. Unfortunately, children sometimes learn negative patterns of conflict in the family of origin and then carry those patterns into their families of procreation.

Research suggests that if children are exposed to parental violence they are more likely to reproduce that violence in their later romantic relationships (Kinsfogel & Grych, 2004; Lichter & McCloskey, 2004). It may seem odd that someone who sees violence as a child (and possibly even experiences that violence visited upon himself or herself) would then become violent with others, but we probably should not be surprised. The things that we see and hear when we are children have a strong impact on us throughout our lives and can become what we revert to when we are unsure of how to proceed. This does not mean that those individuals who were exposed to poor, or even violent, conflict management strategies as children cannot overcome that as adults and choose better ways to handle conflict. They can, and often do. What it does mean is that it is more difficult for people who have not had good conflict management modeled for them as children to "come up" with their own better strategies.

Cultural Patterns

In addition to the impact of family culture on how we "do conflict," the larger cultures in which the family is embedded are also related to conflict patterns. For example, gendered expectations of behavior developed through cultural socialization impact the use of particular conflict strategies. Boxer (2002) suggests that women, being less powerful in the U.S. culture, are more likely to engage in "nagging" than men. This finding is certainly compatible with our commonsense stereotype of women as "nags." From Boxer's (2002) perspective, women are more likely to have their first request ignored, dismissed, or overlooked. Thus, they feel pressed to repeat the request in order to get the desired behavior enacted. When it is again ignored, they are again pressed to repeat. Because women are not expected to be as vocally aggressive as men, each request may be fairly calmly stated (though some degree of increasing frustration is likely reflected in the tone used). So, women become the nags of the relationship. Men, on the other hand, are less likely to nag and more likely to use forceful requests. Because their requests get responded to more quickly, they are not put in a position of needing to repeat themselves again and again (Boxer, 2002). Again, it should be noted that studies that make claims about sex or gender differences are generalized statements. This does not mean that every woman nags or that no man does. Instead, this study simply indicates that, due to our cultural expectations about men and women, women are put in a position that makes it more likely that they will resort to nagging more often.

BOX 6.2 • *Did You Know?*

British Labour politician Lady Edith Summerhill once said: "Nagging is the repetition of unpalatable truths" (www.bartleby.com).

Cultural views about gendered behavior are not the only way that culture affects our conflict management techniques. In a study of individuals in Germany, Japan, the United States, and Mexico, Oetzel and colleagues (2003) found that national culture had an impact on how family members engaged in conflict with one another. Their study indicated that people in more individualistic cultures, like the United States and Germany, tend to be more concerned with maintaining their own face (how they appear to others and their sense of individual power) in conflict and are more defensive than people from collectivist cultures, like Japan and Mexico. Even within the individualistic culture pair and the collectivist culture pair, the researchers found specific differences in conflict management that appeared to be culturally created. German participants were more direct and confrontative in their conflict style than participants from the United States. Japanese participants were more expressive in conflict style than were the participants from Mexico (see also Ting-Toomey, Oetzel, & Yee-jung, 2001).

Differences in culture may also affect how abusive or violent conflict tactics are used and responded to in a family setting. In her 2004 report of research, Gill argues that the South Asian women she studied were reluctant to report violent behaviors in their marital relationships, or even to define these behaviors as abusive. Gill notes that cultural concepts of shame and honor in relation to family were largely responsible for the silence of these women about their situations. Similarly, West (2004), Bent-Goodley (2004), and Kasturirangan, Krishnan, and Riger (2004) argue that sociodemographic, socioeconomic, and sociopolitical factors affect the amount and type of familial abuse experienced by women of minority racial or ethnicity status, as well as impacting how that abuse is responded to by the victims. Anderson (1997) found that cultural expectations of masculinity seemed to be a part of the creation of violent relationships within families. In the families she studied, when men were less economically powerful within their marital relationships (that is, their wives made more money), the likelihood of them becoming violent increased (see also Harrell, 1990). She suggests that this is because manliness, in American culture, is associated with the provider role. When men are unable to take on that role, they may more strongly exhibit other "masculine" characteristics (such as aggression) in order to compensate. In a similar finding, Harrell found that husbands who were less masculine (and therefore perhaps less likely to feel the need to prove that masculinity behaviorally) exhibited less relational aggression and violence. Thus, we can see that culture affects not only how conflict is handled, in general, but also impacts when and if more violent or abusive strategies are implemented within family settings and how that violence is responded to by family members.

The way that family members engage in conflict is impacted by a variety of factors. These factors include individual abilities or differences, family culture and socialization, and the socialization we receive from the larger cultures in which the family is embedded. As you will see in the next part of the chapter, similar issues are in action in how conflicts affect the family members.

What Are the Outcomes of Conflict?

Many researchers suggest that it is not the amount of conflict, or even the issues under discussion, that most impacts how conflict affects our relationships overall. Instead, how conflict is managed and how relational partners respond to that management style are extremely influential with regard to conflict effects (Sillars et al., 2004).

Couple Conflict

In addition to the consideration of overall conflict style, scholars have noted that some conflict management techniques seem to be more effective and positive for couples. In this body of work, they conclude that the use of positive affect messages, like the use of humor and showing verbal and physical affection, both during and preceding conflict, was correlated with better relational stability and satisfaction. Additionally, expressions of support and reassurance for the partner, the use of problem solving, and calm discussion have been found to be effective strategies overall in couple conflict management (for discussions see Cummings & Davies, 1994; Driver & Gottman, 2004; Gottman, Coan, Swanson, & Carrere, 1998; Gottman, Markman, & Notarius, 1977; Julien, Chartrand, Simard, Bouthillier, & Begin, 2003; Notarius & Markman, 1993; Stanley, Markman, and Whitton, 2002).

Researchers have also found particular behaviors to be ineffective in management of couple conflict. For example, the use of negative affect messages was correlated with poorer stability and more dissatisfaction. Other negative strategies noted in research include verbal and nonverbal hostility, threats, physical aggression, personal insults and defensiveness (see, for example, Cummings & Davies, 1994; Driver & Gottman, 2004; Notarius & Markman, 1993). One particular negative management strategy that has received extensive attention is the use of demand–withdraw patterns in conflict. A **demand–withdraw pattern** occurs when one relational partner attempts to talk about an issue ("demands" communication), while the other partner refuses to discuss it ("withdraws" from communication). Scholars such as Caughlin and Vangelisti (1999, 2000), Caughlin and Malis (2004), and Gottman and Levenson (2000) argue that this pattern of conflict management can be harmful to the happiness of relational members. Caughlin and Malis (2004) studied conflicts between adolescents and their parents. Their research revealed that, regardless of the amount of conflict present in the relationship, adolescents and parents reported less relational satisfaction as the incidence of demand–withdraw patterns of conflict management increased. When demand–withdraw patterns exist, one member of the relational dyad repeatedly makes criticisms or requests with regard to the conflict issue, sometimes called nagging (Boxer, 2002), while the other relational partner attempts to avoid discussing the conflict issue at all. This type of pattern is unsatisfactory for both partners in the interaction. The person who is doing the repeated demanding (or nagging) sees the issue as something important that needs to be discussed, and may feel ignored or like the other person doesn't care. The individual doing the withdrawing does not want to talk about the problem (perhaps he or she sees it as a nonissue, or as not solvable) and likely feels that he or she is being pestered by the other in an annoying manner. So, it isn't too surprising that such a pattern isn't good for the satisfaction of either partner.

Which strategies are most effective in particular couple conflict situations is complex and dependent upon a variety of factors. One factor that may impact conflict effects is the sex, or gender, of the participants. Some research has suggested that, in the demand–withdraw pattern, women may be more likely to demand, whereas men may be more likely to withdraw (Caughlin & Vangelisti, 1999). Caughlin and Vangelisti (2000) argue that this may be related to the fact that women, in general, are culturally taught to have greater need for connection, whereas men are taught to have greater need for autonomy. Thus, women are more likely to attempt to discuss the issues, whereas men withdraw from such discussion. Similarly, Roberts (2000) found that men and women were affected differently by various conflict management styles of their spouses. Women's marital satisfaction was more associated with their husband's hostility of response (that is, as husbands' hostility in conflict management increased, wives' satisfaction decreased). Husbands, on the other hand, were more affected when their wives withdrew from the conflict (that is, their satisfaction level tended to decrease as their wives withdrawal increased). This response is probably partly due to our cultural expectations. Women are expected to be emotionally available to others, so men may be particularly surprised when their wives don't want to talk about problems. From findings like this, it appears that, within the adult partner dyad, conflict management styles are more important than the amount of conflict in terms of the health of the relationship. Similar outcomes have been found in relation to how the parental conflict affects children in the family.

Scholars have found that the problem behaviors of youths are more associated with how their parents handle conflict than with the amount of conflict the parents have. That is, having parents that argue frequently does not seem related to poor child behaviors, but having parents who argue destructively does seem to be related to poor child behaviors. Buehler and colleagues (1998) found that hostile parental conflict styles were most predictive of both internalizing (i.e., depression, anxiety) and externalizing (i.e., disruptive behavior) problem behaviors for youth, regardless of whether they were boys or girls, preadolescents or adolescents, in divorced or intact families, or were poor or not poor. Katz and Woodin (2002) also found a strong effect on children and families based on how parents managed marital conflict. They applied one of three classifications to each parental couple, based on conflict style. Hostile–couples were those who showed negative speaker behaviors in conflict. Hostile-withdrawn couples were those who exhibited both negatives speaker and negative listener behaviors in conflict. Engaged couples were those who showed positive behaviors in both speaking and listening. In their study, Katz and Woodin encountered significant differences in the families of these couples. Couples who enacted hostile–withdrawn behaviors during conflict were most likely to have families that were less cohesive and playful. The parents had more problems coparenting their children as well. These couples' children were, as in the Buehler et al. (1998) study, more likely to also exhibit behavioral problems. On the other hand, couples who utilized constructive conflict management strategies were more likely to have happier families and more behaviorally, socially and psychologically well-adjusted children (Beuhler et al., 1998; Cummings, Goeke-Morey, Papp, & Dukewich, 2002; Katz & Woodin, 2002).

Parental Discipline and Decision Making

Another area of conflict management and power negotiation between family members relates to parental discipline and decision making. Disciplining of children is fundamentally related to conflict, as disciplinary moments often arise when there is a perceived conflict between the desires or tendencies of the child and those of the parent (even if the discipline involves a proactive strategy on the part of parents to prevent a child from engaging in particular behaviors in the future). Studies indicate that parents discipline and monitor children using a variety of styles, and that different styles tend to have different impacts on children and on the parent–child relationship (see Wilson & Morgan, 2004, for a review). The four primary parenting and discipline styles that are often referred to in research are authoritarian, authoritative, permissive, and rejecting-neglecting parenting (Baumrind, 1971, 1991). **Authoritarian parenting** is parenting with very high levels of control, but low levels of warmth and responsiveness.

Authoritative parenting is parenting characterized by consistent, warm, and accepting parenting with firm discipline strategies that involve clear explanation of standards for behavior. **Permissive parenting** involves parenting with high levels of warmth, but very low levels of control or discipline. **Rejecting-neglecting parenting** is parenting that has low levels of warmth and acceptance and also discipline and control. Studies have indicated that, generally, authoritative parenting strategies have the most positive outcomes for children and adolescents in psychological, relational, and educational domains (Bronte-Tinkew, Moore, & Carrano, 2006; Dornbusch, Ritter, Leiderman, Roberts, & Fraleigh, 1987; Kauffman et al., 2000; Lamborn, Mounts, Steinberg, & Dornbusch, 1991). However, here too we see the impact of culture, with some studies indicating that very high levels of control (which would generally be seen as authoritarian) may be most effective in African American family settings, and this may be related to socioeconomic issues leading to residing in communities that hold more dangers for children. Additionally, these studies suggest that the extremely strict control is most beneficial when paired with a greater degree of warmth in the mother–child relationship, which would be a style sort of "in between" authoritative and authoritarian (Wilson & Morgan, 2004). Overall, these results suggest that, although discipline is often a source of conflict between parents and children, firm and consistent discipline, if paired with warm and responsive parenting it is helpful to outcomes for children and adolescents in many cultural settings. Of course, that doesn't always mean that the children and teenagers will like it!

Family Violence

When conflict escalates to violence, outcomes can be both troubling and dramatic, **Family violence** can be defined as physical, psychological, or sexual abuse occurring between family members. This definition includes partner violence, child abuse, sibling abuse, elder abuse, and child-to-parent abuse. It also includes violence that occurs both nonverbally (hitting, punching, sexual assault), and verbally (name calling, belittling, threatening). We would all hope that the extent of violence in family settings is limited, but studies suggest that this is not the case.

Family violence is a hidden part of the family experience that occurs throughout the world. The National Center for Injury Prevention and Control (NCIP, a division of the Centers for Disease Control and Prevention) in the United States indicates that over 20 percent of Americans have experienced partner violence (NCIP, 2006). Cantalupo, Martin, Pak, and Shin (2006) note that approximately one in three women in Ghana have experienced physical abuse from a partner, and similar findings have been reported in Spain (Ruiz-Pérez, Plazaola-Castaño, & del Rio-Lozano, 2006) and Tanzania (McCloskey, Williams, & Larsen, 2005). In a study of different countries conducted by the World Health Organization, between 20 percent and 75 percent of women across the countries had experienced intimate partner violence (Fathalla, 2005). Child abuse in family settings is also common. Statistics for child abuse rates are somewhat more difficult to obtain, as the reporting and standards of child abuse varies from culture to culture, and children are less often the participants in research studies. However, in 2004, almost 900,000 children were found to have been abused in the United States, and this number is likely significantly lower than the number of children actually experiencing familial abuse (Administration for Children and Families [ACF], 2004). As considered previously in this chapter, many scholars argue that, in part, the level of family violence in various settings has arisen from cultural acceptance of familial violence, or at least a refusal to acknowledge its existence, that serves to facilitate its continuation. Thus, cultural understandings about family, family roles, and family practices are an important consideration in the study of family violence and abuse.

The potential outcomes of family violence are startling. Violence between domestic partners or from parent to child can lead to physical problems ranging from stress-related illnesses to death (Arias, 2004; Bent-Goodley, 2004). Psychological difficulties, including chronic depression, posttraumatic stress disorder, and suicidal thoughts are also common for victims of domestic violence (Arias, 2004; Bent-Goodley, 2004). For children, domestic abuse and violence is also associated with behavioral problems (Moran, Vuchinich, & Hall, 2004; Salzinger et al., 2002). Family violence impacts how children understand the nature of family as well. Winstok, Eisikovits, and Karnieli-Miller (2004) argue that adolescents who have seen father-to-mother violence in the home are unable to form a coherent mental understanding of their family and its members. Additionally, as the violence escalated, the adolescents studied became more distant from the father. As noted previously, children who observe negative conflict patterns, including violent behavior, in their families of origin are more likely to go on to reproduce those same patterns with their own families (Kinsfogel & Grych, 2004; Lichter & McCloskey, 2004). Cottrell and Monk (2004) also note that adolescents who become abusive to their parents have likely either been abused by them or have witnessed abuse between their parents. So, an additional problematic effect of violent behavior exhibited by parents is that it may then be replicated in other family relationships.

Abusive behaviors in family are not always between adults or perpetrated on children or adolescents by adults. At times, adolescents and children may abuse each other or abuse their parents (Cottrell & Monk, 2004; Eckstein, 2004; Paulson, Coombs, & Landsverk 1990). Eckstein (2004) and Cottrell and Monk (2004) indicate that adolescent-to-parent abuse makes it difficult for parents to feel good about their role as parents. When parents are abused by their children, they may feel both shame and guilt. Shame may stem from the sense of embarrassment that their child (one whom they should have power over) is taking power over them. Guilt can come from feeling that they have done something in the upbringing of the abusive child to make him or her violent in this way. Child-to-parent abuse may be unlikely to be reported due to this combination of shame and guilt, in addition to the love and loyalty the parent feels for the child.

From this portion of the research about conflict effects on family members, it is clear that those effects are rather complicated. Conflict is not, in and of itself, dangerous or problematic to a family and its members; however, how that conflict is managed or enacted can have significant impact on the participants and those around them.

BOX 6.3 • *Family in the News*

Elder abuse, neglect, or violence directed toward the elderly made national news again in July 2006, as the son of Brooke Astor, a 104-year-old multimillionaire and former socialite, was accused of neglecting and abusing her. Although elder abuse in the family is not frequently talked about, it is not as uncommon as you may think. Visit the National Center on Elder Abuse Web site for additional information, at www.elderabusecenter.org/.

Power and conflict in the family setting is an inevitable, and functional, part of life. Families encounter conflicts for a variety of reasons, deal with them in many ways, and the outcomes of those interactions are multiple. In Section 2, you will read about specific research that has been done with regard to family conflict. The articles consider family roles in conflict; adolescent abuse of parents, and how parents attempt to manage and avoid abusive interaction; and the role of culture in the creation of conflict management strategies. As you read these articles, and think about your own conflict interactions and the impact that your family of origin has had on your views of the appropriateness of particular types of conflict styles, and how effective (or not) you find those styles in your own relationships.

References

Administration for Children and Families. (2004). *Child maltreatment 2004*. Retrieved August 1, 2006, from the U.S. Department of Health and Human Services Web site: http://www.acf.hhs.gov/programs/cb/pubs/cm04/index.htm

Anderson, K. L. (1997). Gender, status, and domestic violence: An integration of feminist and family violence approaches. *Journal of Marriage and Family, 59*(3), 655–669.

Andrews, J. A., Foster, S. L., Capaldi, D., & Hops, H. (2000). Adolescent and family predictors of physical aggression, communication, and satisfaction in young adult couples: A prospective analysis. *Journal of Consulting and Clinical Psychology, 68*, 895–915.

Applegate, J. L., Burke, J. A., Burleson, B. R., Delia, J. G., & Kline, S. L. (1985). Reflection-enhancing parental communication. In I. E. Sigel (Ed.), *Parental belief systems: The psychological consequences for children* (pp. 107–142). Hillsdale, NJ: Erlbaum.

Applegate, J. L., Burleson, B. R., & Delia, J. G. (1992). Reflection-enhancing parenting as antecedent to children's social-cognitive and communicative development. In I. E. Sigel, A. V. McGillicuddy-Delisi, & J. J. Goodnow (Eds.), *Parental belief systems: The psychological consequences for children* (2nd ed., pp. 3–39). Hillsdale, NJ: Erlbaum.

Arias, I. (2004). The legacy of child maltreatment: Long-term health consequences for women. *Journal of Women's Health, 13*(5), 468–473.

Barber, C. E., & Haddock, S. A. (2003). Self-perceptions of comparative power and worth in three generational families. *Contemporary Family Therapy, 25*(2), 229–245.

Baumrind, D. (1971). Current patterns of parental authority. *Developmental Psychology Monograph, 4*, 1–103.

Baumrind, D. (1991). Parenting styles and adolescent development. In J. Brooks-Gunn, R. M. Lerner, & A. C. Petersen (Eds.), *The encyclopedia on adolescence* (pp. 746–758). New York: Garland.

Bent-Goodley, T. (2004). Perceptions of domestic violence: A dialogue with African American women. *Health and Social Work, 29*(4), 307–316.

Boxer, D. (2002). Nagging: The familial conflict arena. *Journal of Pragmatics, 34*, 49–61.

Bronte-Tinkew, J., Moore, K. A., & Carrano, J. (2006). The father–child relationship, parenting styles, and adolescent risk behaviors in intact families. *Journal of Family Issues, 27*(6), 850–881.

Buehler, C., Krishnakumar, A., Stone, G., Anthony, C., Pemberton, S., Gerard, J., et al. (1998). Interparental conflict styles and youth problem behavior: A two-sample replication study. *Journal of Marriage and Family, 60*(1), 119–132.

Bugental, D. B., & Johnston, C. (2000). Parental and child cognitions in the context of the family. *Annual Review of Psychology, 51*, 315–344.

Burleson, B. R. (1989). The constructivist approach to person-centered communication: Analysis of a research exemplar. In B. A. Dervin, L. Grossberg, B. J. O'Keefe, and E. Wartella (Eds.), *Rethinking communication: Vol. 2. Paradigm exemplars.* Newbury Park, CA: Sage.

Cantalupo, N., Martin, L. V., Pak, K., & Shin, S. (2006). Domestic violence in Ghana: The open secret. *Georgetown Journal of Gender and the Law, 7*, 531–597.

Caughlin, J. P., & Malis, R. S. (2004). Demand or withdraw communication between parents and adolescents as a correlate of relational satisfaction. *Communication Reports, 17*(2), 59–71.

Caughlin, J. P., & Vangelisti, A. L. (1999). Desire for change in one's partner as a predictor of the demand-withdraw pattern of marital communication. *Communication Monographs, 66*, 66–89.

Caughlin, J. P., & Vangelisti, A. L. (2000). An individual difference explanation of why married couples engage in demand/withdraw pattern of conflict. *Journal of Social and Personal Relationships, 17*, 523–551.

Clark, R. A., & Delia, J. G. (1977). Cognitive complexity, social perspective-taking and functional persuasive skills in second- to ninth-grade children. *Human Communication Research, 3*, 128–134.

Cottrell, B., & Monk, P. (2004). Adolescent-to-parent abuse: A qualitative overview of common themes. *Journal of Family Issues, 25*(8), 1072–1095.

Cummings, E. M., & Davies, P. T. (1994). *Children and marital conflict: The impact of family dispute and resolution.* New York: Guilford Press.

Cummings, E. M., Goeke-Morey, M. C., Papp, L. M., & Dukewich, T. L. (2002). Children's responses to mothers' and fathers' emotionality and tactics in marital conflict in the home. *Journal of Family Psychology, 16*(4), 478–492.

Davis, S. N., & Greenstein, T. N. (2004). Cross-national variations in the division of labor. *Journal of Marriage and Family, 66*(5), 1260–1271.

Delia, J., O'Keefe, B. J., & O'Keefe, D. J. (1982). The Constructivist approach to communication. In F. E. X. Dance (Ed.), *Human communication theory: Comparative essays* (pp. 147–191). New York: Harper & Row.

Deutsch, M. (1973). *The resolution of conflict: Constructive and destructive processes.* New Haven, CT: Yale University Press.

Dornbusch, S. M., Ritter, P. L., Leiderman, P., Roberts, D., & Fraleigh, M. (1987). The relation of parenting style to adolescent school performance. *Child Development, 58*, 1244–1257.

Driver, J. L., & Gottman, J. M. (2004). Daily marital interactions and positive affect during marital conflict among newlywed couples. *Family Process, 43*(3), 301–314.

Dumlao, R., & Botta, R. A. (2000). Family communications patterns and the conflict styles young adults use with their fathers. *Communication Quarterly, 48*(2), 174–199.

Eckstein, N. J. (2004). Emergent issues in families experiencing adolescent-to-parent abuse. *Western Journal of Communication, 68*(4), 365–388.

Fathalla, M. F. (2005). When home is no longer safe: Intimate-partner violence. *Lancet, 366*(9501), 1910–1911.

Fincham, F. D., Beach, R. H., Arias, I., & Brody, G. H. (1998). Children's attributions in the family: The children's relationship attribution measure. *Journal of Family Psychology, 12*, 481–482.

Fitzpatrick, M. A. (1988). *Between husbands and wives: Communication in marriage.* Newbury Park, CA: Sage.

French, J. R. P., Jr., & Raven, B. H. (1959). The bases of social power. In D. Cartwright (Ed.), *Studies in social power* (pp. 150–167). Ann Arbor, MI: Institute for Social Research.

Gill, A. (2004). Voicing the silent fear: South Asian women's experiences of domestic violence. *Howard Journal of Criminal Justice, 43*(5), 465–483.

Gottman, J. (1994). *What predicts divorce: The relationship between marital processes and marital outcomes.* Hillsdale, NJ: Erlbaum.

Gottman, J., Coan, J., Swanson, C., & Carrere, S. (1998). Predicting marital happiness and stability from newlywed interactions. *Journal of Marriage and Family, 60*, 5–22.

Gottman, J., Markman, H., & Notarius, C. (1997). The topography of marital conflict: A sequential analysis of verbal and nonverbal behavior. *Journal of Marriage and Family, 39*(3), 461–477.

Gottman, J. M., & Levenson, R. W. (2000). The timing of divorce: Predicting when a couple will divorce over a 14-year period. *Journal of Marriage and Family, 39*, 461–477.

Harrell, W. A. (1990). Husband's masculinity, wife's power, and marital conflict. *Social Behavior and Personality, 18*(2), 207–216.

Henning, K., Jones, A., & Holdford, R. (2005). "I didn't do it, but if I did I had a good reason": Minimization, denial, and attributions of blame among male and female domestic violence offenders. *Journal of Family Violence, 20*(3), 131–139.

Jensen-Campbell, L. A., Gleason, K. A., Adams, R., & Malcolm, K. T. (2003). Interpersonal conflict, agreeableness, and personality development. *Journal of Personality, 71*(6), 1059–1085.

Julien, D., Chartrand, E., Simard, M., Bouthillier, D., & Begin, J. (2003). Conflict, social support, and relationship quality: An observational study of heterosexual, gay male, and lesbian couples' communication. *Journal of Family Psychology 17*(3), 419–428.

Kasturirangan, A., Krishnan, S., & Riger, S. (2004). The impact of culture and minority status on women's experience of domestic violence. *Violence and Abuse, 5*(4), 318–332.

Katz, L. F., & Woodin, E. M. (2002). Hostility, hostile detachment, and conflict engagement in marriages: Effects on child and family functioning. *Child Development, 73*(2), 636–652.

Kaufmann, D., Gesten, E., Santa Lucia, R. C., Salcedo, O., Rendina-Gobioff, G., & Gadd, R. (2000). The relationship between parenting style and children's adjustment: The parents' perspective. *Journal of Child and Family Studies, 9*(2), 231–245.

Kinsfogel, K. M., & Grych, J. H. (2004). Interparental conflict and adolescent dating relationships: Integrating cognitive, emotional, and peer influences. *Journal of Family Psychology, 18*(3), 505–515.

Koerner, A. F., & Fitzpatrick, M. A. (2002). You never leave your family in a fight: The impact of family of origin on conflict-behavior in romantic relationships. *Communication Studies, 53*(3), 234–251.

Kroska, A. (2004). Division of domestic work. *Journal of Family Issues, 25*(7), 900–931.

Lamborn, S., Mounts, N., Steinberg, L., & Dornbusch, S. M. (1991). Patterns of competence and adjustment among adolescents from authoritative, authoritarian, indulgent, and neglectful families. *Child Development, 62*, 1049–1065.

Lee-Baggley, D., Preece, M., & DeLongis, A. (2005). Coping with interpersonal stress: Role of the big five traits. *Journal of Personality, 73*(5), 1141–1180.

Lichter, E. L., & McCloskey, L. A. (2004). The effects of childhood exposure to martial violence on adolescent gender-role beliefs and dating violence. *Psychology of Women Quarterly, 28*(4), 344–357.

Locke, L. M., & Richman, C. L. (1999). Attitudes toward domestic violence: Race and gender issues. *Sex Roles, 40*(3–4), 227–247.

Manusov, V. (1995). Intentionality attributions for naturally-occurring nonverbal behaviors in intimate relationships. In J. E. Aitken & L. J. Shedletsky (Eds.), *Intrapersonal communication processes* (pp. 343–353). Plymouth, MI: Midnight Oil.

Manusov, V. (2006). Attribution theories: Assessing causal and responsibility judgments in families. In D. O. Braithwaite & L. A. Baxter (Eds.), *Engaging theories in family communication: Multiple perspectives* (pp. 181–196). Thousand Oaks, CA: Sage.

Matthews, L. S., & Conger, R. D. (2004). "He did it on purpose!" Family correlates of negative attributions about an adolescent sibling. *Journal of Research on Adolescence, 14*(3), 257–284.

McCloskey, L. A., Williams, C., & Larsen, U. (2005). Gender inequality and intimate partner violence among women in Moshi, Tanzania. *International Family Planning Perspectives, 31*(3), 124–130.

Moran, P. B., Vuchinich, S., & Hall, N. K. (2004). Associations between types of maltreatment and substance use during adolescence. *Child Abuse & Neglect, 28*(5), 565–574.

National Center for Injury Prevention and Control. (2006). *Intimate partner violence: Fact sheet.* Retrieved August 1, 2006, from the Centers for Disease Control and Prevention Web site: http://www.cdc.gov/ncipc/factsheets/ipvfacts.htm

Notarius, C., & Markman, H. J. (1993). *We can work it out: Making sense of marital conflict.* New York: Putnam.

Oetzel, J., Ting-Toomey, S., Chew-Sanchez, M. I., Harris, R., Wilcox, R., & Stumpf, S. (2003). Face and facework in conflicts with parents and siblings: A cross-cultural comparison of Germans, Japanese, Mexicans, and U.S. Americans. *Journal of Family Communication, 3*(2), 67–93.

Paulson, M. J., Coombs, R. H., & Landsverk, J. (1990). Youth who physically assault their parents. *Journal of Family Violence, 5*(2), 121–133.

Ramsden, S. R., & Hubbard, J. A. (2002). Family expressiveness and parental emotion coaching: Their role in children's emotion regulation and aggression. *Journal of Abnormal Child Psychology, 30*(6), 657–667.

Rinaldi, C. M., & Howe, N. (2003). Perceptions of constructive and destructive conflict within and across family subsystems. *Infant and Child Development, 12*, 441–459.

Roberts, L. J. (2000). Fire and ice in marital communication: Hostile and distancing behaviors as predictors of marital distress. *Journal of Marriage and Family, 62*(3), 693–707.

Ruiz-Pérez, I., Plazaola-Castaño, J., & del Rio-Lozano, M. (2006). How do women in Spain deal with an abusive relationship. *Journal of Epidemiology & Community Health, 60*(8), 706–711.

Salzinger, S., Feldman, R. S., Ng-Mak, D. S., Mojica, E., Stockhammer, T., & Rosario, M. (2002). Effects of partner violence and physical child abuse on child behavior: A study of abused and comparison children. *Journal of Family Violence, 17*(1), 23–52.

Samter, W. (1994). Unsupportive relationships: Deficiencies in the support-giving skills of the lonely person's friends. In B. R. Burleson, T. L. Albrecht, & I. G. Sarason (Eds.), *Communication of social support: Messages, interactions, relationships, and community* (pp. 195–214). Thousand Oaks, CA: Sage.

Sillars, A., Canary, D. J., & Tafoya, M. (2004). Communication, conflict, and the quality of family relationships. In A. L. Vangelisti (Ed.), *Handbook of family communication* (pp. 413–446). Mahwah, NJ: Erlbaum.

Sillars, A. L., Leonard, K. E., Roberts, L. J., & Dun, T. (2002). Cognition and communication during marital conflict: How alcohol affects subjective coding of interaction in aggressive and nonaggressive couples. In P. Noller & J. A. Feeney (Eds.), *Understanding marriage: Developments in the study of couple interaction* (pp. 85–112). Cambridge, England: Cambridge University Press.

Sinclair, S. L., & Monk, G. (2004). Moving beyond the blame game: Toward a discursive approach to negotiating conflict within couple relationships. *Journal of Marital and Family Therapy, 30*(3), 335–347.

Solomon, D. H., Knobloch, L. K., & Fizpatrick, M. A. (2004). Relational power, martial schema, and decisions to withhold complaints: An investigation of the chilling effect on confrontation in marriage. *Communication Studies, 55*(1), 146–167.

Stanley, S. M., Markman, H. J., & Whitton, S. W. (2002). Communication, conflict, and commitment: Insights on the foundations of relationship success from a national survey. *Family Process, 41*(4), 659–675.

Ting-Toomey, S., Oetzel, J. G., & Yee-jung, K. (2001). Self-construal types and conflict management styles. *Communication Reports, 14*(2), 87–104.

West, C. M. (2004). Black women and intimate partner violence. *Journal of Interpersonal Violence, 19*(12), 1487–1493.

Wilson, S. R., & Morgan, W. M. (2004). Persuasion and families. In A. L. Vangelisti (Ed.), *Handbook of family communication* (pp. 447–471). Mahwah, NJ: Erlbaum.

Wilson, S. R., & Whipple, E. E. (2001). Attributions and regulative communication by parents participating in a community-based child physical abuse prevention program. In V. Manusov & J. H. Harvey (Eds.), *Attribution, communication behavior, and close relationships* (pp. 227–247). Cambridge, England: Cambridge University Press.

Winstok, Z., Eisikovits, S., & Karnieli-Miller, O. (2004). The impact of father-to-mother aggression on the structure and content of adolescents' perceptions of themselves and their parents. *Violence Against Women, 10*(9), 1036–1055.

Section 2: Research Examples _____

An Exploratory Investigation into Family Conflict Roles

Patrick C. Hughes

Chelsea A. H. Stow

In Chapter 3, we considered the nature of family roles. In addition to family roles based on positions (mother, father), families also exhibit other roles in their communication processes. In this article, Hughes and Stowe consider the group roles that develop in family conflict situations, and how those roles may serve to diffuse or facilitate conflict situations. An awareness of the roles we play in family conflict, and how those roles impact conflict resolution, can help us develop more effective patterns of conflict management.

L.B.A.

Family relationships are not always easy, and can be extremely challenging and difficult; however, the fact that relationships in general, and specifically family relationships, are complicated is nothing new. Baxter and Montgomery (1996), for example, suggested that all relationships are "messy," or "less logical and predictable than we might expect, and rife with tensions of different sorts" (p. 86). Furthermore, family life itself "is varied and complex and this variation and complexity is very difficult to study" (Bernardes, 1993, p. 41). One aspect of family life that is often difficult to understand is members' experiences during family conflict. This work expands on the discussion of the influences and dimensions of family conflict to include an empirical investigation of the emergent roles during family conflict. First, we briefly point out the many different conceptualizations of "family" from the literature. Second, we describe our method for looking into the emergent family conflict roles. Third, we present our results and analysis, which reveal the role dynamics during family conflicts as recalled by our participants. Finally, we conclude with suggestions for new directions of research on emergent family roles.

Family Types

Many scholars have provided valuable information about different types of families; for example, Afifi and Schrodt (2003) have identified family types such as step- or remarried families, traditional nuclear families, single-parent families, postdivorce families, and first marriage families, to name a few. Although many of these families are considered common in our society, scholars like Turner and West (2003) argue that we should "think outside the box" of commonality to include diverse family configurations like gay and lesbian families, adopted families, and interracial, interclass, or interethnic families. Therefore, whether your personal definition of family is similar to or different from these scholarly definitions, we can be sure that family life is both consistent and changing, both stable and chaotic, and both predictable and emergent.

One conceptualization of family that has received less attention is that of a family as a small group (Whitchurch & Constantine, 1993). Communication in small groups is best characterized as naturally occurring, or "emergent," communication behaviors that are socially constructed through group processes. One area of research in small-group communication that could explain a similar phenomenon in families is the concept of emergent small-group roles. Much of the communication that takes place during the life of a group is called "role formation talk," which is dedicated to the development and assignment of the roles that each member of the group will have (Cragan & Wright, 1993); examples of these roles include the Task Leader, Social-Emotional Leader, Tension Releaser, Central Negative/Devil's Advocate, and Information Provider. Additionally, to the extent that these emergent roles help groups construct their identities, complete tasks, establish rules for interaction, and formulate problem-solving talk (Pavitt & Curtis, 1990), we might also expect *family members* to develop group-type roles during their communication because the family can be considered a small group. That is, we would expect to see roles emerge as in other groups, but to differ in content from nonfamilial group communication (Whitchurch & Dickson, 1999).

Family Conflict and Family Roles

One area in which the emergence of family group roles might be instructive is during family conflict. The family is a unique context for study because "its influence has great longevity. . . . Long after people have moved away from family members geographically, they still feel psychologically and emotionally connected to them" (Sabourin, 2003, p. 39). Relationships with family members have ongoing impacts, and illustrate the importance of the roles filled by those around us (Vuchinich, Emery, & Cassidy, 1988). Regardless of how these roles are formed, the family environment provides its members with a source of support during times of conflict, and often supplies a conflict "template" upon which a person can draw in other stressful situations.

Although there seems to be a general American cultural perception that engaging in conflict is detrimental, conflict often produces beneficial results (McCarthy, Lambert, & Seraphine, 2004; Smetana, 1989). In fact, the presence of conflict has been shown to be less threatening to the relationship than *how* the conflict is managed communicatively (Gottman, 1994). The perception of conflict as nonbeneficial often stems from negative conflict experiences such as role identity confusion, when the family structure changes and individuals are uncertain how to change with it or how to respond to events in their new environment (Marsiglio, 2004). For example, in blended families it is typical for children to be unsure about which parent (the biological parent or the "new" parent) is responsible for discipline (Baxter, Braithwaite, & Bryant, 2004).

Family disagreements are inevitable, and effective conflict management has been recognized as an integral part of family life research (Vuchinich, 1987). Further, some research has pointed to the impact roles may have on promoting or ending conflict; however, this research focuses only on the *structural* aspects of family roles, meaning that little research has been done regarding how family members *socially construct* roles during conflict. Therefore, the purpose of this study is to explore the roles that family members construct during family conflict. The guiding research question of this study is: *What roles emerge for family members during family conflict?*

Method

Participants

One hundred undergraduate students ($n = 46$ males, $n = 54$ females) from a large university in the southwestern United States participated in this study. The participants ranged in age from 19 to 22 years ($M = 21.30$ years). At the time of these interviews, all participants were full-time college students. The cultural backgrounds of the participants were European American (75%), Hispanic (15%), and African American (10%). Most participants were single (90%), but a few were married or engaged (10%). At the time of this study, most of the participants reported that their parents' marital status was married (80%), with fewer being divorced (15%) or widowed (5%).

Procedures

Participants were recruited from the basic public speaking course in the authors' department, and through snowballing procedures (Reinard, 1994); participants were offered extra credit for their participation in the study. Data were collected using an open-ended questionnaire, and participants responded to five questions asking them (1) who they considered members of their families; (2) to recollect a recent family conflict, and describe what each person did and said during that conflict; (3) if they felt the conflict was resolved; (4) how family members participated in this resolution, and if conflicts were typically resolved in this manner; and (5) to describe their family communication patterns since the conflict. All questionnaires were completed during participants' regularly scheduled class time, and took approximately 50 minutes to complete. Data collection continued until saturation was reached—when similar themes in additional questionnaires emerged (Strauss & Corbin, 1990).

Data Analysis

Consistent with the grounded-theory design (Lincoln & Guba, 1985) and following the analytical induction procedures recommended by Glaser and Strauss (1967) and Strauss and Corbin (1990), transcripts and field notes were read for an overall impression of the data. Second, transcripts were read again, and the data were coded into smaller units based on participants' conflict experiences with their families. Third, these units were combined to generate family conflict role themes. Finally, using the constant comparative method of analysis (Strauss & Corbin, 1990), when new themes emerged old themes were reviewed and revised accordingly.

Results and Discussion

The research question guiding this study asked: What roles emerge for family members during family conflict? Our analysis revealed four emergent themes during family conflict: the Avoider role, Mediator role, Instigator role, and Role Construction Contradictions. Examples in support of each theme are given; however, in an effort to be concise, we included only the most representative excerpt for each theme.

Theme 1: Avoider Role

One of the open-ended questions in this study prompted participants to describe what each person in the family did and said during a recent family conflict. Interestingly enough, most of the respondents indicated that many family members (including themselves) wanted to "stay out of it," or otherwise distance themselves from the situation. For example, one participant disclosed:

> There was a fight when my sister decided to drop out of school and my mom was very much against it and my dad wanted to know why she wanted to drop out of school because my sister was a good student. Our parents wanted to involve me because I would be going to school next and they thought that this would set a bad example for me but I just wanted to stay out of it even though it involved my education to a degree because it wasn't my issue and it wasn't my life even though my parents wanted me to talk to my sister about it. I did what I could to not get involved or talk about it with my family.

There are many possible reasons why people avoid conflict, including protecting their relationships and family conflict dynamics. First, Avoiders might distance themselves from a conflict because they feel that their involvement might threaten or jeopardize an aspect of their relationship with the family members involved. Further, avoiding conflict may also reveal a subtle family conflict dynamic. That is, because conflict often temporarily disrupts family life, many family members might avoid conflict in an attempt to maintain homeostasis, or balance. However, research shows that conflict avoidance is an ineffective means of conflict management (Sillars, Canary, & Tafoya, 2004), and family members who avoid conflict to "keep the peace" are probably worsening the situation and causing more imbalance. Further, conflict avoidance in families may also be influenced by a greater cultural need to avoid conflicts in general.

Theme 2: Mediator Role

Participants also reported that someone (themselves or another family member) was often called on to act as a Mediator between conflicting family members. One participant recalled when her mother was mediating a disagreement between her father and herself:

> In my family, the fights were usually just little outbreaks but we would fight a lot. One time I was fighting with my dad, we have a lot of conflicts because we're both stubborn, and I really can't remember what it was we were fighting about but I remember my mom trying to get me and dad to be calm and restate our points of view. I really think she thought we

could figure out what was bothering me and dad, but mom kept trying to get us to "bargain" for what we wanted.

Many responses revealed the Mediator role, and analysis of these excerpts showed that other family members (not just mothers) act as Mediators.

From a family systems perspective, the Mediator role may emerge for similar reasons as the Avoider role: to restore order in the family. However, where the Avoider stays out of it and often increases family disruption, the Mediator gets involved in the conflict to diffuse the situation. Mediation seems to be a more effective tool than avoidance in conflict management, maintaining balance in the family system, and helping family members better understand each others' point-of-view (i.e., find shared meaning). Further, this direct and cooperative form of family communication is considered a highly effective conflict communication strategy (Knudson, Sommers, & Golding, 1980), which suggests that, even though family members may "fight a lot," as the last participant disclosed, a role exists in the family system to help maintain family equilibrium.

Theme 3: Instigator Role

So far, these themes have revealed the relative involvement (or lack thereof) of members during family conflict. Whereas the Instigator role also reveals a level of involvement in family conflict, this role emerged as someone who purposefully contributes to or escalates a situation by manipulating or baiting family members into a conflict with each other. One participant noted:

> Not just in one conflict, but in others we had in our family, there always seems to be someone (especially my brothers and sisters) who whispers in my parents' ears when my mom and dad are having a fight. One time, my brother knew that my mom and dad were fighting about how much time he [Dad] was spending at work because he's in sales and is out of town a lot. My brother overheard my dad talking with his partner about having to miss my sister's game, and my brother told my mom about this before my dad could and started a huge fight because mom thought that my dad wasn't going to tell her. This happens all of the time, my brothers and sisters saying things like "hey mom, guess what Gail is doing?" just to start a fight or keep one going.

This clearly reveals a darker side of family conflict processes. The emergence of the Instigator role in our data suggests that these families may be characterized by a pattern of competition. For example, Gottman (1994) demonstrated that competitive couples often repress ongoing conflicts for a period of time, as the parents seem to do in the previous excerpt, but when one person feels provoked the partners engage in a series of arguments marked by the presence of negative and competitive communication. Therefore, in many cases this competition originates with the parents and is then modeled by their offspring because "children learn how to manage conflicts indirectly by watching their parents and model their behavior and style" (Sillars et al., 2004, p. 426). As seen in the previous example, the children's involvement in this competitive pattern seems almost like a "communication rule" of their family, as "taught" by their parents, which could explain the emergence of an Instigator within the family.

Theme 4: Role Construction Contradictions—Symmetrical versus Complementary Roles

In addition to the Avoider, Mediator, and Instigator roles, our data revealed that the development of roles during conflict may not be as clear-cut as we might think. For some participants, the role they filled during conflict was different from the family's role expectations for that person. For example:

> We were staying home for the summer with our parents and my sister and I forgot we were living under my parents' roof. My sister and I got into a fight with our parents about the curfew issue because we believe we are adults who can come and go as we please, but mom and dad think we are their children still and as long as they are paying the bills we follow their rules.

It is clear from the example that this family is constructing contradictory roles: the children symbolize the construction of symmetrical roles between parent and child, and the parents represent the attempt to enact complementary roles (see Chapter 3 for discussion and definition of symmetrical and complementary behaviors). First, the children claim that they are adults, and have as much authority or power over their lives as their parents (symmetrical roles). However, the parents argue that they have more power over the rest of the family, first by virtue of their "place" as parents in the family structure, and second as having reward power over their children because they "still pay the bills" (complementary roles).

Other occurrences of this theme centered on conflicts between participants' parents that often stemmed from different constructions of power and equality, typically with the father constructing a complementary role and the mother constructing a symmetrical role. Furthermore, in the case of adult dependent children, several excerpts showed that some parents constructed symmetrical roles for certain children and complementary roles for others in the same family, in spite of the similarity in age among the adult children. Therefore, although there is not a clear pattern of these Role Construction Contradictions, it is important to note that these contradictions *can* emerge during family conflicts, often with lasting effects.

Conclusions

The purpose of this study was to conduct an exploratory investigation into the emergent roles during family conflict. Our data revealed four patterns of role development during family conflict: Avoider role, Mediator role, Instigator role, and Role Construction Contradictions; these findings seem to suggest that family members *do* develop particular roles during family conflict. Future research could improve upon and extend this study in at least three ways. First, future research might explore the general pervasiveness of these roles and seek to uncover more types of emergent roles. Second, future research might look at these roles more closely in order to distinguish between the well-being of families in which the various roles emerge (relative [un]happiness, etc.). Finally, the contradiction between the construction of symmetrical and complementary roles could be studied further, especially in the context of parents and their adult dependent children: does the presence of this tension mark the structural transition of a family from one in which the power and authority falls specifically on the parents, to one in which adult children become self-reliant (i.e., adjustment during life changes)? Future research might also ask if this tension helps or hinders this transition.

Questions for Consideration and Discussion

1. In this article, Hughes and Stow use concepts from small-group research and apply these to family communication processes. How well do you think small-group concepts apply to family, and why?
2. This work addresses the emergent nature of roles during conflict. Considering your most recent conflicts with family members, what examples of emergent roles do you see? What causes roles to emerge in conflict situations?
3. The discourse from the participants in this study indicated a divergence in the construction of symmetrical and complementary roles between parents and children. Do you believe this is because these participants are college students, or might this be explained by other factors?
4. This study asked participants to recollect a recent family conflict and base their responses on that recollection. What are some benefits and drawbacks to this method?
5. The participants in this work were college students. How might their age and/or education level have impacted their perceptions of family conflict?

References

Afifi, T. D., & Schrodt, P. (2003). Uncertainty and the avoidance of the state of one's family in stepfamilies, post-divorce single-parent families, and first-marriage families. *Human Communication Research, 29*(4), 516–532.

Baxter, L. A., Braithwaite, D. O., & Bryant, L. (2004). Stepchildren's perceptions of the contradictions in communication with stepparents. *Journal of Social and Personal Relationships, 21*, 447–467.

Baxter, L. A., & Montgomery, B. M. (1996). *Relating: Dialogues and dialectics*. New York: Guilford Press.

Bernardes, J. (1993). Responsibilities in studying postmodern families. In T. C. Sabourin, *The contemporary American family: A dialectical perspective on communication and relationships*. Thousand Oaks, CA: Sage.

Cragan, J. F., & Wright, D. W. (1993). *Theory and research in small group communication: A reader*. Edina, MN: Burgess.

Glaser, B., & Strauss, A. (1967). *The discovery of grounded theory*. Chicago: Aldine.

Gottman, J. M. (1994). *What predicts divorce? The relationship between marital process and marital outcomes*. Hillsdale, NJ: Erlbaum.

Knudson, R. M., Sommers, A. A., & Golding, S. L. (1980). Interpersonal perception and mode resolution in marital conflict. *Journal of Personality and Psychology, 38*, 751–763.

Lincoln, Y. S., & Guba, E. G. (1985). *Naturalistic inquiry*. Newbury Park, CA: Sage.

Marsiglio, W. (2004). When stepfathers claim step children: A conceptual analysis. *Journal of Marriage and Family, 66*, 22–39.

McCarthy, C. J., Lambert, R. G., & Seraphine, A. E. (2004). Adaptive family functioning and emotion regulation capacities as predictors of college students' appraisals and emotion valence following conflict with their parents. *Cognition & Emotion, 18(1)*, 97–124.

Pavitt, C., & Curtis, E. (1990). *Small group communication: A theoretical approach*. Scottsdale, AZ: Gorsuch Scarisbrick.

Reinard, J. C. (1994). *Introduction to communication research*. Dubuque, IA: Brown & Benchmark.

Sabourin, T. C. (2003). *The contemporary American family: A dialectical perspective on communication and relationships*. Thousand Oaks, CA: Sage.

Sillars, A., Canary, D. J., & Tafoya, M. (2004). Communication, conflict, and the quality of family relationships. In A. Vangelisti (Ed.), *Handbook of family communication* (pp. 413–446). Mahwah, NJ: Erlbaum.

Smetana, J. G. (1989). Adolescents' and parents' reasoning about actual family conflict. *Child Development, 60*, 1052–1067.

Strauss, A., & Corbin, J. (1990). *Basics of qualitative research: Grounded theory procedures and techniques*. Newbury Park, CA: Sage.

Turner, L. H., & West, R. (2003). Introduction. Breaking through silence: Increasing voice for diverse families in communication research. *Journal of Family Communication, 3*, 181–186.

Vuchinich, S. (1987). Starting and stopping spontaneous family conflicts. *Journal of Marriage and Family, 49*, 591–601.

Vuchinich, S., Emery, R. E., & Cassidy, J. (1988). Family members as third parties in dyadic family conflict: Strategies, alliances, and outcomes. *Child Development, 59*, 1293–1302.

Whitchurch, G. G., & Constantine, L. L. (1993). Systems theory. In P. G. Boss & W. J. Doherty (Eds.), *Sourcebook of family theories and methods: A contextual approach* (pp. 325–355). New York: Plenum Press.

Whitchurch, G. G., & Dickson, F. C. (1999). Family communication. In M. B. Sussman, S. K. Steinmetz, & G. W. Peterson (Eds.), *Handbook of marriage and the family* (2nd ed.). New York: Plenum Press.

"What Do *You* Do When Your Teenager Hits You?": Exploring Conflict Tactics Used by Parents in Adolescent-to-Parent Abuse

Nancy J. Brule

We often think of abuse as occurring between adult partners, or visited upon children by adults. However, there are numerous instances where teens and adult children abuse their parents or other familial elders. In this article, Eckstein considers the conflict strategies used by parents during teen abusive episodes. Even if you never experience this type of situation, you may find that the same tactics are used in other conflict situations, even those which are not abusive.

L.B.A.

Daily interactions between parents and adolescents often result in conflicts. Family members assume different roles when contributing to the development and enactment of conflict episodes and the basic skills required to resolve conflict involves utilizing a variety of communication tactics (Canary & Spitzberg, 1987, 1989; Cupach & Canary, 1997; Messman & Canary, 1998). An individual's conflict tactics are often reinforced by other family members' responses, and individuals develop patterns of behaviors that others come to expect. These patterns of conflict behaviors may be either constructive or destructive—promoting cooperation and relational growth or power struggles, competition, and unresolved conflicts (Rueter & Conger, 1995; Smetana, 1995). Some destructive conflict between adolescents and parents may escalate into abuse.

Adolescent-to-parent abuse is defined as "actual physical assaults or verbal and nonverbal threats of physical harm" (Harbin & Madden, 1979, p. 1288) directed toward parents by their adolescent children. The National Family Violence Survey reported that adolescents victimized 18% of parents at least once a year; 2.5 million parents are struck by their adolescents, 900,000 of these experiencing severe physical abuse (Cornell & Gelles, 1981; Straus, Gelles, & Steinmetz, 1980). Yet, not all adolescent-to-parent abuse is physical in nature; parents also experience verbal and emotional abuse (Eckstein, 2004, 2005; Price, 1996). Although adolescent-to-parent abuse exists, there is little research in this area of relational violence and as a result the problem often goes unnoticed and more likely unreported.

Because societal norms hold parents responsible for the behavior of their children, parents experiencing abuse often blame themselves for their own abuse (Eckstein, 2004, 2005; Schuett, 1999). Many abused parents fear public victimization (being judged as poor parents), and as a result, become prisoners in their own home, avoid talking about the abusive episodes, minimize the seriousness of the behavior, and are unable to punish the behavior. However, narratives by abused parents reveal that they do attempt to negotiate interactions with their teens in efforts to prevent adolescent-to-parent abuse (Eckstein, 2004, 2005; Price,

1996). The purpose of this study is to identify the specific conflict strategies and tactics used by parents to manage or prevent episodes of abuse.

Defining Abuse

This study defines abuse within a relationship as an "ongoing, repetitive pattern—psychological, emotional, or behavioral—of pain infliction" (Spitzberg, 1997, p. 177). Abuse is conceptualized to include verbal (attacks the self-concept of another individual), physical (acts resulting in physical harm against a person), and emotional (impacts the ability to function in a relational role) behaviors that inflict hurt upon another individual and which violate socially accepted standards.

Conflict and Strategies

Defining Conflict

Interpersonal conflict is defined here as an "expressed struggle between at least two interdependent parties who perceive incompatible goals, scarce resources, and interference from others in achieving their goals" (Wilmot & Hocker, 2001, p. 34). Communication is central to this definition because conflict must be expressed to be an interpersonal conflict. Certain verbal and nonverbal behaviors often lead to, reflect, and express conflict, and can be used to manage or prevent the escalation of conflict (Canary & Spitzberg, 1987, 1989, 1990; Wilmot & Hocker, 2001). When participants are faced with a conflict situation, they consciously or subconsciously make a decision to avoid or engage in conflict.

Strategies and Tactics

Strategies and tactics are the general way individuals behave in a conflict situation. A strategy is an overall plan made up of communication tactics (specific observable actions) that move a conflict in a direction that helps achieve an outcome (Lulofs & Cahn, 2000). Researchers have identified three strategies individuals often use to engage in conflict. First, the integrative strategy (i.e., cooperative confrontation, supportive comments, listening in a supportive manner) encourages both parties to identify and share the goals of conflict and is often considered to have a positive impact on a relationship. Second, the distributive strategy (i.e., threats, demands, coercion, intimidation) is often considered to have a negative impact on a relationship (Sillars, 1986; Wilmot & Hocker, 2001). Third, the avoidance strategy (i.e., giving in to the demands of others, physically withdrawing from the conflict, not voicing thoughts) tries to keep tension at a low level and can have either a positive or negative relational impact. Because tactics are the communicative behaviors that shape conflict strategies, identifying the tactics parents use in attempts to manage and prevent escalation of conflict into adolescent-to-parent abuse becomes important. Thus, the research question is:

> **RQ:** What conflict tactics do parents use when managing and attempting to prevent conflict episodes from escalating into adolescent-to-parent verbal, physical, and emotional abuse?

Methods

Participants

Participants were 20 (male = 7; female = 13) European American parents located in the Midwest, who met the criteria of having been verbally, physically, and emotionally abused by an adolescent child who was living in the home at the time of abuse. Via phone, I contacted 3 parents who met the criteria and asked them if they would be willing to be interviewed. These parents then suggested other parents they knew, and using the purposive snowball sampling method, 10 additional participants were recruited. The final 7 participants were located through a social worker that contacted parents who met the criteria and, if parents consented to being interviewed, I was forwarded their contact information.

Participants ranged in age from 35 to 55 (m = 42). These families averaged 3.4 children; 19 of the families only had one child who was abusive. Nine of the participants were in first marriages (m = 25 years), 9 in second marriages (m = 9 years), and 2 participants were divorced at the time of the interview. Thirteen participants had experienced abuse by biological children, 5 by stepchildren, and 2 by adopted children. Each of the participants had participated in multiple family counseling programs.

Data Collection and Analysis

This study used a qualitative or interpretive approach to data analysis. A semistructured, open-ended interview instrument was developed (Holstein & Gubrium, 1995; McCracken, 1988) composed of questions that asked participants to explain, from start to finish, one experience of each type of abuse episode (verbal, physical, emotional). Before beginning the interview, the three different types of abuse were clearly defined and examples provided for the participants. The use of follow-up questions helped parents provide a full description of each type of abuse episode. Interviews were audio recorded and lasted between 1 and 1 ½ hours yielding 753 pages of 1.5-spaced data.

Data were analyzed in four phases. First the transcripts were listened to and read simultaneously in their entirety to verify the accuracy of the transcription, develop an overall picture of the participants' perceptions, and to start the analysis procedure. Second, Sillars's (1986) conflict strategy and tactic typology guided this analysis. Data were analyzed for the presence or absence of conflict tactics; tactics that did not clearly fit the typology were set aside for further analysis. Third, findings that did not fit the typology were analyzed and additional categories were developed (Creswell, 1998; Miles & Huberman, 1994). Fourth, the transcripts were read again, confirming the findings and locating examples for this study (Miles & Huberman, 1994). For verification of these findings, I performed a member check, which involved presenting my findings to eight of the participants in written form. Participants supported the analysis and stressed the consistency of these tactics, discussing how similar the excerpts were to their own experiences.

Results

Distributive Tactics

Few distributive tactics emerged when analyzing these data, possibly because of the destructive nature of these types of conflict tactics. Regardless of the reasons, the distributive tactics that emerged included personal criticism, ridicule, hit and run, sarcasm, and mirroring.

Personal Criticism, Ridicule, Hit and Run, and Sarcasm.

When personal criticism, ridicule, hit and run, and sarcasm tactics were used, it was often at a point in the conflict episode when parents grew frustrated and had lost control of their emotions. As a result, parents believed these tactics to be reactionary responses and were troubled when using them with their adolescents. A mother reported, "I would try not to ever lose my cool. And as many times as I would get up in the morning and say, 'Today, when he aggravates me I am going to maintain it'. . . . I just couldn't do it. Push that button and bam, gone." Parents also reported that personal criticism, ridicule, hit and run, and sarcasm were ineffective during a conflict and played a role in escalating the conflict into abuse.

Mirroring.

A tactic emerging that was not previously identified as a distributive tactic was mirroring. The mirroring tactic involves parents mimicking, verbally and nonverbally, an adolescent's words and behaviors. Although the initial use of mirroring often was effective in stopping the conflict episode from escalating, parents eventually came to view mirroring as a negative tactic. A mother explained:

> One of the good things is that he would use the language on me and I'd use it back on him. And he'd be shocked, intensely hearing his mother talk in the same language he talked. And that bothered him. . . . He'd bang his fists on something so I'd bang it, and he didn't like that. . . . And in the beginning, when I would do that with him, he would back off. . . . But then he hit a point where that didn't bother him anymore.

Although mirroring was effective when first used, over time it was ignored and thought to contribute to the escalation of the conflict.

Avoidance Tactics

Parents also used a number of avoidance tactics in attempts to prevent escalation of conflict into abuse; tactics included not voicing thoughts, physically withdrawing, giving in to demands, and ignoring.

Not Voicing Thoughts.

Parents frequently used the tactic of not voicing thoughts. A father shared this rationale: "Even though it's hard to do, you have to sit there and take the abuse. I could yell and swear at them back again, but it wouldn't do any good." Participants believed that responding to verbal abuse was not only ineffective, but also contributed to its escalation into more severe forms of abuse.

Physically Withdrawing.   Professional counselors often suggested to parents that they remove themselves from the proximity of the conflict so the adolescent would be unable to escalate it into abuse. Although intuitively this seems like a simple solution, parents reported that, because adolescents often followed parents throughout the house in attempts to continue the conflict, this tactic was extremely difficult to implement. When parents would lock themselves in a bathroom or bedroom, adolescents often pounded or kicked the door while screaming, swearing, and demanding the parent let them in. A parent summed up the failure of this tactic, "Well, unfortunately, it comes with you. It's on the other side of the door pounding. So they [counselors] don't tell you that part of it." Many parents reported these abuse episodes would often escalate and the doors would get broken.

Giving In to Demands.   These parents did not like giving in to the demands of their adolescents. However, parents' emotional exhaustion as well as the length of abuse episodes made this tactic a realistic one. A mother reported:

> He'd be in my face for anywhere from ten minutes to two, three hours . . . he wouldn't leave me alone . . . and he kept on and on. . . . He just wouldn't leave it alone. And I couldn't just let him keep talking to me and not get pulled back. . . . And I'd say, "Yeah, well, whatever." Because I was tired. I didn't want to do it anymore.

Implementing the tactic of giving in to demands was very simple: the adolescent asked for something, the parent said no, the teen verbally abused the parent, and the parent gave in to the adolescent's demands. After years of abuse, these parents reported not having the energy or desire to invest in the conflict episode.

Ignoring.   A tactic that emerged from these data not previously identified as an avoidance tactic was the ignoring tactic; this involved ignoring the verbal, and at times physical abuse taking place during a conversation or activity with the adolescent. For example, a mother who was washing dishes reported continuing to wash dishes even while her adolescent was punching her in the arm. On reflection, parents concluded that this tactic might have contributed to the escalation of the conflict into abuse because adolescents' behaviors become more intense in attempt to get their own way.

Integrative Tactics

Abused parents used integrative tactics the least, even though this strategy is considered a positive approach to dealing with conflict. Parents reported using supportive listening and comments and specific issue tactics.

Supportive Listening and Comments.   These parents used supportive listening and comments to focus on the needs of their adolescent. After an abuse episode, parents arranged a specific time to go for a soda, walk, or lunch with the adolescent. Parents used this time to address conflict issues, using positive verbal and nonverbal language, listening to the frustrations of the adolescent, and encouraging them to "hang in there." One father reported, "that's the times he's staring at you in the eyes, he's talking to you, he's looking at you, you've got your eye contact. . . . Their guard gets totally dropped so you can talk—get them to talk about a bunch of different things." Although this tactic provided opportunity for calm discussion and connection, having a positive effect on the adolescent–parent relationship, it had no evidence of preventing future abuse episodes.

Specific Issue.   A new integrative tactic identified from these data was the specific issue tactic that involved using verbal cues that keep refocusing the parent and the adolescent on the issue of the conflict rather than the behavior of the adolescent. Implementation of this conflict included the use of deflectors such as "nevertheless," "regardless," or "anyway." A mother provides an example of the use of this tactic during a verbal abuse episode when she told her son he could not go out for the night:

> So I said, "no, you can stay home tonight if I don't know who you are going to be with." And he said, "You are such a fuckin' whore, you never trust me, you never let me do things," and things like that. So I simply said, "Nevertheless, you are still staying home tonight." And he kept on verbally abusing me, calling me things, going off on a rampage, and when he finished his statement I would say, "Regardless, you are still staying home tonight." It always made him so mad, he had no response to it and regardless of what he said, I wasn't going to get into it with him and my answer was still no.

Parents viewed the specific issue tactic as being surprisingly effective in preventing the escalation of verbal abuse into either physical or emotional abuse episodes. This tactic allowed parents to maintain control of their emotions, showing adolescents that the parents had heard what they said, but still pointed the interaction back to the issue under dispute.

Engagement Tactics

When placing conflict tactics into the specific context of abuse, a number of conflict tactics emerged that are not previously identified in the conflict typology; these were categorized and labeled as an engagement strategy. The engagement strategy is best defined as tactics used by parents when they have no other option but to engage their adolescent in a conflict situation and are particularly focused on preventing the escalation of conflict into abuse. In fact, these parents believed they were abused because they made decisions that the adolescent did not agree with such as curfew times, not granting permission to go to certain activities, forcing completion of chores, or requiring attendance at certain functions. Engagement tactics identified included (a) warning, (b) good-cop-bad-cop, (c) strategic confrontation, (d) manipulation of physical space, (e) tag-team arguing, (f) physical compliance and restraint, and (g) repetition tactics.

Warning.   These parents learned that although a conflict between one parent and adolescent may have ended earlier in the day, this did not necessarily mean it would not be revisited with the other parent. The warning tactic was used to inform an absent parent of a conflict that had occurred earlier in the day. For example, if earlier in the day a mother and adolescent had engaged in a serious conflict over an issue, the mother would call the father to inform him of what had occurred to prepare him if he was faced with the same question when he got home that evening. When adolescents did engage the other parent, this was the last opportunity to get a yes and often the confrontation with the second parent over the same issue escalated into abuse. A father reported:

> You communicate [with your spouse], because if the kid comes in and says "I want to talk to you," you look at, you know, your husband or wife . . . across the room. . . . But you don't say nothing. You just kind of look . . . and you know this is what the call earlier in the day was about. So you can support each other and kind of be on the same side on this.

Although these episodes often escalated into abuse, the warning tactic helped parents maintain a united front and prevented adolescents from manipulating parents against each other.

Good-Cop-Bad-Cop.   A unique tactic that emerged from these data was labeled the good-cop-bad-cop tactic—a tactic specifically focused on preventing verbal abuse from escalating into physical or emotional. Participants realized that, when having to make decisions that are unpopular with the adolescent, the news was often better received when given by the parent not in the same proximity as the adolescent. When a teen asked a parent to do something, the parent present (good cop) advised the teen to ask the parent who was absent (bad cop). The teen would then call the bad cop on the phone to ask for permission to do something. If the bad cop said no, the conflict episode often escalated into verbal abuse over the phone. Interestingly, these teens focused on only one parent at a time during episodes of abuse. The argument on the phone would continue until the adolescent would either hang up or, in many cases, break the phone. The teen then verbally abused the bad cop to the good cop, who would be supportive of both the teen and the bad cop, using deflectors such as "nevertheless, he is your father and he has made his decision," or "I know this is frustrating for you but you need to just hang in there." A mother explained this tactic:

> My husband and I decided that one of the best ways to deal with him at times . . . was to have the other person call on the phone and be the bad guy. So, say he wanted to go somewhere and we were going to say, "no." I would say, "You'll have to chat with your father about that," so he would call dad at work and dad would say, "No, I've decided you can't go. . . ." And I would be the one at home with him, listening to all of this taking place. . . . He would cuss and he would swear. . . . And they'd go through the argument back and forth like they normally do [on the phone]. But then he was so upset finally he would throw—or hang up the phone and then he'd proceed to beat the phone into a million pieces, throw it and break it. And it was very interesting because the person at home, even though you would hear this outrage and this swearing and this breaking of the phone, it was never directed at you. So, we learned a good way to deal with this type—and to control the level of intensity and keep it from becoming physical abuse toward a person was to have—use the phone. And we went through fourteen, fifteen, more, maybe twenty phones in order to accomplish it.

Parents reported this tactic worked surprisingly well and often diffused what could have been a more serious situation.

Strategic Confrontation.   Another engagement tactic parents used was strategic confrontation. Because the location of the conflict often played a role in how severe a conflict became, some parents strategically chose the location of where to address an issue. For example, if adolescents were more likely to abuse their parents in private, parents often waited to address an issue in public. Other adolescents had a history of being verbally abusive in public so these parents would choose to address the issue in a private setting. Although strategic confrontation did not stop a conflict from escalating, parents believed it helped prevent escalation into physical or emotional abuse.

Manipulation of Space.   When participants were engaged in a conflict episode with an adolescent that had the signs of escalating into physical abuse, they reported being careful to manipulate their physical space. For example, if an adolescent was being verbally abusive, parents would physically position objects (e.g., table, counter, chair) between themselves and the teen to prevent the teen from being able to grab the parent. If a teen moved closer to the parent during an episode, parents often stepped back. Using the manipulation of space tactic often prevented verbal abuse from escalating to physical abuse.

Tag-Team Arguing.   Many times adolescents and parents were engaged in conflict episodes that often lasted up to three hours. Participants used the tag-team arguing tactic rather than give in to an adolescent's demands. Tag-team arguing involved participants taking turns engaging the adolescent so that one parent would not get worn out or overly frustrated. The goal of tag-team arguing was to enable parents to maintain their composure while at the same time wearing out the adolescent until he or she stopped the conflict.

Physical Compliance and Restraint.   The physical compliance and restraint tactic was the use of physical measures to gain compliance or control an adolescent's behavior. This tactic was problematic because adolescents were often larger and stronger than parents and the use of it many times escalated conflict. For example, if a parent asked an adolescent to get in the car and the adolescent refused, the only way the parent was able to get the adolescent into the car was to lead the teen and physically put his or her limbs into the car; this tactic was usually used with girls as they were less likely to respond physically to the parent.

However, parents often used physical restraint when the adolescent was physically abusing a parent or damaging property. Parents may have sat on, lay on, or held the adolescent in a bear hug or hold that prevented him or her from moving until calmed down. As a mother described:

> And he would have to be in holds all the time, where I would have to have him on my lap and wrap my legs around his legs and my arms around his body. . . . And so I ended up laying on him on the floor for like an hour. And the whole time he was hitting me, punching me, biting me, kicking me. And I finally told my little [other] kid, I said, "You need to call the cops." And so he did.

Participants reported using physical compliance when they believed there was no other way of getting the adolescents to comply with their wishes; physical restraint was used to prevent the adolescents from physically harming parents, property, or themselves.

Repetition.   Finally, the tactic of repetition involved parents repeating over and over to an adolescent the reasons for saying no to a request. Participants reported that when they used the repetition tactic, they focused on using calming nonverbal cues such as a soft voice, relaxed body tension, or a slow vocal rate. A mother stated, "And I calmly went over and over the discussion with him, softly and really slowly retelling him why he couldn't do something, over and over while he is yelling until he calms down." Participants reported that the repetition tactic required very deliberate verbal and nonverbal communication and although at times proved effective, at other times, regardless of how long repetition was used, the conflict eventually escalated into other forms of abuse.

Discussion

First, it is important to note that the tactics used by these parents were used in attempts to prevent the escalation of conflict into verbal, physical, and emotional abuse and appear to be unique to adolescent-to-parent abuse episodes. When verbal abuse occurred, it was viewed as an indicator that the conflict was escalating and if not stopped or diffused, then physical or emotional abuse often resulted (Eckstein, 2004, 2005; Price, 1996). These parents considered tactics successful if a verbal abuse episode did not escalate into physical or emotional abuse and were willing to try numerous tactics in attempts to prevent abuse.

Second, the identification of the engagement strategy and its tactics is an important contribution to understanding adolescent-to-parent abuse. Because parents believed it was necessary to engage in some conflict episodes, engagement tactics were specific attempts to maintain parental authority as well as prevent escalation of verbal abuse into physical or emotional abuse. Parents' choice of a conflict tactic was based on the previous history of adolescent-to-parent abuse interactions. Parents realized stopping verbal abuse was virtually impossible and used it as an indicator that a tactic needed to be implemented if escalation of the abuse was to be prevented.

Finally, these parents' reports of conflict episodes reveal the rapid and extreme escalation of conflict into verbal abuse. Participants were very specific in the description of their efforts used to prevent abuse; this may be a sign that experiencing abuse makes parents hypersensitive to the communicative behaviors that play a role in escalating conflict in intensity and as a result, parents may be more willing to experiment with different conflict tactics in attempts to prevent abuse. Because all these participants sought outside counseling and attended parenting classes, they may approach an adolescents' abusive behavior as a puzzle that they should be able to solve. Unfortunately, the majority of these parents were unable to change the behavior of their abusive adolescent and the abuse continued until the adolescent left home.

Limitations and Future Research

All studies have areas that can be improved upon and this study is no exception. First, the homogeneity of the sample is both a limitation and strength. Although generalizability is a problem, because of the early stage of research on adolescent-to-parent abuse, having a homogeneic sample actually provides a strong basis for branching off for future research. Second, these data use retrospective self-reports, and issues of accurate recall may be a consideration. The ideal research situation would be to observe adolescent–parent dyads engaged in conflict episodes escalating into abuse; however, ethical dimensions prevent researchers from doing this.

Finally, these reports are from only one perspective—the abused parent—and do not represent the whole adolescent–parent relationship. I specifically asked these parents to describe a verbal, physical, and emotional abuse episode and as a result, we see only the abusive side of these relationships. Many of these parents expressed great affection for, and gave indications of the good times they experienced with, these teens. Future research should provide descriptions of the entire adolescent–parent relationship such as reports from abusive adolescents, siblings, and others in the family network, the impact on the family, and relational satisfaction.

This study is just a brief glimpse into a phenomenon that impacts many families and yet, family counselors, researchers, and professionals have a long way to go in helping victims of adolescent-to-parent abuse. These parents' reflections on their attempts to prevent abuse episodes should enable us to better understand families experiencing such abuse.

Questions for Consideration and Discussion

1. Brule draws upon research that indicates the superiority of integrative conflict strategies over distributive and avoidance strategies. Based on what has been discussed in this chapter and your own experiences, why do you think integrative strategies are more effective?
2. The parents in this study reported using few distributive tactics with their teens. What might be some causal factors for this choice?
3. Professional counselors had recommended physical withdrawal to many of these parents; however, they found it ineffective. What would be the advantages of physical withdrawal in abusive conflict (i.e., why might counselors recommend it?) and why might these parents have found it ineffective?
4. Brule's study resulted in the creation of a group of tactics she calls "engagement." In these examples, engagement allowed the parent to engage in the conflict, while preventing escalation to abuse. What of other engagement strategies could be used and what are other times when engagement might be useful (besides in parent–teen abuse situations)?
5. Each participant in this study had previously been involved in multiple family counseling programs. What kind of impacts might this have had on the findings of this study?

References

Canary, D. J., & Spitzberg, B. H. (1987). Appropriateness and effectiveness perceptions of conflict strategies. *Human Communication Research, 14*, 93–118.

Canary, D. J., & Spitzberg, B. H. (1989). A model of perceived competence of conflict strategies. *Human Communication Research, 15*, 630–649.

Canary, D. J., & Spitzberg, B. H. (1990). Attribution biases and associations between conflict strategies and competence outcomes. *Communication Monographs, 57*, 139–151.

Cornell, C. P., & Gelles, R. J. (1981, November). *Adolescent to parent violence.* Paper presented at the annual meetings of the American Society of Criminology, Washington, DC.

Creswell, J. Q. (1998). *Qualitative inquiry and research design: Choosing among five traditions.* Thousand Oaks, CA: Sage.

Cupach, W. R., & Canary, D. J. (1997). *Competence in interpersonal conflict.* New York: McGraw-Hill.

Eckstein, N. J. (2004). Emergent issues in families experiencing adolescent-to-parent abuse. *Western Journal of Communication, 68*, 365–388.

Eckstein, N. J. (2005). *Adolescent-to-parent abuse: Abused parents' perceptions of the meaning and goals of adolescents' verbal, physical, and emotional abuse.* Manuscript submitted for publication.

Gelles, R. J. & Straus, M. A. (1988). *Intimate violence.* New York: Simon & Schuster.

Harbin, H. T., & Madden, D. J. (1979). Battered parents: A new syndrome. *American Journal of Psychiatry, 136*, 1288–1291.

Holstein, J. A., & Gubrium, J. F. (1995). *The active interview.* Thousand Oaks, CA: Sage.

Lulofs, R. S., & Cahn, D. D. (2000). *Conflict: From theory to action*. Boston: Allyn & Bacon.

McCracken, G. (1988). *The long interview*. Newbury Park, CA: Sage.

Messman, S. J., & Canary, D. J. (1998). Patterns of conflict in personal relationships. In B. H. Spitzberg & W. R. Cupach (Eds.), *The dark side of personal relationships* (pp. 121–152). Mahwah, NJ: Erlbaum.

Miles, M. B., & Huberman, A. M. (1994). *Qualitative data analysis: A sourcebook of new methods* (2nd ed.). Thousand Oaks, CA: Sage.

Price, J. A. (1996). *Power and compassion: Working with difficult adolescents and abused parents*. New York: Guilford Press.

Rueter, M. A., & Conger, R. D. (1995). Antecedents of parent-adolescent disagreements. *Journal of Marriage and Family, 57*, 435–448.

Schuett, D. (1999, February 25). "I wanted him to be a good child." *Post Bulletin*, p. 7B.

Sillars, A. L. (1986, April). *Procedures for coding interpersonal conflict (revised)* [Manual]. Missoula: University of Montana, Department of Interpersonal Communication.

Smetana, J. G. (1995). Conflict and coordination in adolescent–parent relationships. In S. Shulman (Ed.), *Close relationships and socioemotional development* (Vol. 7, pp. 155–184). Norwood, NJ: Ablex.

Spitzberg, B. H. (1997). Violence in intimate relationships. In W. R. Cupach & D. J. Canary (Eds.), *Competence in interpersonal communication* (pp. 174–201). New York: McGraw-Hill.

Straus, M. A., Gelles, R. J., & Steinmetz, S. K. (1980). *Behind closed doors: Violence in the American family*. New York: Anchor Press.

Wilmot, W. W., & Hocker, J. L. (2001). *Interpersonal conflict* (6th ed.). New York: McGraw-Hill.

Enacting Conflict as Resistance: Urban Indian Women in Hindu Arranged Marriages

Devika Chawla

As considered throughout the text, culture has a strong impact on our family communication patterns. In this article, Chawla considers how cultural factors are a part of family conflict that occurs in the arranged marriages of urban Indian women. The narratives here express how cultural conflict (i.e., the more traditional Hindu family practices meeting more liberal modern urban views of family and individual power) can become an important factor in family experiences, and exhibit the attempts of family members to cope with this conflict. As you read, consider the ways in which culture, as well as cultural changes, have affected family conflict in your experiences.

L.B.A.

The Context: Hindu Arranged Marriages

Arranged marriages are a norm in Asian cultures such as India, China, Japan, and Korea (Applbaum, 1995). Premised upon similarity of social standing, which often includes the caste, class, religion, and education of the prospective couple, the arranged marriage is the most popular form of organizing a marital relationship among Hindu Indians in India (Mullatti, 1995). Despite forces of modernization, urbanization, and liberalization, the number of arranged marriages in India far outnumbers "love" marriages. In fact, an estimated 95% of all Hindu marriages in India are still arranged marriages, thus making them a norm rather than an exception (Bumiller, 1990; Kapadia, 1958; Kapur, 1970; Mullatti, 1995).

Contemporary arranged marriages are generally organized by parents and elderly kin (Sur, 1973). In earlier times, intermediaries called sambhalas, or traditional matchmakers, were employed to keep the genealogical history of each family, and make sure that the bride and groom were not related from five to seven generations (Sur, 1973). In more recent times, these criteria have stretched to include other characteristics. Mullatti (1995) outlines seven criteria that are currently followed by matchmakers, kin, parents, and relatives: caste, social structure, moral value compatibility, academic compatibility, occupational compatibility, the family's moral history, and horoscope compatibility (though not necessarily in this order). In the past two decades, parents have begun looking for matches for their children through matrimonial columns in newspapers, magazines, and now even the Internet (Mullatti, 1995).

Originally, the most appropriate form of Hindu marriage was a union arranged by parents and kin, and is said to be derived from laws interpreted in the *Dharmashastras* which in turn have their roots in the 3,000-year-old hymns called *Vedas* and *Smritis*, the oldest surviving documents of the Indian civilization recorded between 4000 B.C. to 1200 A.D. (Kapadia, 1958). A general theme across these scriptures was that marriage was a duty and a religious sacrament that was required of all human beings for the well-being of the community. In fact, marriage and procreation are one of the four necessary stages in a

Hindu's life. Marriage constitutes the second stage, *grahastha*, aimed at progeny and sexual activities.

However, there is no evidence that any of these life stages were structured toward women. Therefore, although marriage was required of all Hindus, its advantages were enjoyed only by men, who benefited from both the spiritual and economic understandings of the Hindu marriage (Mukherjee, 1978). Spiritually, men benefited because they married in order to beget sons who would light their funeral pyre. This ensured the male line a place in heaven, rebirth in the next life as a human being, as well as the liberation of future generations of the family (*moksha*). The need for a male heir was also an economic necessity—a male heir was desired because he alone could continue the family line and inherit ancestral property.[1] Therefore, historically, the Hindu arranged marriage was "male-emphasized" (Mukherjee, 1978). It has even been suggested the word *wife* was often used interchangeably with *household* (Mukherjee, 1978; Sastri, 1972, 1974). In other words, a woman's role in her own home as well as in her marital home was largely objectified.

Once married, an Indian woman would typically enter a joint family system. An ideal Hindu joint family in contemporary India consists of a man and wife, their adult sons, their wives and children, and younger children of the parental couple (Gore, 1968; Sharma, 1997). A joint family can often be looked upon as a multiplicity of genealogically related nuclear families living under the same roof and sharing in worship, food, and property.[2] Very often, a joint family has been described as a group of adult male coparceners and their dependents—the dependents being wives and children (Gore, 1968). For instance, if a father has two sons and one daughter, the sons would be considered joint heirs (coparceners); but, a daughter would not inherit property (see endnote 1). According to Hindu law, an adult male and his sons were coparceners in ancestral property (Gore, 1968).

The very structure of the joint family contributed to an overall subordinate status of women. Formal authority was always centered on the oldest male and thereby hierarchically bound by age. This hierarchy occurred on many levels. Women were married and brought into the family that consisted of men who were all related by blood. They were not only biologically on the outside, but also they were treated as "symbolic-outsiders" until they gave birth to a son. Daughters-in-law would be completely included in the family only once they begot a son. And, if they did not beget a son, then a new wife could be *brought into the family* (although this changed with the Hindu Divorce Bill in 1952; Kapadia, 1958). Once married, the conjugal relationship between couples was discouraged from becoming too romanticized because the emphasis was on the socioeconomic welfare of the family. This contributed to the degradation of women's status in the family, which in turn was supported by denial of property rights to women and by women's inability to achieve economic independence (see endnote 1). Role and authority segregation of men and women were therefore essential to the economic well-being of a joint Hindu family. Even though women remained necessary to the family, they remained powerless, property-less, and dependent within the household which they symbolized.

It is evident from this discussion that women were largely seen as an instrument of procreation in the Hindu marriage system. Not only were they a "silent" voice in the historical literature, but their experiences of marital life remain largely unexplored. This is true even of social scientific literature which has continued to focus on variable-analytical studies that explore marital adjustment, attitudes, marital satisfaction, comparisons to love marriages, and so on (see Chandak & Sprecher, 1992; Dhyani & Kumar, 1996; Kapadia, 1958; Kapur 1970; Rao & Rao, 1975; Ross, 1961; Yelsma & Athappilly, 1988). Moreover, many of these studies are dated. The most recent longitudinal study to focus on arranged marriages was a sociopsy-chological survey published by Promilla Kapur in 1970, now over three decades old.

Given the scarcity of literature on the marital experiences of Hindu women in arranged marriages, I designed a narrative study that would access marital narratives of women who had been involved in arrange marriages in the last three decades. In the follow-ing section, I briefly describe the research practices that I undertook for the study. Follow-ing this, I explore the main sites of conflict and negotiation in the family that emerged from the interview narratives of my participants. Finally, I offer a brief discussion of the implica-tions of such conflict in the study of diverse family systems.

Research Practices and Thematic Analysis

Aided with this historical and sociological knowledge, I traveled to Delhi, India, in the summer of 2003 to conduct life-history interviews with urban middle-class north Indian women who had chosen to have their marriages arranged for them. Broadly described, I centered my research practices around an ethnographic qualitative interviewing frame-work. Such approaches are especially sensitive to context, dynamic processes, and subjec-tive perspectives, and allow us to understand experiences that are inaccessible from survey methods (Denzin & Lincoln, 2000; Strauss & Corbin, 1998).

My participants included 20 urban, working and nonworking, middle-class women who ranged in age from 27 to 44 and were married either in the early 1980s, the 1990s, or the early 2000s. I accessed the groups using a word-of-mouth and snowball strategy. A majority of the women were referred to me by families in the Delhi community where I myself reside. Their occupations ranged from homemakers to corporate executives, med-ical doctors, teachers, special education counselors, sexual rights activists, journalists, day care workers, and private entrepreneurs.

I designed a chronological interview protocol that was structured around three broad domains—girlhood, premarriage, and marriage. It comprised 25 open-ended questions that focused on socialization processes, family interactions, events, and turning points. Once completed, each interview was treated as a case. The interviews were all audiotaped and transcribed by me. After doing so, I conducted a thematic analysis to search for shared experiences that were common to the stories.

Seven broad themes, two of which focused upon conflict, emerged from my analysis. Through my participant's narratives, I found that family and marital conflict seemed to be rooted in one authority figure, that of the mother-in-law. Therefore, addressing the mother-in-law as a power-authority figure emerged as the primary site of conflict in the women's marital stories. My participants named her as a threat and coped with her by "performing resistance" which emerged in the form of a "material embodied resistance" and "silence." In the follow-ing section, I rely on my participants' self-stories to explore the aforementioned themes.

Addressing the Mother-in-Law

When a Hindu woman marries and moves to her new home, she joins a world in which all men are related by blood and the women are unrelated to each other (unless one is the daughter of the house who eventually does leave home). Within this world of the women, there exists a matriarchal hierarchy with the mother-in-law as the most significant person in terms of authority. In fact, a woman's marital experience often begins with encountering the mother-in-law. At least 60% of my participants were married into joint or semijoint families (see endnote 2), and the mother-in-law was invariably the first person they encountered. This figure merged as the first site and figure of conflict in my participants' narratives. All participants, regardless of age or year of marriage, spoke about the persisting presence of the mother-in-law. They portrayed her as a "monstrous" character who dominated their marital relationship. Her presence was so continuous that there seemed to be an acceptance of her interfering presence.

This process can be seen in Anita's story.[3] Twenty-nine-year-old Anita, who was married into a very traditional extended family, repeatedly referenced her mother-in-law in her story. In the course of her marriage, Anita's parents-in-law had disapproved of her wearing non-Indian or Western clothes. Anita explained that, although her mother-in-law never verbalized her disapproval, Anita nevertheless sensed the disapproval in her silence. Addressing this, she explained:

> No, she doesn't say anything, but you can make out. Because my mom-in-law is like that, no? I don't know sometimes I feel that she doesn't say anything, because she knows that I will not take any nonsense. That's why she doesn't speak up. But, it's okay because I don't like to cross her. If I cross her I cross him [my husband], and I don't want to do that. His whole happiness is connected with the parents. If I keep his parents happy he is very happy, you know?

In this exchange, Anita illustrated the importance of her mother-in-law in her marital life. In fact, as the interview progressed her relationship with her mother-in-law took more space in the story than her own marital relationship.

A resonating experience was related by Reema, a 37-year-old woman who had been married for 18 years. Reema's narrative was saturated with stories about her mother-in-law. She charted a trajectory that spanned a description, an explanation, and the consequence of the mother-in-law's presence in her life. Upon speculating on the "whys" of the conflict with her mother-in-law, Reema explained that the troubles were rooted in the beginning years of her marriage:

> Maybe because my husband is the only son (male) as my father-in-law expired very early. My mother-in-law must have been very attached to him or something. Then after the marriage the husband looks after more about the wife, that is there among newlyweds anyway. So she must be feeling that thing—left out. Maybe the problem started that way.

By suggesting that the problem starts "that way," Reema was generalizing that perhaps this was the reason for mother-in-law conflicts in most homes. Describing her verbal altercations with her mother-in-law, Reema attributed them to power struggles in the home:

> Yeah there are many. It's always a little thing, of no consequence. The fight starts about just anything. If I reply back then it becomes big. Then she says, "She doesn't listen to anyone, she doesn't agree with anything." Then they call up [my parents] and say, "She replied back and she did this." So they [my parents] used to say that, "We will make her understand, we can take her home for a while." Even now it's still there, but very less. I keep myself very busy. Now I don't involve in these things. I make it a point to go out, have my kitty parties

and all. Otherwise I go to the Avon store. I do this to make myself busy. There is not much money in it. You don't have any earning, but it keeps me occupied.

Reema's mother-in-law was a discipliner in the home, and if Reema did not "behave well," her "misdeeds" were reported to her parents. In whatever verbal or nonverbal ways the conflict occurred, there was a sense of foreboding about this matriarchal presence. Only some of the participants had been able to make spaces for themselves, both symbolically and physically, in their own homes. However, most of them were bitter about their continuing struggles with their mothers-in-law. This bitterness shadowed Suparna's story.

Thirty-seven-year-old Suparna's story was more old-fashioned. She had been married to her husband for spiritual reasons. Her mother's guru had suggested a match with a man who was one social class lower than her natal family, but belonged to the same religious community. Blindly believing the spiritual consul, her mother had urged her to marry this man not realizing that Suparna was unaccustomed to doing household chores. Suparna's mother-in-law expected a daughter-in-law who knew how to manage the household. Describing her inability to work in her in-law's kitchen, which was small and dirty compared to the one in her parental home, Suparna described some early altercations with her mother-in-law:

> She would say, "Why don't you work in the kitchen? Did your parents not see initially that we don't have a servant? Did they not prepare you for this?" I was like all young girls. I would like to get up late. I would get up at eight and I would find her scary eyes looking at me. I was asked not to get out of my room without taking a bath and I could not get out in a dressing gown. I had to get up early in the morning. They would get up at five, so I was expected to do the same. Things like that, you know? My husband would not say anything, and ours was not a very pleasant relationship. We used to have a lot of fights because of my in-laws. He would not accept his parents' mistakes. He thought that they were the best. She is my husband's soft spot. You know he never said "no" to her for anything. That's something very wrong I feel for my husband.

Suparna's story involved power struggles with her mother-in-law over chores, space, and her husband's attention. These eventually led to a property split in the family, leading to the literal emergence of two spatial units as they each moved into different family homes. During the time of the interview, her struggles with her mother-in-law continued.

Anita, Reema, and Suparna's stories illustrate that the mother-in-law is a power-authority figure in the Hindu joint family. A conflict with her is comparable to a conflict with the entire family. Not only is she the first matriarchal figure that a daughter-in-law encounters, but she also becomes a conduit to the rest of the family. Rather than get involved in overt conflict with her, my participants utilized and enacted a strategy of resistance to her interference.

Performing Resistance

In my study, I used the term *resistance* as a conflict resolution and negotiation strategy employed by my participants. Even though none of the participants used the terms *negotiation* or *resolution*, their stories seem to suggest that they had performed resistance to accomplish these very goals. In other words, they used resistance to carve literal and emotional spaces for themselves in their homes. As a response to conflict in the stories of my coparticipants, I defined resistance very loosely—it constituted material embodied resistance and silence against filial structure. Both qualities of resistance were articulated in distinct ways by the participants.

Material Embodied Resistance

By a material embodied resistance I am implying that some participants relied on external objects to enact resistance. As already explored, Anita had been discouraged from wearing Western clothes such as jeans, skirts, or dresses. As a new bride, the north Indian traditional dress, such as a sari or the salwar kameez, had been imposed upon her by her mother-in-law. For about five years, Anita adhered to these rules, but on occasion she would slip outside the house unnoticed in her jeans. She was materially resisting filial norms. On one such occasion she was caught by her father-in-law, who complained to her husband. Revealing her response to being disciplined about clothing, Anita told me:

> I didn't say anything, but I told my husband, look I am married to you, I'm not married to them. I will wear what I want. He said, "Okay agreed." He was agreeable to the idea that a human being should be able to wear clothes of their choice.

This negotiation with her husband was a resistant act against material norms which Anita successfully accomplished. Such material resistances might seem small, but they seemed to shape Anita's story.

Later on in the interview, Anita spoke of other restrictions that she had encountered. When single, she was used to dining out. Both her mother- and father-in-law had imposed a rule that required every family member to eat dinner together. Not one to be deterred by this, Anita began a bodily rebellion against the rule and was able to negotiate new rules of dining out with her husband. In doing this, she was able to make her marriage take precedence over the family. She reflected on this when she said:

> I just kept losing weight. There was a time when I was 38 kilograms [84 pounds] because I stopped eating at home. I don't like eating at home, and on top of it, it was a sort of rebellion. I was trying to show my husband that I will not eat at all.

This embodiment of material resistance was a recurrent theme in the narratives. Meena, a 27-year-old doctor, was married into a semijoint family. At the time of the interview she was living alone with her husband, but her in-laws often stayed with her. Meena spoke of beginning to wear "cut-sleeve" blouses even though her mother-in-law disapproved. Wearing those clothes in front of her husband's family was a resistant act through which she was sending the message that she was a "differentiated self," and that she would make her own rules while adhering to some of theirs.

> My own father never stopped me from wearing any type of dresses. My mother-in-law thinks that girls shouldn't wear jeans and sleeveless blouses. Once I shifted to my own home, I started wearing my normal clothes. I loved wearing shorts. When they are here, to not make them unhappy, I wear a nightgown over them.

Meena felt that she was able to resist because of the support she received from her husband.

> When they asked me not to wear these clothes, I told my husband, "So what should I do?" He said, "You wear whatever you want, don't worry I'll talk to them." He was supportive. He could have said, "No, my parents don't like it, so you shouldn't wear it." Instead he said, "No I like it and you should wear what everyone is wearing nowadays."

There were two factors that influenced Meena's resistance—support from her husband and beginning to live in her own home. Both Anita and Meena had involved their husbands in their resistant acts, thus garnering support from them. Although Anita and Meena embodied resistance in material ways, other women told stories of performing resistance through silence.

Silent Resistance

Neeta, a 44-year-old woman entrepreneur, was married into a joint family in which she was required to live not only with a mother-in-law, but also a grandmother-in-law. Her personal history as a single person had been a source of conflict with her mother-in-law. As an unmarried woman, Neeta had been "picky" about whom she would marry. Word of this had reached her husband's home. Her grandmother-in-law and mother-in-law were aware that she was "outspoken," and that she had rejected many men before she chose their son. Therefore, when Neeta got married they were determined to keep her "in check." They imposed rules on her that involved learning how to cook, how to obey them, and how to do household chores. Neeta coped with these rules via silence. Describing this, she said:

> I already knew that I was known to be very "outspoken." I did not want to do anything that would aggravate this. Yet I did not know what to do. I was not happy. Then my grandmother-in-law came to stay with us and that was a major adjustment because she was very clever and she had heard that I was sharp. She knew that if they don't keep me suppressed then I will speak out too much. So, the initial year was very difficult. I would cry sometimes—in hiding.

In trying to disprove her previous reputation to her in-laws, Neeta remained silent. In those early years she grew closer to her husband, who had been a stranger to her. Her silence with his family pushed them closer, and she gained his emotional support. In her silence, Neeta managed to shift the focus from family to marriage. In becoming closer to her husband, she had started helping him out in his business, which was undergoing a rough patch. During all this time, she carried on working in the household and also took over the reins of the business. In starting to help her husband economically, Neeta had emerged from the silence, and/or defeated the silence that had been imposed upon her. Neeta explained this transformation and her new self very succinctly:

> I think after marriage for a few years I really tried hard to be like a typical wife. Later, I was just trying to survive. I was busy with my house, my work, my children and I was trying to run the whole show. I think I was trying to be a superwoman, but at that time I was trying to be the best at whatever I was doing. My children had to be the best. In my work whatever I could do, even at home *I tried you know to do all the work that I can do.*

Silence emerged as strength in Neeta's narrative. Along similar lines, 44-year-old Naina, an economically independent corporate executive, was married into a joint family in which her mother-in-law tried to keep her in check. Naina utilized silence as a deliberate resistant strategy in dealing with conflict with her mother-in-law and other members of the family.

Naina entered her marriage as a confident and financially independent woman. However, she soon began to be harassed by her husband's family because they expected a traditional Indian wife. At first, she responded by replying and fighting back. When this did not solve the problem, she addressed the issue with her husband, thus shifting their story from family to marriage. She stopped overt resistance and handed the conflict over to her husband, thereby attaining a silent resistance:

> He took over and that was the only way we saved our sanity. Whenever I tried doing things on my own it never used to work. His family used to outplay me. They are much sharper, more politically minded, wiser about silly games. I think Mahesh latched on to the fact that I was cracking up. He told me, "You may be a communications expert, but you don't know how to communicate with this clan and I know how to communicate with them, so now you stay out. If they ask you anything just keep quiet and either you say we'll talk in front of Mahesh or don't say anything, just keep quiet."

Both Neeta and Naina used silence as a shield against the mother-in-law, which in turn brought them closer to their husbands. Anita and Meena used a material embodied resistance, with a similar goal—to garner support from their husbands. Resistance worked in a two-dimensional way in these marital stories. First, it shielded these women against the mother-in-law. Second, resistance brought these women closer to their husbands because they began confiding in their spouses to resist the matriarchal figure.

Final Thoughts

It is evident from the previous examples that the structural configuration of the Hindu joint (and semijoint) family creates two concentric circles of power in the household. The outer circle consists of the male line in which all men are bound by blood. The inner circle or the interior world of women, with the mother-in-law as the ruling matriarch, consists of women unrelated not only to each other but also to the men. In a typical situation, a daughter-in-law first experiences the inner circle and encounters the mother-in-law. This allows us to understand a type of marital conflict that is located outside the husband–wife relationship. It resides in a figure of authority in the family. Interestingly, even as this figure comes to represent conflict, it is clear that in resisting the mother-in-law, women gain access to marital support from their husbands, thus solidifying their marriage. The mother-in-law, even as she creates conflict, opens up channels for the daughters-in-law, allowing them access into the outer circle of men in which their husbands reside.

Questions for Consideration and Discussion

1. The topic considered in this research is somewhat sensitive in nature. What elements of the methodology do you think might have made participants more at ease discussing these issues?
2. Chawla's work considers, in part, a cultural conflict between more conservative mothers-in-law and their less conservative daughters-in-law. What would be other examples of times when cultures may conflict within family settings?
3. The narratives of these participants reflect upon issues of family power and the importance of the mother-in-law in Hindu family culture. In your family experiences, what specific family roles or positions have been culturally established as powerful, and why do you think that is the case?
4. Chawla's respondents used both silence and material embodied resistance in their efforts to reject the power of the mother-in-law. What examples of these strategies have you seen in family settings?
5. What do you see as the overarching value of this type of research for our understandings of family?

Endnotes

1. Hindu women were not entitled to any property rights until 1956, and therefore were economically dependent on their fathers, husbands, and later sons (Gore, 1968; Kapur, 1970). With the amendment of Hindu property laws in 1956 that allowed for female inheritance, and increased levels of women entering the workforce by choice in the latter half of the twentieth century, there was some change in gendered roles within families (Gore, 1968; Kapadia, 1958; Kapur, 1970). Further, in the 1980s and 1990s the liberalization of developing world economies created new jobs for women throughout the world, including India (Government of India, 2001). In particular, the last two decades saw an upsurge of women in both the urban and rural workforces. Of the 314 million Indians currently in the workforce, 89 million are women (Government of India, 2001). Despite the promise and arrival of economic independence, many urban Hindu women continue to choose arranged marriages. It would seem that the breakdown of economic disparities would lead to an increase in self-arranged or love marriages, yet that has not been the case.

2. In this study I have used the words *joint* and *semijoint* to refer to family structure and cohabitation patterns. A semijoint family could mean one in which one son and his family live together with his parents while the other siblings live elsewhere.

3. In this chapter, all the women's names have been changed to pseudonyms in order to protect their privacy.

References

Applbaum, K. D. (1995). Marriage with a proper stranger: Arranged marriage in metropolitan Japan. *Journal of Ethnology, 34,* 37–51.

Bumiller, E. (1990). *May you be the mother of 100 sons: A journey among the women of India.* New York: Fawcett Columbine.

Chandak, R., & Sprecher, S. (1992). Attitudes about arranged marriage and dating among men and women from India. *Free Inquiry in Creative Psychology, 20*(1), 59–69.

Denzin, N. K., & Lincoln, Y. S. (2000). *Handbook of qualitative research* (2nd ed.). Thousand Oaks, CA: Sage.

Dhyani, J., & Kumar, P. (1996). Marital adjustment: A study of some related factors. *Indian Journal of Clinical Psychology, 23*(2), 112–116.

Gore, M. S. (1968). *Urbanization and family change.* New York: Humanities Press.

Government of India. (2001). National Commission for Women Report. New Delhi, India: Ministry of Education and Social Welfare, 2001.

Kapadia, K. M. (1958). *Marriage and family in India.* Calcutta, India: Oxford University Press.

Kapur, P. (1970). *Marriage and the working woman in India.* Delhi, India: Vikas.

Mukherjee, P. (1978). *Hindu women: Normative models.* New Delhi: Orient Longman Ltd.

Mullatti, L. (1995). Families in India: Beliefs and realities. *Journal of Comparative Family Studies, 26*(1), 11–25.

Rao, V. V., & Rao, N. (1975). Arranged marriages: An assessment of the attitudes of college students. *Journal of Comparative Family Studies, 7*(3), 433–453.

Ross, A. D. (1961). *The Hindu family in the urban setting.* Bombay, India: Oxford University Press.

Sastri, H. C. (1972). *The social background of the forms of marriage in ancient India* (Vol. 1). Calcutta, India: Sanskrit Pustak Bhandar.

Sastri, H. C. (1974). *The social background of the forms of marriage in ancient India* (Vol. 2). Calcutta, India: Sanskrit Pustak Bhandar.

Sharma, K. L. (1997). *Social stratification in India: Issues and themes.* New Delhi, India: Sage.

Strauss, A., & Corbin, J. (1998). *Basics of qualitative research (2nd* Ed.). Thousand Oaks, CA: Sage.

Sur, A. K. (1973). *Sex and marriage in India.* Bombay, India: Allied.

Yelsma, P., & Athappilly, K. (1988). Marital satisfaction and communication practices: Comparisons among Indian and American couples. *Journal of Comparative Family Studies, 19,* 37–54.

Section 3: Conclusions and Application—
Power and Conflict in Your
Family Experience _____

This chapter has introduced you to some theoretical conceptions of conflict and power, ideas about where our conflict management styles and strategies come from, information about conflict outcomes, and discussion of abuse and violence in family strategies. As you attempt to relate this information to your own life, you may need to begin by rethinking your concept of conflict. This will help you consider how you engage in conflict (the positive and negative), as well as thinking about the possibility of change for negative conflict patterns you might have or observe.

Changing the Way You Think about Conflict

One change that is hard for most people to make, when they learn about conflict theory and research, is to stop thinking of conflict as always a bad thing, and as a situation where one party must win and the other lose (or one party be right and the other wrong). As is indicated in this chapter, conflict is not about right and wrong. Conflict instead is about differences we perceive and how we interact in relation to those differences. Conflict is created in interaction between family members. Although the word *conflict* has negative associations, it is a natural part of our family processes. People are different from one another, thus it is natural that they will have different perceptions, desires, values, and so forth. Conflict is not only natural, but it can also be beneficial. Think about the last big positive change that happened in your family. Were there any conflicts associated with that change? It is likely that, big or small, there were. Often conflict is what encourages us to make change. At some point you may have expressed to your adult caregivers that your curfew (or some other rule) was too strict. This conflict may have resulted in a change of that rule (if you were lucky). When we express our points of difference in the family, it allows us to create changes and that is a growth process for the family and its members. This is the positive value of conflict.

Of course, conflict can at times be a negative experience. Due to the cultural differences in the perception of conflict and beliefs about conflict, engaging in conflict may be more problematic in some cultures than in others. Thus, we must keep in mind that, even though it is not always negative, conflict is not always positive for the interactants either.

When we can begin to think of conflict in this way, not as inherently negative or bad (nor always positive or good) but rather as an ubiquitous part of our family process, it may help us fear conflict less and attend more to how we engage in conflict. As noted by the many scholars referenced in this chapter, it is how we *manage* conflict that has the most effect on relational outcomes, not the amount of conflict itself. Thus, conflict is not something to be feared or simply avoided, but it is worthwhile to think about the ways that we deal with conflict as we interact with family members.

Considering How You Engage in Conflict

As with many other communication patterns, the way we handle conflict is likely due to a variety of factors. Researchers suggest that there are individual factors, cultural and family factors, and role factors that impact our management strategies.

One of the individual factors that researchers believe may be related to our ability to engage in conflict in a productive manner is cognitive complexity. This concept, based on constructivism, relates to the degree to which we think of others in multifaceted, complex ways. From this perspective, individuals who are more cognitively complex are able to create more person-centered messages; however, that doesn't mean they always will (sometimes they may not want to). The concept of complexity and how it relates to conflict management can be used to inform our interactions with others. It can help us understand why children, and even adolescents, may not be able to create messages that are compelling for the other. (Have you ever heard a 13-year-old try to argue with his or her parents based only on what he or she wants and not at all thinking about what the parents might be thinking or wanting?) It also may point to the issue of intentionality in conflict management. Even people who are capable of producing compelling person-centered messages may not always want to. This concept can provide us a lens of understanding for our own conflict choices and also those of others.

In addition to individual factors, the family culture and the larger societal culture impact the ways we interact during conflict. Family conflict patterns are developed through interaction, as members take on particular conflict strategies and roles. Considering the conflict roles exhibited in your family, as discussed by Hughes and Stow, may provide insight into how conflicts proceed in your family interactions, and some alternative role positions you may want to adopt in conflict management. Additionally, children in families learn the way to engage in conflict in part from their parents. When parents manage conflict in ways that are primarily constructive, their children are likely to learn to manage conflict in similar ways (and vice versa). As adults, this information should certainly influence how we engage in conflict with and in the presence of children, and also allows us to understand more about how we arrived at our own patterns of managing conflict.

The larger cultures in which the family is embedded also impact the way members engage in conflict management. Research suggests that gendered patterns, such as women nagging and men withdrawing, have something to do with our expectations of men and women and the relative power differences (and types of power) for the two groups. Scholars also indicate that cultural expectations about individuality, collectivism, and so on may impact our face management strategies in conflict (the extent to which we are concerned with preserving our own position or that of others). As in the Chawla article, culture can strongly impact the power bases held by members of families and who is allowed to use what conflict strategies. And when two cultures clash, conflict can be more difficult to manage due to differing positions and expectations. Thinking about cultural impacts and expectations provides us another method for understanding our own communication in conflict and that of others.

Although the most useful and constructive ways to manage conflict in any family or any particular situation depend on the aspects of that family and situation (and the participants), there seem to be some communicative behaviors that are more destructive than constructive in conflict. The research we addressed in this chapter suggests that some conflict management strategies are more effective than others, and result in better relational outcomes.

One conflict behavior that often seems to have negative repercussions is the refusal to acknowledge or engage in communication about the conflict when other relational partners are seeking to do so. This is discussed in this chapter in terms of demand–withdrawal patterns and the Avoider role discussed by Hughes and Stow. There are likely a variety of factors that impact why individuals engage in withdrawal from conflict. Some research suggests that men are more likely to withdraw from conflict in family settings because of cultural expectations that men should not discuss their feelings. Other individuals may avoid or withdraw from conflict because of a fear that conflict is bad, or because they see themselves as powerless in the conflict situation.

Another set of conflict behaviors that have been shown to have negative outcomes for relationships are those which represent extreme negativity (hostility, name calling, contempt, etc.). Negative affect behaviors in conflict have been shown to have poor effects on relational satisfaction as well as the emotional health of the relational partners. Of course, the extreme form of such negative behaviors is abuse and violence. As discussed in this chapter, cultural patterns are also related to the extent to which abuse is perpetrated in some families, and who is most likely to be the victim of abuse. Abusive relationships have extremely troubling outcomes for victims, abusers, and observers, as can be seen in Eckstein's article.

Some family patterns are extremely negative, but can be prevented or changed with effort. The writings of Chawla and Brule explicitly show how some family interactants have attempted to change or alter negative patterns within their family settings, and how difficult that can be. Additionally, the research studies included in this chapter point to the existence of more positive conflict management strategies that appear to have a more positive impact on relationships and relational interactants; for example, support-reassurance, expressions of caring, calm discussion, and problem solving. As family members, we may want to engage in increased use of such strategies in our interactions. It is important that we consider the ways that we deal with conflict in our families so that we can make changes where necessary in order to achieve the benefits of conflict interactions, but avoid the potential troubling outcomes for all family members.

Questions for Consideration and Discussion

1. In general, how do you think people feel about conflict in family settings? Where does this perception come from and how might we adjust it to be more functional for families?
2. In the most recent family conflict you experienced, what power did you have? What power did your relational partners have? Who do you feel had more power in the situation? Why?
3. Gottman and Fitzpatrick have developed typologies of couples with regard to their communication patterns, including conflict management. What do you see as the benefit of developing such typologies? What drawbacks might there be?
4. How does the larger culture in which you live impact the way your family engages in conflict? In what ways do you see your family corresponding to cultural expectations and in what ways do you see your family diverging? Why?
5. When conflict turns into family violence, it can be very detrimental to family members. As a society, how can we help families learn strategies to avoid and/or manage conflict that threatens to become violent or abusive?

Key Terms and Concepts

attribution theory
authoritarian parenting
authoritative parenting
coercive power
cognitively complex
conflict
conflict avoiding couple
conflict management

constructivist
demand–withdraw pattern
expert power
family violence
independent couple
legitimate power
permissive parenting
power

referent power
rejecting–neglecting parenting
reward power
separate couple
social construct
traditional couple
validating couple
volatile couple

7

Race, Ethnicity, and Family

Chapter Outline

Section 1: Overview of Issues of Race, Ethnicity, and Family
    Defining Race and Ethnicity
    Race, Ethnicity, and Family Culture
    Race/Ethnicity Socialization
    Interracial and Multiracial Families

Section 2: Research Examples
    "What Shall I Tell My Daughters That Are Black?": Oral History Reflections of Middle-Class African American Motherhood in a Culturally Diverse Community

    The Mother–Adolescent Daughter Tug-of-War: Ethnicity's Impact on the Connection–Autonomy Dialectic
    Parenting in the Interracial Family: More Alike Than Different

Section 3: Conclusions and Application—Issues of Race and Ethnicity in Your Family Experience

Chapter Objectives

1. To be able to define race and ethnicity and understand the difference between them
2. To develop understanding of how race/ethnicity impact family culture and experience and thus family practice
3. To understand the relationship between socialization practices and racial/ethnic impacts on family
4. To critically address how messages about race/ethnicity have affected your understandings of self and others, as well as the family behaviors of self and others

Section 1: Overview of Issues of Race, Ethnicity, and Family _____

- If you were to casually describe yourself to someone you had never met, what descriptors would you use?
- If you were asked about your ancestry, what categories would you mention?
- If your college or university offered a scholarship program "based on race," would you assume yourself to be eligible? On what racial category or categories would you make that assumption?

Looking at your answers to these questions, did your racial/ethnic characteristics appear the same in answer to each question? Would you be more likely to think about yourself as belonging to a particular racial/ethnic group under some situations than others? Keep these thoughts in mind as you read this chapter and think about the complexity of race and ethnicity.

Defining Race and Ethnicity

The U.S. Census of 2000 asked respondents to select their race from the following categories (Grieco & Cassidy, 2001):

White
Black or African American
American Indian or Alaska Native
Asian
Native Hawaiian and other Pacific Islander
Some other race

Many of these categories had subcategory choices (i.e., Asian Indian, Chinese, Filipino, Japanese, Korean, Vietnamese, and Other Asian were subcategories for the race categorized as Asian). In addition to those choices, participants were asked to indicate whether they were Spanish, Hispanic, or Latino (this choice could then be combined with any previous option given). Individuals could also select more than one race or subcategory, allowing for many possible combinations of categories. It's a fairly complex system of attempting to capture how individuals understand their own race/ethnicity. Each time the census is conducted, the methods used to assess race are shifted somewhat in an attempt to more accurately capture citizens' beliefs about their racial category. After many years of conducting the census, these changes continue, and likely there will be some alterations in the race component for the next census. This is due to the difficulty of clearly defining the boundaries of racial categories and the labels that are appropriate to those categories.

Race as a Category of People Perception

Race and ethnicity are difficult terms to define because they signify so much that cannot be captured in a simple definition. But, for the sake of this reading, I provide definitions of

BOX 7.1 • *Internet Connection*

The U.S. Census Bureau Web site provides a variety of information about race, as well as a discussion of how race is defined and calculated in government surveys. You can reach the race page of the census site at www.census.gov/population/www/socdemo/race.html.

each here. Wilkinson (1999, p. 18) defines a **race** as "a category of people who are related by a common heredity or ancestry and who are perceived and responded to in terms of external features or traits." It is important to note in this definition that race is a social concept, not a biological one. What this means is that, although we often think about race as a genetic trait, there is no race gene. People of the same race have similarities in appearance because of evolutionary changes related to their location of national origin, not because they have a "White gene" or a "Black gene." It is important to understand this because it speaks to the idea of variability, similarity, and difference within and between races. Two people of the same racial category are as likely to be genetically dissimilar as two people of different racial categories.

This is not to say that race isn't "real." It is real, because it is a very real part of the way we respond to each other socially. Because racial division is based on external features and traits, race is a social marking that we use when communicating with and about others. We categorize others into racial groups, and apply beliefs about those groups to others as we attempt to understand them and their behavior. Thus, the experience of living life for individuals of one race is different from the experience of living life for individuals of another race, because those racial categories impact how others respond to us and what sort of opportunities are more and less available to us. How we think about race, and the categories into which people are divided based on external markers, are also related to issues of power. This is part of why, over the course of history, what has "counted" as a race has changed. At one point in U.S. history, Black men and women who had been enslaved and Black men and women who were free were considered to be of different races (Fields, 1990). Historically, in the United States and across the world, race has often been used as a way to keep some groups of individuals in power, while denying power to other groups. Negative racial stereotypes provide "justification" for treating one race as inferior in some way to others. Thus, even though race is not a genetic characteristic, it is certainly part of the reality of our experience as individuals and as family members.

Ethnicity as Culture of a Group of People

Ethnicity can generally be referred to as those cultural beliefs and behaviors that a group of people, originating at some point of their family history in a particular location, share, which make them distinct from other groups (Wilkinson, 1999). So, like race, ethnicity isn't biological. Ethnicity is largely an issue of shared culture that develops in a particular geographic region over a long period of time. As members of that culture leave and go on to other places, they and their families carry the traditions and beliefs of that culture with them. For example, Italian Americans are immigrants or descendants of immigrants who originally lived in Italy. In Italy, they or their ancestral family developed a culture, and then that culture has gone on with them (and been passed down to their children and grandchildren in somewhat altered forms) as they relocated. Ethnicity is not equal to race; the two represent different ideas, though they may be connected by location. This means that people within a particular race (e.g., White) can still be of different ethnic groups (like Irish or French).

"White" as Race

As noted by Walker (1993), Frankenberg (1993, 2001), Bonilla-Silva (2003), and other scholars, one issue with race is that people often forget that White is also a race. We often treat White as an absence of race. For example, if a politician is White, news stories about him or her will generally not mention race. However, if he or she is Black, that will often be mentioned in some way. The same is often true for stories about crime, where race is not mentioned if all of the involved individuals (perpetrators and victims) are White.

This tendency to view White as a nonrace happens both for individuals in everyday interaction and for family communication scholarship. Thus, thinking about the impact of race on family is largely focused on how non-White families behave. This is unfortunate, in that it may limit our scholarly understandings of race and ethnicity in family settings, but it is partly a reflection of the reality that families of color face. Individuals and families who are White are not without race; however, because White is so often seen as an absence of race, their race is not often a focus of attention, or prejudice, from others. Thus, race is a more salient issue in the experience of non-White family members. In addition, White families are disproportionately reflected in family communication research. Studies often involve subjects of a variety of racial groups (and are not, thus, *only* about Whites), yet the predominant race of participants is typically White. So, in some ways, it does make sense that research explicitly about race is largely focused on families that are not White. Even though that is the case, in this chapter the authors discuss research that considers individuals of a variety of races and ethnicities.

Difficulty of Discussing Race and Ethnicity

To engage in a discussion of race is not always easy, and may seem like it is an acknowledgment of difference in a way that is itself prejudicial. You've probably heard people say that they "never notice" race or that race is completely unimportant to them. This perspective likely springs from a good place (wanting to avoid any aspect of racism); however, it runs the risk of denying the real social and structural differences that occur on the basis of racial categorization. The attempt to be "colorblind" arises in part from a desire to avoid racism, and in part from a discomfort with "wrangling with" the complexity of race and the potential recognition that racial categories result in some individuals having more opportunities than others (Bonilla-Silva, 2003; Frankenberg, 1993; Knowles & Peng, 2005). However, to ignore race is not to avoid racism. Race is a fundamental part of our experience of humanity. Although racial categorization has been, and will likely continue to be, used as a way to oppress particular groups and empower others, a discussion of race and its impacts on our lives is not itself inherently racist. It is only through a frank consideration of race and ethnicity, and their impact on us, that we can hope to understand and avoid the potential negative outcomes of racial and ethnic categorization.

This section of the chapter discusses some of the ways that race and ethnicity relate to beliefs and interactions in family and the creation of family culture. Second, it addresses issues of racial/ethnic socialization in the family system. Finally, this section considers interracial and multiracial families.

Race, Ethnicity, and Family Culture

Early research in family process typically did not consider how race and ethnicity impact or relate to family interaction. Race was mentioned only as a demographic variable of the participants and little attention was given to how race is related to culture, family process, and thereby communication. In the past few decades, more family scholars have addressed the importance of race and ethnicity in the creation of family practices (Diggs & Socha, 2004; Kotchick & Forehand, 2002; Turner & West, 2003). This is important, Turner and West (2003) note, because without attention to these issues of diversity, the study of family is partial and makes a faulty assumption of homogeneity in family structure and process. Kotchick and Forehand (2002) note that, even more recently, researchers have begun to pay attention to within-group variations and the parenting strategies that represent particular strengths for that culture. Such a focus gives us a better sense of family experiences and successes, because a parenting style that works well in one culture may work less well in another. One example of this relates to parental discipline styles, as discussed in Chapter 6. Although many studies have found authoritative parenting to be most effective, some research has indicated that for particular ethnic/racial groupings, authoritarian styles may have more positive effects (for example, Chao, 1994; Lamborn, Dornbusch, & Steinberg, 1996). From this we can see the importance of thinking about how race and ethnicity contribute to family culture, and how that culture then relates to family processes and outcomes. It would be faulty to assume that what works for one family culture is best for all others, partly because of the family beliefs and values that develop from larger cultural influences, such as race and ethnicity.

Race, Ethnicity, and Family Values

Racial and ethnic culture impacts what families most value, and is the "glue" that helps sustain family togetherness. We learn in our cultural settings, including race and ethnicity, what is valued for individuals and for families. We are assessed by members of our cultures on the degree to which we are able or willing to act in a way that corresponds to those values. For example, in mainstream U.S. culture of the 1950s, divorce was considered a failure and an embarrassment. When parents were divorced, people looked askance at them and at their family because of this perceived failure to uphold the value of marital and family commitment. Today, that expectation has changed somewhat in mainstream culture, and we are less surprised or judgmental about families of divorce. Racial and ethnic culture has similar effects on our family values.

Families may hold particular values more strongly because of the influence of racial/ethnic culture. In a study of Mexican American families in California, Aoki (2000) found that participants focused on the importance of family in their lives and how family members must support and sustain one another even when they would rather not. Aoki's respondents also discussed the way that religion was an anchor point for the family. These

BOX 7.2 • *Did You Know?*

Living in nuclear family households is not the norm in all cultures. For example, in sub-Saharan Africa, about 50 percent of older adults live with grandchildren and/or adult children (Zimmer & Dayton, 2005). In northern Vietnam, 75 percent of newly married couples reside with the groom's parents (Hirschman & Nguyan, 2002). And, in Taiwan, 50 percent of young teens were raised in households with their grandparents (Yi, Pan, Chang, & Chan, 2006).

---

ideas, Aoki argued, served as forces that unified the family members and provided them with a strong sense of family identity, as well as ethnic identity. In a similar study, Mosely-Howard and Evans (2000) found seven prominent themes in the narratives of African American families: relying on family tradition to raise children, the value of kinship bonds, pride in cultural heritage, overt teaching about racism, negotiation between two cultures, education, and the role of spirituality. The authors argue that these themes indicate the value placed on relationships in these African American families.

Sometimes the values affected by racial/ethnic culture are general beliefs, and in other instances they may be more specifically related to beliefs about family responsibilities. For example, Burr and Mutchler (1999) considered how Black, Hispanic, and White participants felt about the provision of financial support and coresidence between adult children and their parents. The authors found that older Black and Hispanic respondents were more supportive of the idea that generations should live together when necessary than were older White respondents. These results were the case with regard to both adult children living with their parents, and parents living with their adult children. Black and Hispanic participants were also more likely to feel that adult children should provide financial support to their parents when needed than White participants. The three groups had more similar beliefs about parents providing financial support when necessary to their adult children. Lee, Peek, and Coward (1998) also found that older Black respondents believed that children had a greater obligation to help support and assist their parents than did older White respondents. The authors of these two studies suggest that these differences are likely related to cultural differences in ideas about family responsibility, particularly the responsibility of children to their parents. Such beliefs may impact the likelihood of intergenerational support being offered, and also affect how family members feel about it being offered. Family members from cultures where such support is considered an obligation may see it as a natural part of the family history. Family members from cultures where such intergenerational support is less valued may see it as more burdensome or have no model of how to engage in such exchanges.

Race, Ethnicity, and Family Behavior

In addition to affecting our beliefs about family and our values with relation to family issues, racial and ethnic culture impacts how we actually "do family." Penington (2004) studied mother–adolescent daughter pairs in European American and African American families. As you will see in Section 2 of the chapter, her research revealed many similarities between the pairs, but also differences that appeared to be related to how each racial group saw family and their role in it. Phinney, Kim-Jo, Osorio, & Vilhjalmsdottir (2005) considered similar issues of autonomy and connectedness in their analysis of independence, compliance, and assertion for adolescents and young adults in families. Their study involved European Americans, Armenian Americans, Mexican Americans, and Korean Americans. They found many similarities between the groups, as well as some differences. One major similarity that the authors noted was that the groups did not differ in terms of autonomy (independence) in their family relationships. One major difference was that the non-European participants were more compliant with parental requests or commands than the European participants. The authors argue that these differences are likely related to cultural expectations about family, children, and the process of becoming adult.

At times, we may see the intersection of race/ethnicity with other cultural factors, such as religion. Sherif (1999) argues that the rules of the Qur'an (the Islamic holy book) and Islamic culture impact how children are raised in Islamic families. Children are considered very important to the life of the family, and are brought into the adult social circle early in life. The interaction with adults produces a consistent emphasis on displaying gender-specific behaviors. Parents will correct young boys from an early age for displaying feminine behaviors, and girls are taught early to be soft spoken and dress modestly. Islamic children are also taught to respect their parents and not question the parents' decisions or argue with the parents. This extends into young adulthood and beyond with the selection of a major in college and even a spouse.

From these studies and examples, it seems clear that the cultures related to race and ethnicity impact the beliefs and values that families hold about their relationships and obligations. They also affect the behaviors that families engage in when interacting with one another. As the culture impacts the family, so the family creates and recreates the culture; within the family, socialization is provided with regard to family culture and racial/ ethnic culture.

Race/Ethnicity Socialization

As we have discussed previously, one part of family life is socialization. Family members socialize each other with regard to both family expectations and the expectations of the larger culture. Through **race/ethnicity socialization,** parents pass on to their children the racial and ethnic cultural beliefs, values, and behaviors that they have learned. Children likewise affect their parents' understandings of self and culture.

At times, adults may offer specific explicit messages about race/ethnicity to their children. Frabutt, Walker, and MacKinnon-Lewis (2002) studied African American families with a young adolescent child. They investigated connections between the extent of explicit racial socialization messages a mother provided (ranking them as high, moderate, or low), and various family factors including warmth, negativity, and involvement. These researchers found that mothers who showed moderate racial socialization seemed to have the most involved, warm, and positive relationships with their children. Whereas this relationship may not be causal (that is, the researchers can't claim that the socialization leads to the relationship or vice versa), it is interesting to note that the research seems to suggest that moderate explicit racial socialization efforts (not talking about race with extremely high frequency, but not ignoring it either) were connected to the most positive family patterns. This study addresses the frequency of socialization efforts, but it focuses exclusively on explicit messages, and doesn't address how families felt about or experienced their own socialization processes. Other authors, however, have talked about these issues.

Members of families may believe passing on messages about race/ethnicity to be more or less important due to cultural expectations and the positioning of that race/ethnicity within larger social settings. Kawamoto and Cheshire (1999) interviewed American Indian mothers and preadolescents from Oregon. Though the families were living in an urban environment, the mothers indicated the importance of teaching the practices and beliefs of the culture. The researchers noted that the transmission of such information occurred in many ways, including observing cultural phenomenon (tribal dance), telling stories, and so on. The mothers felt that such efforts were vitally important in their cultural and family lives.

Similarly, other scholars have found that race socialization is particularly important in some family settings. Hughes and Chen (1997) found that African American families engaged in a variety of socialization about race issues. In their study, they indicate that families primarily attempted to teach children about African American culture. A second type of socialization that was common in the families related to preparing children for encountering racism and prejudice of others. Finally, they noted that only a small number of parents also provided their children with messages indicating that they should not trust people of other races (see also Garcia-Coll, Meyer, & Brillon, 1995). Marsiglia and Holleran (1999) consider the role of Mexican American mothers in passing along cultural socialization messages to their daughters. The researchers found that the mothers of their adolescent respondents were passing along traditional messages from Mexican culture, which prominently placed women in a subordinate yet morally superior role to men, but were also providing more feminist messages of independence and strength to their daughters. The families studied by all of these authors believed in the importance of passing on information about racial and ethnic culture. However, not all families feel the same need to explicitly socialize their children with regard to racial/ethnic issues.

As discussed earlier in the text, family stories are an important way that socialization messages are passed on. Bylund (2003) found both similarities and differences in family stories told by her European American, Mexican American, and African American participants. Although her study was too small to make generalizations, she noted that only the African American family explicitly stated that there were lessons about race, and racism, to be learned in family stories. Bylund noted that this is likely due to the family's history in the United States and the complex nature of Black–White race relations in this country.

Talking about race in very explicit ways may seem to be more important for families whose race/ethnicity is more "marked" within a larger social setting. McAdoo (2001) argues that socialization messages about race and ethnicity are vitally important. Parents have to walk a thin line between preparing their children for racial issues and overemphasizing the problems or dangers of race and discrimination. Because of the racial/ethnic stereotypes and prejudices that exist in the larger culture, however, most parents whose children are not of minority status do not feel the same need to expressly address issues of race with their children.

Family socialization can become particularly complex when the racial/ethnic culture of the family seems to be in contrast or conflict with the mainstream culture of the society it exists within. This is often the case in families where immigration has been recent. In some situations, families may change as they adapt to the new culture. Jain and Belsky (1997) considered the role of acculturation (adapting to and accepting the expectations of a new culture

BOX 7.3 • *Reading about Immigration and Family*

If immigration is something that is distant from your own experience, you may find it reveal-ing to read autobiographical or fictional accounts of the intersections between family, race, and ethnicity within the context of immigration. Some titles to consider include:

The Namesake by Jhumpa Lahiri (2004)
On Gold Mountain by Lisa See (1996)
The Fortunate Pilgrim by Mario Puzo (1965)
American Chica by Marie Arana (2005)
Lost in Translation by Eva Hoffman (1990)
Crossing Over by Ruben Martinez (2002)
Children of Loneliness by Anzia Yezierska (1923)
The Plot Against America by Phillip Roth (2004)
Paper Fish by Tina DeRosa (1980)
Brown Girl, Brownstones by Paule Marshall (1959)

and interweaving those expectations into the previously existing cultural beliefs) in the fathering behaviors of Indian immigrants. They found that the acculturation process did have an impact on parenting behaviors. Fathers in the study who were more acculturated to the United States were more involved and engaged in child care than those who were not. The authors argue that this is because the Indian culture places virtually all responsibility for child care on the mother, whereas U.S. culture has shifted toward more shared responsibility. Thus, as the fathers adopted the U.S. culture in their lives, they also changed their parenting style.

The acculturation of the fathers in Jain and Belsky's (1997) study seems to have resulted in a positive outcome for the family (more involved parenting), but other studies related to the issue of immigration, family, and acculturation have pointed to the tensions that can arise as a result of cultural shifts. In Li's 2004 study of Chinese immigrant families living in Canada, he found that parents placed a heavy emphasis on learning and on the development of moral character. Additionally, the parents also promoted the idea that children should become culturally integrated into the larger Canadian culture in order to be more successful in life. Li (2004) notes that at times these two competing values (retaining of a traditional Chi-nese culture, while becoming part of the larger culture in Canada) caused tensions for the children in these families. In a similar study, Farver, Narang, and Bhadha (2002) considered the influence of families on the acculturation and ethnic identity (as well as psychological characteristics) of Asian Indian adolescents who had been born in the United States (but whose parents were immigrants). The authors found that those families who felt more mar-ginalized, or less integrated into mainstream culture, and/or had not found a way to integrate their ethnic identity with their national culture, experienced more family conflict. Addition-ally, when parents and children had similar levels of acculturation, the adolescents had greater self-esteem and less anxiety than when there were differences between parent and adolescent integration into the culture. Aoki (2000) also found, in his study of Mexican American fami-lies, that changing socialization and acculturation of generations produced conflict for family members because children and grandchildren, as they became acculturated to the larger society, were less inclined to see the importance of a strong family connection or religion than their parents and grandparents were (see also Silverstein & Chen, 1999).

Socialization is an important, and in fact inevitable, part of family life. As discussed here, families may feel more or less urgency to impart specific messages to their children related to race. Studies seem to suggest that European American families (whose race/ethnicity is less marked) may stress racial/ethnic learning in the family less than non-White families. Cultural socialization in the family may be even more complex when there are different, and even contradictory, values, beliefs, and behaviors being promoted by the racial/ethnic cultures and by the larger culture in which the family is embedded. Issues of socialization and how to "deal with" race may be even more complicated for families that are composed of more than one race or ethnicity.

Interracial and Multiracial Families

The terms *interracial* and *multiracial* are used to designate families where members represent more than one racial grouping. This may be two White parents who adopt a Black child. It may be an African American parent and a Chinese American parent who together have children. There are endless variations of racial/ethnic composition we can find in family systems. Being in a family that is composed of multiple races presents unique challenges and opportunities for family members. There are many ways that a family may be multicultural (e.g., two religions, two ethnicities), but racial differences are somewhat unique in that they are apparent not only to those inside the relationship, but also to observers.

Interracial Couples

In the United States, interracial marriage was illegal or somehow limited in many states up until the 1960s. It wasn't until 1967 that the Supreme Court, in the case of *Loving v. Virginia*, ruled that antimiscegenation laws were unconstitutional. Although this forced all of the states that still had laws against interracial marriage on their books to retract them, it did not create an automatic acceptance of such relationships (for a discussion see Wallenstein, 2002). Even today, social sanctions against interracial relationships are a common occurrence in the United States. Thus, it may be harder for interracial couples and families to maintain happy and satisfying relationships in the face of both cultural differences and the disapproval of others.

Achieving a satisfying and stable relationship may be somewhat more difficult for interracial couples; however, research suggests that it is certainly possible. Leslie and Letiecq (2004) studied interracial couples (where one partner was Black and one partner was White). They found that partners who had a strong sense of pride in their own race, but were also willing to accept people of other races, were the most satisfied with their marital relationship. Foeman and Nance (1999) concur with this view, arguing that interracial couples who are able to go through a series of four stages of adjustment are more likely to be successful and satisfied. First, the relational partners must have an awareness of four perspectives on race: their own, their partner's, their racial group, and their partner's racial group. Communication about these perspectives helps partners develop this understanding.

Second, the couple must find a way to deal with the social perceptions of others in regard to race. They need to decide together how to respond to racial insults or slights. Third, the partners need to develop a way to understand and define themselves and their relationship that is not based on negative ideas or the downsides of interracial relationships. Perhaps they may reach a definition that allows them to see how much richness there can be in bringing together the rituals, beliefs, and values of two cultures. Finally, couples have to learn how to sustain and maintain their relationship with regard to race issues by returning to the discussion when they need to. Ignoring race and race issues does not make them go away; it is through communication that we manage problems related to race.

Children in Multiracial Families

As with adults in interracial relationships, discussion of race and race issues is also important for biracial or multiracial children. Fukuyama (1999) writes about her experience being a biracial (Japanese and Anglo American) child in the 1950s and beyond. She states that it was difficult for her, as a child and well into her adult life, to find a way to claim both cultural heritages, but that eventually doing so made her a more emotionally healthy person. Fukuyama says that discussions about race and racism were not a part of her childhood experience with her parents, and this made it difficult for her to develop a way to approach these issues (see also Williams, 1999). Stephan and Stephan (1991) and Suyemoto (2004) argue that, once biracial and multiracial children have developed this sense of positive self-identity, they may be particularly responsive and respectful of the diversity of others. Thus, even though some see biracial status as a negative for children, these authors argue that it can be a positive, if self-concept is strong.

Similar, yet different, issues may arise when parents and children do not share race/ethnicity. Galvin (2003) considers some of the particular challenges faced by families where a child or children is adopted **transracially** (across races) and internationally. Families in such situations (for example, when a Korean child is adopted by a set of White parents) face an interesting and complex set of dynamics. Galvin notes that issues of family identity development are affected by the transracial and international nature of the family. Among other concerns, families may need to deal with racism in attitudes of other family members, may not have creation stories to share with the child, need to be prepared to address the physical differences between the child and other family members both within and outside the family, and may struggle to define and describe their family cultural identity. Additionally, Galvin states that such families must discover how they will (or will not) discuss their adoption story with outsiders, and deal with incidents of racism from others. Finally, Galvin indicates that socialization may be particularly complicated

---

BOX 7.4 • *Family in the News*

Although recent stories about stars like Angelina Jolie have made transracial adoptions seem relatively commonplace, their history is more complex than you might think. The Adoption History Project offers information about transracial adoptions across time at http://darkwing. uoregon.edu/~adoption/topics/transracialadoption.htm.

in transracial international adoptive families, because families must decide how, when, and how much to expose the child to the culture of origin as well as the adoptive culture. This may be even more difficult because adoptive parents may have little firsthand knowledge of the child's culture of origin. Children who had been adopted transracially and their parents, interviewed by deHaymes and Simon (2003), supported Galvin's claims, noting that they faced criticism and comments from others, as well as making their own adjustments and deciding how to deal with issues of culture and socialization.

Multiracial families can be a site of opportunity to create unique cultural/ethnic identities; to explore the diversity of cultural attitudes, beliefs, and practices; and even to help others outside the family see race in more complex ways. Family members, however, do have to learn together how to cope with their differences and with the reactions they receive from others. This process occurs through communication.

Overall, in this section we have considered the definitions of race and ethnicity and how difficult it is to clearly define these concepts. Additionally, you read about some of the ways that race/ethnicity intersects with family beliefs and processes and how families participate in the socialization process with regard to race/ethnicity and culture. Finally, we've considered some of the situations that affect multiracial families. Section 2 discusses research examples that relate to how race and ethnicity are experienced in family settings. The first article considers racial and gender socialization in African American middle-class families. The second considers interactional patterns in mother–daughter relationships for Black and White families, whereas the third article addresses research about parenting in interracial families. Section 3 concludes with a discussion of how this material can be applied to your life.

References

Aoki, E. (2000). Mexican American ethnicity in Biola, CA: An ethnographic account of hard work, family, and religion. *Howard Journal of Communications, 11*(3), 207–227.

Bonilla-Silva, E. (2003). *Racism without racists: Color-blind racism and the persistence of inequality in the United States.* Lanham, MD: Rowman & Littlefield.

Burr, J. A., & Mutchler, J. E. (1999). Race and ethnic variation in norms of filial responsibility among older persons. *Journal of Marriage and Family, 61*(3), 674–687.

Bylund, C. L. (2003). Ethnic diversity and family stories. *Journal of Family Communication, 3*(4), 215–226.

Chao, R. K. (1994). Beyond parental control and authoritarian parenting style: Understanding Chinese parenting through the cultural notion of training. *Child Development, 65,* 1111–1120.

deHaymes, M. V., & Simon, S. (2003). Transracial adoption: Families identify issues and needed support services. *Child Welfare, 82*(2), 251–272.

Diggs, R. C., & Socha, T. (2004). Communication, families, and exploring the boundaries of cultural diversity. In A. L. Vangelisti (Ed.), *Handbook of family communication* (pp. 249–266). Mahwah, NJ: Erlbaum.

Farver, J. A. M., Narang, S. K., & Bhadha, B. (2002). East meets West: Ethnic identity, acculturation, and conflict in Asian Indian families. *Journal of Family Psychology, 16*(3), 338–349.

Fields, B. J. (1990, May/June). Slavery, race and ideology in the United States of America. *New Left Review,* 95–118.

Foeman, A. K., & Nance, T. (1999). From miscengenation to multiculturalism: Perceptions and stages of interracial relationship development. *Journal of Black Studies, 29,* 540–557.

Frabutt, J. M., Walker, A. M., & MacKinnon-Lewis, C. (2002). Racial socialization messages and the quality of mother/childhood interactions in African American families. *Journal of Early Adolescence, 22*(2), 200–217.

Frankenberg, R. (1993). *White women race matters: The social construction of whiteness.* Minneapolis: University of Minnesota Press.

Frankenberg, R. (2001). The mirage of an unmarked whiteness. In B. Brander Rasmussen, M. Klinenberg, I. J. Nexica, & M. Wray (Eds.), *The making and unmaking of whiteness* (pp. 72–96). Durham, NC: Duke University Press.

Fukuyama, M. A. (1999). Personal narrative: Growing up biracial. *Journal of Counseling and Development, 77*(1), 12–14.

Galvin, K. (2003). International and transracial adoption: A communication research agenda. *Journal of Family Communication, 3*(4), 237–253.

Garcia-Coll, C. T., Meyer, E. C., & Brillon, L. (1995). Ethnic and minority parenting. In M. H. Bornstein (Ed.), *Handbook of parenting: Biology and ecology of parenting* (Vol. 2, pp. 189–210). Mahwah, NJ: Erlbaum.

Grieco, E. M., & Cassidy, R. C. (2001). *Overview of race and Hispanic origin: Census 2000 brief.* Retrieved from the U.S. Census Bureau Web site: www.census .gov/prod/2001pubs/c2kbr01–1.pdf 1/1/2005.

Hirschman, C., & Nguyen, H. M. (2002). Tradition and change in Vietnamese family structure in the Red River Delta. *Journal of Marriage and Family, 64,* 1063–1079.

Hughes, D., & Chen, L. (1997). When and what parents tell children about race: An examination of race-related socialization among African American families. *Applied Developmental Science, 1*(4), 200–214.

Jain, A., & Belsky, J. (1997). Fathering and acculturation: Immigrant Indian families with young children. *Journal of Marriage and Family, 59*(4), 873–883.

Kawamoto, W. T., & Cheshire, T. C. (1999). Contemporary issues in the urban American Indian family. In H. P. McAdoo (Ed.), *Family ethnicity: Strength in diversity* (2nd ed., pp. 94–104). Newbury Park, CA: Sage.

Knowles, E. D., & Peng, K. (2005). White selves: Conceptualizing and measuring a dominant-group identity. *Journal of Personality and Social Psychology, 89*(2), 223–241.

Kotchick, B. A., & Forehand, R. (2002). Putting parenting in perspective: A discussion of the contextual factors that shape parenting practices. *Journal of Child and Family Studies, 11*(3), 255–269.

Lamborn, S. D., Dornbusch, S. M., & Steinberg, L. (1996). Ethnicity and community context as moderators of the relations between family decision making and adolescent adjustment. *Child Development, 67,* 283–301.

Lee, G. R., Peek, C. W., & Coward, R. T. (1998). Race differences in filial responsibility expectations among older parents. *Journal of Marriage and Family, 60*(2), 404–412.

Leslie, L. A., & Letiecq, B. L. (2004). Marital quality of African American and White partners in interracial couples. *Personal Relationships, 11*(4), 559–574.

Li, J. (2004). Parental expectations of Chinese immigrants: A folk theory about children's school achievement. *Race, Ethnicity & Education, 7*(2), 167–183.

McAdoo, H. (2001). Point of view: Ethnicity and family dialogue. *Journal of Family Communication, 1*(1), 87–90.

Mosley-Howard, G. S., & Evans, S. B. (2000). Relationships and contemporary experiences of the African American family: An ethnographic case study. *Journal of Black Studies, 30,* 428–452.

Penington, B. A. (2004). Communicative management of connection and autonomy in African American and European American mother–daughter relationships. *Journal of Family Communication, 4*(1), 3–34.

Phinney, J. S., Kim-Jo, T., Osorio, S., & Vilhjalmsdottir, P. (2005). Autonomy and relatedness in adolescent–parent disagreements: Ethnic and developmental factors. *Journal of Adolescent Research, 20*(1), 8–39.

Sherif, B. (1999). "Islamic Family Ideals and Their Relevance to American Muslim Families." In *Ethnic Families: Strength in Diversity,* ed. H. P. McAdoo. Newbury Park, CA: Sage.

Silverstein, M., & Chen, X. (1999). The impact of acculturation in Mexican American families on the quality of grandchild–grandparent relationships. *Journal of Marriage and Family, 61*(1), 188–198.

Stephan, W. G., & Stephan, C. W. (1991). Intermarriage: Effects on personality, adjustment, and intergroup relation in two samples of students. *Journal of Marriage and Family, 53,* 241–250.

Suyemoto, K. L. (2004). Racial/ethnic identities and related attributed experiences of multiracial Japanese European Americans. *Journal of Multicultural Counseling and Development, 32*(4), 206–221.

Turner, L. H., & West, R. (2003). Breaking through the silence: Increasing voice for diverse families in communication research. *Journal of Family Communication, 3*(4), 181–186.

Walker, A. J. (1993). Teaching about race, gender, and class diversity in United States families. *Family Relations, 42*(3), 342–350.

Wallenstein, P. (2002). *Tell the court I love my wife: Race, marriage, and the law.* New York: Palgrave Macmillan.

Wilkinson, D. (1999). Reframing family ethnicity in America. In H. P. McAdoo (Ed.), *Family ethnicity: Strength in diversity* (2nd ed., pp. 15–60). Thousand Oaks, CA: Sage.

Williams, C. B. (1999). Claiming a biracial identity: Resisting social constructions of race and culture. *Journal of Counseling and Development, 77*(1), 32–35.

Yi, C., Pan, E., Chang, Y., & Chan, C. (2006). Grandparents, adolescents, and parents: Intergenerational relations of Taiwanese youth. *Journal of Family Issues, 27*(8), 1042–1067.

Zimmer, Z., & Dayton, J. (2005). Older adults in sub-Saharan Africa living with children and grandchildren. *Population Studies, 59*(3), 295–312.

8

Sexuality and the Family

Chapter Outline

Section 1: Overview of Family Communication and Sexuality

Partner Sexuality and Relational Satisfaction

Parent–Child Communication about Sex and Sexuality

Sexual Orientation and the Family

Section 2: Research Examples

Communication about Sex as a Daughter, Parent, and Teacher

The Social Context of Lesbian Family Identity

Section 3: Conclusions and Application— Sexuality, Family, and You

Chapter Objectives

1. To become more cognizant of the role of sexuality in the family
2. To understand how covert and overt communication about sexuality in family settings impacts children and adolescents
3. To develop an awareness of particular issues faced by gay- and lesbian-parented families and families with gay/lesbian children
4. To use material to analyze communication in your own family of origin, understand the families of others, and plan for your future

Section 1: Overview of Family Communication and Sexuality

- If you were watching television at 8:30 on a Wednesday night, and you saw an advertisement that had a somewhat sexual overtone (a flock of women and one man following an attractive man with a diet soft drink), what kind of reaction would you have?
- If you saw a gay couple holding hands in front of their children, how would you respond?
- If you saw a mother and father kiss in front of their children, what would you think?
- If you heard a four-year-old child use the word *sex*, how would you react? What thoughts might go through your head?

The ways in which we respond to, and communicate about, issues of sexuality are certainly multifaceted. In these examples, some individuals might find themselves saying they would be more shocked or appalled by the four-year-old child saying "sex" than by the risqué advertisement on television during a time when children are likely to watch. Other people may not be particularly shocked that a four-year-old would speak about sex, but would be disturbed that a gay or lesbian couple might show physical affection in front of a child. Some individuals might not have a particularly strong reaction to any of these situations, whereas others might find them all inappropriate in some way. The responses we have to issues related to sexuality come from our histories in family cultures, friendship and romantic relationship cultures, and larger social settings.

Let's begin by addressing, generally, the role of sexuality and sexual communication in family settings. The family system is imbued with sexuality. Parents and adult caregivers enact their sexual relationship within the family setting. That relationship impacts their happiness and satisfaction, which then affects the family system. Parents and children socialize each other about sex-role/gender expectations (what it means to be male or female) in the family. This learning then becomes a part of their understanding of self that they carry with them, in some form, throughout their lives. Messages are given to children, in the family setting, about sexuality generally, sexual orientation, the appropriateness of particular physical behaviors, and how to respond to issues of sexuality. As children grow, and their own sexual nature becomes more apparent (though it is always there), children also communicate to family members about their own concerns, impressions, and values related to sex roles, sexual orientation, and sexuality. As we are all sexual beings, so too are families sexual entities.

In this text, we have already considered some information related to sex-role/gender socialization and sexual orientation. In this chapter, we focus on issues of sexuality in the family including adult sexuality and relational satisfaction, parent–child communication about sexuality, and parent and child sexual orientation.

Partner Sexuality and Relational Satisfaction

As we discussed in Chapter 2, the adult romantic/sexual relationship is often seen as the foundation of family. For most family settings, the adult caregivers are involved in a romantic/sexual relationship. In intact nuclear or blended families, the parents (and/or stepparents) maintain a romantic/sexual relationship with each other. In single-parent or solo-parent families, the parent may maintain a romantic/sexual relationship with a dating partner or partners. Though this relationship is about the adult caregivers, and not the family as a whole, because families are systems, the outcomes and interaction patterns in the marital/partner relationship reverberate throughout the family system. Sexuality is no exception.

Numerous studies have indicated a positive correlation between **relational satisfaction** (an overall happiness with the relationship) and **sexual satisfaction** (happiness with the sexual aspects of the relationship). That is, studies seem to indicate that as sexual happiness increases, so too does relational happiness (for discussion see Byers, 2005; Purnine & Carey, 1997). However, what isn't fully clear is the order of causation. Byers (2005) suggests a number of ways this relationship could be explained.

It could be that couples who are more satisfied sexually are more satisfied relationally. In a study of Chinese families, Guo and Huang (2005) found that the level of sexual satisfaction a couple had was predictive of their marital satisfaction, and concluded that greater education about sexuality is likely to produce more satisfying sexual relationships, and thus more satisfying marriages.

A second possibility is that couples that are more relationally satisfied with each other become more sexually satisfied. Young, Denny, Young, and Luquis (2000) examined sexuality and relational questionnaires completed by 641 married women. They found that relational satisfaction factors (general relationship satisfaction, satisfaction with the non-sexual elements of the relationship) were correlated with and predicted significantly the amount of sexual satisfaction experienced. The authors conclude that sexual interactions and satisfaction need to be considered within an understanding of evaluations of the relationship as a whole (see also Lawrance & Byers, 1995).

A third possibility is that the two factors impact each other. In a study of romantic couples, Sprecher (2002) found that there was a positive correlation between sexual satisfaction and relational satisfaction, such that when one improved, so did the other, and when one suffered, so did the other. But, in her study, which was done over five waves of data gathering in an attempt to look for temporal change, it was not clear that either variable "came first" in changing. Thus, Sprecher argues that it is possible that the two factors simultaneously impact one another.

Finally, it may be that a third factor contributes to both relational and sexual satisfaction. An increase in communication intimacy has been shown to be related to both relational and sexual satisfaction (Byers, 2005; Byers & Demmons, 1999; Cupach & Comstocks, 1990; Litzinger & Gordon, 2005). Litzinger and Gordon examined the relationship between these two factors in a group of 387 married couples. Their study indicated that both communication and sexual satisfaction were positively correlated with marital satisfaction. However, they also found that if couples are communicating well, this seems to be the primary factor of importance, and thus may lead to both relational and sexual satisfaction.

It is possible that there is not a single explanation for how relational and sexual satisfaction relate to one another. Based on the variety of studies that suggest different causality in this relationship, Byers (2005) suggests that the connection between sexual and relational satisfaction may vary based on the couple involved. What does seem clear is that there is some relationship between sexual happiness and relational well-being for romantic partners. And, given that we know that when parents have a happier relationship, there are

BOX 8.1 • *Internet Connection*

A television program that has received much interest in 2006 is *Strictly Dr. Drew*. The show, which has fared well in viewer ratings, focuses on ways that adults can increase their sexual satisfaction in relationships. Read more at http://health.discovery.com/fansites/dr_drew/dr_drew.htm.

positive results throughout the family system, this is indicative of the importance of sexuality in family settings.

Parent–Child Communication about Sex and Sexuality

Just as sexuality impacts on the parental/adult caregiver romantic relationship, so too does it reverberate through the parent–child relationship. Though the study of family communication about sexuality is a relatively new area of focus (Warren, 1992, 1995), a variety of studies in communication and other family fields have indicated that family communication can have an impact on the sexual beliefs, knowledge, values, and behavior of family members. It is important to note that families cannot "not communicate" about sex and sexuality. Family interactions inevitably "say something" about sexuality, even if the discussions are never explicitly held.

From the time a child is born, his or her parents or adult caregivers communicate with him or her about sex and sexuality. This occurs in a variety of ways. Parents communicate with children about sex through **sexual modeling** (the ways that they behave with one another or with other adult romantic partners in the case of single parents). Parents who are relatively open about their own nature as sexual beings (i.e., kissing in front of the children) may communicate to their children about the naturalness of sexual attraction. Parents who never touch at all in front of their children may communicate that physical affection and attraction are inappropriate, or to be hidden.

In addition to communicating via their behavior with each other, parents communicate with their children in how they respond to the behaviors of the child, and how they interact with the child or children. When fathers show less physical affection to sons than to daughters, as discussed in Chapter 5, this may send a message that physical intimacy between males is "off limits." When a parent or adult caregiver observes a child fondling his or her own genitals, the response of the parent tells the child something about sexuality (maybe that it is natural, maybe that it is "dirty," maybe that it is private). When a parent turns off the television if a scene shows sexuality in any form, that action communicates something to the child about sexuality.

Family communication that may seem to be unrelated to sex often is. For example, the tasks of raising a child, including diapering, toilet training, bathing, and so on, call for some degree of conversation about genitalia. And, children are naturally curious about their own body parts and the body parts of others. Thus, family **body talk** is a common occurrence.

Many families develop euphemisms with which to talk about genitalia ("wee-wee," "pee-pee," "down there"). Although the purpose of such talk may be about toilet training or learning body parts, it nonetheless communicates something about sexuality.

Of course, parents and adult caregivers may also communicate with children through **overt sexuality communication.** Whether this occurs in the context of a child-led discussion ("Mom, where do babies come from?"), casual comments, or "the talk," many families engage in some form of overt talk about sexuality. Thus, communication about sexuality in the family takes many forms. In this text, however, we focus on the obvious discussions of sexuality, as those have been more completely studied than the more "hidden" types of sex communication just discussed.

Overt Parent–Child Communication about Sexuality

Overt and ongoing communication about sexuality in the family is a relatively rare phenomenon, with some studies reporting that only around 10 percent of families participate in such discussions (Warren, 1992, 1995). Conversations that do occur are often limited to particular family dyads. Studies have often indicated that mothers and daughters are the family dyad that primarily engages in talk about sexuality (Fox, 1981; Heisler, 2005; Hepburn, 1983; Hutchinson & Cooney, 1998; Rosenthal & Feldman, 1999). Mothers and daughters talk more about sexuality in general, but other scholars have also found that fathers are more likely to be the ones speaking with their sons (Fisher, 1993). Taken together, this seems to suggest that boys receive less overall talk about sexuality from their parents and adult caregivers.

So, you might wonder, exactly what and how often are parents explicitly communicating to their children about sexuality issues. Work done by scholars such as Heisler (2005), Hutchinson and Cooney (1988), and Fox and Inazu (1980) suggest that, in most families, some explicit communication about sexuality does occur. However, their studies also indicate that some topics are harder for parents to discuss with their children. These scholars argue that parents are more likely to talk about general issues like relationships, morals, menstruation, pregnancy, postponing sex, and resisting sexual pressure (with most of that talk being done by mothers). Talk about topics such as sexually transmitted diseases (STDs) is less common, with Hutchinson and Cooney finding only half of mothers and less than one-quarter of fathers participating in such talks. Hutchinson and Cooney concluded that parents may be less comfortable discussing such issues than they are less sensitive concepts like menstruation. This type of finding has been replicated in other research, such as Jordan, Price, and Fitzgerald's (2000) study that indicated 20 percent of parents were "somewhat" or "very" uncomfortable talking about sexuality and that the more sensitive the topic, the less inclined parents were to discuss it (with topics like pornography, masturbation, and prostitution the least likely to be talked about) (see also Rosenthal & Feldman, 1999).

From these studies, we see that some parents do discuss sexuality issues with their children (though mothers do so more than fathers), but the topics discussed may be restricted and limited due to parents' (and possibly the teen's) discomfort with discussing particular topics. This understanding is important because of the potential effects of parent–child communication about sexuality on adolescent and young adult sexual behavior and health.

Family Communication about Sexuality and Impact on Child Behavior

Studies have indicated that the relationship between explicit parent–child communication about sexuality and adolescent behavior is very complex. Moore, Peterson, and Furstenberg (1986) found that when parents who had traditional or conservative attitudes talked to their adolescents about sex, teenage girls were less likely to be sexually active (see also Newcomer & Udry, 1985), but teenage boys were more likely to be more sexually active. On the contrary, Fisher (1989) found that increased explicit communication about sexuality seemed to be unrelated to the sexual behavior of adolescent males, but was positively correlated to the sexual behavior of adolescent girls (that is, more communication was associated with more sexual activity). She found this correlation for both liberal and conservative parents. Fingerson (2005) studied mother–adolescent relationships, mother–adolescent communication, and adolescent sexual activity. She found that when mothers and teens had a stronger relationship, the teens were less likely to have had sex. However, when mothers and teens talked more about sex, the teens were more likely to have had sex. From these studies, we can see that the connection between explicit communication about sexuality and adolescents' likelihood of becoming sexually active is complicated and hard to predict. Miller (2002) suggests that some of the difficulty may lie in addressing causality. Do adolescents whose parents talk more about sex have more sex, or is it that when parents suspect their adolescent is having or will have sex, they start talking more about it? It's not an easy relationship to untangle.

Though the effects of parent–child communication on amount of sexual activity and the age at which such activity begins is unclear, research has indicated somewhat more consistent results with regard to how talk about sexuality affects safe sex behaviors. Miller, Levin, Whitaker, and Xu (1998) found that when parents and adolescents had conversations about condom use before the adolescent's first sexual encounter, the adolescent was far more likely to use a condom during that encounter and to continue to practice condom use thereafter (see also Fisher, 1987; Handelsman, Cabral, & Weisfeld, 1987; Newcomer & Udry, 1985). Additionally, the quality of that talk is also important. Whitaker, Miller, May, and Levin. (1999), Booth-Butterfield and Sidelinger (1998), and Powell and Segrin (2004) found that when parents talk openly and comfortably to their children about sexual risks and condom use, those children, as adolescents, are more likely to discuss safe sex with their sexual partners and use condoms. Similarly, Warren (1995) and colleagues have argued that when parents approach sex communication with a supportive stance, and integrate that communication throughout the children's lives,

BOX 8.2 • *Family in the News*

A Centers for Disease Control and Prevention (CDC) report issued in late summer 2006 indicated that fewer high school students were having sex than in the early 1990s, the ones that were had fewer partners, and more were using condoms. The study findings can be seen at www.cdc.gov/HealthyYouth/yrbs/pdf/trends/2005_YRBS_Sexual_Behaviors.pdf.

teens are more likely to discuss sex and birth control with their dating partners in a way that leads to safer sex behavior.

Overall, the evidence about the effects of sexual discussions with children are somewhat mixed; however, research does tend to indicate that, the more parents discuss sexuality with their children, the more the children's beliefs and values about these topics become similar to their parents. Additionally, the research supports the theory that parent–child communication about sexuality must occur over time, rather than being isolated to the teen years, and be supportive and open in nature if it is to result in better judgments on the part of teens with regard to safe sex behavior. Because communication is at the heart of the creation and negotiation of shared meanings, this claim certainly makes sense.

In addition to discussions of sexuality and the impact those have on family members, a second sexuality-related concept that has been studied in family communication research relates to the sexual orientation of family members. Although most studies in family communication studies have assumed a heterosexual orientation for parents (and rarely discussed the sexual orientation of children), more recently the issue of sexual orientation of family members has begun to be an object of interest in family studies.

Sexual Orientation and the Family

To discuss family in terms of sexual orientation is more difficult than it may appear at first. We tend to think of **sexual orientation** as being "fixed" (you are either homosexual or heterosexual and once you become sexual you know for sure which one), but research suggests that how individuals define themselves in terms of sexual orientation may be more fluid than that. It is not uncommon for an individual to identify himself or herself as heterosexual, and even marry, but then later identify as homosexual (Wyers, 1987). Thus, identifying which families have members who are gay or lesbian isn't always simple.

Allen and Demo (1995) analyzed over 8,000 articles published about family relationships between 1980 and 1993. They found that, in that time, families headed by gay or lesbian adults were extremely underrepresented in family research. These authors contend that one of the problematic issues in research and theory relating to gay and lesbian families is definitional. If a family has one gay or lesbian member, is it a gay or lesbian family? Does that label apply only if the parents/adult caregivers are gay or lesbian? Additionally, an individual may operate in a heterosexual family and a gay or lesbian family at the same time (where one is the family of origin and the other is the family of procreation/partnership). This further complicates the issue. These authors suggest that the label **gay/lesbian family** should be used for families where there are two adult partners who are gay/lesbian, with or without children, and families where there is one adult who is gay/lesbian raising at least one child. We will adopt this definition, and begin our discussion of sexual orientation and the family by discussing gay/lesbian families.

Gay/Lesbian Families

Culturally, in the United States there is public debate over gay/lesbian families. Some of this concern stems from religious or moral beliefs. Although this debate is certainly an important issue, it falls outside the purview of this text. Whether we condone or accept homosexuality as a life pattern, we cannot deny the presence of significant numbers of gay and lesbian individuals around the world. Thus, this discussion does not focus on whether individuals "should" or "should not" be gay/lesbian (or even whether sexual orientation is a matter of choice or a trait that is outside our control). Rather, we consider some of the specific issues under debate with regard to gay/lesbian families.

Before we begin discussing gay/lesbian families, you might be wondering how many families in the United States are parented by homosexual individuals. This isn't totally clear (partly due to the fluidity of sexuality discussed previously). However, the American Psychiatric Association (2000) estimates that between 1 and 4 million lesbian women are mothers. The number of children living in gay- and lesbian-parented households is estimated to be between 6 and 14 million (American Civil Liberties Union, 1999).

Concerns about gay/lesbian families tend to revolve around three particular issues. First is the idea that children who have gay or lesbian parents are more likely to be homosexual themselves. Second, individuals sometimes indicate concern that if a child does not have a parent of both sexes, he or she will not achieve appropriate socialization or have a satisfactory childhood. This is most often mentioned as a concern related to the sons of lesbian women. Third, because of a lack of acceptance for homosexuality in U.S. culture, there is question about the social stigma that may attach to the children of gay/lesbian parents. Let's consider these issues in turn.

The first concern often indicated about gay/lesbian families is that children raised in such families are more likely to be gay or lesbian. Of course, this is only an issue to the extent that we believe homosexuality to be a problem (that is, as a society, we aren't concerned if parents "pass on" heterosexuality to their children, but we are concerned that they may pass on homosexuality). We certainly learn many of our relational patterns in our families of origin, as discussed in previous chapters, but research does not indicate that sexual orientation is such a learned behavior. Allen and Burrell's 1996 overview of previous research related to the children of gay and lesbian parents concluded that they were no more likely to be homosexual themselves than children of heterosexual parents. Stacey and Biblarz (2001) similarly argue that their respondents, adult children of gay and lesbian parents, were no more likely to identify themselves as gay or lesbian; however, they were more accepting of homosexuality and nontraditional gender roles. Thus, it appears that, whereas children of gay/lesbian parents may be less troubled by the idea that they could possibly be attracted to someone of the same sex, they are no more likely to actually self-identify as homosexual.

The second concern about gay/lesbian families often mentioned is the lack of a father or mother figure in the family to provide socialization, and so on. Silverstein and Auerbach (1999), based on a large study of fathering across family forms, argue that "father absence" in lesbian families is not, in and of itself, detrimental to the children in those families. These scholars do note that father absence may at times result in a decreased socioeconomic status that could affect child outcomes. However, when socioeconomics are controlled for, having a household without a father does not result in an overall reduction in child well-being (see also Crockett, Eggebeen, & Hawkins, 1993; Phares, 1999). Silverstein and Auerbach's research indicated that children need at least one responsible parent who cares for them on a consistent basis in order to have positive outcomes. In homes where there are two parents, this may be easier to manage simply because when one parent is unavailable (emotionally or physically) to the child or children, the other parent is there. However, their research did not indicate a difference with regard to families where there were heterosexual or homosexual parents. Additionally, these authors and others note that children receive socialization from individuals other than their parents. It would be erroneous to assume that a child with lesbian parents would not have male family members (or close family friends) who would participate in the socialization process. The same is true for households headed by gay men.

The third concern mentioned that is often leveled against families headed by gay/lesbian parents is that children will suffer from the social stigma of having "two moms" or "two dads" and thus will have psychological and social adjustment issues. **Social stigma** exists when an individual has a characteristic or set of characteristics that are seen as significantly undesirable socially (Goffman, 1963; Link & Phelan, 2001). It is likely the case that children in families of gay/lesbian parents are sometimes teased by others, or questioned about their family life. There is social stigma related to being in a gay/lesbian household (Herek, 1991). However, this is a societal problem, not a problem of the families themselves. If homosexuality itself was not stigmatized in U.S. culture, children of gay/lesbian parents would not be teased, or worse, about their family situation. Although social stigma related to homosexuality is an important issue, Allen and Burrell (1996), in their review of various studies of children from gay/lesbian families, found that children of homosexual parents did not have poorer social or psychological adjustment than children of heterosexual parents. This suggests that, although stigma is likely present for such families, it does not seem to have a strong detrimental effect on the children. It would be better for children of gay/lesbian families to not be teased or bullied by others due to their family structure, but such problems can also occur for single-parent families, families who are of lower socioeconomic status, interracial families, and families where a member has a disability. Thus, the issue of stigma is not something that is unique to gay/lesbian families.

Even though the primary concerns that are often voiced regarding gay- and lesbian-parented families do not appear (based on research) to be as serious as we may have thought, there are some issues that occur in gay- and lesbian-parented families that do not occur in heterosexual families. One of these issues is disclosure, by the parents, of homosexuality (West & Turner, 1995). This issue is unique to gay- and lesbian-parented families because in a culture where heterosexuality is the assumed norm, children of heterosexual parents do not need to be told about their parents' sexual orientation. As previously discussed, social penetration theory (Altman and Taylor, 1973) and other interpersonal theories suggest that disclosure is an important part of the creation of closeness and connection between relational members. Research related to parental disclosure of homosexual orientation to children tends to suggest that there is a positive effect on the parent–child relationship after disclosure; however, homosexual parents indicate that knowing when, if, and how to disclose to children is often a struggle (West & Turner, 1995). This relates back to the privacy–openness dialectic considered in Chapter 3. Deciding when to be open, what information to share and what information to conceal, and so forth is an active dialectic in the issue of disclosure in gay/lesbian families.

Overall, research about gay/lesbian families suggests that those families are much more similar to than different from heterosexually parented families. Although there are issues that gay/lesbian families face that are distinct from heterosexual families, outcomes for children do not appear to be dramatically different. Of course, sexual orientation is not something that only adults in a family have. Gay/Lesbian adolescents, as they come to understand their sexual orientation, also face a number of challenges as they engage in the "coming out" process within the family setting.

Gay/Lesbian Adolescents and Family

Some scholars (for example Armesto & Weisman, 2001; Beaty, 1999) have discussed the difficulty involved for an adolescent or adult to come out to his or her family. **Coming out** refers to the times at which a gay or lesbian individual acknowledges homosexual orientation to his or her family, friends, peers, colleagues, or larger social groups. The process of informing family members of homosexual orientation can be difficult for many reasons, depending on the family situation, the age of the individual who is coming out, and characteristics of the family members and the family system.

One issue involved with the coming out process for adolescents is that the individual himself or herself must first be aware of and accepting of his or her own sexual orientation (Beaty, 1999; Troiden, 1989). This process occurs gradually, over time, and involves the development of understandings related to sexuality in general, heterosexuality or homosexuality more specifically, and self-identification. Because U.S. culture is heterosexually oriented, it may be difficult for the adolescent to accept that he or she is different from others (DiPlacido, 1998). In fact, many gay/lesbian individuals go though a period of denial related to sexuality, and also a period when they feel that their orientation is wrong or shameful. Thus, one reason that gay and lesbian preadolescents and adolescents may not tell their parents (or others) about their sexual orientation is that they are still working through the process of understanding it themselves. Once an adolescent is comfortable enough to come out to his or her family, the reactions of the family members become a concern.

Armesto and Weisman (2001) studied parental reactions to the coming out of a gay or lesbian adolescent. They found that parents who believed that homosexuality was controllable were much more likely to be rejecting of the child who parents who believed it to be uncontrollable. This is likely because parents who believe that their child has intentionally made what they see as a negative, or abnormal, life choice are more inclined to feel anger toward the child. Additionally, Armesto and Weisman found that when parents felt a higher degree of shame, they were more likely to be rejecting. But when they felt a higher degree of guilt, they were more likely to be accepting. **Shame** refers to a general negative feeling related to self-worth ("I am bad"), whereas **guilt** is a negative feeling related to a particular behavior ("That was wrong to do"). Parents who are more likely to experience shame may

BOX 8.3 • *Internet Connection*

Because hearing that a family member is gay/lesbian can be very difficult. Parents, Families & Friends of Lesbians & Gays (PFLAG) offers support groups, information about how to respond to coming out, information about sexuality, and more. You can find a PFLAG group or read their articles at www.pflag.org/.

see themselves as bad parents because their child is gay, or may see the child himself/herself as a bad person for being gay. Parents who are more inclined to feel guilt, rather than shame, may feel some guilt about the situation ("Did I do something that caused my child to be gay?"), but that guilt doesn't transcend into beliefs about their personhood (or that of their child). Of course, parents who don't see homosexuality as particularly problematic are unlikely to experience either shame or guilt about the situation.

Parental and family acceptance of an adolescent or young adult's sexual orientation is important because, without acceptance, social support is unlikely to follow. As we considered in Chapter 5, research related to theories of social support indicate that it is linked with a variety of positive outcomes for individuals, and a lack of social support may contribute to negative outcomes. Fontaine and Hammond (1996) and other scholars have considered the higher rates of depression, suicide risk, anxiety, and substance abuse for homosexual adolescents who feel rejected by family and peers. D'Augelli (2002), in a study of 542 gay and lesbian adolescents, found that adolescents had more mental health problems, including suicide attempts, when both parents had a negative reaction to a child's homosexuality, or when the parents did not know because the child felt unable to tell them due to the anticipation of a negative reaction. Because gay and lesbian adolescents often experience rejection in peer settings (D'Augelli, 2002; Fontaine & Hammond, 1996), the support of family is even more important.

Whether considering homosexual men and women as parents, or the coming out process of gay/lesbian adolescents, sexual orientation is a part of family life. Although scholars have often "ignored" orientation, by assuming heterosexuality of all family participants, consideration of the role of sexual orientation and associated processes (familial and societal) has become a more prominent part of the study of family communication in recent years, and this trend will likely continue into the future.

In this section, we considered the parental sexual relationship, family talk about sexuality, and issues related to sexual orientation. Sexuality is a complex issue and communication about it is fraught with embarrassment, insecurity, confusion, and even fear. However, it is important to realize how much a part of family life such communication is. Section 2 discusses how to communicate with children about sexuality, and the construction of family identity in lesbian-parented families. Finally, in Section 3 we consider how information about sexuality and the family might impact your life now and in the future.

References

Allen, K. R., & Demo, D. H. (1995). The families of lesbians and gay men: A new frontier in family research. *Journal of Marriage and Family, 57*(1), 111–127.

Allen, M., & Burrell, N. (1996). Comparing the impact of homosexual and heterosexual parents of children: Meta-analysis of existing research. *Journal of Homosexuality, 32*(2), 19–35.

Altman, I., & Taylor, D. A. (1973). *Social penetration.* New York: Holt, Rinehart Winston.

American Civil Liberties Union. (1999). *Fact sheet: An overview of lesbian and gay parenting, adoption, and foster care.* Retrieved March 5, 2005, from the American Civil Liberties Union Web site: www.aclu.org/ LesbianGayRights/

American Psychiatric Association. (2000). *Fact sheet: Gay, lesbian and bisexual issues.* Retrieved March 5, 2005, from the Body: The Complete HIV/AIDS Resource Web site: www.thebody.com/apa/apafacts. html

Armesto, J. C., & Weisman, A. G. (2001). Attributions and emotional reactions to the identity disclosure ("coming out") of a homosexual child. *Family Process, 40*(2), 145–161.

Beaty, L. A. (1999). Identity development of homosexual youth and parental and familial influences on the coming out process. *Adolescence, 34*(135), 597–601.

Booth-Butterfield, M., & Sidelinger, R. (1998). The influence of family communication on the college-aged child: Openness, attitudes and actions about sex and alcohol. *Communication Quarterly, 46*, 295–308.

Byers, E. S. (2005). Relationship satisfaction and sexual satisfaction: A longitudinal study of individuals in long-term relationships. *The Journal of Sex Research, 42*, 113–118.

Byers, E. S., & Demmons, S. (1999). Sexual satisfaction and sexual self-disclosure within dating relationships. *The Journal of Sex Research, 36*, 1–10.

Crockett L. I., Eggebeen, D. J., & Hawkins, A. J. (1993). Father's presence and young children's behavioral and cognitive adjustment. *Family Relations, 14*, 355–377.

Cupach, W. R., & Comstock, J. (1990). Satisfaction with sexual communication in marriage: Links to sexual satisfaction and dyadic adjustment. *Journal of Social and Personal Relationships, 7*, 179–186.

D'Augelli, A. R. (2002). Mental health problems among lesbian, gay, and bisexual youths ages 14 to 21. *Clinical Child Psychology and Psychiatry, 7*(3), 433–456.

DiPlacido, J. (1998). Minority stress among lesbians, gay men, and bisexuals: A consequence of heterosexism, homophobia, and stigmatization. In G. M. Herek (Ed.), *Stigma and sexual orientation: Understanding prejudice against lesbians, gay men, and bisexuals* (pp. 138–159). Newbury Park, CA: Sage.

Fingerson, L. (2005). Do mothers' opinions matter in teens' sexual activity? *Journal of Family Issues, 26*(7), 947–974.

Fisher, T. (1987). Family communication and the sexual behaviors and attitudes of college students. *Journal of Youth and Adolescence, 16*, 481–493.

Fisher, T. (1993). A comparison of various measures of family sexual communication: Psychometric properties, validity, and behavioral correlates. *The Journal of Sex Research, 30*(3), 229–238.

Fisher, T. D. (1989). An extension of the findings of Moore, Peterson, and Furstenberg (1986) regarding family sexual communication and adolescent sexual behavior. *Journal of Marriage and Family, 51*(3), 637–639.

Fontaine, J. H., & Hammond, N. L. (1996). Counseling issues with gay and lesbian adolescents. *Adolescence, 31*, 817–830.

Fox, G. L. (1981). The family's role in adolescent sexual behavior. In T. Ooms (Ed.), *Teenage pregnancy in a family context* (pp. 73–130). Philadelphia: Temple University Press.

Fox, G. L., & Inazu, J. K. (1980). Mother–daughter communication about sex. *Family Relations, 29*(3), 347–352.

Goffman, E. (1963). *The presentation of self in everyday life.* Garden City, NY: Anchor Books.

Guo, B., & Huang, J. (2005). Marital and sexual satisfaction in Chinese families: Exploring the moderating effects. *Journal of Sex & Marital Therapy, 31*(1), 21–29.

Handelsman, C., Cabral, R., & Weisfeld, G. (1987). Sources of information and adolescent sexual knowledge and behavior. *Journal of Adolescent Research, 2*, 455–463.

Heisler, J. M. (2005). Family communication about sex: Parents and college-aged offspring recall discussion topics, satisfaction, and parental involvement. *Journal of Family Communication, 5*(4), 295–312.

Hepburn, E. (1983). A three-level model of parent–daughter communication about sexual topics. *Adolescence, 18*(71), 523–534.

Herek, G. M. (1991). Stigma, prejudice and violence against lesbians and gay men. In J. C. Gonsiorek & J. D. Weinrich (Eds.), *Homosexuality: Research implications for public policy.* Newbury Park, CA: Sage.

Hutchinson, M. K., & Cooney, T. M. (1998). Patterns of parent–teen sexual risk communication: Implications for intervention. *Family Relations, 47*(2), 185–194.

Jordan, T. R., Price, J. H., & Fitzgerald, S. (2000). Rural parents' communication with their teen-agers about sexual issues. *Journal of School Health, 70*(8), 338–344.

Lawrance, K., & Byers, E. S. (1995). Sexual satisfaction in long-term heterosexual relationships: The interpersonal exchange model of sexual satisfaction. *Personal Relationships, 2*, 267–285.

Link, B. G., & Phelan, J. C. (2001). Conceptualizing stigma. *Annual Review of Sociology, 27*, 363–385.

Litzinger, S., & Gordon, K. C. (2005). Exploring relationships among communication, sexual satisfaction, and marital satisfaction. *Journal of Sex & Marital Therapy, 31*(5), 409–424.

Miller, B. C. (2002). Family influences on adolescent sexual and contraceptive behavior, *Journal of Sex Research, 39*(1), 22–26.

Miller, K. S., Levin, M. L., Whitaker, D. J., & Xu, X. (1998). Patterns of condom use among adolescents: The impact of mother–adolescent communication. *American Journal of Public Health, 88*, 1542–1544.

Moore, K., Peterson, J., & Furstenberg, F. (1986). Parental attitudes and the occurrence of early sexual activity. *Journal of Marriage and Family, 48*, 777–783.

Newcomer, S. F., & Udry, J. R. (1985). Parent–child communication and adolescent sexual behavior. *Family Planning, 17*, 169–174.

Phares, V. (1999). *Poppa psychology: The role of fathers in children's mental well-being*. Westport, CT: Praeger.

Powell, H. L., & Segrin, C. (2004). The effect of family and peer communication on college students' communication with dating partners about HIV and AIDS. *Health Communication, 16*(4), 427–449.

Purnine, D. M., & Carey, M. P. (1997). Interpersonal communication and sexual adjustment: The roles of understanding and agreement. *Journal of Consulting and Clinical Psychology, 65*, 1017–1025.

Rosenthal, D. A., & Feldman, S. S. (1999). The importance of importance: Adolescents' perceptions of parental communication about sexuality. *Journal of Adolescence, 22*, 835–851.

Silverstein, L. B., & Auerbach, C. F. (1999). Deconstructing the essential father. *American Psychologist, 54*, 397–407.

Sprecher, S. (2002). Sexual satisfaction in premarital relationships: Associations with satisfaction, love, commitment, and stability. *The Journal of Sex Research, 39*, 190–196.

Stacey, J., & Biblarz, T. (2001). (How) does the sexual orientation of parents matter? *American Sociological Review, 66*(2), 159–183.

Troiden, R. R. (1989). The formation of homosexual identities. *Journal of Homosexuality, 17*, 43–73.

Warren, C. (1995). Parent-child communication about sex. In T. L. Socha and G. H. Stamp (Eds.), *Parents, children, and communication: Frontiers of theory and research* (pp. 173–201). Mahwah, NJ: Erlbaum.

Warren, C. (1995). Perspectives on international sex practices and American family sex communication relevant to teenage sexual behavior in the United States. *Health Communication, 4*(2), 121–136.

West, R., & Turner, L. H. (1995). Communication in lesbian and gay families: Building a descriptive base. In T. J. Socha & G. H. Stamp (Eds.), *Parents, children and communication: Frontiers of theory and research* (pp. 147–169). Mahwah, NJ: Erlbaum.

Whitaker, D. J., Miller, K. S., May, D. C., & Levin, M. L. (1999). Teenage partners' communication about sexual risk and condom use: The importance of parent–teenager discussions. *Family Planning Perspectives, 31*(3), 117–121.

Wyers, N. L. (1987). Homosexuality in the family: Lesbian and gay spouses. *Social Work, 32*, 143–148.

Young, M., Denny, G., Young, T., & Luquis, R. (2000). Sexual satisfaction among married women. *American Journal of Health Studies, 16*, 73–84.

Section 2: Research Examples _____

Communicating about Sex as a Daughter, Parent, and Teacher

Amber E. Kinser

In Section 1, we addressed some of the difficulties that family members face in the attempt to talk overtly about sexuality. For this article, Kinser uses an autoethnographic approach (a study of self) to explore this issue from the perspective of the child in the family, the parent in the family, and a professor of family communication as well. This piece is an illustration of both the concepts we have discussed in this chapter and the power of carefully constructed autoethnography as a scholarly tool.

L.B.A.

Family communication about sex is exceedingly complex. Research suggests most parents agree that talking with children about sex is important, but it also suggests that many parents speak with young people about sex at best indirectly, or ineffectively, from the point of view of the children. The purpose of this section is to explore some of the everyday life complexities of family talk, and other communication, about sex and the body. Using an autoethnographic approach (writing about the culture of the self), I explore here some of the multiple layers of sex communication by examining with a critical eye the practices in my family when I was growing up, in my family now that I am raising children, and in my students' families based on what they have shared in class. It is my hope that autoethnography's pointed focus on the frank and the particular of an individual perspective, in this case my own, might illuminate possible paths for inquiry and critique that can inform more general perspectives about family sex communication. Ideally, I would like to help lift some of the stigma and discomfort from family sex communication by sharing some of the intimacy, ambiguity, and humanity of my own story.

Sex Talk Metaphors

The metaphors we use to refer to conversations with children about sex are revealing. They reveal our discomfort about the topic, our insistence that the most important thing to know about sex is the science of it, our resistance to letting children in on the human relationship dimensions of sexuality, our fear of being or appearing sexually inappropriate, our dissatisfaction or guilt about our own sexual decisions, and our deficient preparation for handling sexual matters. Most people probably understand the phrase "the facts of life," for example, to represent discussion about "where babies come from," about how a female and male engage in sexual intercourse and how that often enough results in pregnancy, and consequently decisions about parenthood. It represents a focus on the clarity of seemingly indisputable biological "sexual urges" rather than the murkiness of passion, desire, choice, need, regret, guilt, and power. A discussion about sex that sticks to the "facts" is significantly easier to navigate for the discussion leader (usually the parent or parents), though its usefulness for the other participants in the discussion (usually the children) is limited. Its advantage, of course, is that it allows us to feel like we are talking about the important stuff of sex without actually having to talk about the important stuff. It is interesting to note that we find sexual matters important and central enough to warrant the status of the title The Facts of Life, yet not important or central enough to include with its discussions these murky and uniquely human dimensions. At the same time, we may discuss issues such as respect, obedience, integrity, race, justice, work, and love with our children, yet do not view these as important or central enough to warrant the status of The Facts of Life, even though they are probably no less so, and perhaps more so, than sex.

Talk about "the birds and the bees" is also revealing. Here again, we seek to reduce sexual matters to the biology and science of them alone. This metaphor has the additional advantage of keeping the discussion out of the realm of everyday human living altogether. Further, the images of the nonhuman animals conjured by The Birds and the Bees complicate our ability to focus on just what it is these birds and bees are *doing*. If we were able to picture these flying animals having sex, it is unlikely to pose the threat of leading to thoughts and mental images of *humans* having sex. It is no coincidence that we don't refer to sex talk as being about "the dogs and the horses;" too many people already know and have seen or can easily picture precisely what is going on there. The distance between picturing images of these animals and picturing similar images of human animals is a short one; if it weren't, we wouldn't take such note of, or be so embarrassed by, finding horses or dogs engaging in sexual behavior. If instead we used a metaphor like "the bottlenose dolphins and the bonobo chimps," we would be able to talk more clearly, for example, about same-sex behavior because these are among the minimally 10 percent of the animal kingdom that practice same-sex sexual behavior. But again, using our current metaphors allows us to *not* talk about much of anything. So birds and bees it is.

A third popular phrase for referring to sex communication, particularly to that taking place in families, is "the talk." This is probably understood by many to refer to a necessary but often discomfiting conversation that is withheld until a child reaches puberty, at which point, it is widely held, bodily changes threaten to awaken sexual awareness for the first time—or at least in more overwhelming and exigent ways than before. This metaphor makes clear the assumption that what a person needs to know about the sexual body not only can be *condensed* to a single talk, but also can be *learned* in a single talk. It suggests that the person who initiates The Talk will know when and how to give it at such a precise and identifiable single moment in another person's life. In fact, that someone is giving a talk makes clear its monologic nature: there is little conversational exchange going on, no reciprocity of listening or speaking. One person lacks the knowledge, now suddenly needs the knowledge, and the other person possesses, distills, and transfers it to her or him. The Talk suggests that a child has not been learning about sex and bodily intimacy since she or he was born; that years of messages about privacy, nudity, hugs, personal space, and kisses have not been about sexuality at some level; and that billboards, magazines, the Internet, peers, television, song lyrics, commercials, radio, and film have not been overwhelming the child with sexuality information for years. The idea of The Talk, though it may feel uncomfortable while it is going on, is in the long run for many parents a comforting idea. It simplifies the complexities of sexual matters, and helps parents feel powerful in an area where they are finally powerless: dictating their children's sexuality. This metaphor allows us to pretend that we really only have to talk about sexuality once, at which point we fortunately can invoke the facts of life and the birds and the bees, and talk very little about sexuality ever. So the first points of confrontation for us in studying family sex communication are the multiple alternatives already in place for sending a lifetime of messages about sexuality while never actually *talking* about it.

Talking and Thinking about the Body

The first time I asked my students to contribute to our discussion on the impact of language by sharing some of the ways their families talked about sex, I was surprised. Even now when I pose this question every semester, I am struck by their responses. One of the ways I begin this part of the module on language is to suggest that the way our parents talked about our bodies shaped in part how we have come to view our bodies and bodily intimacy; I ask them to share some of the terms that were used in their families to refer to body parts, specifically genitalia. Most often, no one responds to that question, which probably does not surprise you. I then suggest that surely their parents used *some* kind of terms when, for example, they were teaching about bathroom behavior like using the toilet or bathing. At this point, some students gradually recall, or gradually admit, what terms they were taught as children, usually with awkwardness. I am struck that they have a hard time getting comfortable with this conversation even as college adults.

They are embarrassed partly by the unique, sometimes comical, sometimes even bizarre terms their own families used and the terms they use even now. The mother of one of my students, for example, used the term "bug" to refer to female genitalia, whereas her father "never addressed sexuality ever." She is chagrined to realize that she ended up referring to her daughter's genital region as a "tootie." The family of another student used "bird-dog" and "pecker" to refer to the penis, and "goose" or "down there" to refer to "all the female sexual organs." My students also are uncomfortable partly because they never have thought about terms like these as a topic for open discussion. Still other students remember that their families did not use any names to refer to what are considered to be sexual body parts because there *were* no such references made in their home. They report that their parents did not talk about genitals, about sex, about reproduction, or about menstruation. My students can see how such silence communicated powerful sexuality messages that stuck with them. These class sessions strike me both because I know that healthy sexuality and identity are significantly influenced by family communication, and because my experiences with these issues in my own family are markedly different from those of my students.

I grew up in a home that was very comfortable talking about genitals, sex, reproduction, and menstruation. This is surprising given that my parents sent us to a religious school for years and were surrounded by friends and neighbors who had a twofold lesson about sex communication with their kids: don't talk about it and don't do it. I lived with my mother and father, then grew up from two years old on with my mother and stepfather, and maintained a good relationship with my biological father for a long time. It was largely my mother who taught me most of what I know about the body, including feeling comfortable talking about it. As I've explained in other writing: "She taught me to be bold about my body—to look at it, talk about it, ask questions about it. She taught me to be bold about my sexuality. She did not hide her sexual playfulness with my [step]father; she was unconcerned about other people's responses to the mirrors on her bedroom ceiling" (Kinser, 2004, p. 126). If I was not feeling like my usual self because I was menstruating, I could comfortably tell my stepfather that I had my period and he seemed fine with this openness. It was my father who drew the picture of the fallopian tubes, the ovaries, the uterus, and the vagina while he was explaining what getting a period means. My family used terms like "testicles" fairly easily, and when I asked my mother at a very young age what an "orgzm" was—I knew neither what it was nor how to pronounce it—she explained it to me without hesitation. Even though "climax" and "juices flowing" were not notions I could do much with at the time, what I learned in that conversation with my mother, and others like it, is that a person is entitled to know and understand her body and how it works and how that relates to other people.

My family was not without its hang-ups. We had our share of dysfunction and we were not comfortable talking about *everything*. I did not know what a clitoris was until my young adulthood, though I was unwittingly introduced to how it worked and how that felt when I was climbing up a pole to slide down it while on the playground in elementary school. I knew nothing of circumcision or foreskin until I became sexually active as a young adult; I knew of no terms to refer to the labia. Also in elementary school, it was my slightly younger cousin and not my parents who explained the bodily specifics of heterosexual intercourse, which she learned from her mother, my mother's sister. It was then, I think, that I learned the terms "penis" and "vagina." Though the memories would not surface until my young adulthood, I was unwittingly introduced to this too as a victim of sexual abuse by a man down the street when I was five years old. I didn't mention it to my parents until after several repeated incidents and I don't know quite why. There was no conversation about birth control until after I already was sexually active. I don't recall conversations about STDs (sexually transmitted diseases). Although my parents, especially my mother, were direct and comfortable and honest in much of their treatment of family sex communication, we did miss some important components.

Even with these various complexities in my own family's sex communication, I am amazed at how many of my students report minimal or no concrete interactions about sex or the sexual body. Perhaps I should not be surprised then, even though I am, that my students typically "get the willies" at the thought of their parents having a sex life. I always have a small handful of people in class who are very clear that their parents are sexually active beings and who are quite comfortable with that, though they are uninterested in spending time talking or thinking about it, which makes sense to me. But a majority of my students shudder, physically, at the thought. They can never quite explain why they react this way. Somehow they manage to separate being a parent from having sex. Perhaps that is one reason the United States leads all other developed nations in unintended pregnancy (Warren, 1992). Here, too, my childhood was notably different from that of my students. My parents taught my two older sisters, my younger brother, and me that their bedroom was to be of no concern to us and that, for the most part, we had no business being in there. We also knew that when their door was shut they were off limits to us and we were clear on the fact that this was because they were having sex. I was annoyed in these moments at not having immediate access to my parents precisely when I wanted it, as I suppose most children would be; my sisters and I rolled our eyes at the thought. But I never got the willies about what they were doing behind that door. I imagine some of my students learned from their parents and developed the same head-in-the-sand approach to their parents' bodies that their parents seem to have developed about theirs. I find it interesting that my students critique their parents' puritanical attitudes regarding their sex lives, but display similar puritanical attitudes toward that of their parents.

Sex Communication and My Sexual Decision Making

The relative openness and honesty with which my family engaged in sex communication in large part enabled me to start having intercourse no earlier than I did at 16, and to make choices that were in my long-term best interest, like deciding, most of the time, to be sexual only with people I cared deeply about, using reliable birth control consistently, and seeking regular gynecological care where my decisions could be informed by health care expertise and where I could be checked for and treated for STDs. When my mother first discovered I had become sexually active upon finding a condom wrapper I had failed to throw away, her immediate response was about birth control. I was more concerned that she knew I was having sex and sobbed through that conversation; she was more concerned about my preventing pregnancy and kept asking me why I was crying. We set up a gynecological appointment and I started taking "the pill." At this time, we were not focused as a culture on STDs, and certainly not on AIDS/HIV, which had not yet touched the public nerve, so what talk there was with kids about sex tended to focus on birth control or abstinence.

Still, no one variable can determine an outcome; sex communication between parents and children is not the only variable that influences sexual decision making. Mine was influenced by multiple variables. For example, I was fortunate enough and, I like to think, smart enough to have usually dated young men who were equally prepared for long-term healthy decision making, and sometimes even more prepared than I was. One boyfriend refused to have sex with me because we were too young, and a later boyfriend would never have sex with me unless we used a condom or my diaphragm. Relatively healthy relationships, direct conversations with responsible partners, access to and the means to afford birth control, and the good fortune to have my birth control never fail so far, plus multiple other variables that I probably never will know about all worked together with my family's sex communication, resulting in my having two children at points in my life when I was ready and prepared to be a parent. Family sex communication can be a powerful predictor of the sexual decisions young people make, but it is not the only predictor (Nelson, 1997; Walters & Walters, 1983).

Sex Communication with My Children

Perhaps because I have recognized the limited role families might play in shaping sexual attitudes and behaviors, I have been mindful of sexual socialization since my first of two children, my daughter, was an infant. I have wanted badly to get right whatever role I might play. My parents set good examples in many ways and I want to continue in that tradition. I also have made a number of choices in this area that my parents would never have made. Sometimes I feel confident about those choices; other times I am not so sure. As a parent, I want to be open about and comfortable with sex and body talk in our home like my parents were, but I want to go even further than they did. I want to talk about birth control and STDs before my children begin sexual activity. I want to be more attentive to their personal body boundaries and more respectful of their personal space. I want to work harder to counter the negative messages in the various media when they portray sexual relations as grounded in manipulation, and portray sex as primarily about power. I want to counter the hateful and damaging cultural message that homosexuality is less human or less loving or less beautiful than heterosexuality. I want to teach them somehow that, as Eisler (1995) has argued at length, sex is both more important and less important than the culture would have us believe.

I think I have raised my daughter so far to feel comfortable with her body and talking about it. She knew the word for labia about as early as she learned the words for nose and eyes, and learned about clitoris and vagina, as the subjects arose, not long after that. It was a little tricky when she used these terms out loud at the grocery store, needless to say, because few people, I've discovered, share my commitment to open and direct family sex communication. In fact, few of my adult female friends at the time knew what my daughter was referring to when they overheard her say "labia," as do few of my students now. Since preschool, she has been different from her peers in sexual knowledge, and I guess I am comfortable with that.

My first direct conversation with my daughter about sexual behavior was prompted at three years of age when she walked in on her father and me having sex. We were caught by surprise, thinking we had locked the door. Despite my surprise, I was able to avoid shouting for her to get out and instead was able to focus calmly on the house rule about knocking on closed doors. I was conflicted by thoughts of telling her to go out, of picking her up and making it not such a big deal, and that this is one of the most monumental moments in a child's life that will have reverberations throughout it and I needed to handle it well. Plus, of course, I was trying to figure out just how long she was there and how much she saw. When she finally did leave the room, I followed her out into the hall and asked her if she was all right. To my unprecedented terror she asked me "How come Daddy was on you like that?" Now the interesting point for me as I write this story is that I truly thought, given how much I think and read and teach about this very kind of family sex communication, that I would have some earthly idea of how to respond to this question. But words seemed to fail me. Finally, I was able to tell her that her father "was loving on me," and that what she saw is one of the ways that moms and dads love on each other.

The conversation went on for a bit as I tried to adhere to two principles that I have come to see as critical components of parental sex communication: Do tell children what they want to know, and don't tell them more than they are able to handle at a given point in their development, which is quite often more than parents think. But I had a hard time in that moment sorting out what to tell her that honored both of those principles. In the end, we talked about love and affection, and that big people often love one another with their bodies, and that it is good and that it made her father and me happy and that everything was all right. It was a moment I will never forget. In retrospect, I am pleased that her first direct lesson about sex was primarily about love, affection, and intimacy, rather than "where babies come from," because the latter is but one of many components of sexual relations in general, and the former is what *most* sex *is* about. I think I did the best I could do in the moment in my daughter's sexual socialization, but I probably never truly will know.

As a family communication professor and feminist scholar interested in sexuality studies, not to mention book collector, I have an abundance of books and resources related to sex, most of which are in our home. Yet even with ready access to plentiful sexuality information, my preteen daughter sought out other, culturally sanctioned resources. When she took more than the normal amount of time to answer her bedroom door one evening, I suspected she was online on some site she did not want me to see. I asked her what she was doing and she said she was emailing. I said, "Well let's take a look at where you've been lately," and clicked on her online history. As I thought, she was checking out visual pornography sites. She was embarrassed and sheepish. I asked her why she was embarrassed and she didn't know. I told her there was nothing embarrassing about being curious—everyone is curious, especially about sex. I said, "Your dad, stepdad, and I have all looked at those sites out of curiosity. But there is nothing there worth seeing, finally. If you want to look at nude bodies and people being sexual there are images that are worth seeing and you won't find them on those sites. We have plenty of books here you can look at. If you want something of your own, I'll buy you a book of nudes rendered by artists. Some depictions of sex and the body are beautiful and enlightening and others are not. Expose yourself to the beautiful ones instead of that. Do something more intelligent with your mind." We continued to talk about what she saw online and it was a good conversation, I think. I suppose she has revisited those sites some, to my disappointment, but the lure of secrecy and the forbidden is lifted some, and she leaves her door open much more often than she used to. Sometimes I feel comfortable with how this interaction turned out. Other times I wonder about it.

Even though moments like these with my daughter have been tricky, I have discovered that body talk was easier for me with her than it is with my son. When he was three, their father and I divorced. When I started seeing someone else, I learned that my new partner lived, when he was a boy, with an adult female family member who had been sexually inappropriate with him and that it has greatly affected him to this day. So I have been particularly vigilant about my behavior with my son, wanting very much never to make him feel uncomfortable, but still wanting very much not to fail in my responsibility to help him understand his body. We have had conversations from the beginning, so that I was sure he knew how to care for his body; also, I know that he will look different from most of his peers and I wanted to begin early helping him feel comfortable with his body regardless of how other boys look. I learned from my own research that circumcision was medically unnecessary and his father and I decided that, for us, any choice about circumcision should be made by our son when he is capable of making it himself. One of the consequences of that decision is that my son and I often are in the position of talking openly and directly about things that are very personal and private for him. His father takes care of this when our son is at his house, and although my current husband, his stepfather, is willing to help me on this front, their relationship has not developed enough yet to keep such interactions from being more awkward than they already are. So my son and I are having more sexually sensitive discussions than most mothers and sons are having, I suspect. I wonder if fear or uneasiness with this discussion is why many families avoid it through circumcision. The topic never feels completely comfortable for me. I do know that the few times he has had concerns about his body, he has felt at ease enough to talk with me so we can take care of it. That never feels completely comfortable for me either, and I doubt it does for him.

Some Implications for Family Sex Communication Research

As an academic, and unlike most parents I suspect, I am familiar with the research about family sex communication and what thousands of adolescents, teens, college students, and parents are reporting about how their families communicate about sex and how that relates to the sexual behaviors of the young people in those families. What I wish is that I could read through these hundreds of studies and come to some definitive conclusions about how to interact with my kids in order to bring about the sexual attitudes and behaviors that I believe are important. I am willing to modify my current thinking and methods, and adopt some others that are proving to work. To my dismay, however, the research has not proven to be quite that conclusive.

Much of the difficulty, from a research perspective, in exploring how families socialize children about sexuality lies in the fact that families are communicating about sexuality even when they are not sitting down and discussing it. Issues of privacy and personal space, expectations for intimate contact with others, a parent shooting "a look" to a child in response to something he or she is wearing or has said or asked, what the children are allowed to watch on television and why are all oblique forms of sexual socialization. Family sex communication includes untold numbers of tiny messages, "unspoken, indirect, and nonverbal," that accumulate over a long time—12, 15 years and more—that represent parental attitudes and values (Fox, 1980, p. 22). These are nearly impossible to "research." Furthermore, parent-child interaction is only one of many variables influencing adolescent and teen behavior. Mediated messages, peer relationships and expectations, sex education in school, friendships, observations of parents' relationships, sibling relationships, fashion, individual personality, religion, and how the parents' parents addressed sexuality in their home all play a part in shaping a young person's behavior.

One of the important things to keep in mind about young people's sexual behavior is that the point in a child's life when the parents want most for the child to follow their teaching, is the point at which they are most likely to follow that of their peers. So if the parent–child conversation about sex and the body begins at puberty, it is too late to accomplish the parents' goal. I have argued for a long time in the classes I teach that if parents find themselves having The Talk, they have done it wrong. Nietzsche (1878) has argued that marriage is a long conversation. If it is true of marriage, it is no less true of parenting, and in particular of parenting about sexuality. Family sex communication begins in infancy when the child first learns about touch and need and the feeling of skin against skin. When a child *has* to give Grandma a kiss, for example, she or he learns, among other things, that other people get to decide how and with whom she or he will be intimate and how. If children have no space to call their own, designated for example by the right to close their bedroom doors and to expect that others usually will knock, they are learning here too about how little power they have to control their lives. Moments like these send important messages that reverberate throughout the child's sexual decision making.

We cannot expect that persons who have been taught that others control their body and space will feel empowered to make smart sexual decisions. We cannot expect that children will be willing to bring their sexuality concerns and questions to adults who have no time or patience to answer their other childlike questions. We cannot expect children to develop a healthy sense of their own sexuality when their every curiosity and intrigue is judged and corrected. I suspect that parents are spending too much time trying to figure out how to simplify and wrap up the sex conversation instead of embracing the fact that it has been going on since the child's first day. It neither started recently nor will end soon and it has taken and will take myriad forms, most of which do not look or sound like sex talk at all.

One of the most important contributions we could make to the sexual well-being of young people is to see more clearly the multiple and varied ways we are communicating about sexuality when we are *not talking* about it. Another important contribution would be to reexamine the multiple ways we have devised as a culture to claim we are talking about sexuality and appear to be doing so, but actually and conveniently avoid addressing the sexual matters that matter most. We need to find alternative metaphors for sex talk that, unlike The Facts of Life, The Birds and the Bees, and The Talk, get at the humanity of sex and actually confront its murkiness and ambiguities. Without these contributions, the stacks of research conducted on family sex communication since the mid-1960s will be of little use, and we will be no closer to discovering what is best for the sexual well-being of young people and the adults they will become than if we had never asked the research questions at all.

Questions for Consideration and Discussion

1. In this piece of work, Kinser discusses the metaphors facts of life, birds and the bees, and the talk with regard to family communication about sex. Which of these terms had you heard and/or used prior to this reading? What do these terms suggest to you about sexuality?
2. As noted here, families often construct their own terminology to use when describing genitalia and other body issues. Thinking back to your own childhood, what terms were used and how did those make you feel about your body? When did you first note that other people had different terms, and how did you feel about that?
3. Kinser discusses some hopes that she has for communicating about sexuality with her children. Looking back on your family experiences, what were the positive parts of the communication you received from your parents/caregivers? What do you wish they had done differently?
4. In this work, Kinser says that she hopes such writings will help reduce some of the discomfort or stigma of family communication about sexuality. Having read this piece, do you feel your attitudes about family sex communication have changed? Explain.
5. This work is autoethnographic in nature. What do you see as the benefits and drawbacks of an autoethnographic approach?

References

Eisler, R. (1995). *Sacred pleasure: Sex, myth, and the politics of the body.* San Francisco: HarperSanFrancisco.

Fox, G. L. (1980). The mother–adolescent daughter relationship as a sexual socialization structure: A research review. *Family Relations, 29*(1), 21–28.

Kinser, A. E. (2004). Negotiating spaces for/through third wave feminism. *National Women's Studies Association Journal, 16*(3), 124–153.

Nelson, M. C. (1997). *Community and media influences on adolescent sexual abstinence.* (Doctoral dissertation, University Microfilms International). Dissertation Abstracts International, *58*(5), 2721. (UMI No.

AAM9734630). Retrieved August 24, 2004, from PsycINFO (1840-Current) database.

Nietzche, F. (1878). *Human, all too human: A book for free spirits.* Retrieved April 12, 2006, from www.public appeal.org/library/nietzsche/Nietzsche_human_all_ too_human/index.htm

Walters, J., & Walters, L. H. (1983). The role of the family in sex education. *Journal of Research and Development in Education, 16*(2), 8–15.

Warren, C. (1992). Perspectives on international sex practices and American family sex communication relevant to teenage sexual behavior in the United States. *Health Communication, 4*(2), 121–136.

The Social Context of Lesbian Family Identity

Elizabeth A. Suter

Karla Mason Bergen

Karen L. Daas

As we discussed in Chapter 1, family has been defined in a variety of ways across time and subject matter. Generally, however, definitions have often focused on the legal union between a man and woman and their offspring. This means that some families, including gay- and lesbian-parented families, may need to work harder to be seen as family, or even to feel confident in their own family status. In this work, Suter, Bergen, and Daas discuss some of the strategies used by lesbian parents to construct family identity. As you read, consider how cultural understandings and expectations have contributed to the strategies noted here, as well as to your own family identity experiences.

L.B.A.

More children are raised in lesbian and gay households than ever before. Most estimates agree that in the United States today between 6 and 12 million children are being raised by gay parents (Patterson, 1995; Woosley, 2003). In the lesbian community, in particular, having children is so common that many refer to it as the lesbian baby boom (Chabot & Ames, 2004; Kershaw, 2000). In fact, somewhere between 1 and 5 million lesbians are now mothers (Johnson & O'Connor, 2002). Some lesbian mothers have children through previous marriages and heterosexual relationships, but many lesbians are now having children through artificial insemination by donor (Kershaw, 2000). As the number of lesbian families continues to grow, it is clear these understudied and less traditional families need to be studied.

Our study contributes to an understanding of lesbian family life by exploring how lesbian families use rituals and symbols to communicate they are a family. We explore how these lesbian families use rituals and symbols to communicate both external and internal family identity. Communicating an external sense of family identity refers to how families make clear that they are a lesbian family to others, including extended family, neighbors, and strangers. Communicating an internal sense of family identity refers to how families make clear that they are a lesbian family to one another, particularly to the child(ren).

Rituals and Symbols as Communicative of Identity

Rituals help families express their family identity. Family rituals include holiday celebrations, family traditions, and everyday patterned interactions (Wolin & Bennett, 1984).

Likewise, symbols help communicate family identity. Family symbols include objects and words that show family ties (Goffman, 1971).

Symbolic Interactionism

We use a symbolic interactionist perspective (Mead, 1943; Perinbanayagam, 2003) to help explain the ways lesbian families communicate that they are a family. Communication is the primary way identity is negotiated. In other words, individuals and families do not necessarily get to be who they want to be. Instead, they are defined through their interactions with others. Persons are uncertain if others will accept or reject the identity they present. Role is also closely tied to identity. The role a person performs, such as joint motherhood, partly defines who one is (Goffman, 1959). Therefore, the research question for our study was: How do lesbian families use rituals and symbols to create and negotiate their identity?

Method

We invited lesbian families to be a part of our study by making announcements at community groups and placing advertisements in public places. We interviewed 21 lesbian families in their homes. We analyzed the interviews in the qualitative tradition using a form known as constructivist grounded theory, which argues that there is not an objective reality to be "discovered," but rather that research provides "an *interpretive* [italics in original] portrayal of the studied world, not an exact picture of it" (Charmaz, 2002, p. 678). Our study focuses on 16 of these families who all had their children via donor insemination. However, we used data from all 21 interviews to create an educational brochure and Web site.

Findings and Discussion

We found that lesbian families use rituals and symbols to communicate family identity externally (to others) and internally (to themselves). We first discuss how lesbian families communicate their identity externally. We then discuss how these families communicate their identity internally.

We found that the symbols of last names and donor choice and the ritual of doing family helped these lesbian families communicate their family identity to others. We also found that the symbol of names for two mommies and the rituals of attending a same-sex parenting group and doing family helped these lesbian families communicate their family identity to one another, particularly to the children. In this section, we discuss how families used these rituals and symbols to show others that they are a family.

Externally Communicating Family Identity

Last Names.   We found that last names are one key symbol that communicates an external sense of family identity. In 12 families, the child's name included the last name of the nonbiological mother (the nonbirth mother). One family took the biological (birth) mother's last name as a shared family name. The remaining three families gave their children the biological mother's last name. Sharing a family name supports a family's identity, particularly when others use the family name (Suter & Oswald, 2003). For instance, Cami and Bray reported that receiving cards and packages addressed to their family name "Olson" validates their identity as a family. Cami explained, "It is traditional assessment that you're a family. . . . You have the same last name. People just click that that's a family."

Last names also make the lesbian family form clear to acquaintances and strangers (Suter, 2004). Robin described how "when we go places, the hospital or emergency room or something like that, when we say, 'This is Jacob Miller-Wilson' and then they go, 'Which one of you is the mom?', and we say, 'We are both the mom.'" The child's hyphenated last name highlights the connection both mothers have with their child and shows others that they are a family unit.

By contrast, Annette's hesitation to take her partner and child's last name serves as a powerful reminder of how easily these families' identities can be disconfirmed. Because of her family's lack of support, Annette is keeping her family name until her parents die, in hope that her parents will be there as grandparents for her and Jamie's son. Although Theresa and Brenda gave their child a hyphenated name, they did not merge their names because of the potential threat to Theresa's military job. This threat underscores the power last names have to communicate family to outsiders, which as these examples illustrate, can sometimes be positive and other times negative.

Last names also externally communicate roles to others. For instance, Angie and Lisa's twins' hyphenated name communicates their joint motherhood to others. Angie explained, "[The reason] we wanted to do hyphenated names was that it just showed, you know, maybe school administrators or doctors or whatever that they belong to both of us." For this family and others, sharing a last name helps show others that they are a family.

Donor Choice.   We found sperm donor choice is a second key symbol that communicates an external sense of identity. Families chose donors from sperm banks, which provide families access to donor files that include descriptions of the donor's physical features, family medical history, level of education, and occupation. Some files also include photographs and personal essays.

Most families chose donors because of their physical appearance. Choosing a donor based on desired physical traits nonverbally communicates family by creating family resemblance. Families chose donors who had similar traits to the nonbiological mother to increase the likelihood that the child would look like a blend of the two mothers. Sandra explained, "So that we would all look related." Traits of importance included skin tone, eye color, hair color, and ethnicity. Jamie talked about how this is like what naturally occurs when heterosexual couples have a biological child, "Your heterosexual couples that have children have the biological connection and the physical characteristics." Looking related paints the picture of family.

A few families went beyond physical appearance and factored in nonphysical traits, such as values or personality characteristics they learned through the donors' essays. For Jenny, honesty was the most important value. She chose the donor she thought was the most honest because he admitted he had suffered a period of depression, whereas other donors claimed to be perfectly healthy. Likewise, Michelle and Susan chose a donor because they were won over by his personality. In his personal essay, he described himself as someone who likes to drink coffee on Sunday morning, a "regular guy."

Doing Family.   We found that a primary ritual that communicates family identity to others is patterned everyday interactions—ordinary family activities that happen regularly (West & Zimmerman, 1987 Wolin & Bennett, 1984;). Ellen described how, "when they see us together with her, I think they know automatically that we are a family. We don't act any different than any other family."

Families reported that everyday activities, such as shopping, family walks, interacting with neighbors, and attending church, expressed their family identity to others, who either accepted or rejected that identity. Carol identified shopping as a key ritual that announces familyhood to others. She said, "Shopping, because it doesn't matter where we go, somebody has to, they see the intimacy between the two of us, the three of us, really, and need to define it, and it happens a lot." Family walks can function in the same way. Sarah spoke about how being together on nightly walks shows familyhood. She explained, "It's a joining of all three bodies at one time doing an activity . . . the closeness and proximity of us together." Lynn recalled how they were "doing the stroller thing, the dog thing" and an interaction with a neighbor made clear "we, the whole group of us walking together, dog, child, live in that house over there. And you could see the wheels turning." Likewise, attending church services shows family identity to others. For example, Angie and Lisa's pastor asked them to speak during a Sunday service about life as a lesbian family. Angie and Lisa felt the parishioners' reactions supported their family identity. Angie recalled, "This young girl came up and told me, 'Thanks for being brave.'"

In summary, this section used the perspective of symbolic interactionism to explain how rituals and symbols help lesbian families show family identity to others. A shared family name signals that the two mothers and their child or children consider themselves a family unit, careful selection of donors' traits create physical resemblance, and everyday activities, like shopping or nightly walks, communicate family status. The negotiated nature of identity is illustrated when interactions with others either affirm or disconfirm lesbian family identity. We now discuss how the symbol of names for two mommies and the rituals of attending a same-sex parenting group and doing family communicate internal family identity.

Internally Communicating Family Identity

Names for Two Mommies.   We found that the names children call their mothers communicate internal family identity. Cami explained the importance of these names: "[At] one of our first meetings of our same-sex parenting group, everybody was like, 'What are you going to have your kids call you?' you know, because it's uncharted territory." Most families chose to use different variations of *mother*, such as *mom* and *momma* for both mothers. Other families drew a term from another culture such as *ama, nay,* or *aunee* for one mother. Some families chose parallel names, such as *Momma M* and *Momma R* or *Mama Tina* and *Mama Wanda*.

Choosing separate names for the two mothers helps clarify the child's internal sense of family identity. Michelle and Susan struggled over what to have their daughter call them.

Susan compared using *mom* for both mothers to naming two children the same first name. Likewise, Patty said, "We figured we had to distinguish so that our child wouldn't be so confused."

On one hand, others can support internal family identity by using the chosen mother terms. Maria and Robin have chosen to be called *Momma M* and *Momma R*. Maria explained, "Our names carry over through to preschool: the kids refer to us and they will say, 'Jacob, Momma M's here.'" By distinguishing between Momma M and Momma R, the preschool teacher and classmates support Jacob's family identity. On the other hand, others can confuse the child's internal sense of family identity. For instance, Pam described an interaction between her son and a child at day care. Pam explained how her son Drew said, "'I have two mommies; and then this one kid goes, 'You can't have two, you know, mommies.' He goes, 'Yes I can. I have 'Mommy' and 'Momma.'" This example illustrates how easily lesbian family identity can be rejected.

Same-Sex Parenting Group. We found that attending a same-sex parenting group was a key ritual that supports a family's internal sense of identity. Many families attend a group primarily so that their children can see and interact with other families with two mothers. Many parents go so that their children will not feel isolated. Wanda wanted to show her daughter "that she wasn't just the lone ranger at school with two moms." Families also go so their children do not feel that their family is abnormal. Sarah observed, "We are the only same-sex couple on this block of eight or ten houses. So, if you figure that and you want to base that as your norm, then we can appear abnormal to her."

Families hope that the group will create a set of friends that the children can rely on, if they are later teased, harassed, or shunned because they have lesbian parents. Sandra explained, "To have other kids as they grow that they can talk to and kind of have as a resource like you know. They are going to go through a lot of stuff that we didn't have to go through growing up."

Families also attend a same-sex parenting group to support the mothers' own sense of family identity. Interaction with other lesbian mothers provides support. As Holly said, "We benefit just having other people around that are going to be going through those same things." Interaction with a group that shares a similar family identity validates internal family identity.

Doing Family. We found that patterned everyday interactions (West & Zimmerman, 1987; Wolin & Bennett, 1984) were important family rituals that communicated family not only to others but also to the family members themselves. Recurring daily interactions, such as shared meals and bedtime rituals, help support internal family identity. Shannon and Ellen make eating dinner together every evening a priority because they feel family meals are a time and place to build family. Likewise, nightly bedtime rituals help lesbian families feel like a family. Maria revealed the almost-sacred quality of their family bedtime ritual. She stated, "If the phone rings, we don't answer it." Dina and Libby's nighttime ritual with Hannah includes lying in bed together and saying their prayers. Dina and Libby lead the traditional, "Now I lay me down to sleep . . ." and Hannah fills in the blanks at the end. She always adds "Mommy" and "Momma."

Families also discussed the importance of recurring weekly interactions. Maria and Robin described how their Sunday morning ritual of blueberry pancakes and sausages helps build a sense of family. Carol and Lynn stressed how passing down rituals they had grown up with creates familyhood. Carol grew up with music blaring in the background during Saturday morning house-cleanings. She said, "When we have the music on when we are cleaning the house, to me does feel like family because . . . Saturdays, when I was growing up, that's what we did. We had Barbra Streisand blaring in the background and we cleaned." Likewise, Michelle passes down a family ritual by singing her mother's special song to her own child. Singing this song carries on a tradition that established a bond between Michelle and her mother and now establishes a special bond between Michelle and her child.

In summary, we used the perspective of symbolic interactionism to explain how rituals and symbols help lesbian families construct their own family identity. Two distinct names for the biological and nonbiological mother help clarify the child's sense of family, seeing other children who also have two mothers may lessen a child's sense of social isolation, and everyday patterned interactions create a heightened sense of family. The negotiated nature of identity is illustrated when a child's family identity is challenged by another's child's questioning the possibility of having two mommies.

Conclusion

We studied rituals and symbols to understand how lesbian families communicate their family identity externally and internally. We found that families chose shared last names to show others they are a family. The parents in these families also selected donors who resembled them in order to nonverbally communicate family to others. Finally, these families interacted as families in public (shopping or taking walks together) to show others that they are a family. In addition to using symbols and rituals to show others they are a family, these families also reported using symbols and rituals to show each other, especially their children, that they are a family. Parents chose names for both mothers to communicate their parental roles to their children. Families also attended a same-sex parenting group so that they would be in contact with other families that resemble their own. Finally, families had everyday rituals, such as eating meals together, to show each other that they are a family.

Our study demonstrates how lesbian families use rituals and symbols to communicate family identity. In so doing, our study illustrates the symbolic interactionist claim that communication is the primary way identity is negotiated between self and other. Interactions with others shape the family's identity. Identity is a social process in which lesbian families negotiate acceptance or rejection of their family identities with others. Our study shows how others, particularly children's peers, can challenge lesbian families' identities.

In response to the finding that children from heterosexual families often challenge the family identity of children from lesbian families, we created and distributed resource materials for elementary school educators. Our desire to make a difference in the community led us to develop a brochure and Web site that address problems children of lesbian families may face in the classroom. We have received positive feedback from administrators and teachers who find the materials timely and practical.

Finally, our study shows the need for additional research on how speech acts such as teasing and questioning impact the children of lesbian and gay parents. Although Rankin (2003) documents the teasing, harassing, shunning, and verbal threats gay, lesbian, bisexual, and transgender students experience on college campuses, future research needs to gain access to elementary-aged children of lesbian and gay parents and understand the climate in schools from their perspective.

Questions for Consideration and Discussion

1. What particular cultural forces contribute to the need for lesbian families to communicate family identity to outsiders?
2. In addition to lesbian/gay families, in what situations might family names be important for the construction of internal and external family identity?
3. The authors note the importance of "doing family" for lesbian family identity. How might we apply these findings to the study of other family forms?
4. This study focuses on lesbian-parented families. Do you believe that families parented by gay men would be similar? What different identity issues might they face?
5. In this study, the participants were 16 lesbian-parented families, all of whom used donor insemination. How might this have affected the results of the study?

References

Chabot, J. M., & Ames, B. D. (2004). "It wasn't 'let's get pregnant and go do it'": Decision making in lesbian couples planning motherhood via donor insemination. *Family Issues, 53,* 348–356.

Charmaz, K. (2002). Qualitative interviewing and grounded theory analysis. In J. F. Gubrium & J. A. Holstein (Eds.), *Handbook of interview research: Context & method* (pp. 675–694). Thousand Oaks, CA: Sage.

Goffman, E. (1959). *Presentation of self in everyday life.* New York: Doubleday.

Goffman, E. (1971). *Relations in public: Microstudies of the public order.* New York: Basic Books.

Johnson, S. M., & O'Connor, E. (2002). *The gay baby boom: The psychology of gay parenthood.* New York: New York University Press.

Kershaw, S. (2000). Living in a lesbian household: The effects on children. *Child and Family Social Work, 5,* 365–371.

Mead, G. H. (1943). *Mind, self, and society.* Chicago: University of Chicago Press.

Patterson, C. J. (1995). *Lesbian, gay and bisexual identities over the lifespan.* New York: Praeger.

Perinbanayagam, R. S. (2003). Telic reflections: Interactional processes, as such. *Symbolic Interaction, 26,* 67–83.

Rankin, S. R. (2003). *Campus climate for gay, lesbian, bisexual, and transgender people: A national perspective.* New York: The National Gay and Lesbian Task Force Policy Institute.

Suter, E. A. (2004). Tradition never goes out of style: The role of tradition in women's naming practices. *The Communication Review, 7,* 57–88.

Suter, E. A., & Oswald, R. F. (2003). Do lesbians change their last names in the context of a committed relationship? *Journal of Lesbian Studies, 7,* 71–83.

West, C., & Zimmerman, D. H. (1987). Doing gender. *Gender and Society, 1,* 125–151.

Wolin, S. J., & Bennett, L. A. (1984). Family rituals. *Family Process, 23,* 401–420.

Woosley, L. (2003, March 9). Family ties. *Tulsa World,* p. D1.

Section 3: Conclusions and Application—Sexuality, Family, and You _____

In this chapter, you read about the parental sexual relationship and how it relates to marital satisfaction. From this review, it is clear that, although we can't be quite sure about the direction of causation, sexual satisfaction and marital happiness are linked for many couples. Thus, adult partner sexual interaction impacts the family system as a whole.

We also addressed how parents communicate about sexuality to their children, both implicitly and explicitly. You read about the impacts that parent–child communication about sexuality seem to have on adolescent behavior. These impacts are part of why it is so important for us to consider how parents and children talk about (or don't talk about) sexuality in the family.

The final major theme of this chapter was related to homosexuality in the family. Attention to the particular dynamics of sexual orientation in family interaction has been a relatively recent phenomenon in research. Additionally, the issue of gay/lesbian parents has become more of a point of societal focus in the last decade, with many public debates and strong feelings about the issue from a variety of viewpoints.

Now that you have read about these issues, how might they impact you in your life as a member of families? How might you use this information to understand families (yours and others)? In this section, I suggest three ways to utilize your new knowledge: to gain understandings of your family of origin and how it impacted you; to get insight into the experiences of others; and to think about how you might use these understandings and insights in your communication with others.

Sexuality Communication in Your Family of Origin

Who in your family talked to you about sexuality? Research would tend to suggest that, when parents do talk about sexuality, they talk to the child of the same sex. If that was not true in your family, think about why. One of your parents may have been more comfortable speaking about sexuality issues. Or, it may have been that one of your parents felt that talking about sexuality was largely unnecessary. As you read earlier in the chapter, girls are spoken to more explicitly about sexuality than boys. So, if you are male, it is possible that neither parent felt that a talk about sexuality was particularly important for you. If there were both male and female children in the family, comparison of how parents spoke to each might give you insight into why a particular parent or adult caregiver spoke to you about sexuality most often.

If your parents did explicitly talk to you about sexuality, what was the focus of the conversation? As discussed here, research tends to indicate that often explicit communication about sexuality centers on issues such as how conception occurs and contraception, and talk about issues such as masturbation and having a healthy sex life are rarely spoken of. Frequently, the discussion is about what not to do (i.e. "Don't have sex!"). Were your conversations about sexuality similar to this. If not, you might ask yourself why? Do you think your parents were more or less comfortable than "the average" parent in talking about sexuality? As Kinser discusses, even parents who have a desire to be open with their children about sexuality may experience discomfort when attempting to talk about sexuality with their children. Regardless of whether your conversations with your parents/adult caregivers were similar to what has been shown in research, consider the extent to which you felt satisfied with the information you received from your parents. Did you want more information? Less? Different?

In addition to thinking about how your adult caregivers communicated overtly to you about sexuality, consider how they communicated more subtly about this issue. As you grew up, how much exposure to sexuality were you allowed? If there was a scene in a television show or movie involving sexuality, did your parents turn it off? How did your parents/adult caregivers behave toward each other in your presence? Did you have a sense of their physical interest in each other, or was that largely hidden? As you ponder these questions, you can consider what you learned from these implicit messages.

Finally, think about what you learned in your family of origin about sexual orientation. Most parents and other adult caregivers proceed from the assumption that every child will grow up to be a heterosexual adult. As a child, you may remember being teased by adult family members about your cross-sex friends ("Oh, is he your little boyfriend?"). You may have had an adult say that you had a "crush" on someone of the opposite sex. In these ways, adults, without ever explicitly saying it, teach children that heterosexuality is normal, male–female relationships are about romance, and male–male or female–female relationships are about friendship. In many families, explicit conversations about homosexuality are rare. In some families, to be sure, discussion of sexual orientation is more open. If your family was one of those families, why? Were your parents particularly adamant in their views about homosexuality and thus wanted to be sure you understood? Is someone in your family openly gay or lesbian and that prompted more discussion of sexual orientation? Did cultural events occurring at that time that lead you to ask about homosexuality, or lead your parents to discuss it more?

Once you have thought about how you experienced communication about sexuality in your family of origin, you can apply those understandings to thinking about your own sexual behavior. Research suggests that talking about sexuality with children and adolescents has outcomes on their later sexual behavior and attitudes. Although it is hard to isolate the effects, because of the many other things that impact our sexual lives, it is likely that the way your family of origin dealt with sexuality had some impact on you as you grew up. Reflecting on the connections between family communication about sexuality and your own behaviors and attitudes may provide you with some interesting insights. In addition to helping you think about and understand your own experiences, this knowledge can also be applied to considering the experiences of others.

Understanding the Experiences of Others

As children, and often even beyond, the ways that our family interacts become so "normal" for us that when we see or hear others behaving in ways that are different, we may feel that they are doing it "wrong" or are "weird." That's natural, particularly when we are young, because our own experiences are really all we know. As we get older, and learn more about the diversity of family experience, it may help us appreciate the variations in families, including diversity with regard to communicating about sexuality.

Throughout life, you will develop relationships with people from many different families, and each one of those individuals will have his or her own attitudes and behaviors in relation to sexuality. At times, the behavior or beliefs of another may be hard to understand. If the person is an acquaintance, this may not present much of an issue. However, if a close friend or romantic partner seems to have very different ideas than you do about sexuality, it can cause confusion, or even conflict in the relationship. Understanding the role of family of origin in helping us develop our sexual selves can give you a way to think about these differences between people and accept them as not necessarily better or worse, just different.

Thinking about Your Future in the Family

As you continue on in your life, you will likely engage in long-term romantic relationships. The research that we considered here suggests that attention to the impact of sexuality on a romantic relationship is important. At times, we may feel that sexual happiness should just happen naturally. However, that is often untrue for couples, and knowing how sexual satisfaction relates to relational happiness may help you to work on your sexual relationship and seek help if and when needed.

Additionally, many of you either do have or will have children. Even if you do not plan to have children of your own, it is likely that you will interact with children as an aunt or uncle, or close family friend. As you continue to consider the role of communication about sexuality in the family, ask yourself how your knowledge may guide your future communication with children and adolescents in your life. Most adults would agree that they want the children they care about to grow up and become sexually healthy and well-adjusted adults. Will you talk to these children about sexuality? How will you? What do you wish your adult caregivers had said to you that they didn't? What did they say to you that you want to pass on to the children you are close to? Thinking about what you have learned in this chapter may help you understand how, even when you aren't talking explicitly with children about sexuality, you are teaching them about it. This may not be always comfortable, but such consideration can help us be more reflective adults in our interactions with children and therefore may lead to subsequent generations who have a good understanding of their own sexuality, and the sexuality of others, and can make wise life choices as they embark upon their own adulthood and their own relationships with future generations of children.

Questions for Consideration and Discussion

1. Reflecting upon your own experiences, how did family communication affect your sexual behavior as you became an adolescent and adult?
2. How do you think that culture (larger societal culture, racial/ethnic culture, religious culture) impacted your family of origin's communication about sexuality? What do you see as the positive and/or negative outcomes of that impact?

3. Kinser's article, as well as other research cited here, points to the complex nature of communicating with children about sexuality and the discomfort that may arise for both parents and children. Can you see any ways that parents might be able to lessen this discomfort for themselves and their adolescents?

4. As laws regarding homosexuality and gay/lesbian relationships change and evolve over time, how do you think this may affect gay- and lesbian-parented families?

5. Drawing from the work in this chapter, what specific recommendations would you make to new parents as they approach the issue of sexuality in their families?

Key Terms and Concepts

body talk
coming out
gay/lesbian family
guilt

overt sexuality communication
relational satisfaction
sexual modeling
sexual orientation

sexual satisfaction
shame
social stigma

Appendix A

How to Read a Scholarly Research Article

If reading scholarly work is new to you, it may seem somewhat difficult or confusing. However, once you get accustomed to the form and style of such work, it really isn't as difficult as it might appear at first. In this appendix, I introduce you to the "genres" (general types) of work you see represented in this text, and some of the terminology that is used in scholarly work, as well as considering the typical parts of a research report. Although the articles in this text have been written specifically for you, the undergraduate student, you will likely read other articles directly from scholarly journals and this information will help guide and inform that reading.

Worldviews: Social Science and Humanism/Interpretivism

One area of distinction between types of research in communication relates to the perspective, or worldview, of the researchers. Some researchers proceed from a *social scientific* view, whereas other scholars adopt a more *humanist* or *interpretive* perspective.

The difference between social scientific scholars and humanist/interpretive scholars begins in how they understand the nature of truth and reality. In general, social scientists believe that there is a Truth (a *fundamental reality*) and that reality can be found through research if that research is done carefully and repeatedly. Humanist/interpretivist scholars argue that there are truths (*multiple realities*) and that reality can be understood only through the lens of our own experiences.

Following on this difference in understanding of reality, these two types of scholars understand human behavior in different ways. Social scientists believe in a concept called determinism. *Determinism* reflects a belief that human behavior is determined by a combination of genetic factors and environmental factors. Thus, if we know enough about people's heredity and environment, we can predict behavior. Humanist/interpretivist scholars don't believe in determinism. Instead, they argue that human behavior is fundamentally affected by *free will*. As humans we make choices about our behavior (and can choose to do things that seem contradictory to both heredity and environment). So, humanists/ interpretivists do not try to make predictions about human behavior.

Because these types of scholars have different viewpoints on truth and human behavior, they also have different primary values in terms of research. Social scientists value *objectivity* in their work. Being certain that a piece of research is carefully done and doesn't reflect any bias—that is, is objective—is very important from a social scientific stance. Given that humanist/interpretivist scholars don't see Truth as accessible, but rather seek truths, they value work that emancipates ideas, voices, and people. *Emancipation* refers to freeing. Thus, humanist/interpretive scholars hope to free new ideas, hear voices that are not typically heard, and increase the power and visibility of people often rendered silent or invisible.

All of these differences lead to a distinction in the end goal of these groups of scholars. Social scientific scholars hope to be able to reach *general statements of relationships* between one variable of human experience and another. The more people these statements can be applied to, and the more situations in which they can be seen to apply, the better the results are. Each bit of research done about a topic has the potential to contribute to these general statements of relationship (sometimes called "covering laws"). Interpretivist/ humanist scholars hope to provide *new understandings*. They want to be able to show something about human experience that is new and compelling. The finding may apply to a small group of people or a large group, a very specific situation or more general sets of situations.

A final difference that can be seen between these two groups of scholars is how research is conducted. Social scientific research is typically done using *experimental design* or *surveys*. Humanist/interpretive research is usually accomplished through *ethnographic study* (studying a group of people closely in an attempt to understand their culture), or *textual analysis* (carefully looking at communicative phenomenon in an attempt to see themes, patterns, etc.).

So, why is it important for you to understand these differences? First, because in order to really understand a piece of research, it is best to know from what worldview the researchers are operating. Although research can have elements of both stances, most research is identifiable as being primarily one or the other. Having a clear understanding of the beliefs that ground the research will help you fully appreciate the claims being made by the authors (and also prevent some confusion).

Second, a clear understanding of the stances taken by communication researchers will allow you to be better prepared to engage in critical analysis of the work. When reading research, it is most fruitful to critically analyze and assess its quality by comparing it to the standards of the stance it represents. Assessing social science based on humanist/ interpretive standards will not really help critique it fairly because those are not the standards of the researchers. Likewise, assessing humanist/interpretive work on the basis of social scientific standards will get in the way of your ability to see its value for what its authors were attempting to do.

You may find that one or the other of these approaches is more appealing to you, and that's fine. But knowledge of both will equip you to really grasp the material you are presented with in communication scholarship.

Quantitative and Qualitative Methodology

A second distinction that can be made between types of research relates to the methods that scholars use to study the phenomenon they are interested in. The two types of methods you will encounter in this text are *quantitative methods* and *qualitative methods*. Interpretivist/humanists most commonly use qualitative methods, and social scientists often (but not always) use quantitative methods, but the two methodological categories can cross the two worldview categories previously discussed.

Before we turn to the differences between the two types of methods, there is a set of terms you will need to understand when reading either quantitative or qualitative research: *reliability* and *validity*. Not all researchers discuss these things, and some humanist/interpretive scholars would argue that they are not of real concern to them. However, these terms are still important for you to know.

The *reliability* of a finding reflects the extent to which, if the same experiment was performed in the same way a number of times, the results would be the same. If I completed a study of how much my children liked tofu, and when they tasted it, all of them were repulsed, but when I repeated the study one hour later only one third of them were repulsed, that study wouldn't be very reliable. We can also talk about intercoder reliability. *Intercoder reliability* refers to agreement between the different researchers who are analyzing the data. When a study has more than one researcher doing analysis of the material gathered, we want them to analyze it in the same way. Measures of intercoder reliability are a way to show that this is happening.

Validity is that the values in the study represent what they are trying to represent. *Internal validity* means that, within the study, measurements are indeed assessing what they were designed to assess. If I was attempting to study how much my children liked tofu, but I had soaked the tofu in wasabi soy sauce, my study would not have good internal validity because it could be the sauce, rather than the tofu, that they were responding to. *External validity* means that the measurements within the study represent the phenomenon outside the controlled analysis that they mean to represent. If my children ate tofu happily during the study (because they were being studied) but then would never eat it again, that measurement would have poor external validity.

Although these terms are used by scholars conducting various types of communication research, discussions about qualitative and quantitative methods also have their own particular terminologies and understanding some of those ideas will help clarify what the writers are saying.

Qualitative methods are those that consider the qualities of a particular communicative phenomenon, rather than doing numerical analysis. Qualitative methodology can be done in a number of ways. Frequently, qualitative analyses involve looking for themes, or patterns in communication. Often, the terms used with regard to qualitative methods are relatively self-explanatory (or easy to understand with a brief discussion). However, to get you started, let us consider two concepts often present in qualitative research reports.

Inductive analysis is an attempt to look at a body of communicative data (interviews, texts, etc.) and from that find the themes or patterns that seem to emerge in the discourse. Rather than beginning with a set of categories that are applied to the communicative phenomenon, the researchers allow the discourse itself to drive the creation of categories or particular understandings. As *thematic analysis* occurs, researchers return to the discourse again and again as they create the categories, themes, and so on to be sure that those ideas really represent the phenomenon.

Observational role is another idea that is often important to qualitative research. When engaging in ethnographic (study of the cultural practices of a particular group) or other naturalistic studies, scholars must decide how they will interact with the individuals being studied. Generally, there are four possible positions of observation. First, the researcher may be a *complete participant*. This means that he or she functions fully as a member of the group under study, and the group members are not aware that he or she is conducting research (this sometimes happens because the scholar was or is part of the group first and only later decides to analyze that group). Second, the researcher may be a *participant-observer*. This means that he or she participates as fully as possible in the group, but the members of the group are also aware that they are being studied. Third, the researcher may be an *observer-participant*. In this role, he or she would mostly just observe the individuals under study and try to stay out of the way for the most part, but there would sometimes be interactions. Finally, the researcher may be a *complete observer*. In this case, he or she would not interact with the members of the group at all, but would only observe them. Understanding what observational role the researcher assumed in the study will help you comprehend how he or she gained understanding of that situation.

Quantitative methodologies are those that rely on numerical computations in the accomplishment of research. In this text, you will see several examples of quantitative methodology being used. Quantitative methods are sometimes daunting to students because they don't understand the equations or what the numbers mean. The exact numerical analyses completed and the way that those are reported depend on the nature of the study. Thus, the scholars who have written for this text have attempted, in each article, to explain clearly the numerical analyses that are important for you to understand their findings. But, for now, we will address two basic terms to get you started.

One term you will commonly see in qualitative analysis is *correlation*. A *correlation* is a relationship between two values (numbers assigned to some variable). As one value changes, so does the other (in some way). A *positive correlation* means that as one number goes up or down, so does the other number. If the amount of hours I exercise is positively correlated to the amount of ice cream I eat, that means that the two will both go up or down together. A *negative correlation* means that as one number goes up, the other number goes down. If the amount of hours I exercise is negatively correlated to the number of pounds I weigh, that means that as one increases the other decreases. Correlations are written from a 0 (no connection between the numbers) to a + 1 or a − 1. A correlation of +1 means that the two numbers move in the same direction at exactly the same rate. So, if I exercise for 1 hour, I eat 2 bowls of ice cream; if I exercise for 2 hours, I eat 4 bowls of ice cream. A correlation of −1 means that the two numbers move in opposite directions at exactly the same rate. If I exercise for 2 hours, my weight decreases by 8 oz; if I exercise for 3 hours, my weight decreases by 12 oz. It is important that you note that correlation doesn't mean causation. Because two variables are correlated, that does not mean that one causes the other (and certainly not that we know which one causes the other). It could be the case that I eat more ice cream because I'm hungry after exercising. Or, it could be the case that when I eat more ice cream I feel guilty and exercise. Or, it might be that my gym has an ice cream shop where the ice cream is really good. So, the more often I go to the gym, the more often I exercise and the more often I eat ice cream.

Finally, researchers using quantitative methodology will often speak of *statistical significance*. Whether or not a correlation is statistically significant depends on a variety of factors. The computation of statistical significance is complex, so I won't go into it here. What you need to understand is that when researchers say that a measure is statistically significant, what they mean is that it is unlikely that the connection between the two variables is simply due to chance, so this is a connection we should pay attention to in the findings. Correlations that are not statistically significant might still be connections, but it isn't quite clear whether they are or whether the connection that was seen is accidental.

This is an introduction to a few terms that you might see in quantitative and qualitative research. As you read the research sections in this text, you will encounter other terms. Read carefully and look for the definitions, and you will find that they are not as difficult as they may appear on the surface.

The Parts of a Research Report

As you read reports of research, you will find that there are typically several parts represented in the work. The organization of those parts varies depending on the work itself (social scientific work tends to follow a more regular format, whereas humanistic/interpretive formats are more varied). However, regardless of the organizational structure, there are elements that are usually present.

Introduction to the Topic

Reports of research begin with some introduction to the topic. This clarifies for you what is being studied in the piece of research. It also points out why this particular phenomenon is important to study.

Review of Other Research or Theory

In the writing, you should expect to see the scholars referring to previous research that has been done about the topic, or theoretical concepts that are related to the issue under study. This may appear at different points in the writing (usually after the introduction in social scientific work, but sometimes dispersed throughout in humanistic/interpretive work). The *literature review* gives you a sense of where this piece of research is positioned within the larger field, provides background information that you need in order to understand the work, and also points you to other articles that you might want to read for further discussion of the topic.

Research Questions or Hypothesis

At some point in the article, you can expect to find a statement of the research questions or hypothesis that the researchers had going into the work. These may be stated in various ways. What the research questions and hypothesis tell you is the purpose for doing the research, what the researchers hoped to answer, or the concepts that they wanted to test with the study.

Methods

The methods of the research will also be described in some way. This is the "who, where, and how" of conducting research. The researcher typically describes the people or texts that were studied and possibly address how those were selected. How and where the research was conducted generally also are considered in the writing. It is important for you to know how the research was conducted because this will help you contextualize the results.

Results and Discussion

Eventually, the work addresses what the authors found in their research. In quantitative research, this is often divided into *results* (which present the results of the statistical analyses that were run with the data) and *discussion* (which is the interpretations that the researchers made of those statistical findings). When reading research presented in this way, you may find that the results section seems kind of confusing at first, particularly if your background in statistics is limited. If this is the case, you may wish to read the discussion first (so you understand how the authors interpreted those numbers) and then go back to the results section. In qualitative research these two can be combined or separate. The results and discussions section or sections tell you what the researchers concluded from their work and what they find most important for you to know. Often researchers also discuss both the benefits and the liabilities of their particular study, and what studies they feel should be done in the future about this topic.

As previously stated, research reports won't always follow this format exactly, but most of these elements will exist somewhere in the writing. Looking for them as you read will help you organize your understandings of what the authors are saying.

Scholarly research writing is an acquired taste. There is no doubt that it is more difficult than reading *USA Today*, or a nice Stephen King novel. However, reading reports at research can be interesting, exciting, challenging, and confirming. If you persevere, it is worth the effort.